a memorable year

Concept: Isabella Dôthel
Layout and Design: Leftloft
Translation: Suleima Autore
Quality control: Barbara Barattolo

ISBN 978-88-6965-196-0

Printed and bound in Italy

Distribuited by Thames & Hudson - www.thamesandhudson.com

1989

The Year in Pictures

contrasto

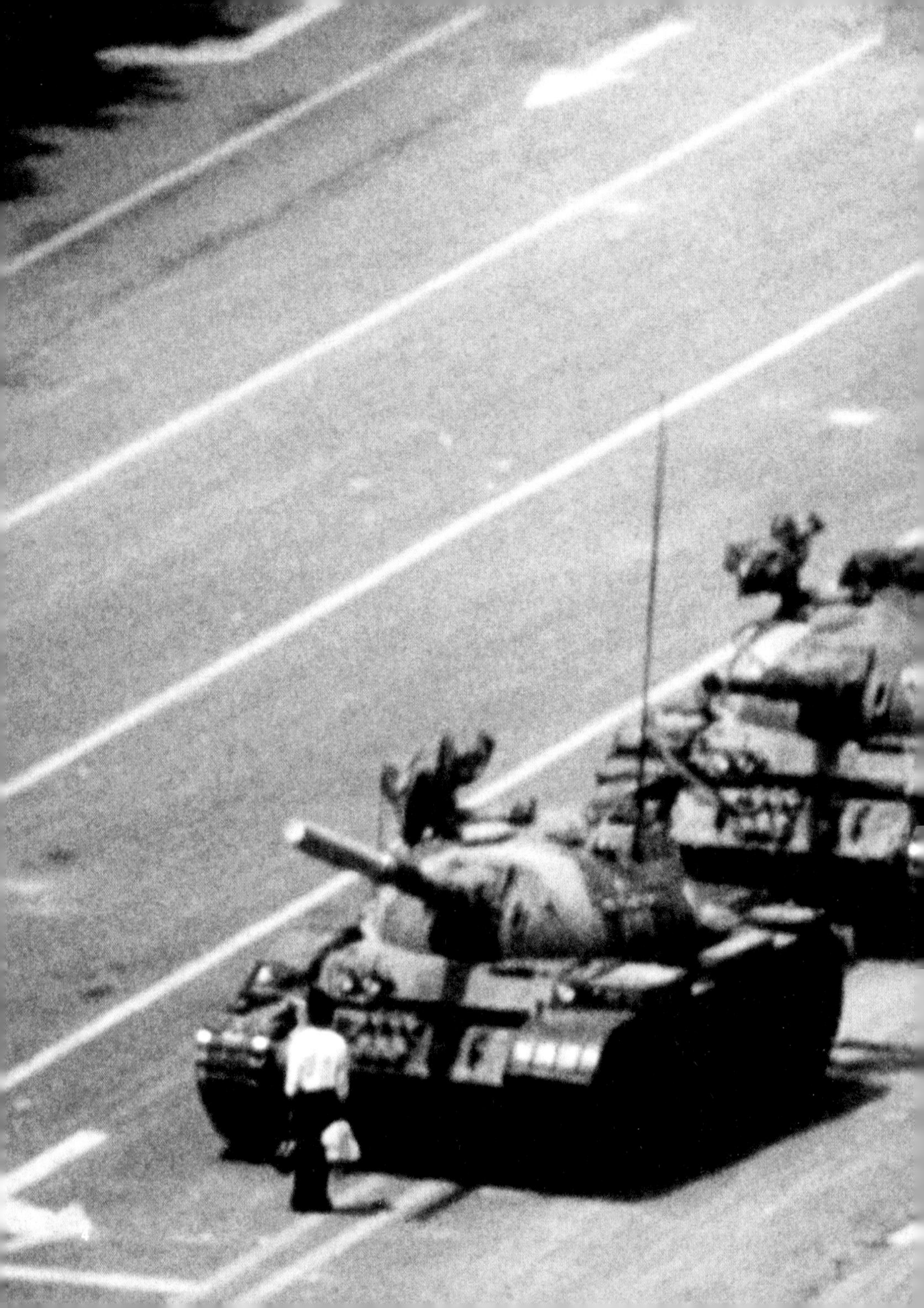

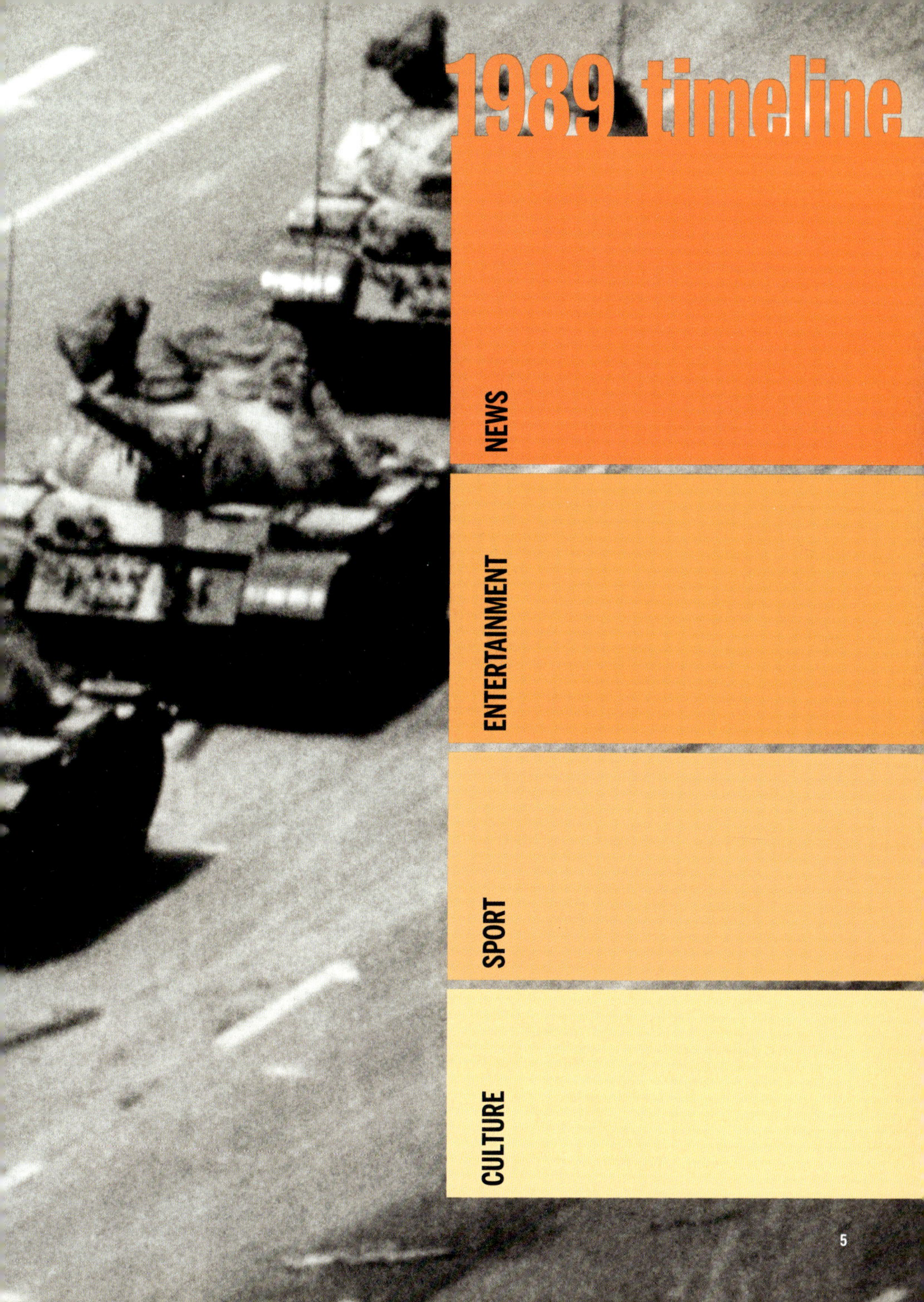
1989 timeline
NEWS
ENTERTAINMENT
SPORT
CULTURE

01

04 Libya: two Libyan MiG-23 "Floggers" are shot down by two US F-14 Tomcat in the skies above the Sidra Gulf.

07 Japan: emperor Hirohito dies in Tokyo.

15 Czechoslovakia: during the commemoration of Jan Palach's death, hudreds of protesters are arrested. Among them Václav Havel, future president.

18 Poland: the Polish Communist Party acknowledges Solidarność, the autonomous worker's catholic union led by Lech Walesa.

20 United States: George H. W. Bush becomes the 41st President of the United States of America.

ENTERTAINMENT

01 Great Britain: release of "She Drives Me Crazy" by the Fine Young Cannibals.

12 Great Britain: release of "The look" by Roxette.

28 United States: 46th edition of the Golden Globes.

SPORT

22 United States: the XXIII Super Bowl.

CULTURE

18 France: writer Bruce Chatwin dies in Nice.

23 Spain: surrealist painter Salvador Dalí dies in Figueres.

02

03 Paraguay: a coup d'etat overthrows Alfredo Stroessner, dictator since 1954.

15 Afghanistan: the Soviet Union announces the official withdrawal of the troops begun on the 2nd of February.

24 Iran: Ayatollah Ruhollah Khomeini issues a fatwa against Salman Rushdie, author of "The Satanic Verses".

11 United States: release of "Eternal Flame" by The Bangles.

22 United States: 31st edition of the Grammy Awards. Bobby McFerrin wins Record of the Year and George Michael wins Album of the Year.

28 United States: release of "Like a prayer" by Madonna.

17 France: couturier Guy Laroche dies in La Rochelle.

03

13 Canada: a magnetic storm causes the collapse of Québec's electrical network with a nine-hour blackout for six million people.

14 Lebanon: General Michel Aoun announces a "war of liberation" to push out Syria and its allies.

24 United States: oil tanker Exxon Valdez hits a cliff in Alaska, scattering over 42.000 m³ of crude oil into the environment.

29 United States: 61st Academy Awards in Los Angeles. "Rain man" of Barry Levinson is the absolut protagonist.

11 Japan: Marc Girardelli is the overall winner of the Alpine Skiing World Cup in all disciplines.

09 United States: photographer Robert Mapplethorpe dies in Boston.

23 United States: Stanley Pons and Martin Fleischmann announce the experimental production of cold fusion in the laboratories of the University of Utah.

30 France: the new entrance to the Louvre, Paris, a glass pyramid designed by architect Ieoh Ming Pei, is unveiled.

04

04 Belgium: the 40th anniversary of NATO is celebrated in Brussels.

07 Barents Sea: the Soviet submarine K-278 Komsomolets sinks killing 41 people.

9 Georgia: the Red Army kills over 20 people in Tbilisi's main square during a pacifist demonstration.

15 Great Britain: 96 football supporters lose their lives at the Hillsborough Stadium in Sheffield.

21 China: Tian'anmen Square's protest begins.

17 United States: release of "Doolittle" by Pixies.

26 United States: actress Lucille Ball dies in Los Angeles.

30 Italy: director Sergio Leone dies in Rome.

12 United States: boxer Sugar Ray Robinson dies in Culver City.

05

06

NEWS

02 Hungary: first breach in the Iron Curtain, 240 km of barbed wire are dismantled along the border with Austria.

14 China: The students' protests and the government's reaction become stronger. The Martial Law is established.

03 Iran: ayatollah Khomeini dies in Teheran.

04 China: the army approaches Tian'anmen Square. Confronted with the protesters' resistance they open fire and reach the square.
Poland: Solidarność wins the elections, it is the first anti-communist movement to impose itself in Eastern Europe.

21 Great Britain: British police arrest 250 people celebrating the Summer solstice at Stonehenge.

ENTERTAINMENT

01 Great Britain: after 20 years the last episode of "The Benny Hill Show" is broadcast.
Great Britain: release of "Disintegration" by The Cure.

11 United States: Dynasty's last episode is broadcast.

21 United States: the last episode of Miami Vice is broadcast.

23 France: 42nd edition of the Cannes Film Festival.

24 United States: release of "Indiana Jones and the Last Crusade" by Steven Spielberg.

02 Stati Uniti: release of the "Dead Poets Society" by Peter Weir.

16 Austria: conductor Herbert von Karajan dies in Anif.

23 Stati Uniti: release of "Batman" by Tim Burton.

SPORT

24 Spain: at the Camp Nou stadium in Barcelona, A.C. Milan wins the European Cup.

CULTURE

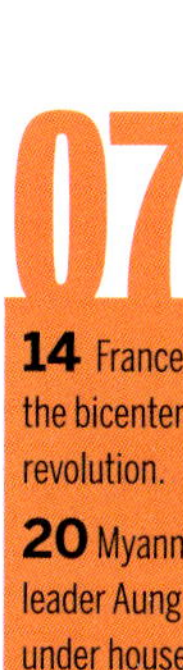

07

14 France: celebrations for the bicentenary of the French revolution.

20 Myanmar: opposition leader Aung San Suu Kyi is kept under house arrest.

07 United States: release of "Lethal Weapon 2" by Richard Donner.

11 Great Britain: actor Laurence Olivier dies in Steyning.

14 United States: release of "When Harry met Sally..." by Rob Reiner.

15 Italy: Pink Floyd's concert in Venice is broadcasted worldwide.

23 Gran Bretagna: actor Daniel Radcliffe is born in London.

23 Greg LeMond wins the Tour de France. He crossed the finishing line only 8 seconds before the French Laurent Fignon.

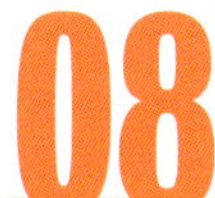

08

19 Poland: President Wojciech Jaruzelski appoints Tadeusz Mazowiecki, of Solidarność, as Prime Minister, the first non-communist in 42 years.

23 Baltic States: two million people in Estonia, Latvia and Lithuania protest against Soviet occupation.

25 Solar System: space probe Voyager II reaches Neptune.

29 Great Britain: release of "Personal Jesus" by Depeche Mode.

09   10

09

10 Hungary: the government opens the borders with Austria, thus creating the first passage in the Iron Curtain, through which many DDR refugees entered the country.

20 South Africa: Frederik Willem de Klerk is the new President who opens the path to the abolishment of apartheid.

10

13 United States: black Friday in Wall Street. The crash will influence all stock markets in the world.

17 United States: earthquake in Loma Prieta, 7.1 degrees on the Richter Scale, hits the San Francisco Bay, 63 people die.

18 Germany: Erich Honecker, President of the DDR, discharges for health reasons.

23 Hungary: President Mátyás Szűrös officially declares the birth of the Republic of Hungary and the end of the People's Republic of Hungary.

ENTERTAINMENT

01 Germany: Bill and Tom Kaulitz singer and guitarist of music band Tokio Hotel, are born in Liepzig

02 United States: release of "The best" by Tina Turner.

15 Italy: 46th edition of the Venice Film Festival.

22 United States: the first episode of "Baywatch" is broadcast.

06 France: actress Bette Davis dies in Neuilly-sur-Seine.

13 United States: release of "Look Who's Talking" by Amy Heckerling.

SPORT

CULTURE

04 Switzerland: writer Georges Simenon dies in Lausanne.

05 Sweden: Nobel Peace Prize goes to the 14th Dalai Lama, Tenzin Gyatso.

11

09 Germany: East Germany's government declares that visitors are allowed to enter West Germany and Berlin. The Wall is assaulted by a joyful crowd.

12 Brazil: first democratic elections after 25 years of dictatorship.

17 Bulgaria: communist leader Todor Zhivkov is replaced by Petar Mladenov.

17-28 Czechoslovakia: the "Velvet Revolution" begins. 500.000 peacefully protest obtaining the resignation of the entire party's leadership.

22 Lebanon: a bomb explodes in the western part of Beirut at the passage of President René Moawad's parade, killing him and other 63 people.

05 United States: pianist Vladimir Samoylovich Horowitz dies in New York.

22 United States: release of "Back to the Future Part II" by Robert Zemeckis.

05 Australia: Alain Prost wins the Formula One Championship.

12

03 Malta: Bush and Gorbachev sign an agreement to end the Cold War.

14 Chile: after 16 years the first democratic elections are held.

17 Romania: a wide protest explodes in Timişoara.

20 Panama: US troops invade the country and overthrow Manuel Noriega's dictatorship.

22 Romania: during Ceauşescu's speech in a rally in Bucarest, some gunshots trigger the Revolution against the dictator.

25 Romania: Nicolae and Elena Ceauşescu are executed.

29 Czechoslovakia: Václav Havel is elected President.

06 Great Britain: the serial "Doctor Who" ends after 26 seasons.

07 Great Britain: actor Nicholas Hoult is born in Wokingham.

08 United States: release of "The War of the Roses" by Danny De Vito.

15 United States: release of "Driving Miss Daisy" by Bruce Beresford.

16 Spain: actress Silvana Mangano dies in Madrid. United States: actor Lee Van Cleef dies in Oxnard, California.

20 United States: "Born on the 4th of July" by Oliver Stone opens.

14 Russia: nuclear physicist and Nobel Peace Prize Andrej Dmitrievič Sakharov dies in Moscow at the age of 68.

22 France: playwriter and Nobel Prize Samuel Beckett dies in Paris.

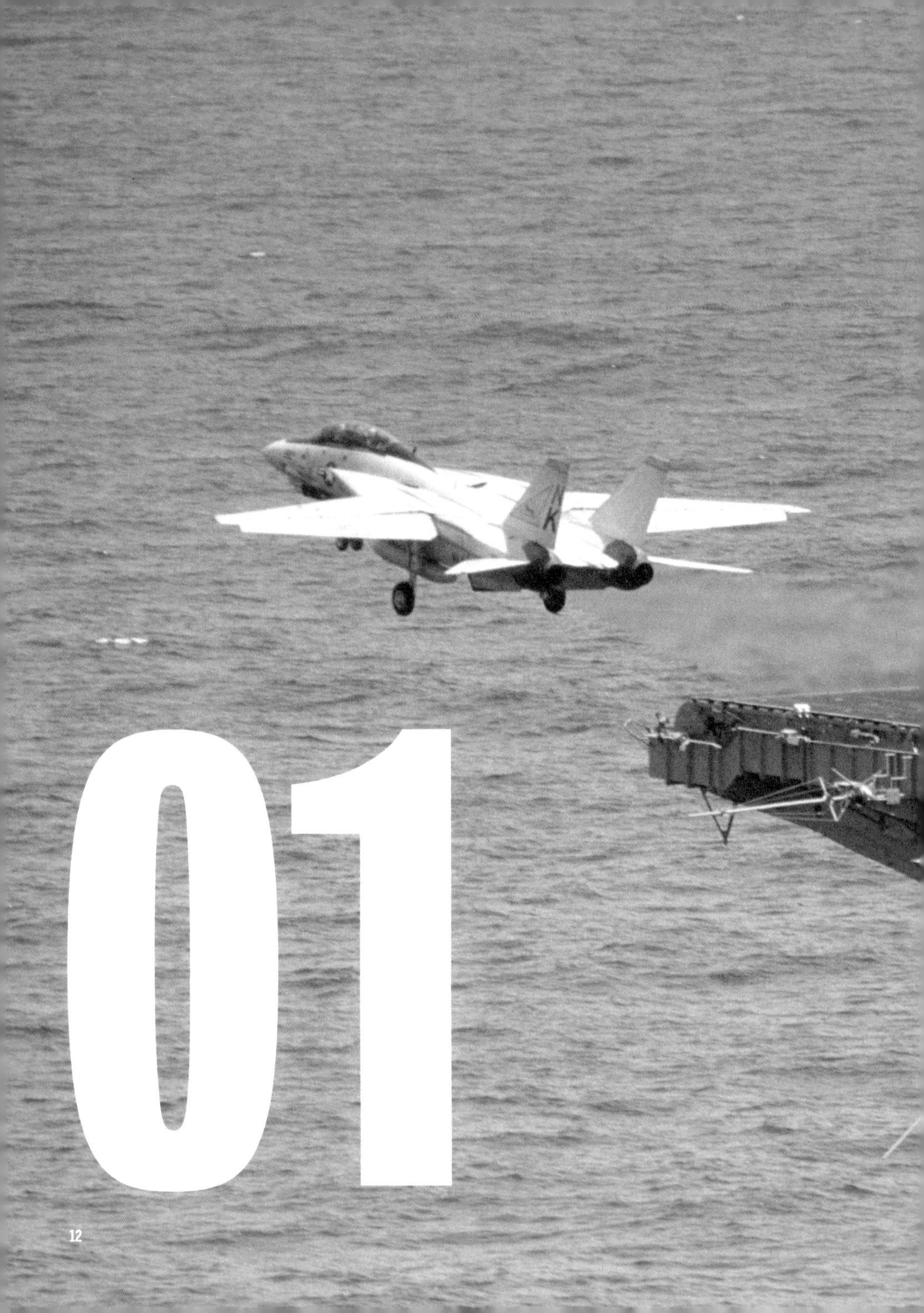

01

01

Great Britain: release of "She Drives Me Crazy" by the Fine Young Cannibals.

04

Libya: two Libyan MiG-23 "Floggers" are shot down by two US F-14 Tomcat in the skies above the Sidra Gulf. It is the peak of a tension between the two countries started in 1973.

07

Japan: at the age of 88, emperor Hirohito dies after 62 years and 14 days of reign. It has been the longest reign in Japanese history.

12

Great Britain: release of "The look" by Roxette, one of the year's international hits.

15

Czechoslovakia: during the commemoration of Jan Palach's death, hudreds of protesters are arrested. Among them Václav Havel, future president.

18

Poland: the Polish Communist Party acknowledges Solidarność, the autonomous worker's catholic union led by Lech Walesa.

France: at the age of 48, writer Bruce Chatwin dies in Nice.

20

United States: George H. W. Bush succeeds Ronald Reagan and becomes the 41st President of the United States of America.

22

United States: for the first time the XXIII Super Bowl is played in Miami. The San Francisco 49ers beat the Cincinnati Bengals 20-16. The match, with a surprising overturning of the result in the last 34 seconds, has been listed, in 2006, among the top 10 matches of all times.

23

Spain: surrealist painter Salvador Dalí dies in Figueres at the age of 84.

24

United States: the serial killer Theodore Bundy is put to the electric chair in Florida. Bundy had confessed the murder of 28 people, but the exact number of his victims is still a mystery.

28

United States: 46th edition of the Golden Globes. "Rain man" by Barry Levinson is awarded as Best Motion Picture - Drama; "Working Girl" by Mike Nichols wins Best Motion Picture - Comedy. Both actors, Dustin Hoffman and Melanie Griffith, are awarded as best actor and actress in their category.

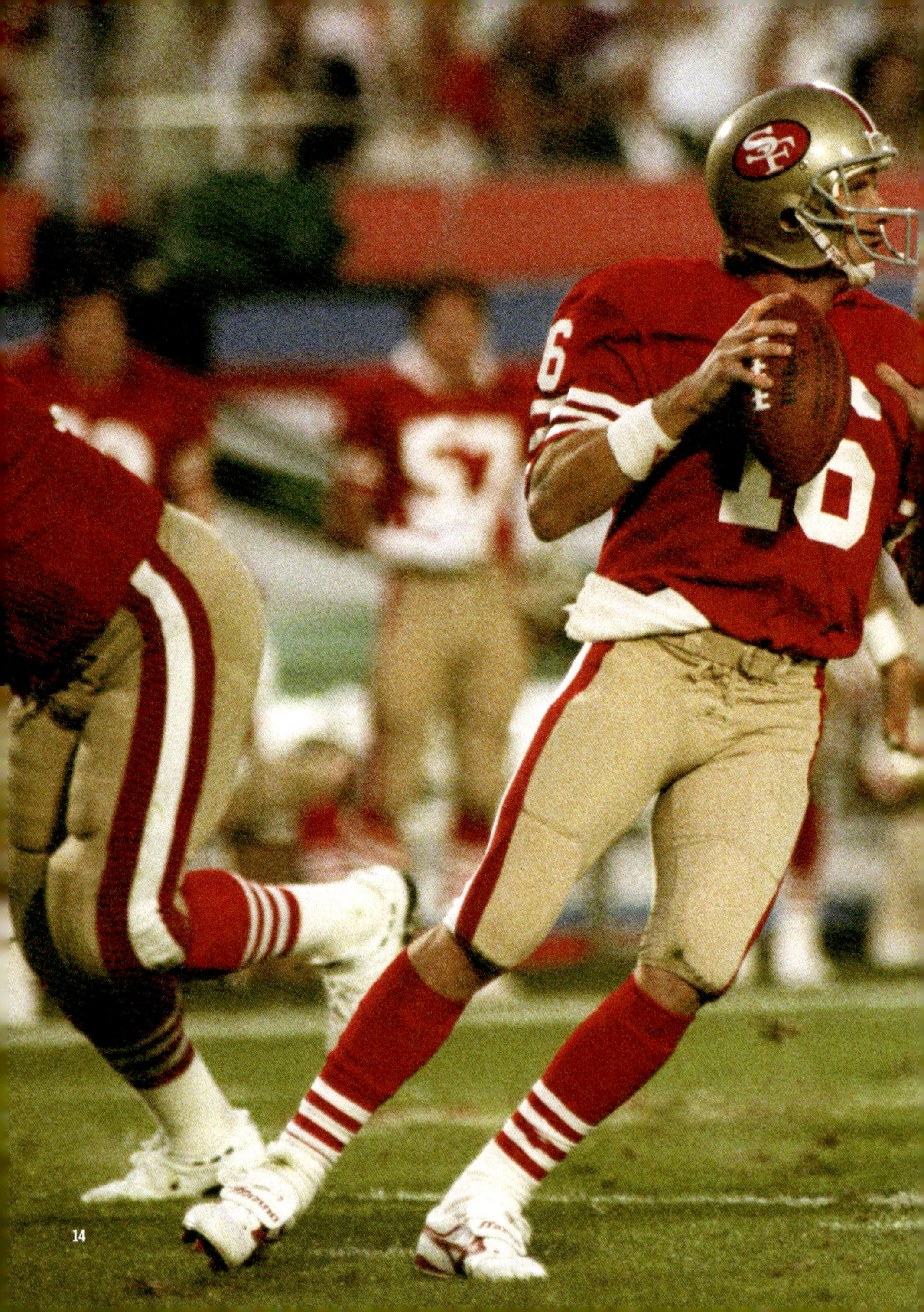

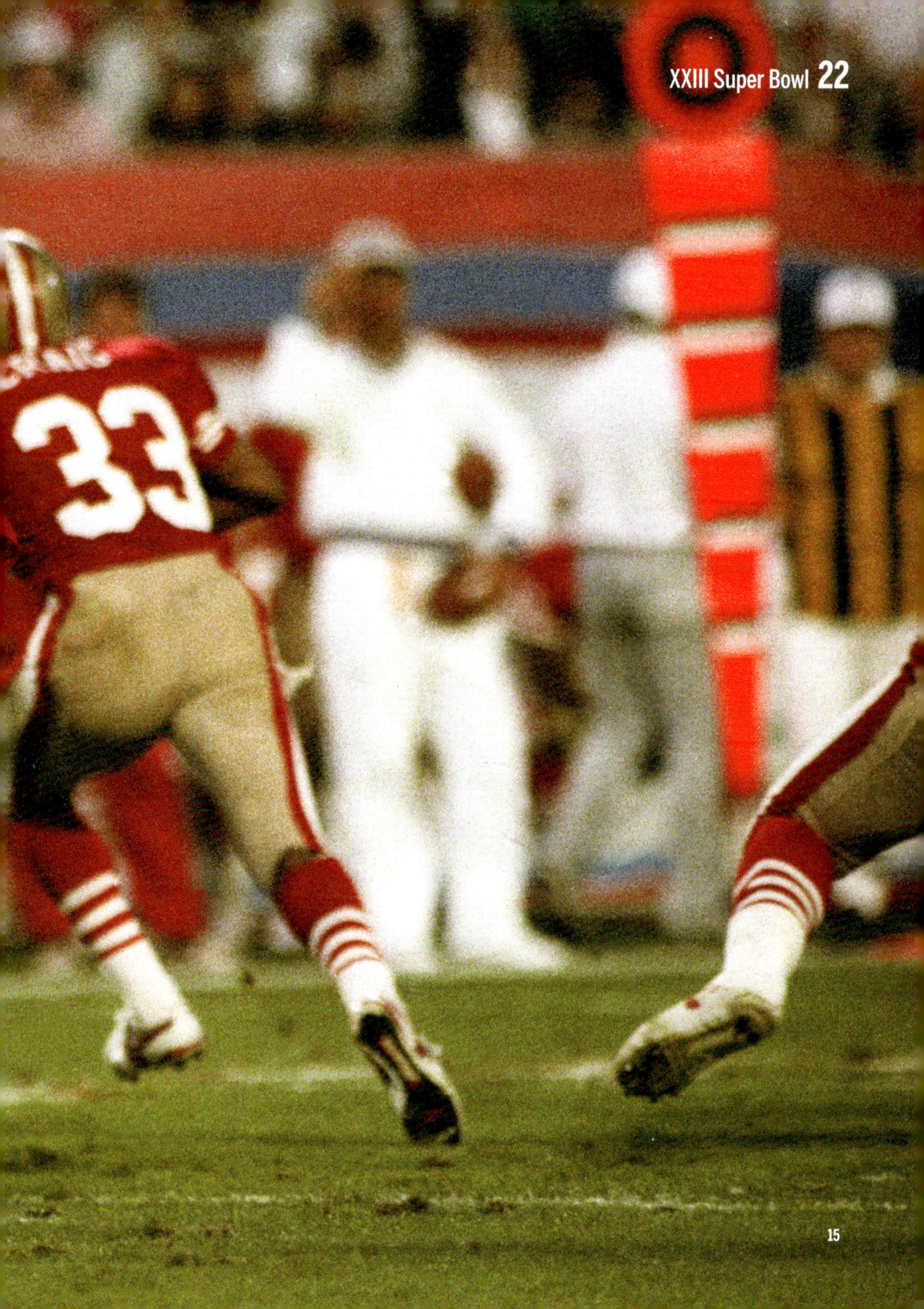

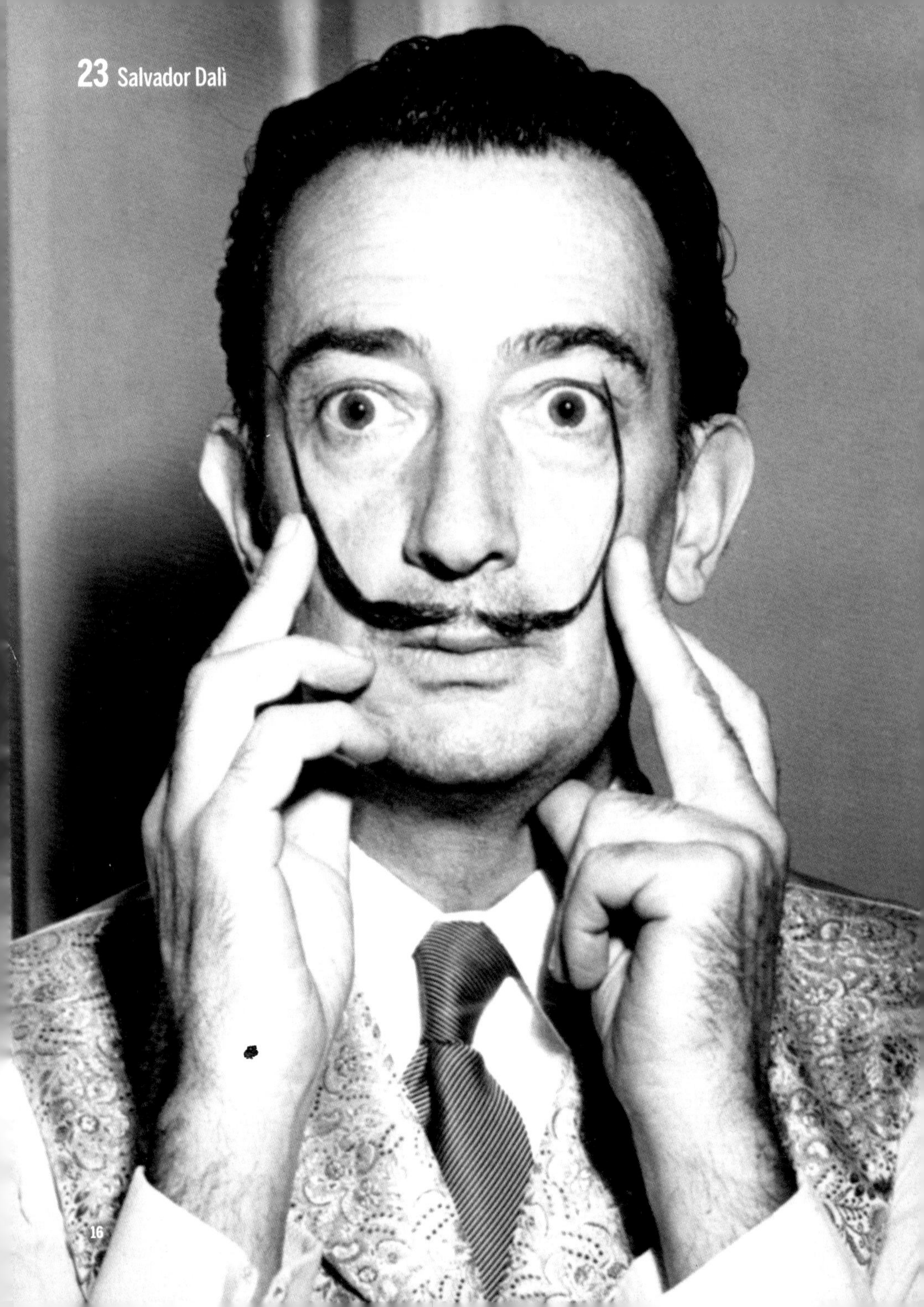

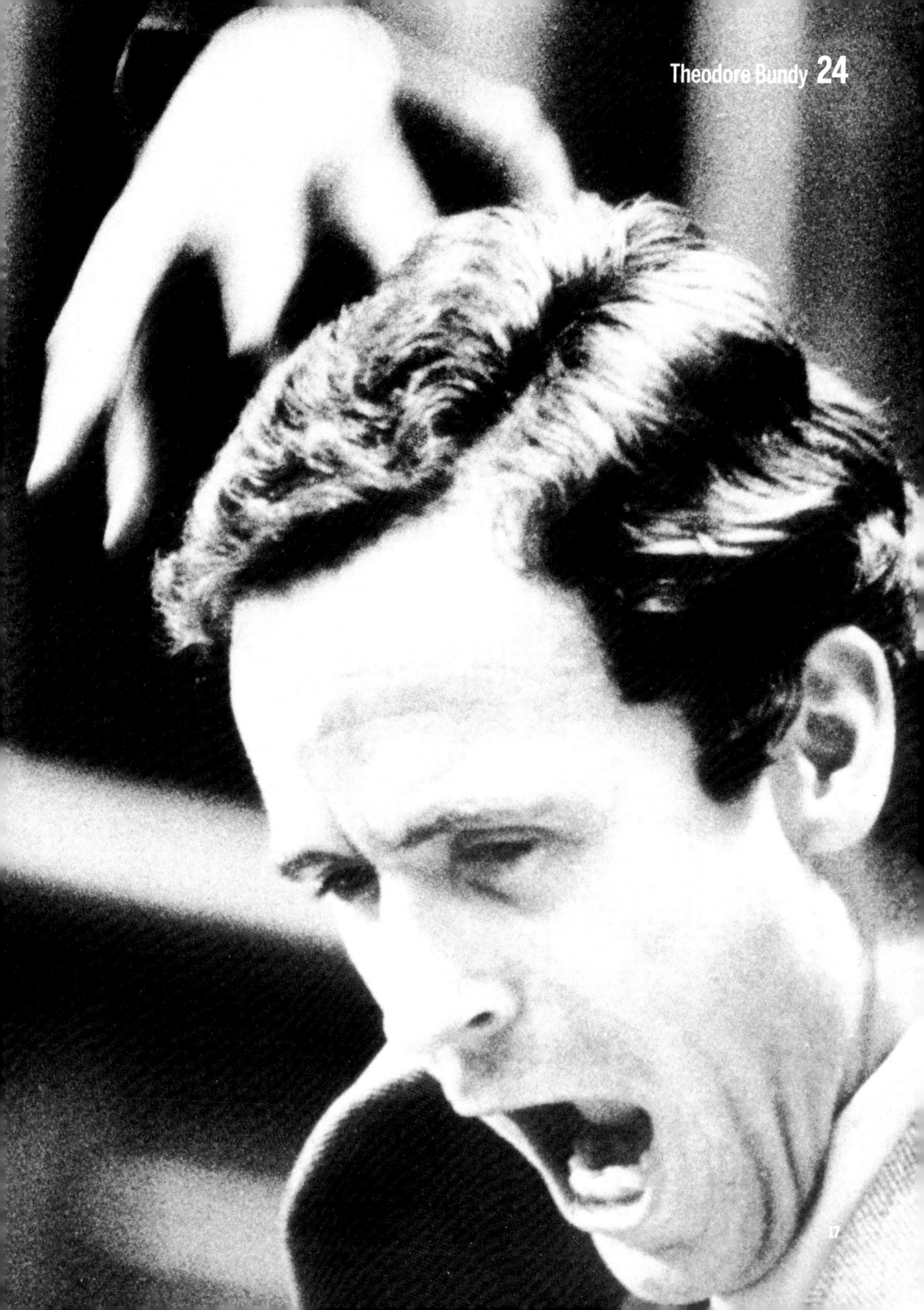

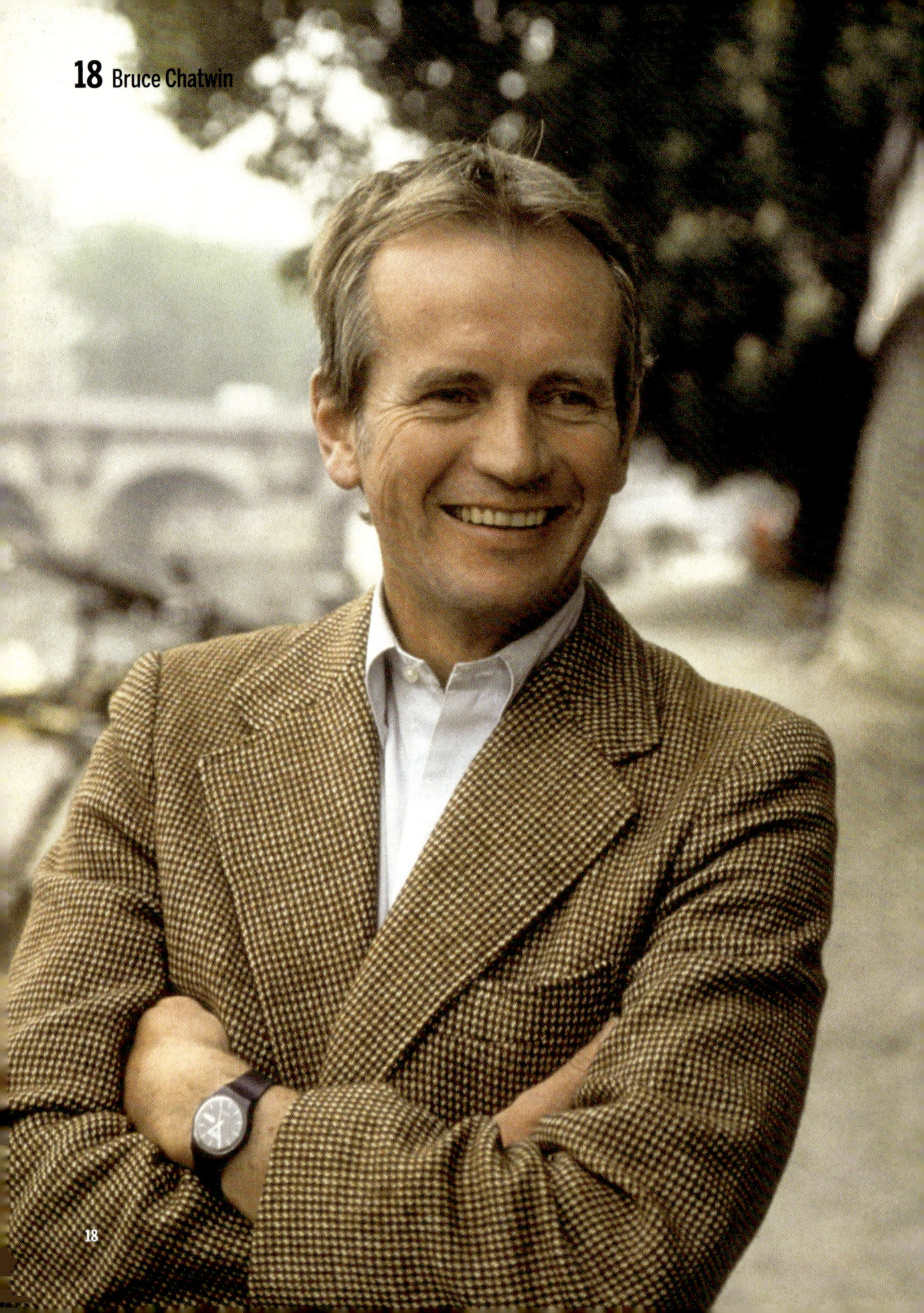

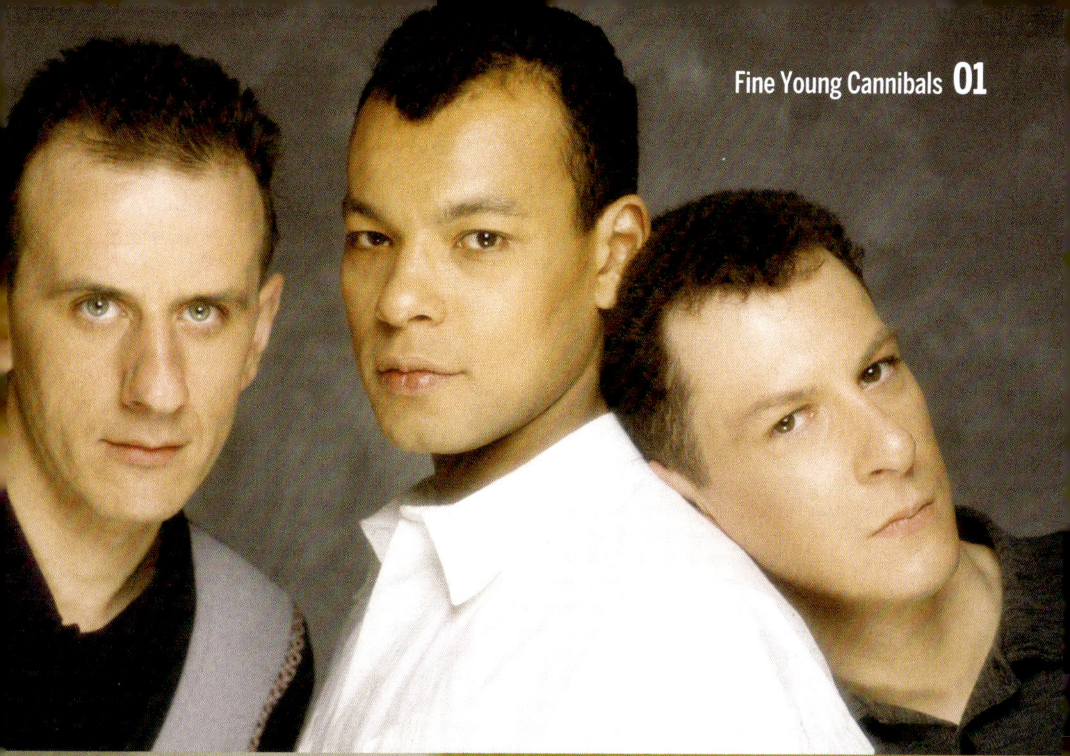

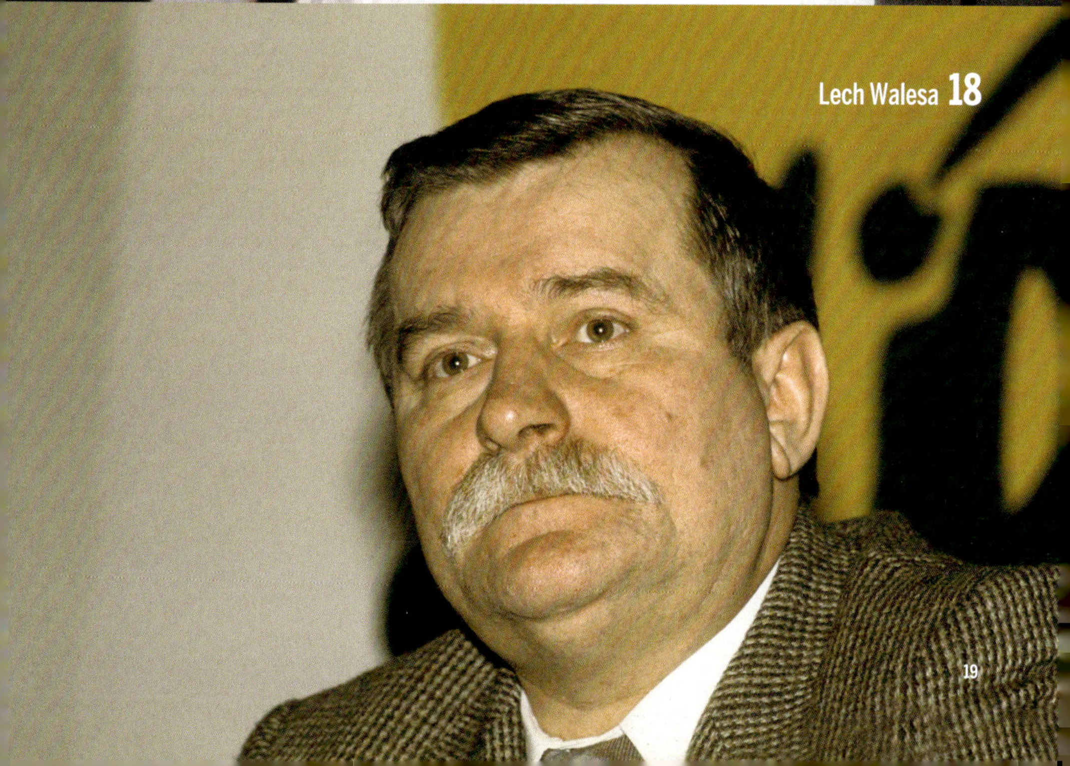

Lech Walesa **18**

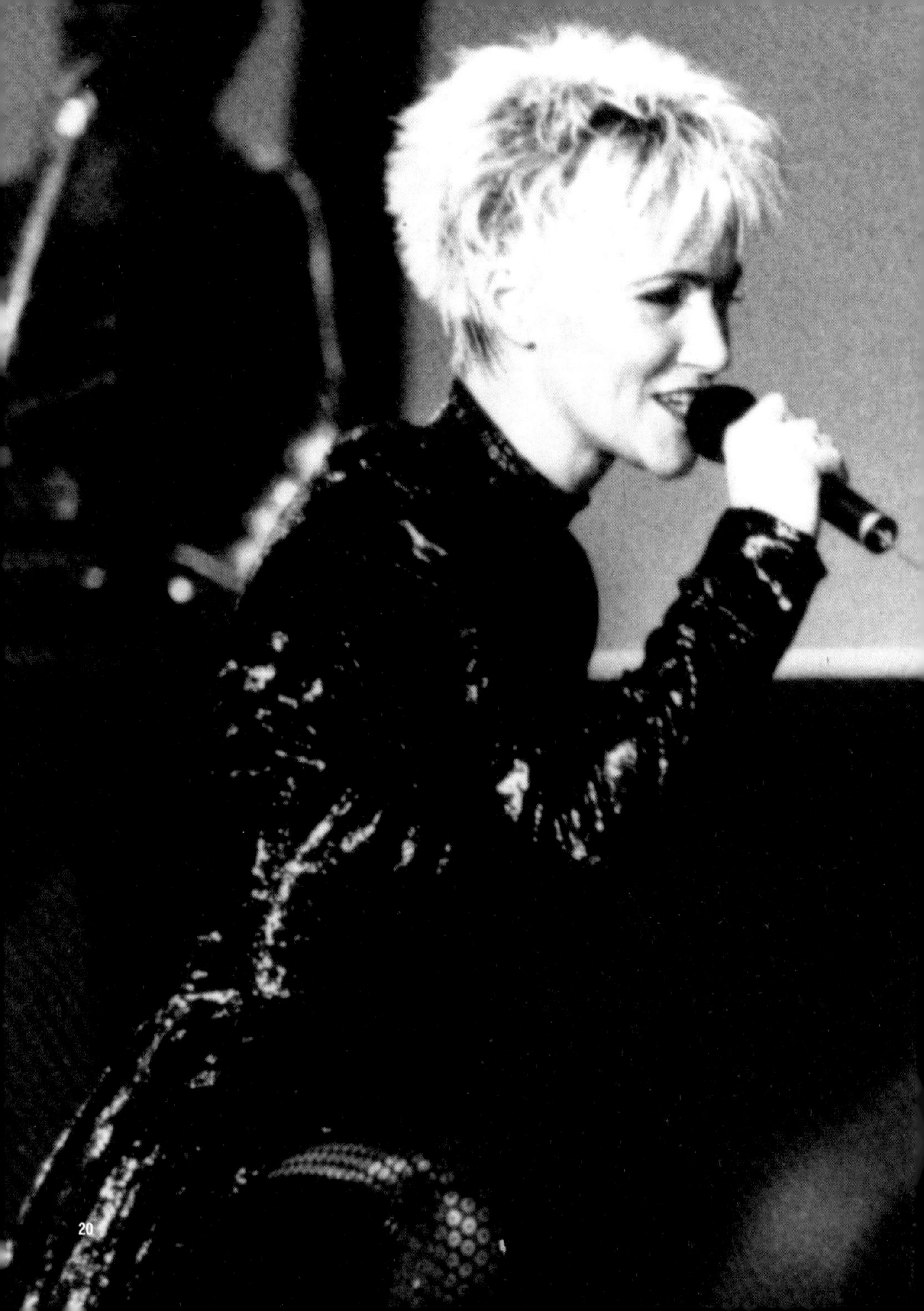

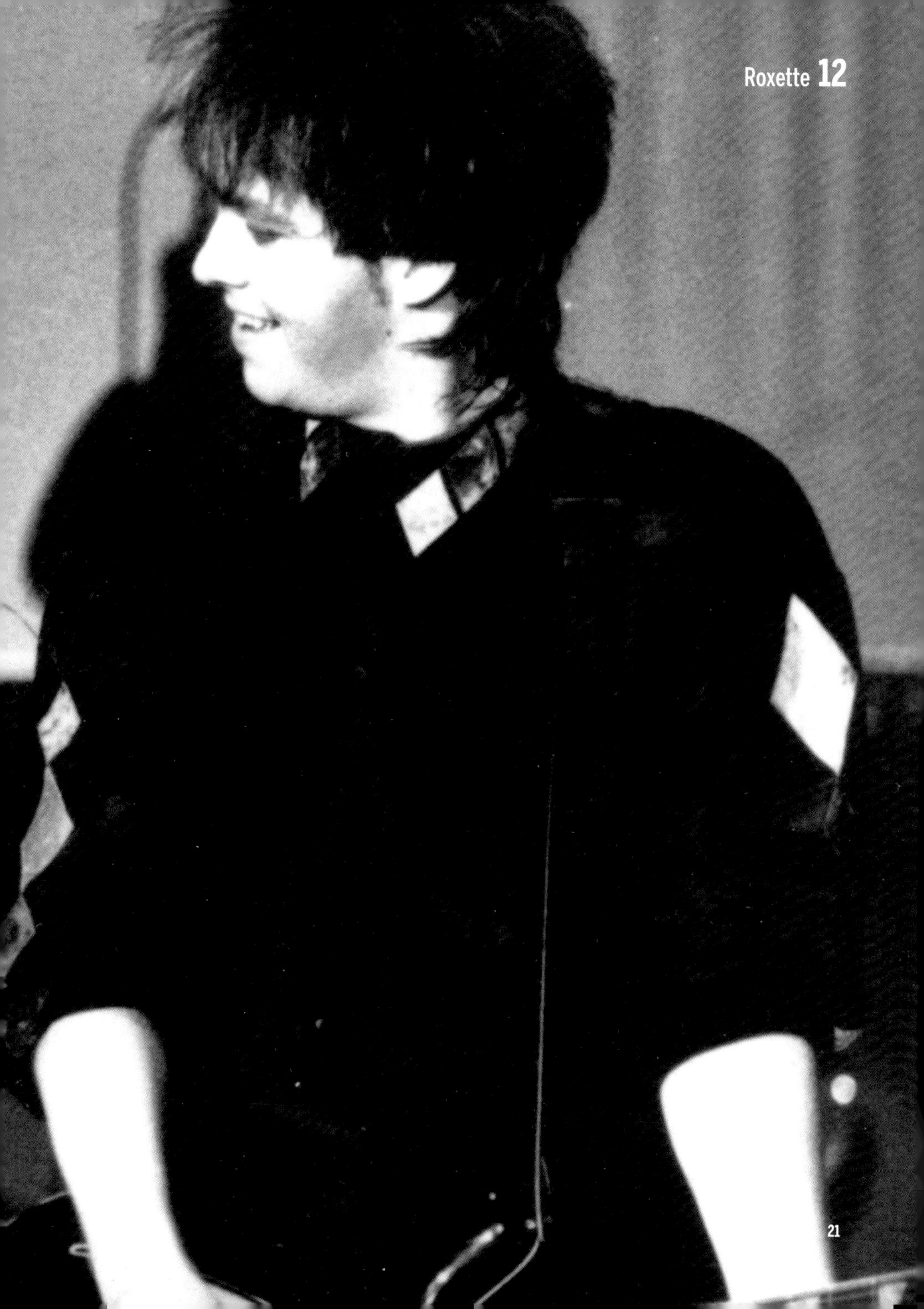

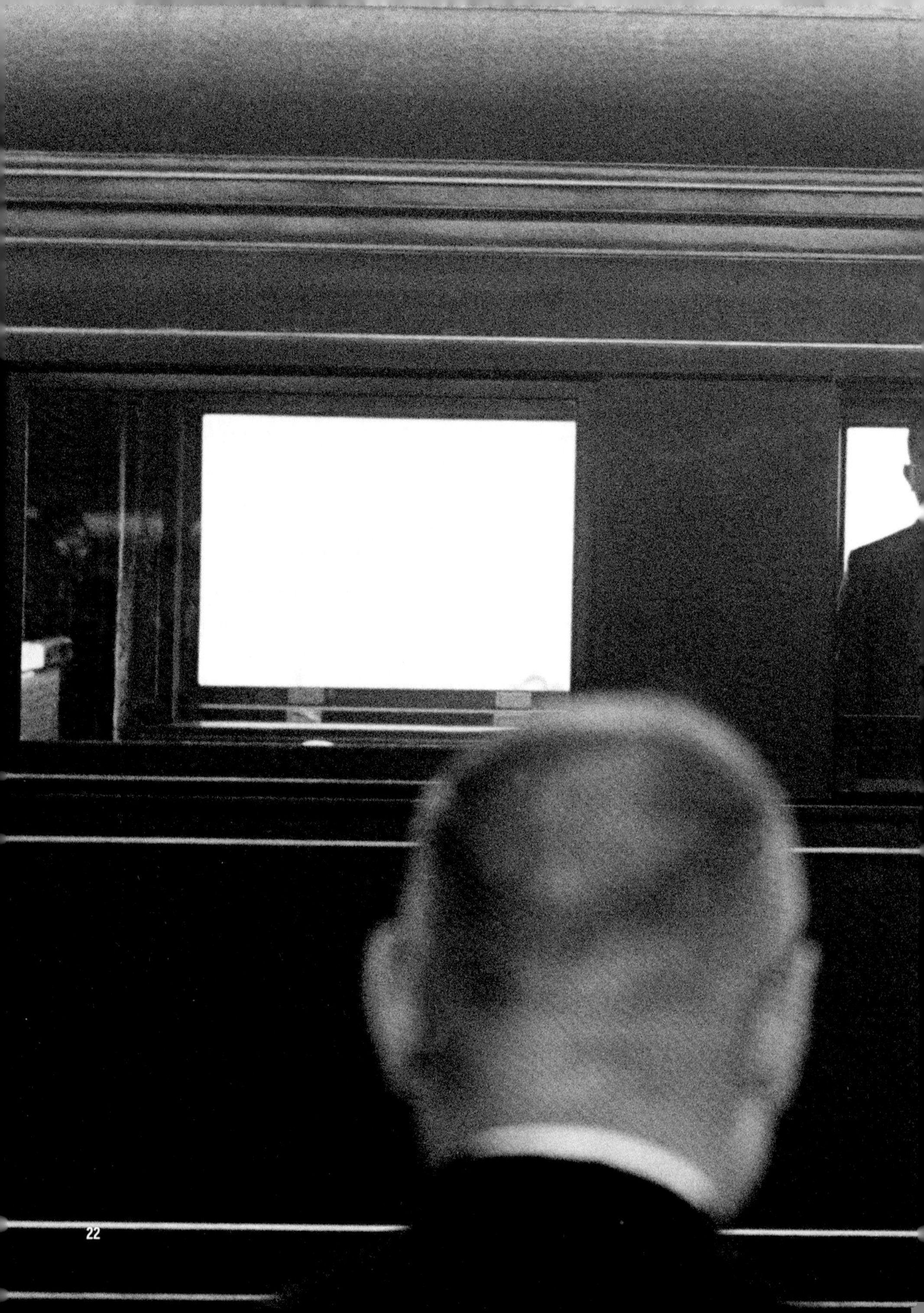

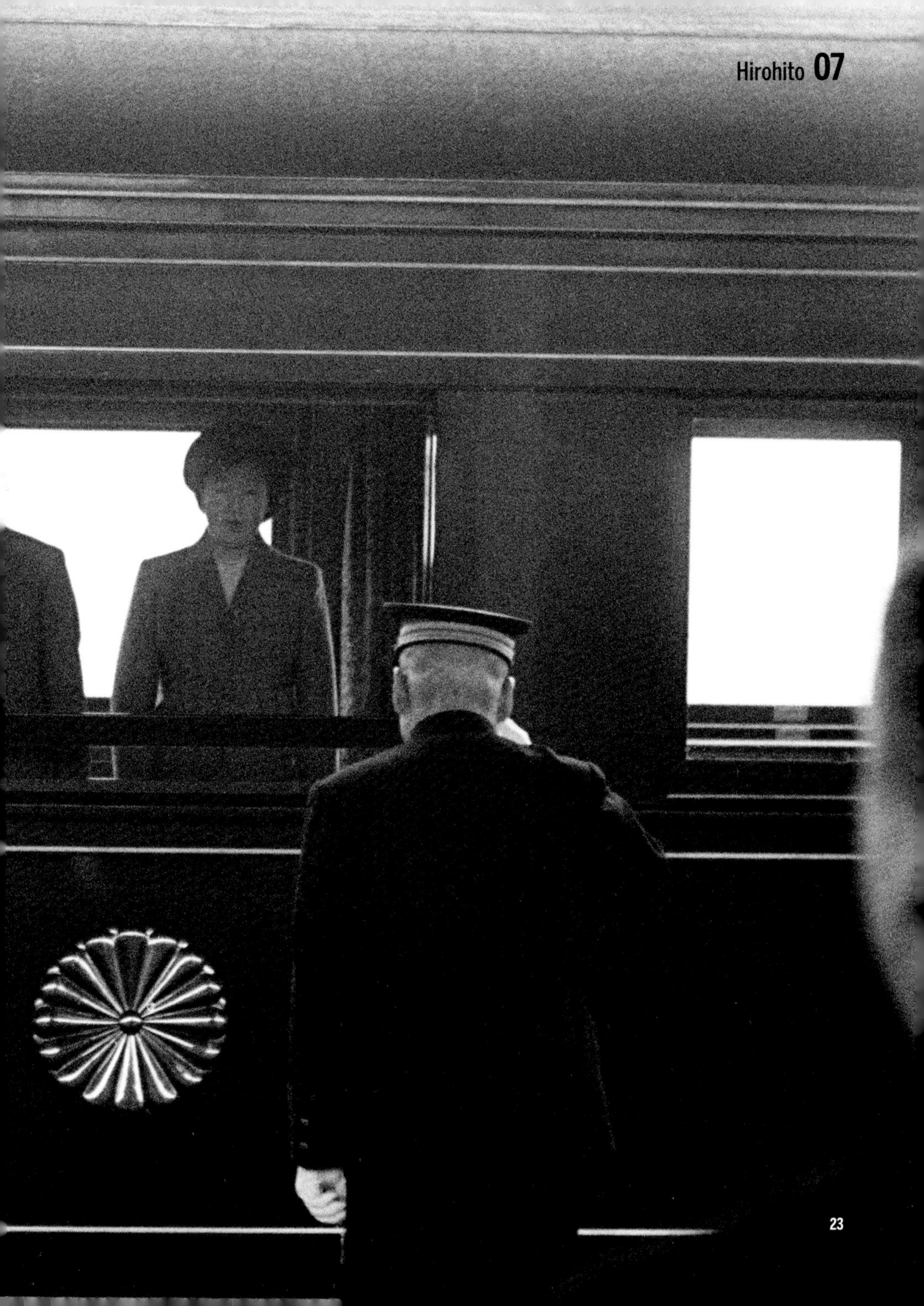

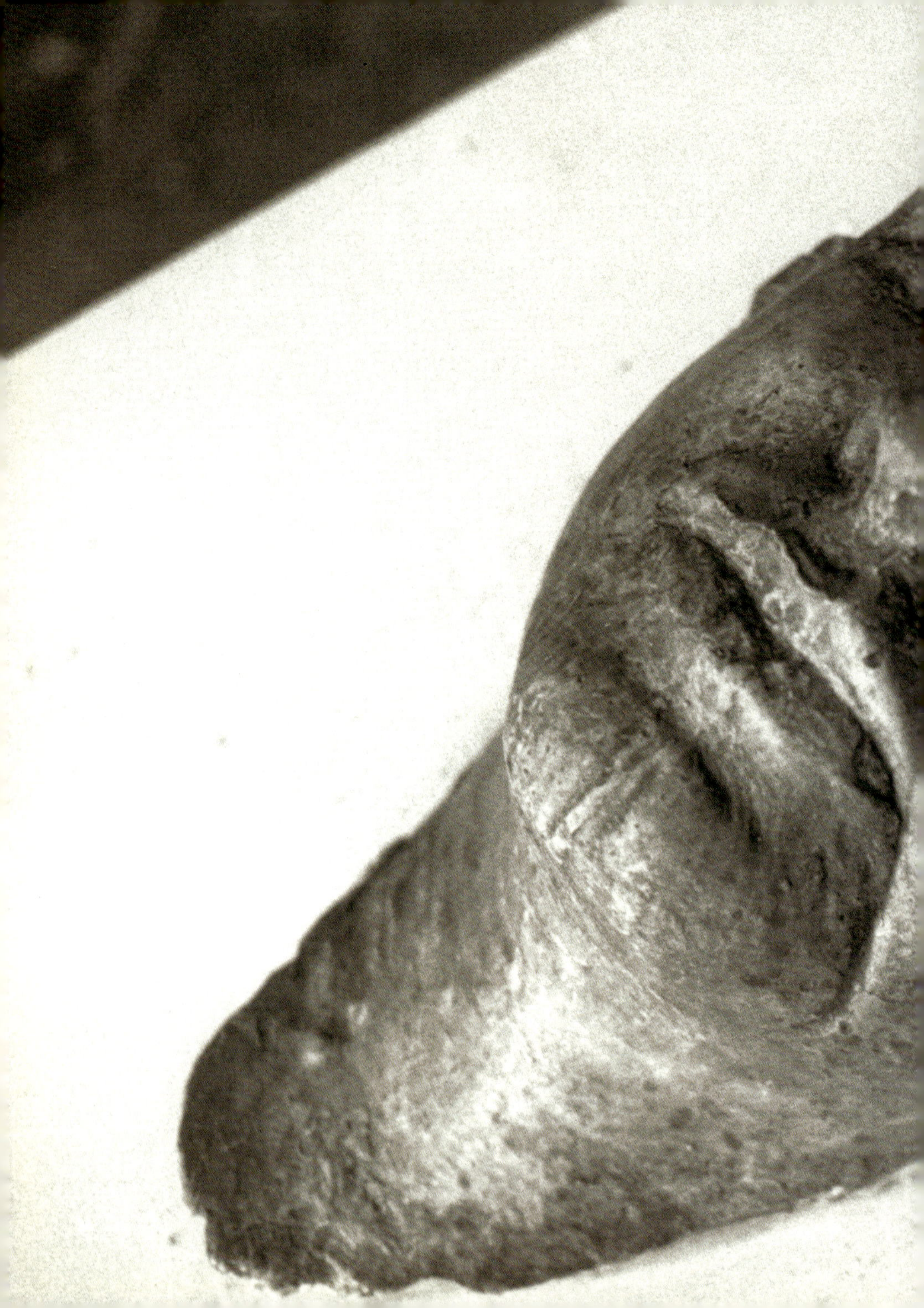

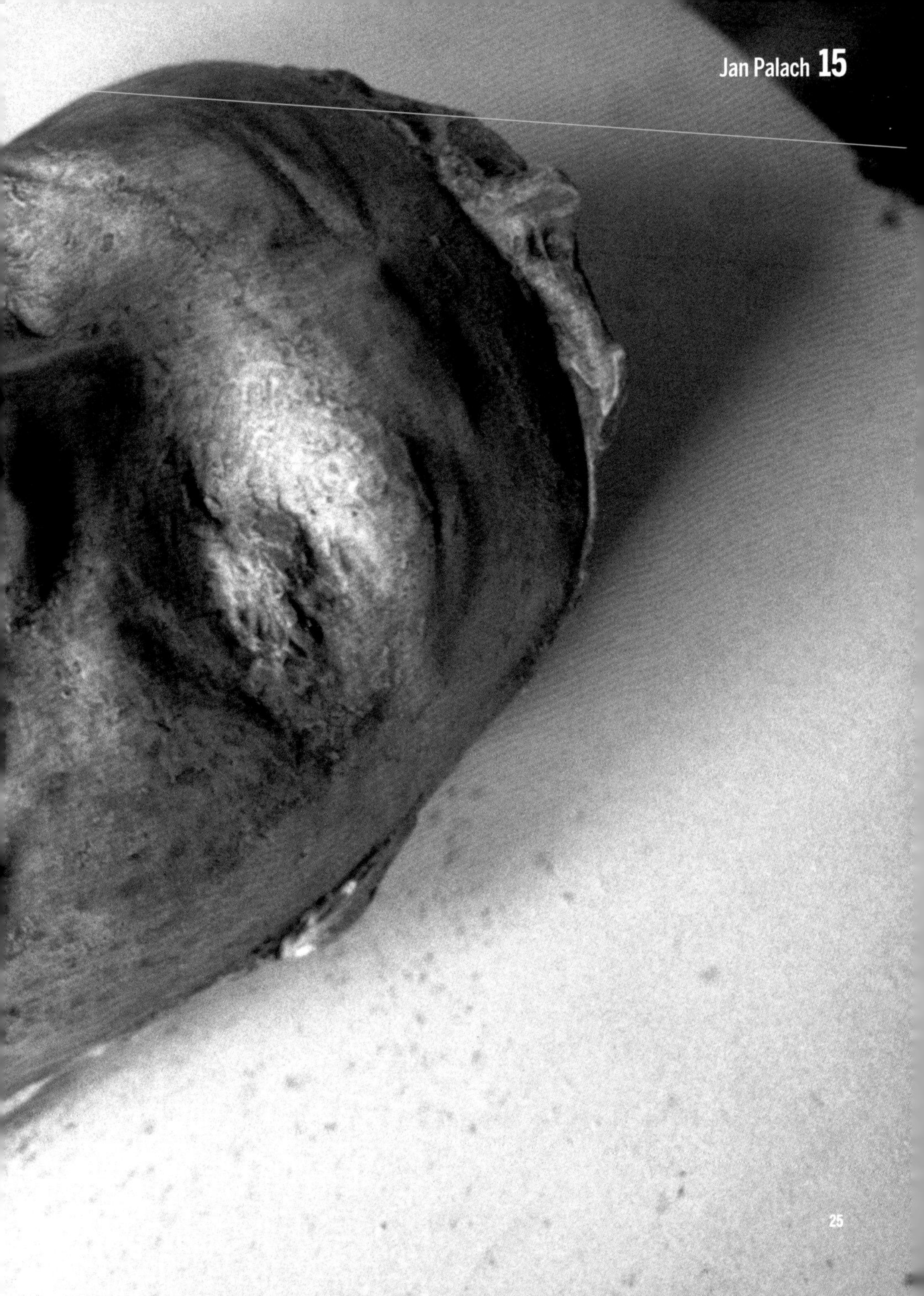

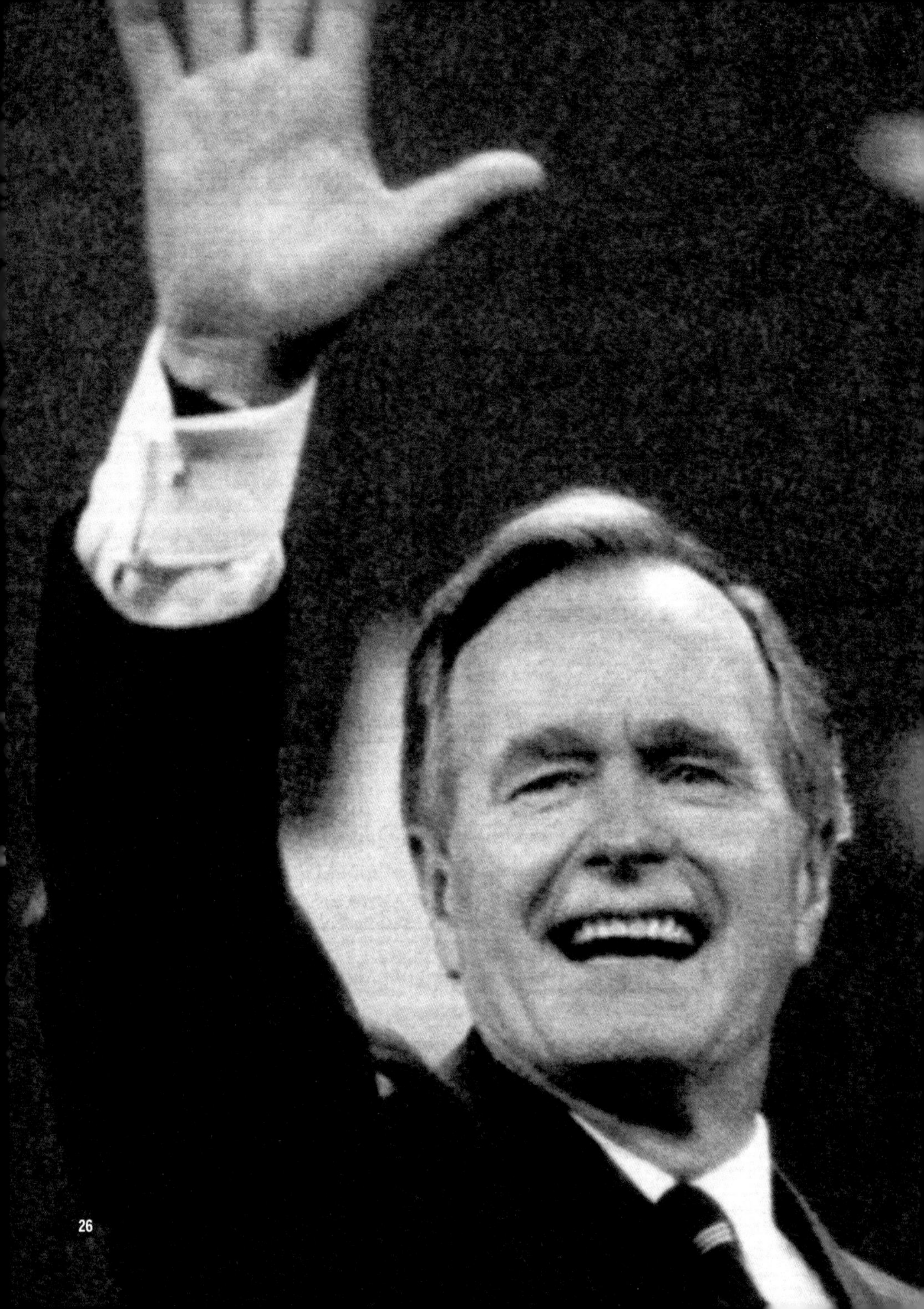

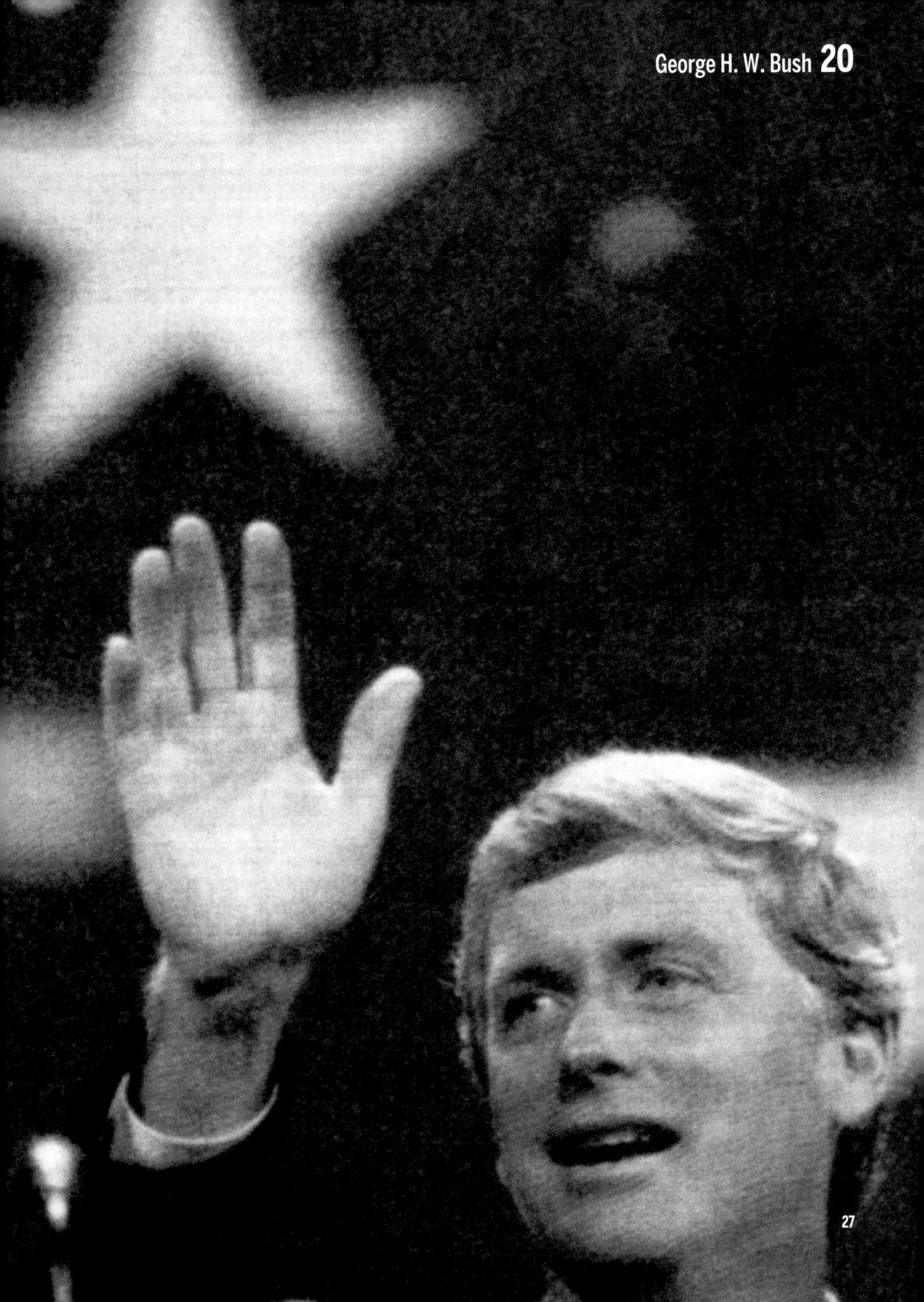

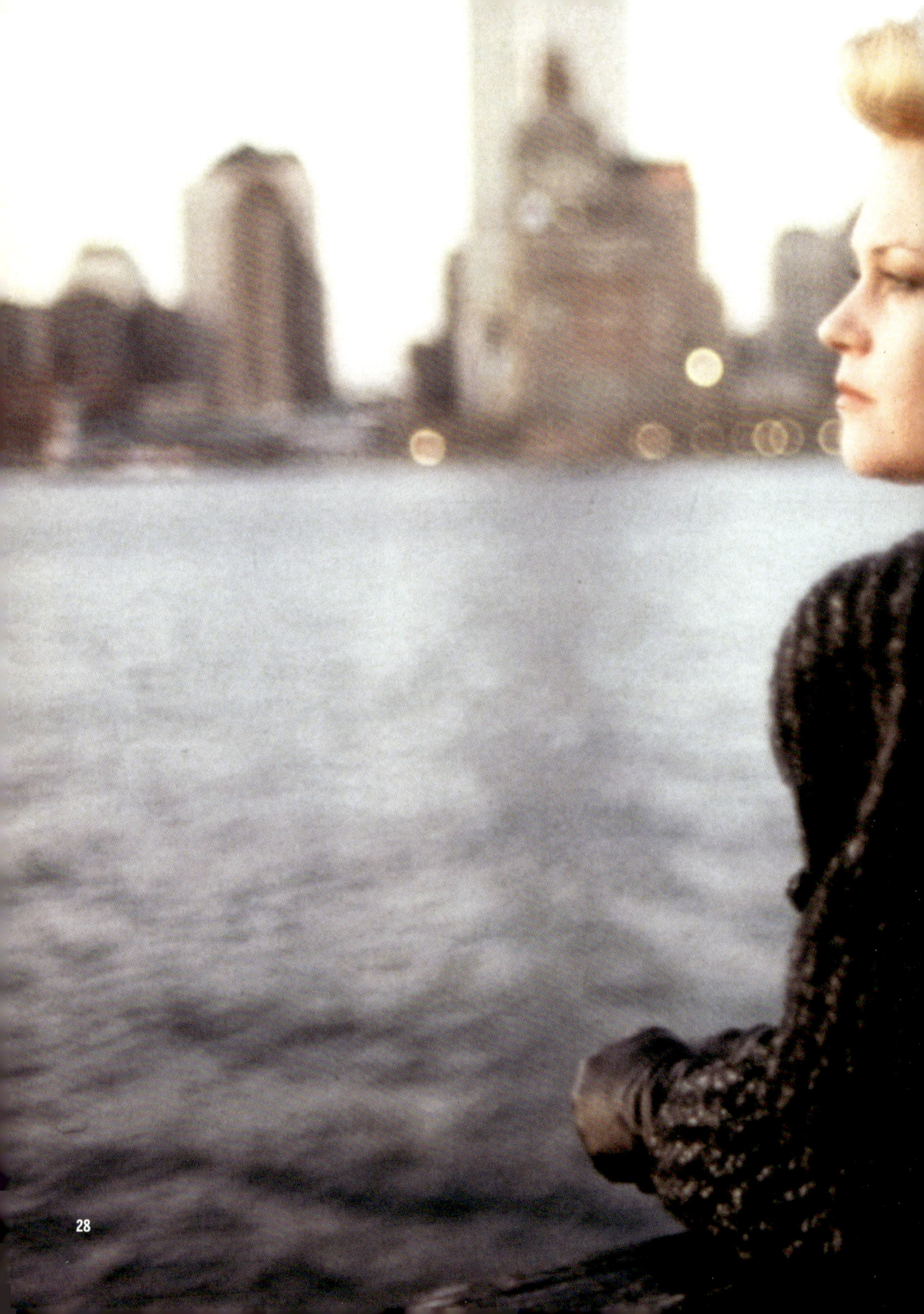

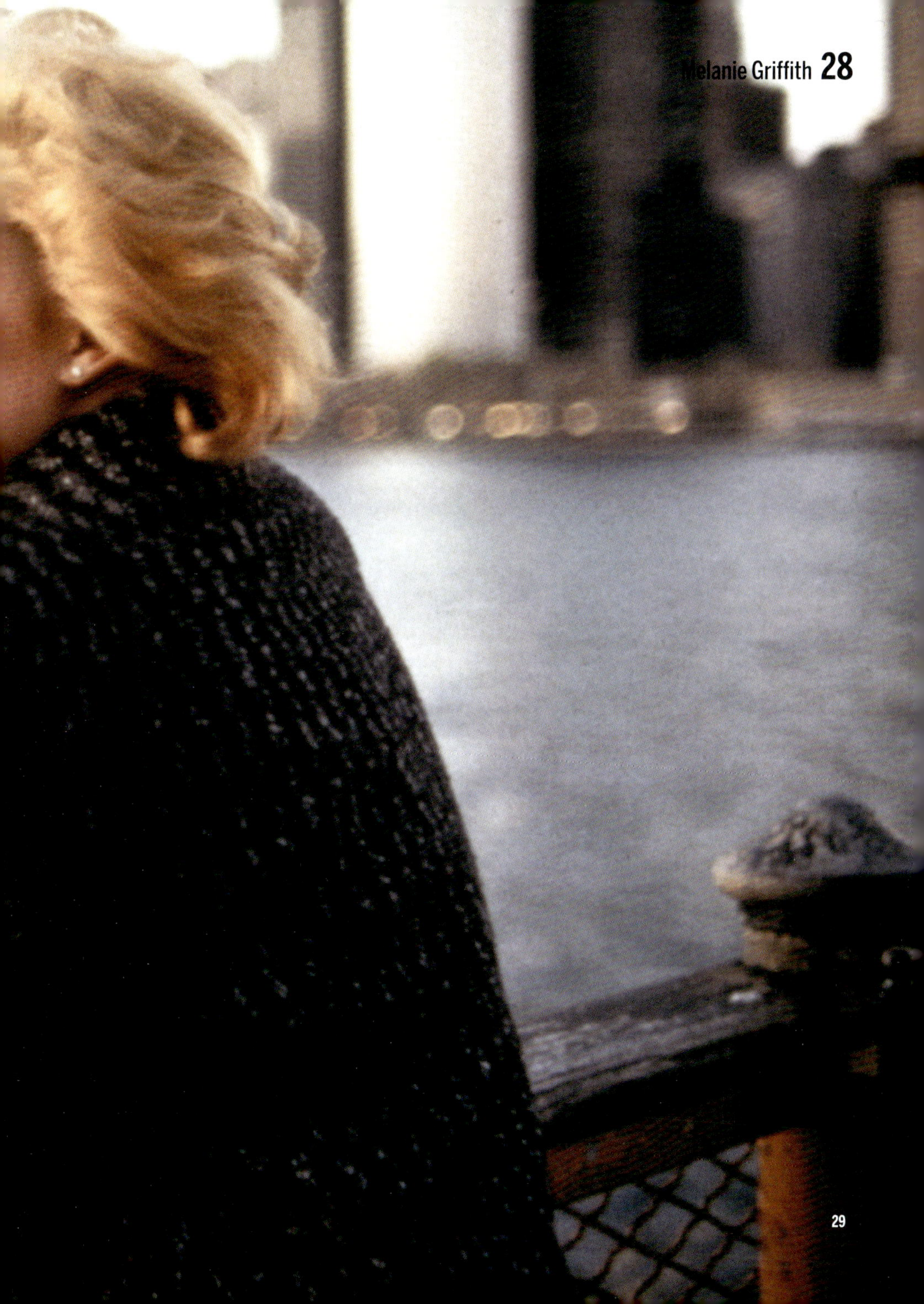

Melanie Griffith 28

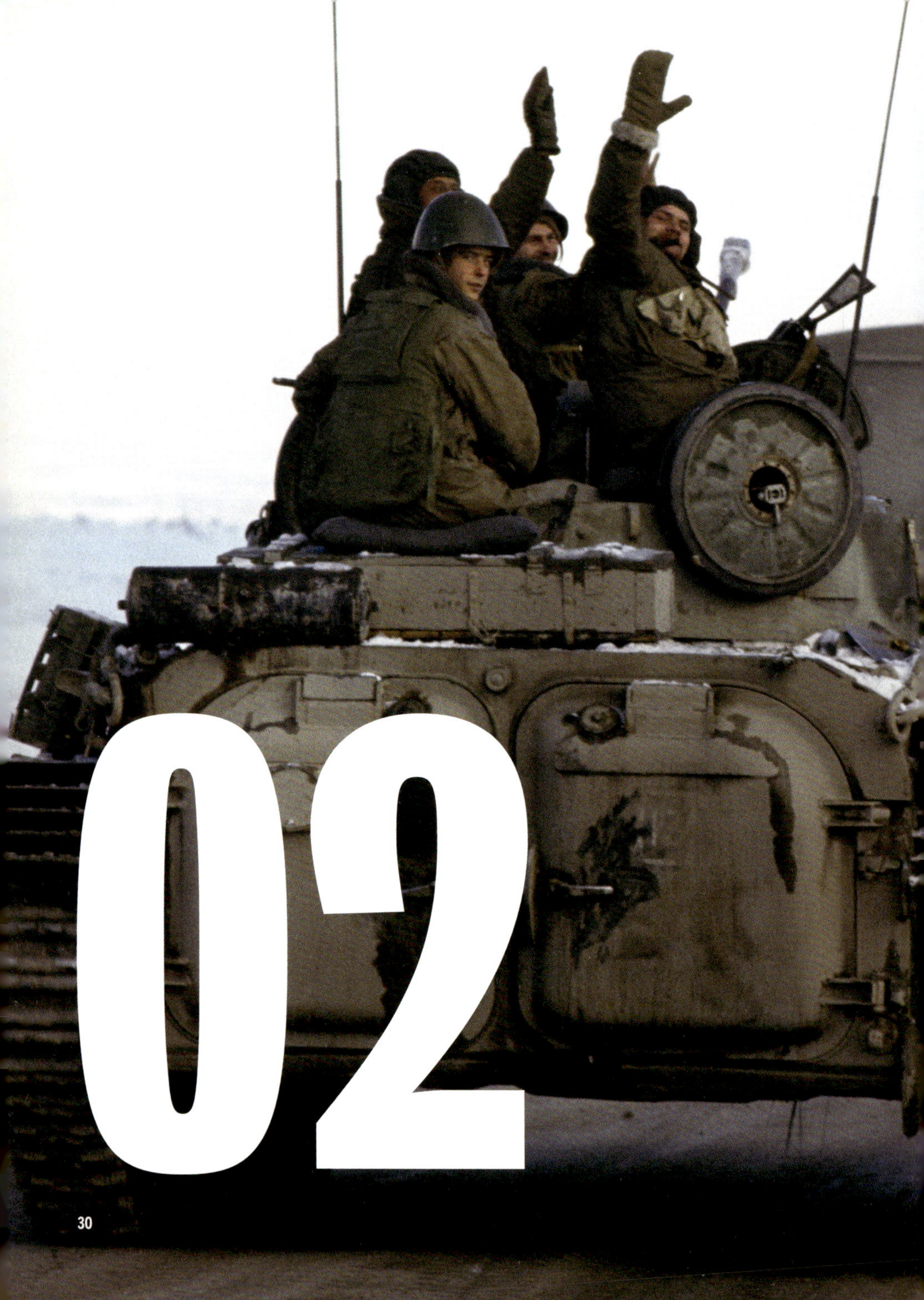

02

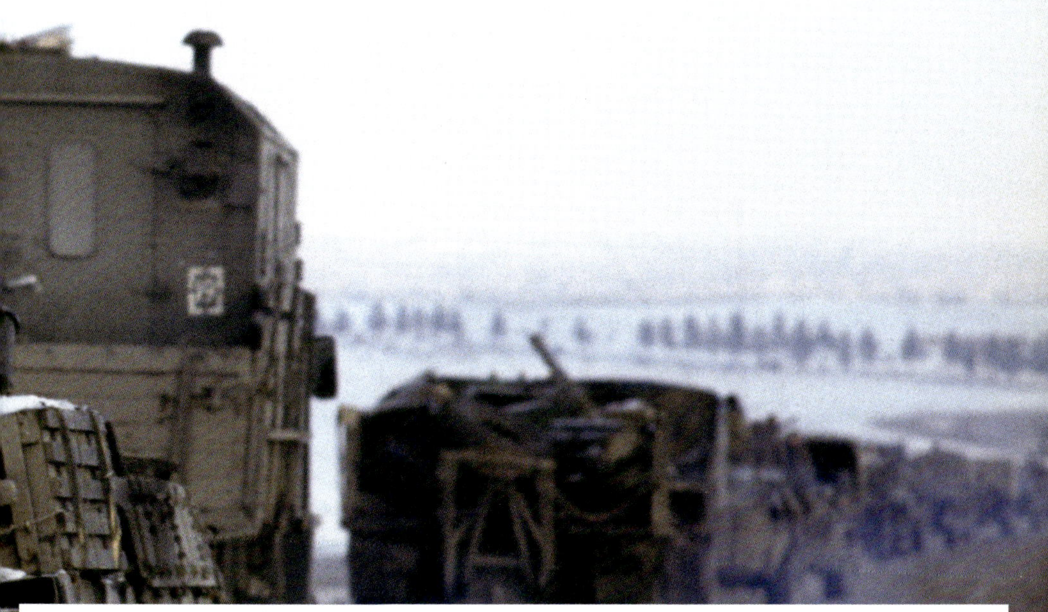

03

Paraguay: a coup d'etat overthrows Alfredo Stroessner, dictator since 1954.

11

United States: release of "Eternal Flame" by The Bangles, a hit in six countries including United States, Great Britain and Australia.

15

Afghanistan: the Soviet Union announces the official withdrawal of the troops begun on the 2nd of February. A 20 year long conflict finally ends.

17

France: couturier Guy Laroche dies in La Rochelle, at the age of 68.

22

United States: Bobby McFerrin with "Don't Worry, Be Happy" wins Best single at the 31st edition of the Grammy Awards; "Faith" by George Michael is Album of the year and Tracy Chapman is the Best new artist.

24

Iran: Ayatollah Ruhollah Khomeini issues a fatwa against Salman Rushdie, author of "The Satanic Verses" and sets a price of 3 million dollars on his head.

28

United States: release of "Like a prayer" by Madonna, the best selling single of the year with over 5 million copies. It still is recognised as one of the singer's undisputed hits.

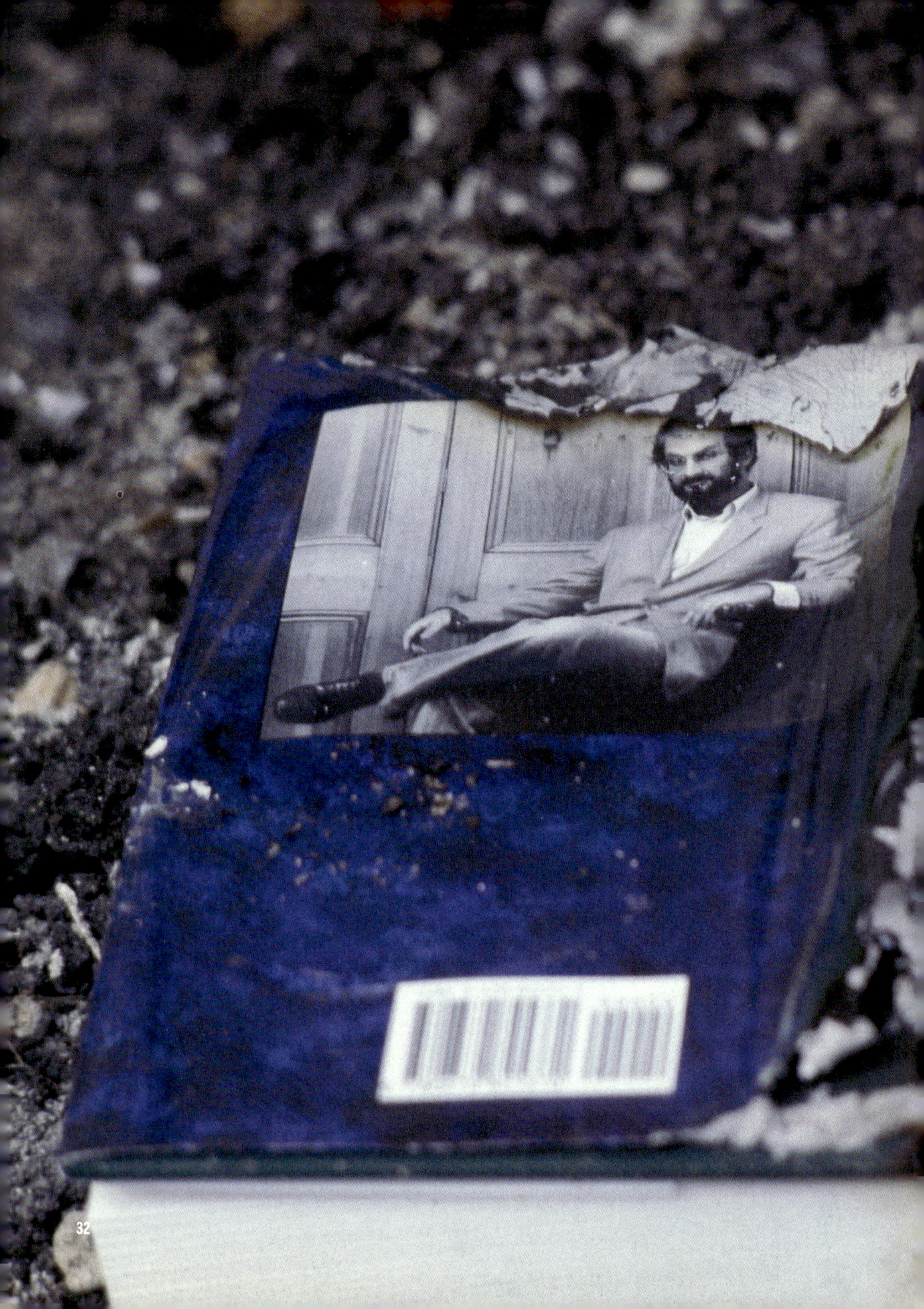

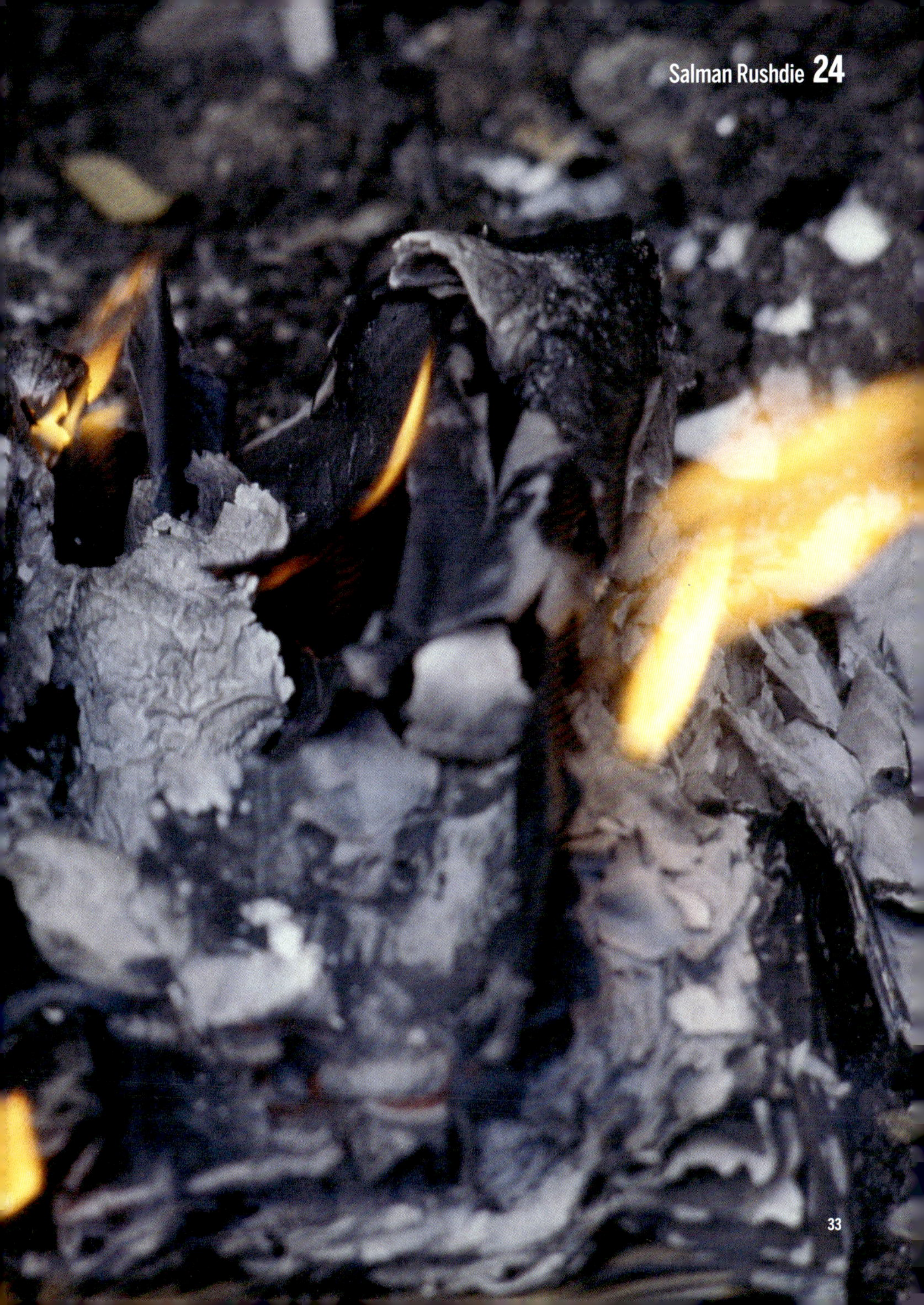

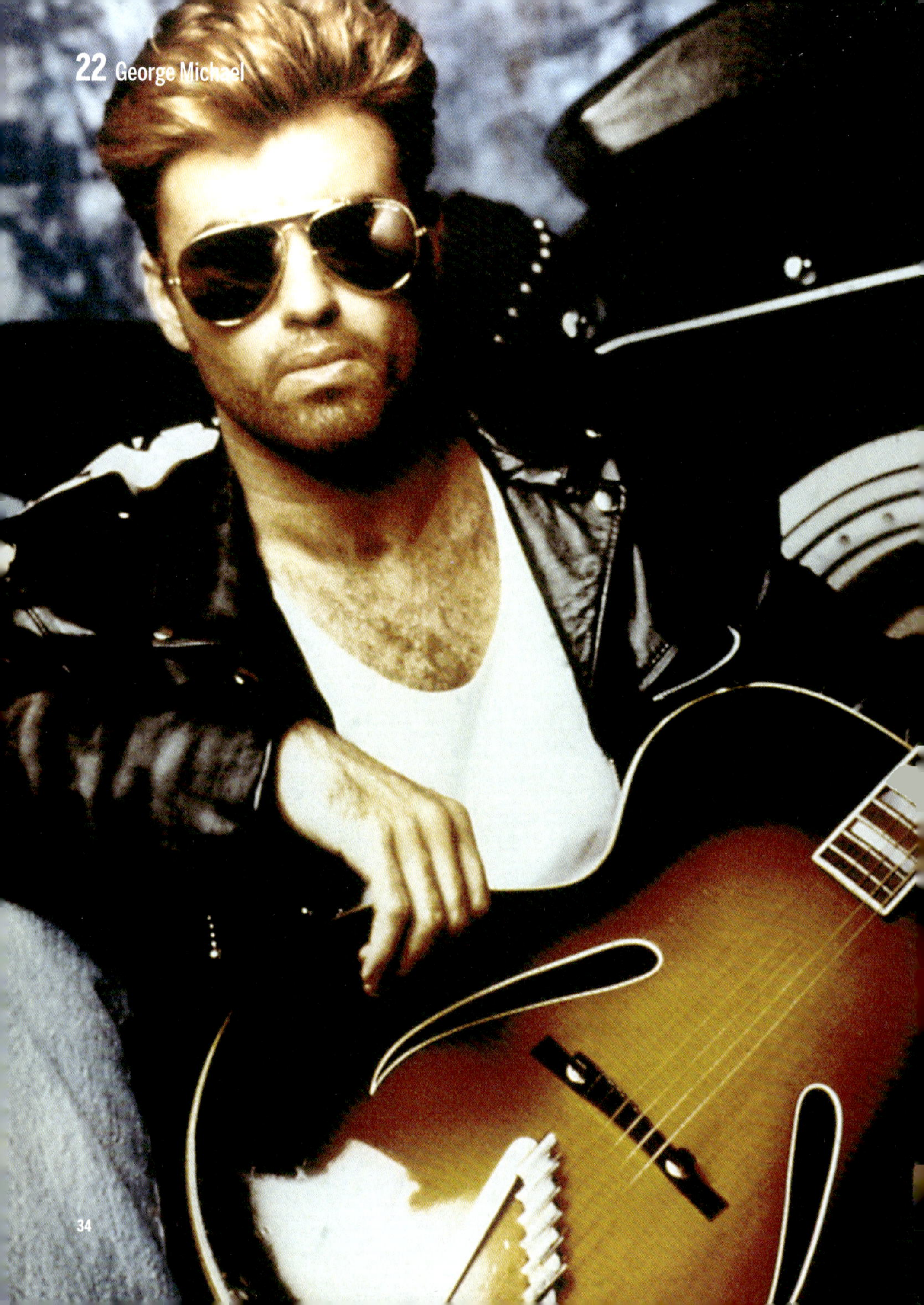

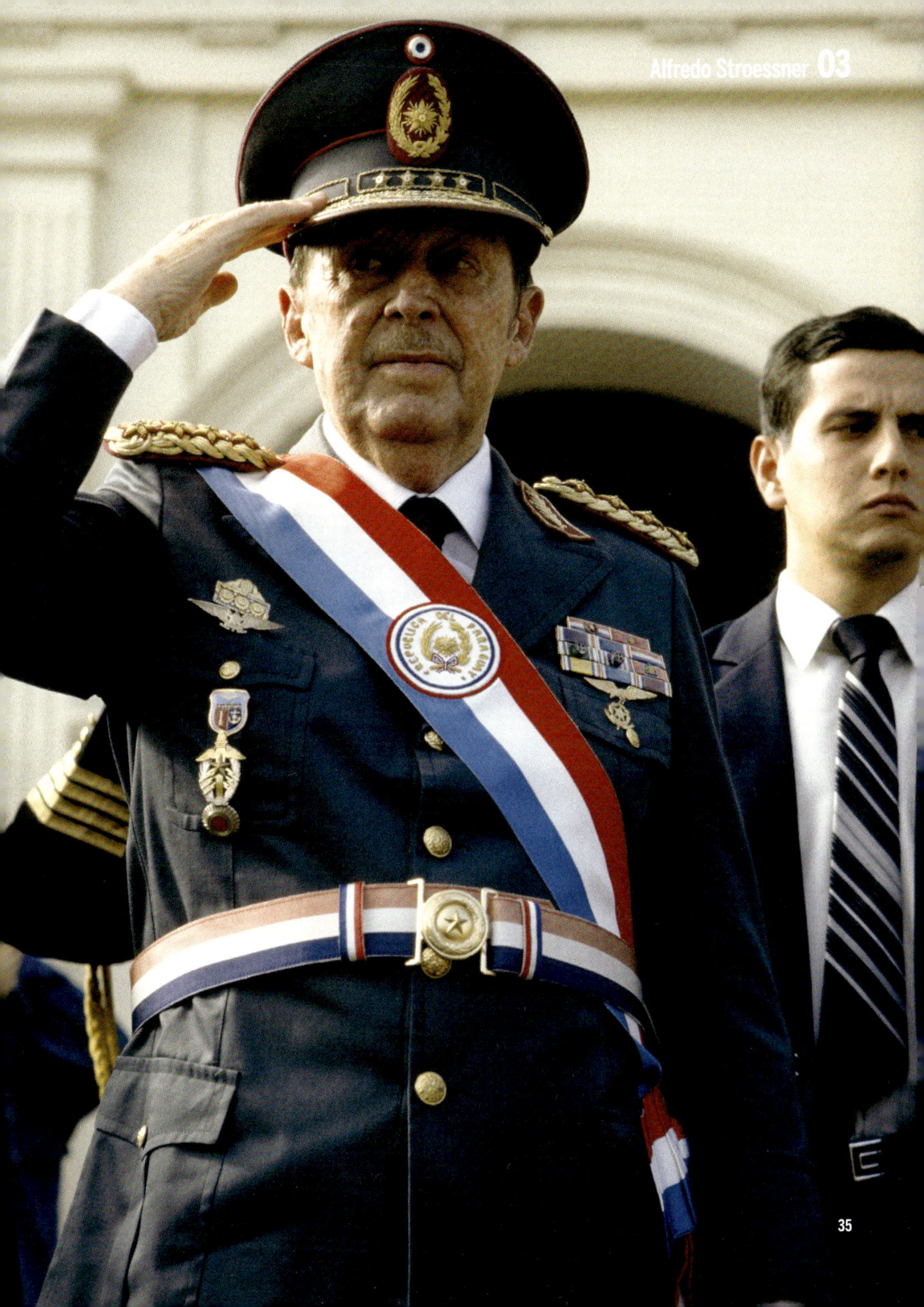

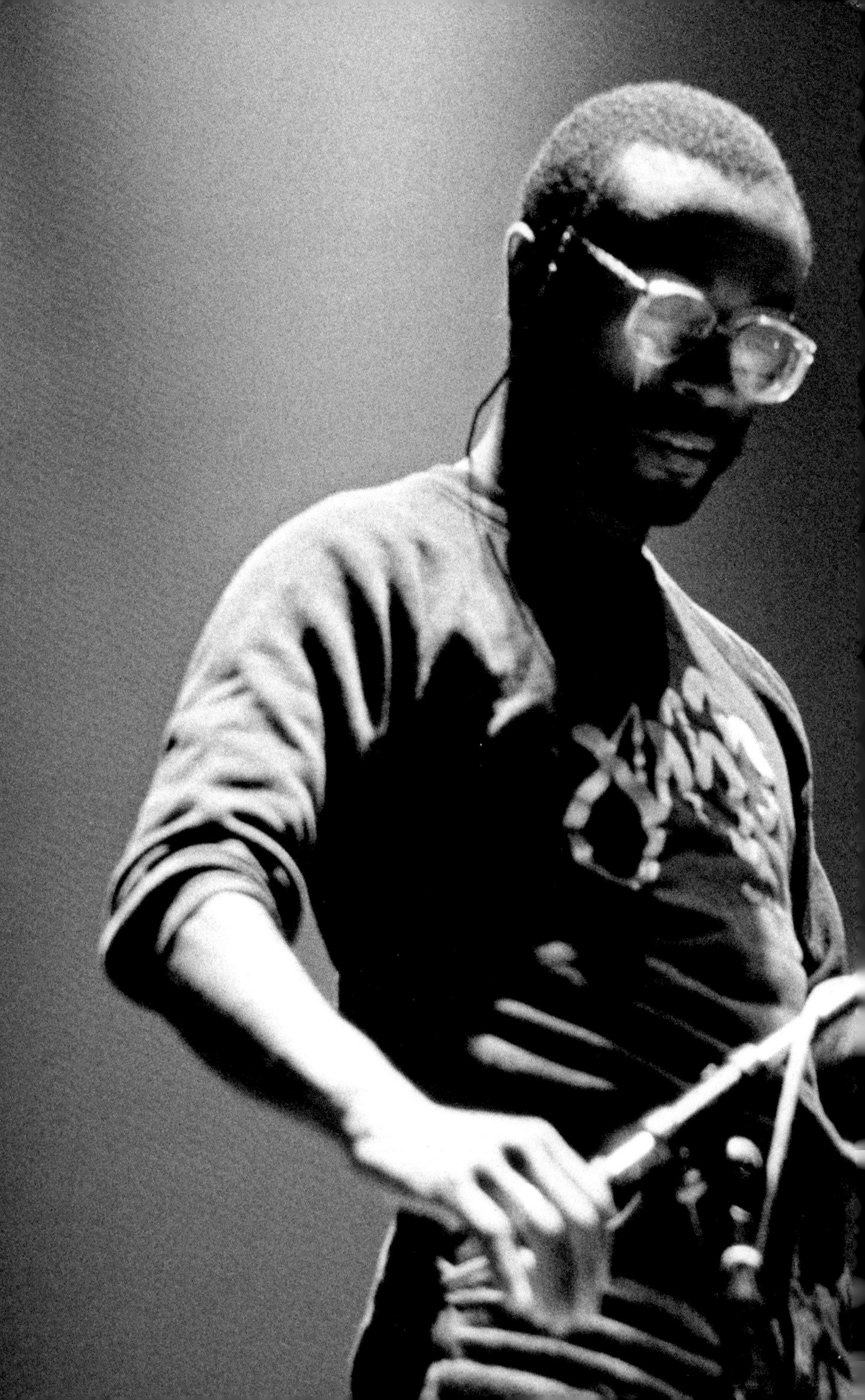

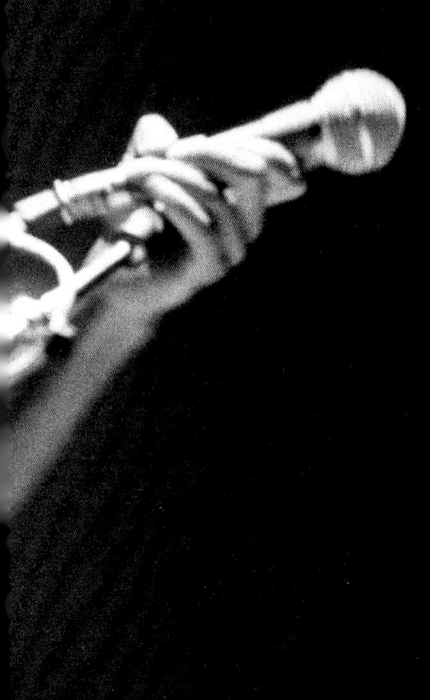

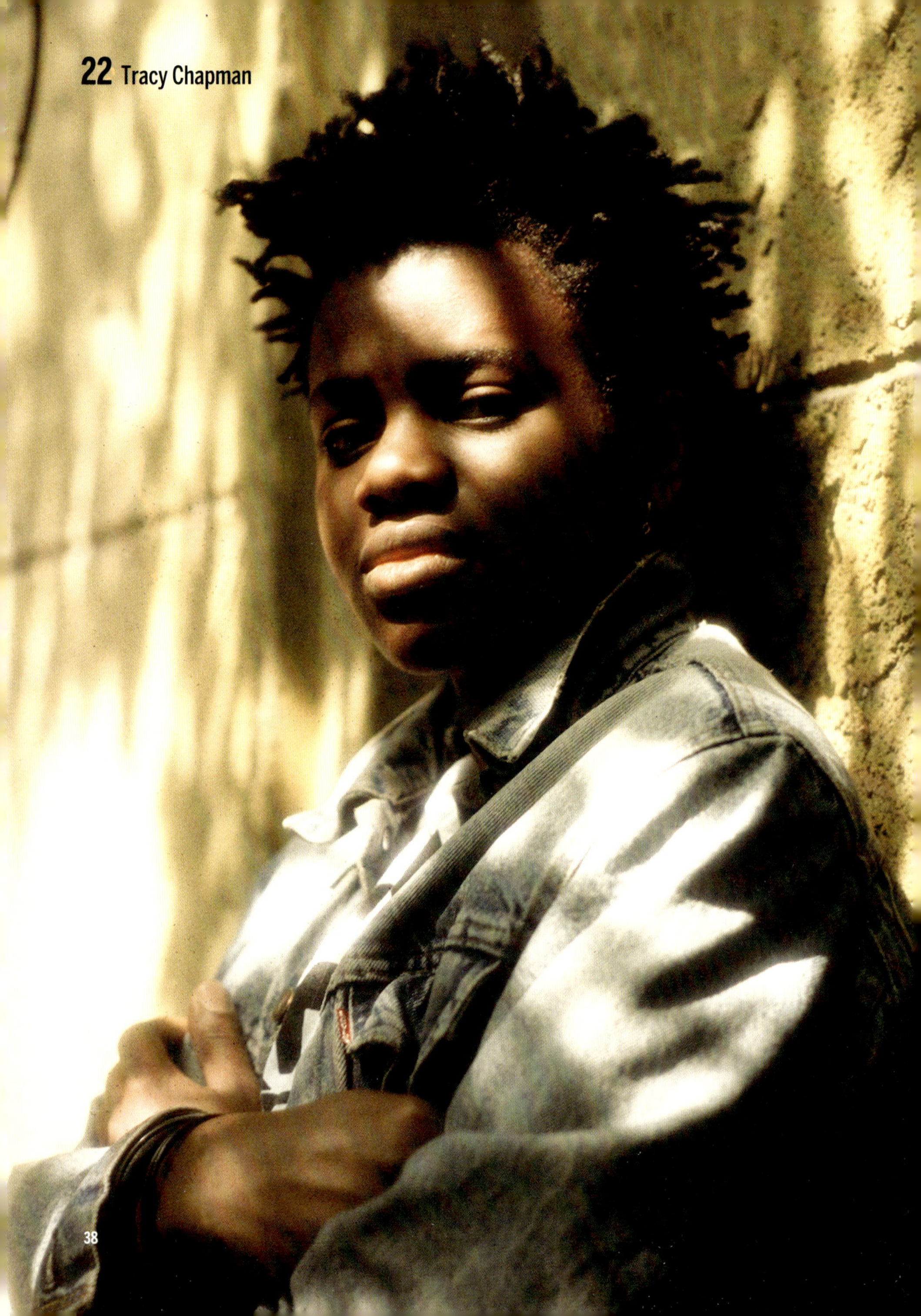

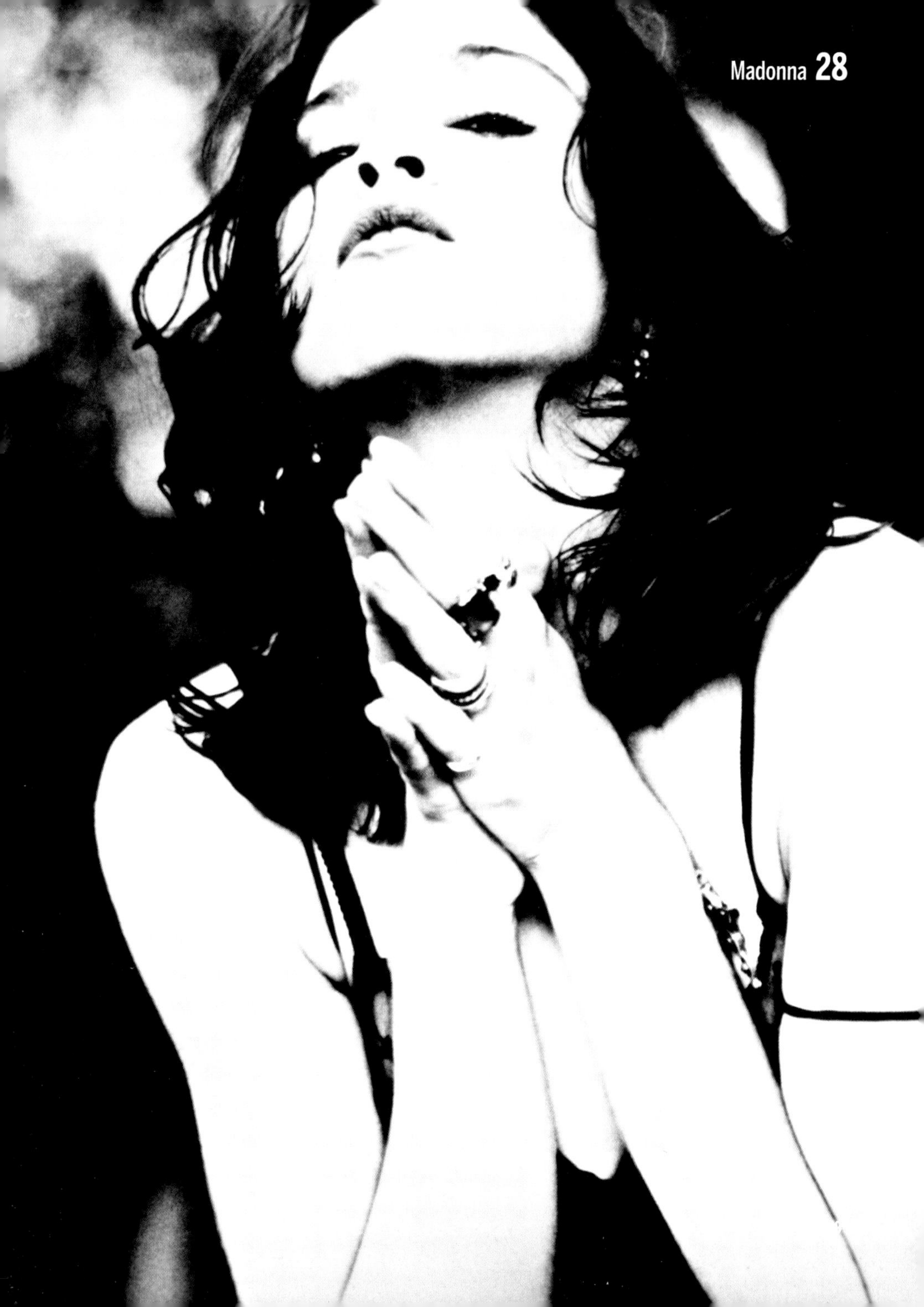

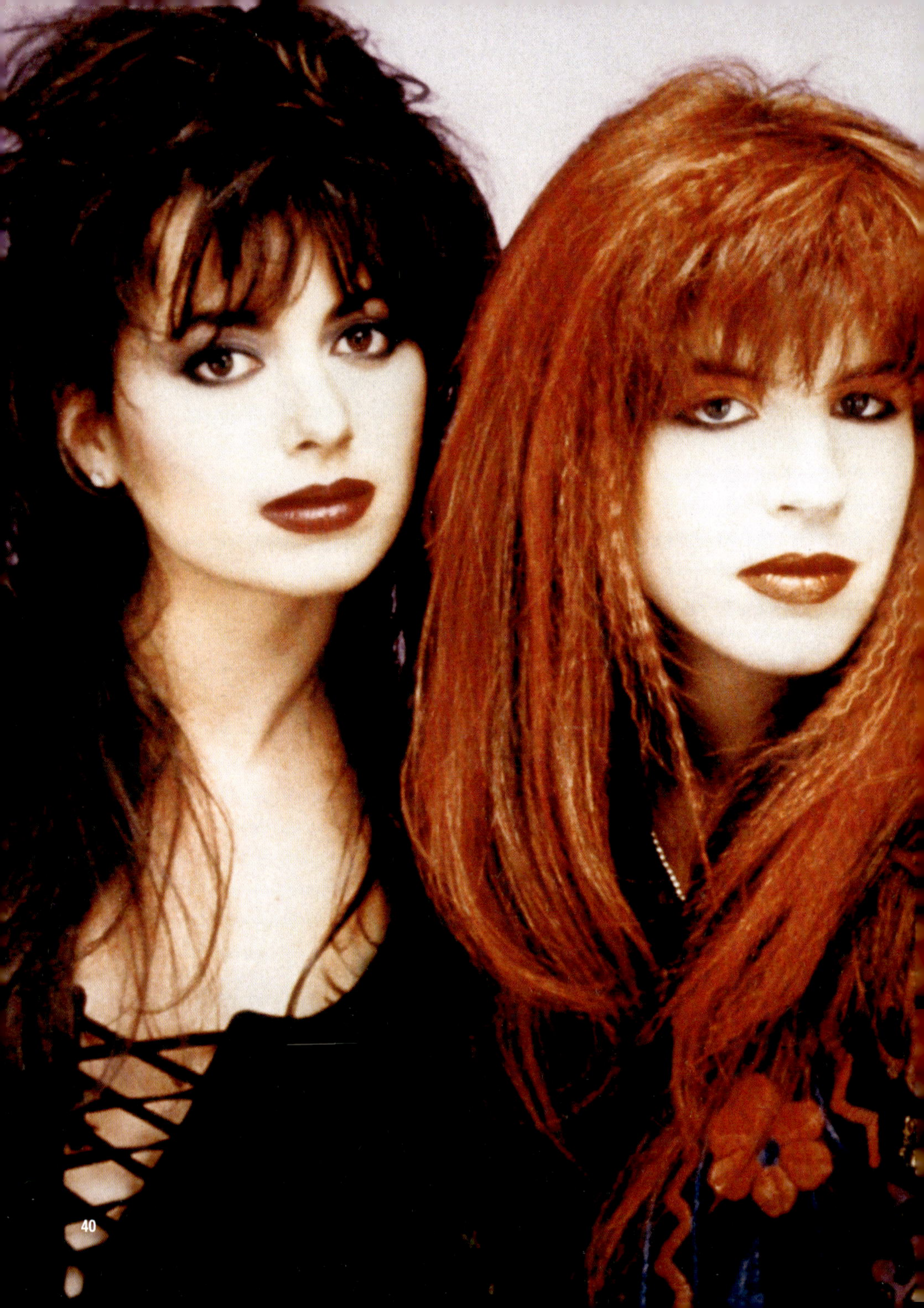

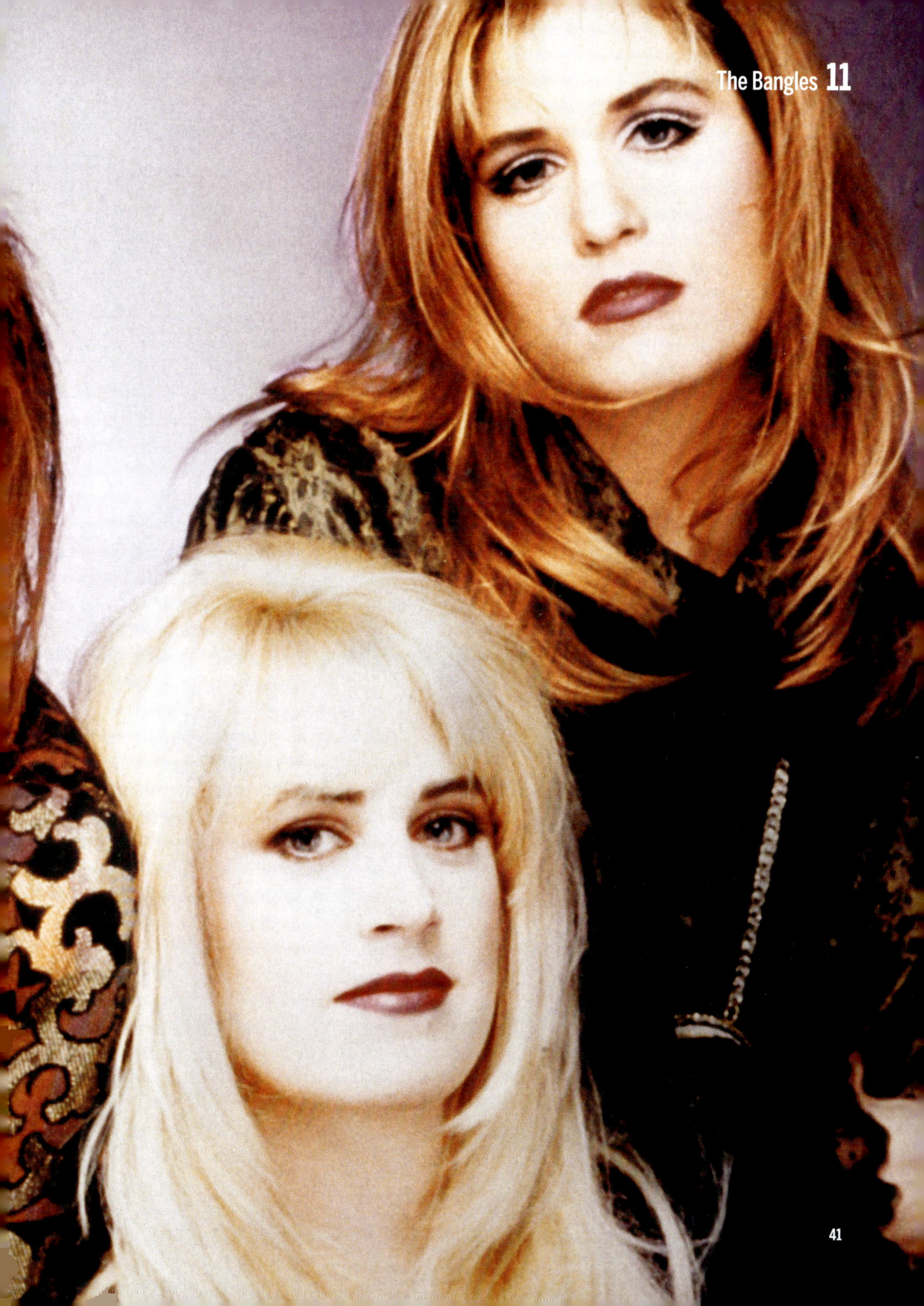

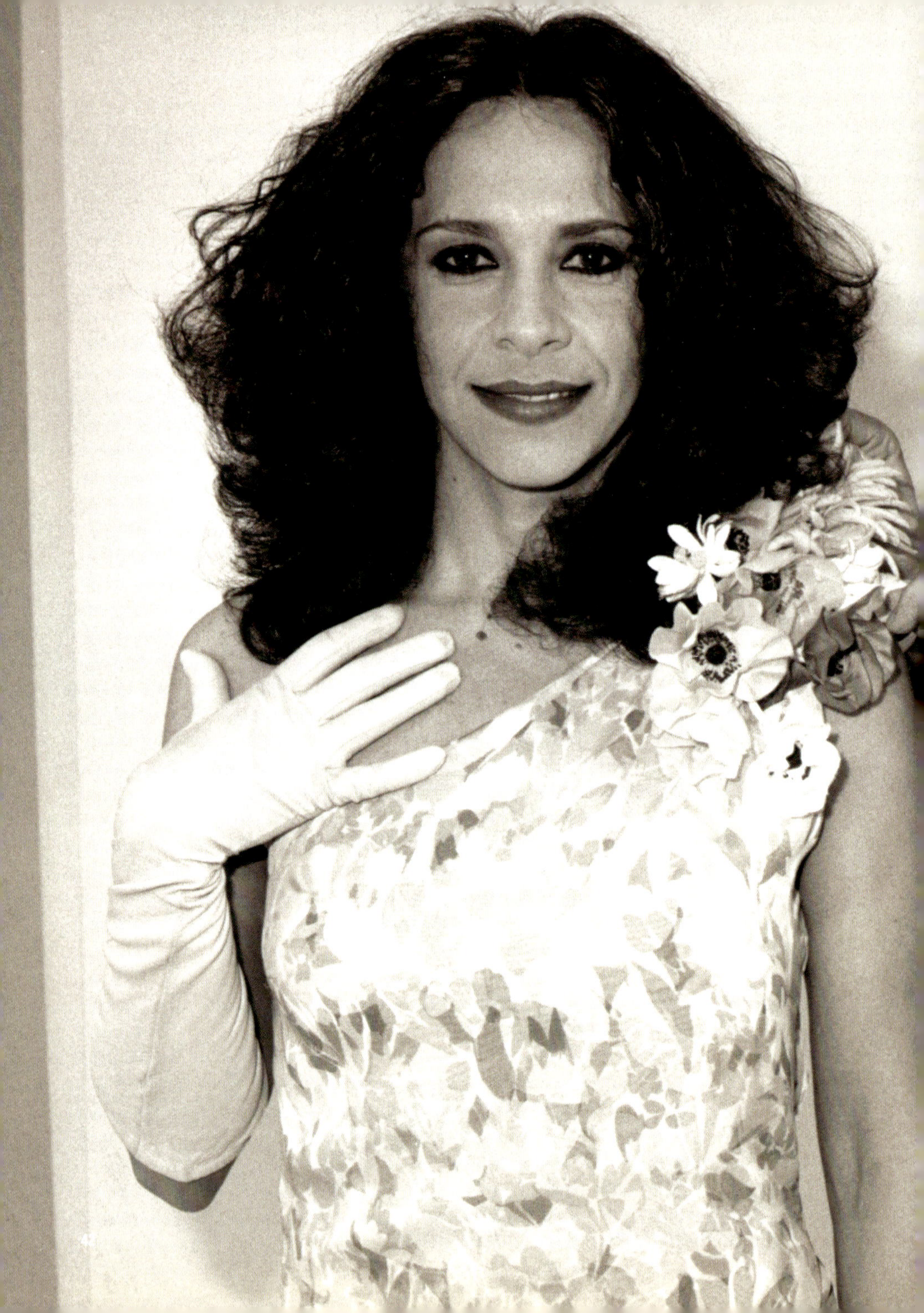

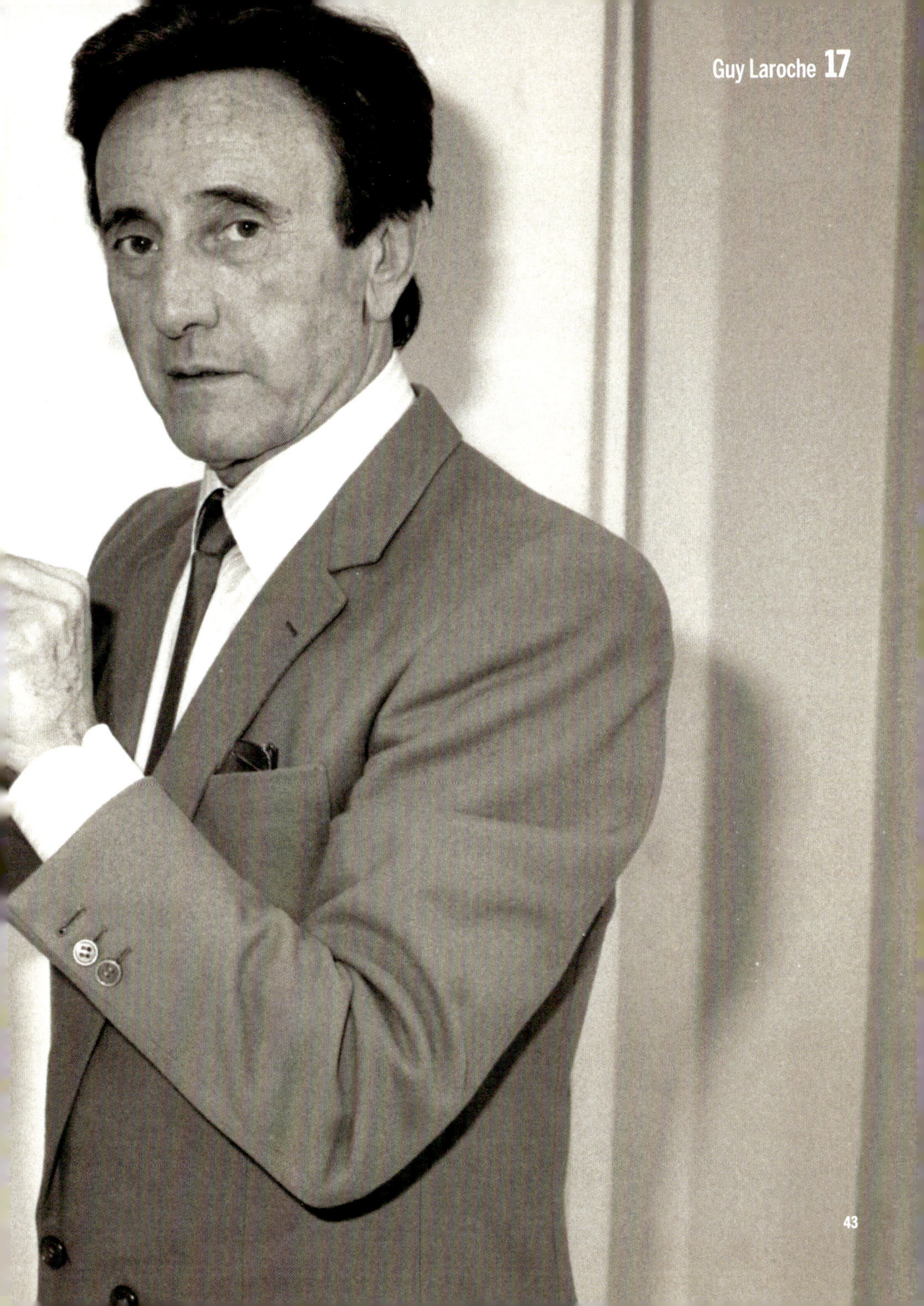

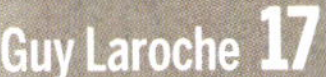

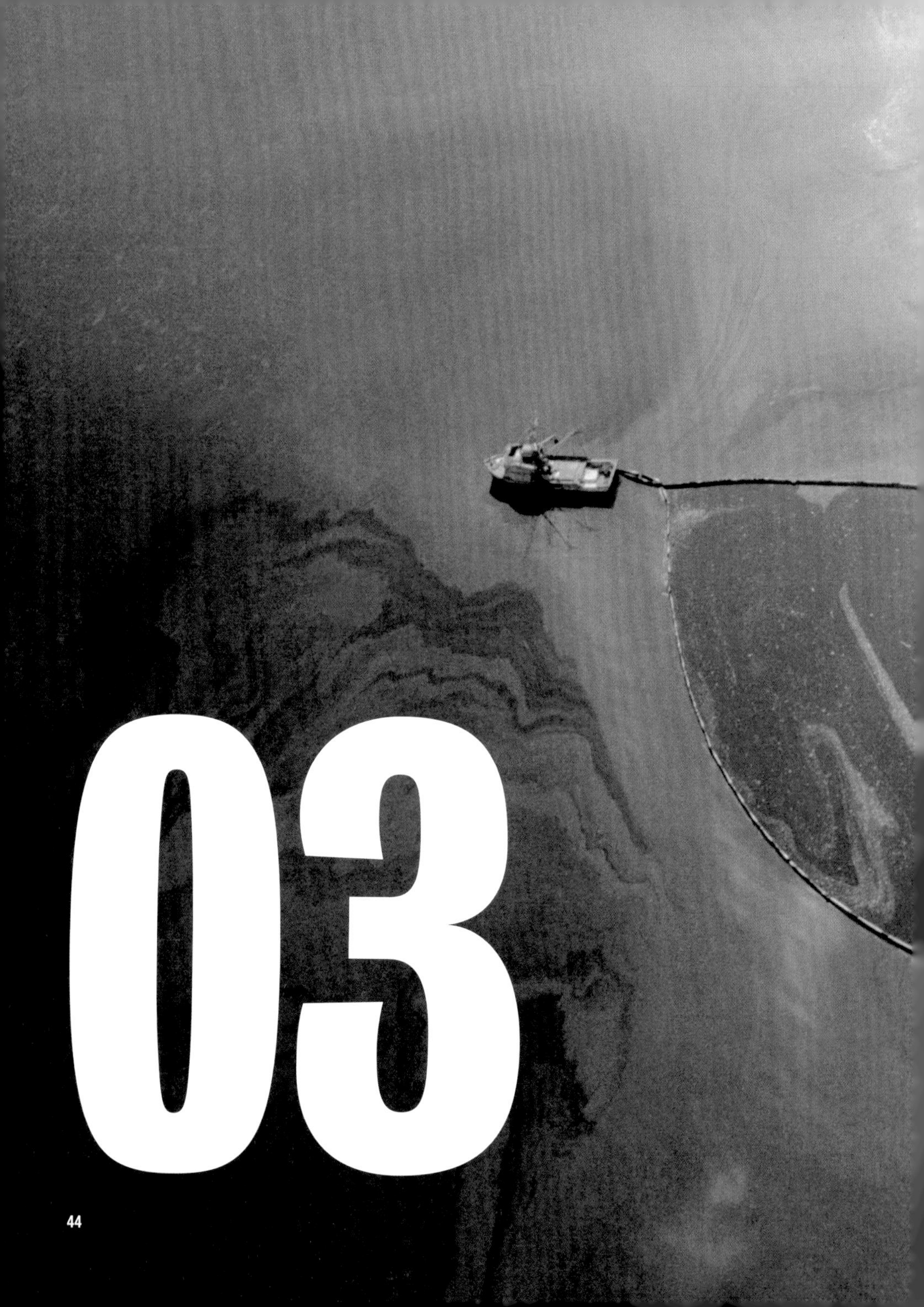

03

09

United States: photographer Robert Mapplethorpe dies in Boston at the age of 43.

11

Japan: Marc Girardelli is the overall winner of the Alpine Skiing World Cup in all disciplines. With the five victories in his carreer, he is the only skier to have won five times the "Crystal Sphere".

13

Canada: a magnetic storm causes the collapse of Québec's electrical network with a nine-hour blackout for six million people. Some areas of northeastern USA and Sweden are also involved. The aurora borealis is seen as far as Texas.

14

Lebanon: General Michel Aoun announces a "war of liberation" to push out Syria and its allies.

23

United States: Stanley Pons and Martin Fleischmann announce the experimental production of cold fusion in the laboratories of the University of Utah.

24

United States: oil tanker Exxon Valdez hits a cliff in the strait of Prince William, Alaska, scattering over 42.000 m³ of crude oil in the waters and polluting a 1.900 km long coast.

29

United States: 61st Academy Awards in Los Angeles. It is the year of "Rain Man" by Barry Levinson, a feature film that will be remembered for Dustin Hoffman's superb interpretation and for Tom Cruise's first "mature" performance. It wins Best Picture, Best Actor, Best Original Screenplay and Best Director awards. Best actress is awarded to Jodie Foster in "The Accused", and Kevin Klein is awarded Best Actor in a Supporting Role, in "A Fish Called Wanda".

30

France: the new entrance to the Louvre, Paris, a glass pyramid designed by architect Ieoh Ming Pei, is unveiled.

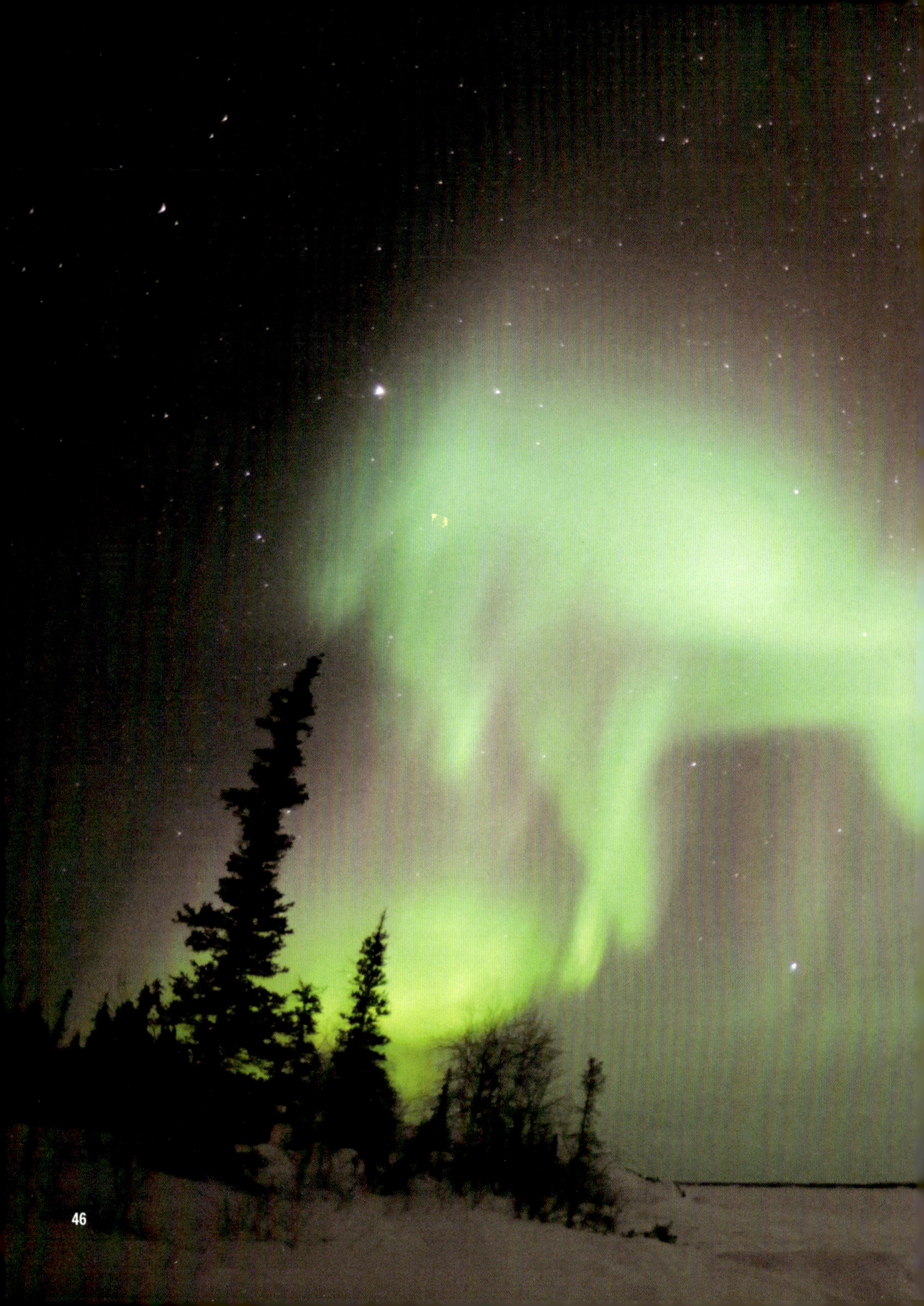

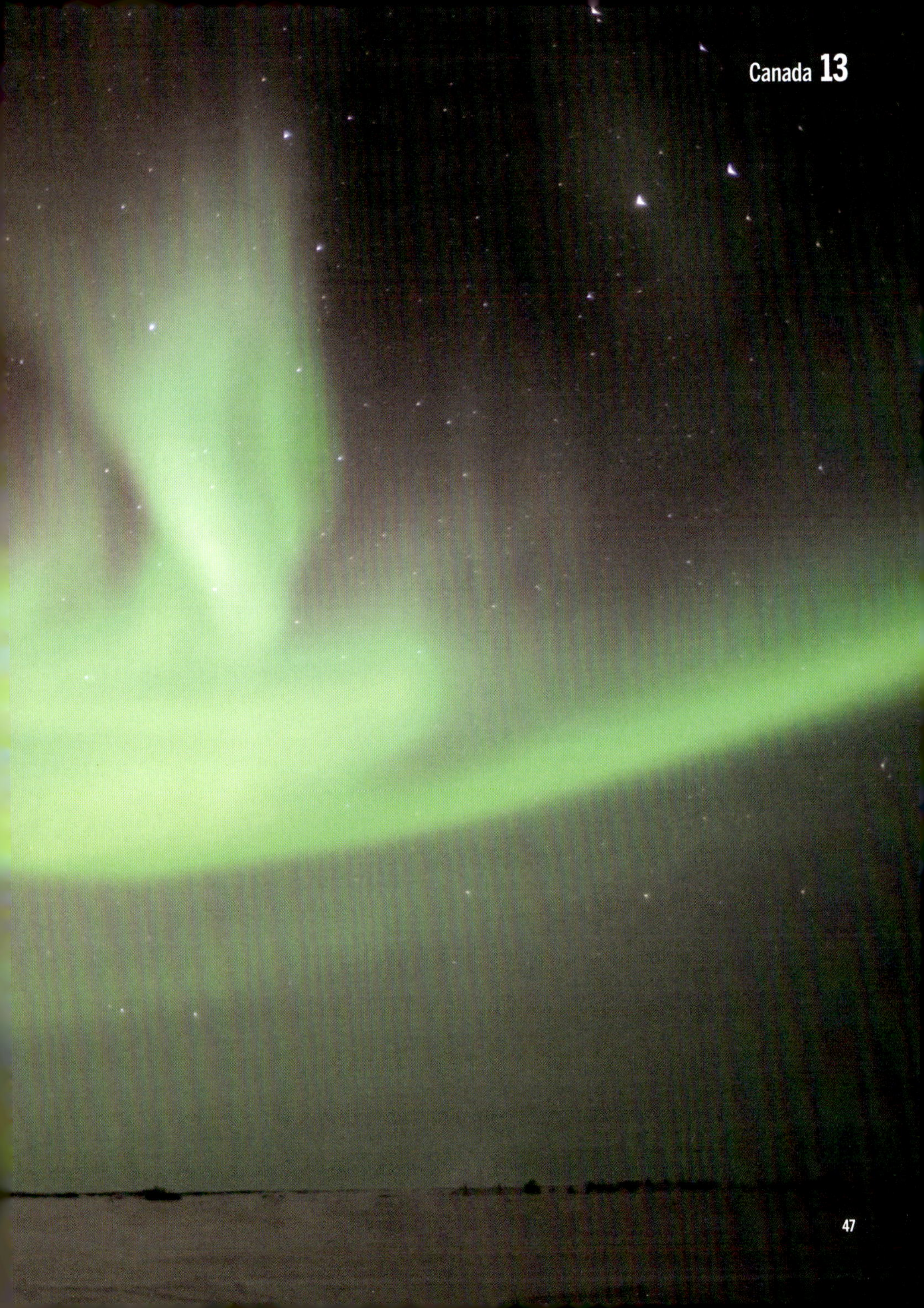

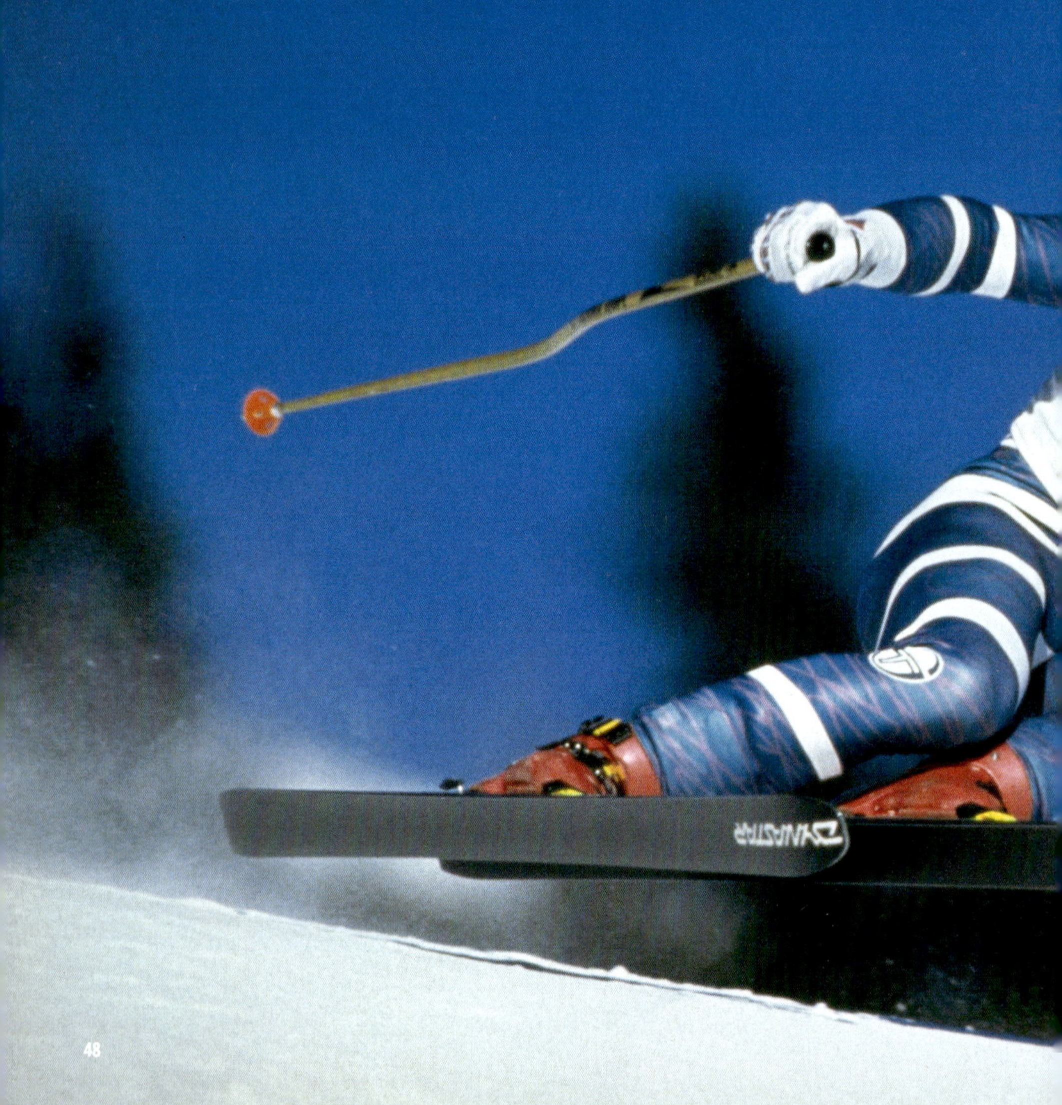

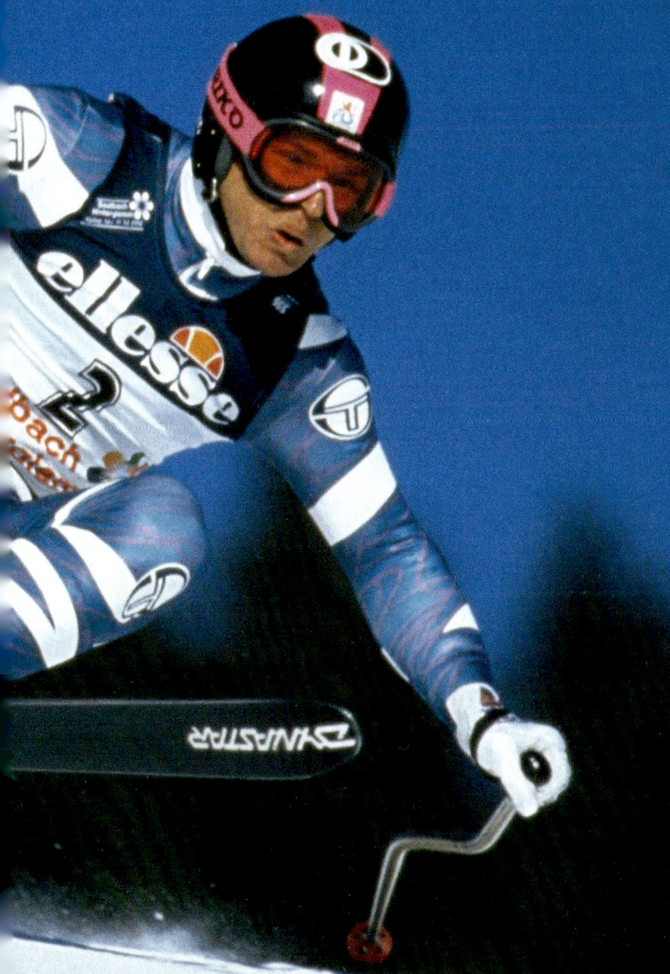

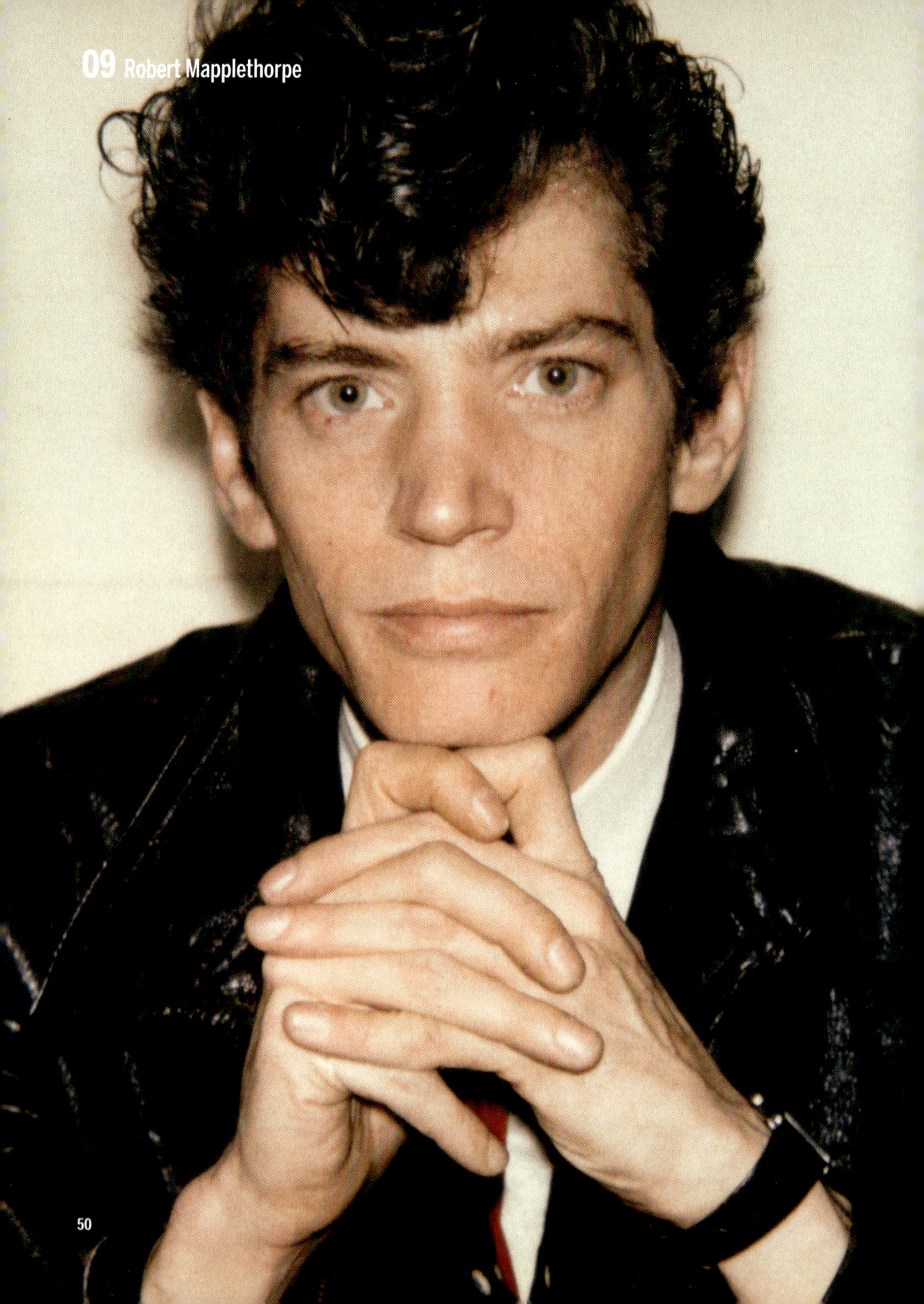

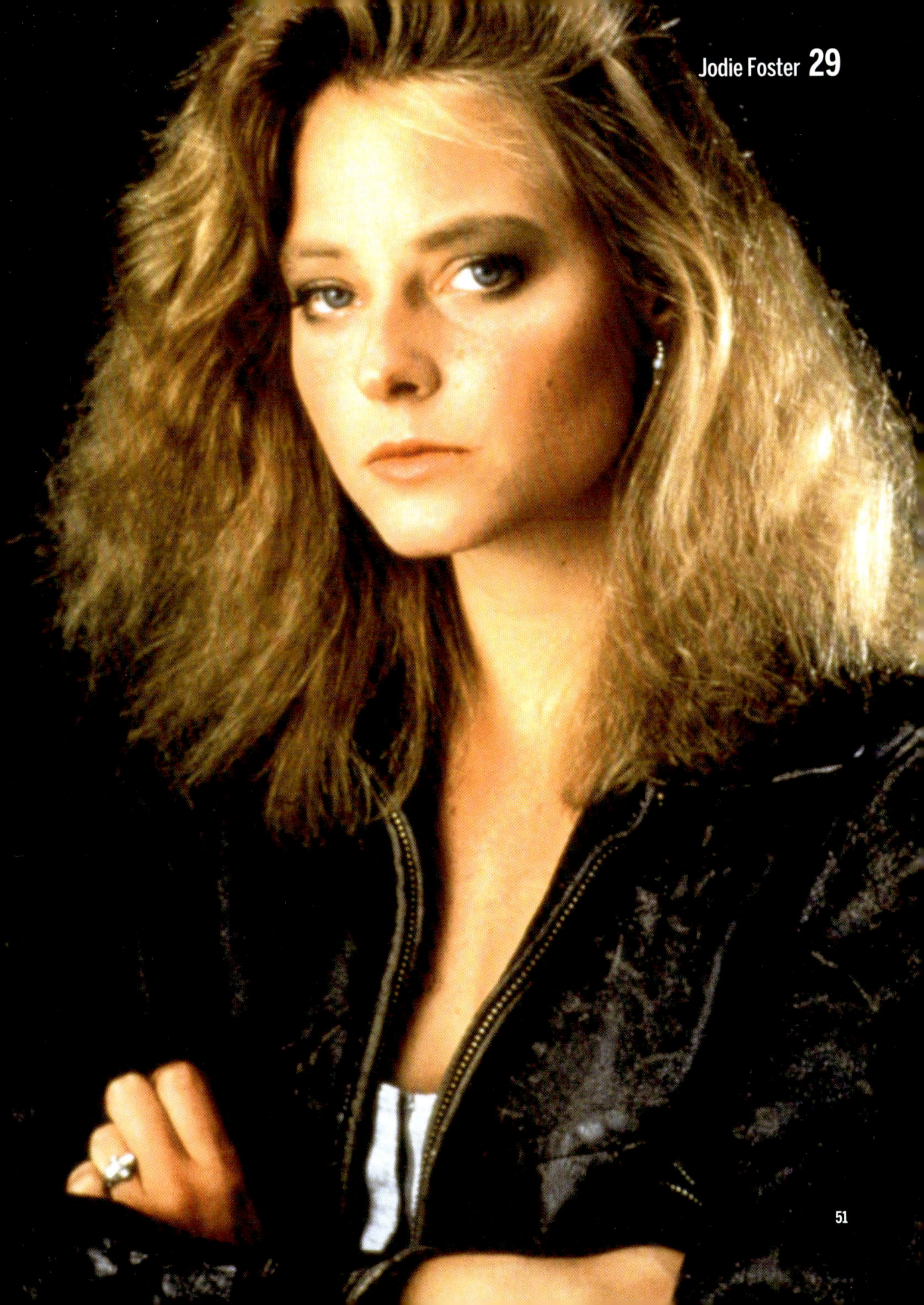

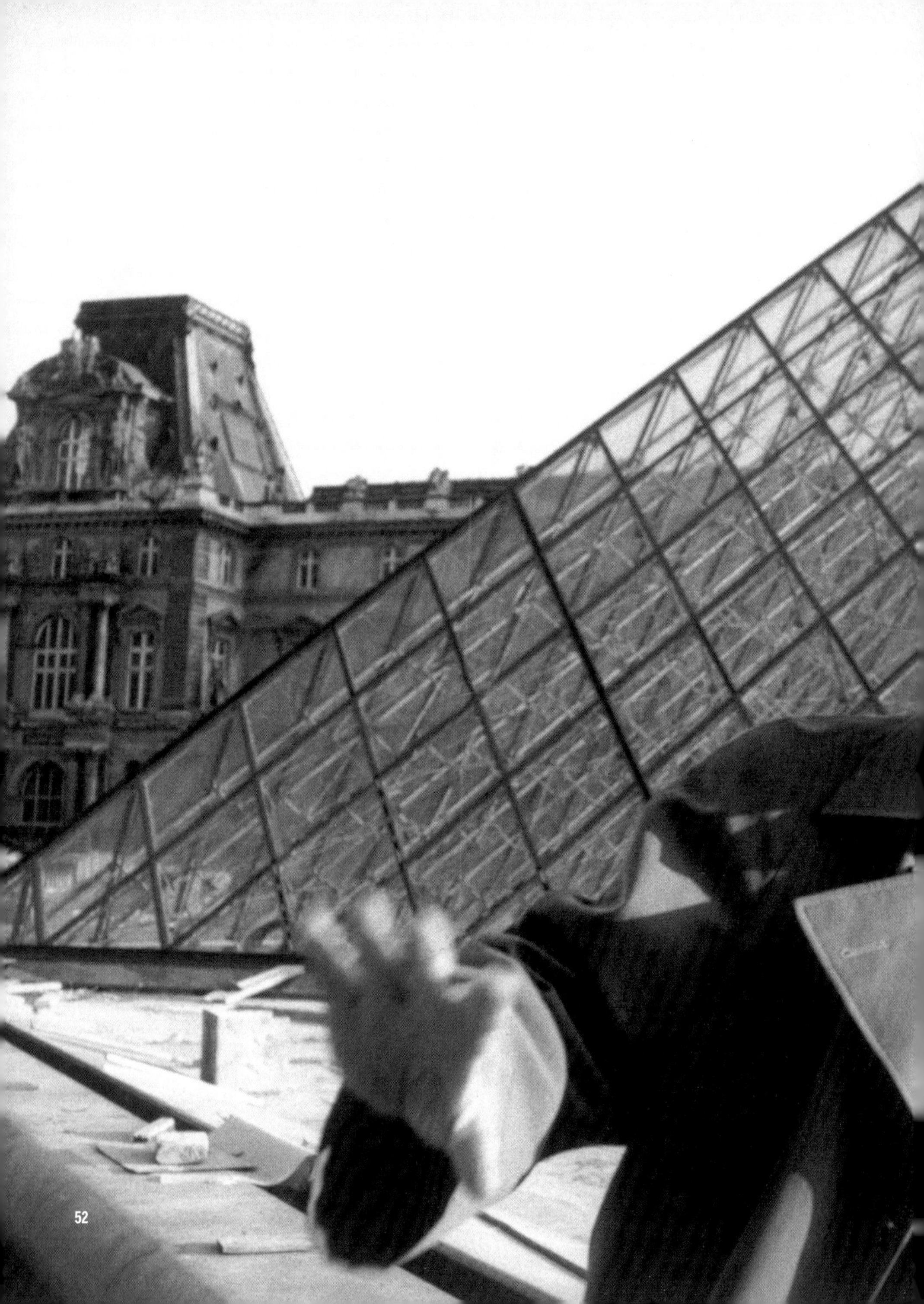

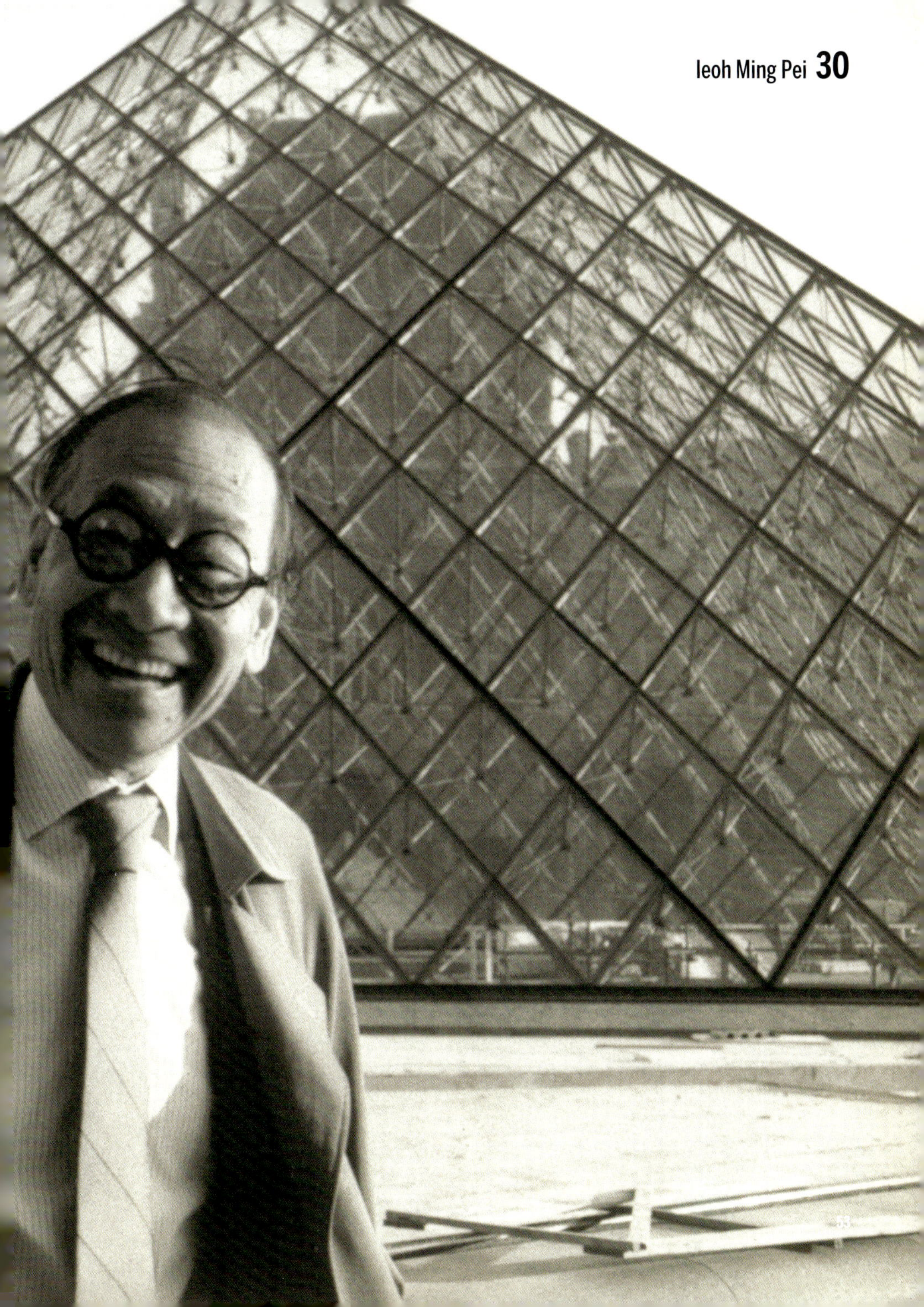

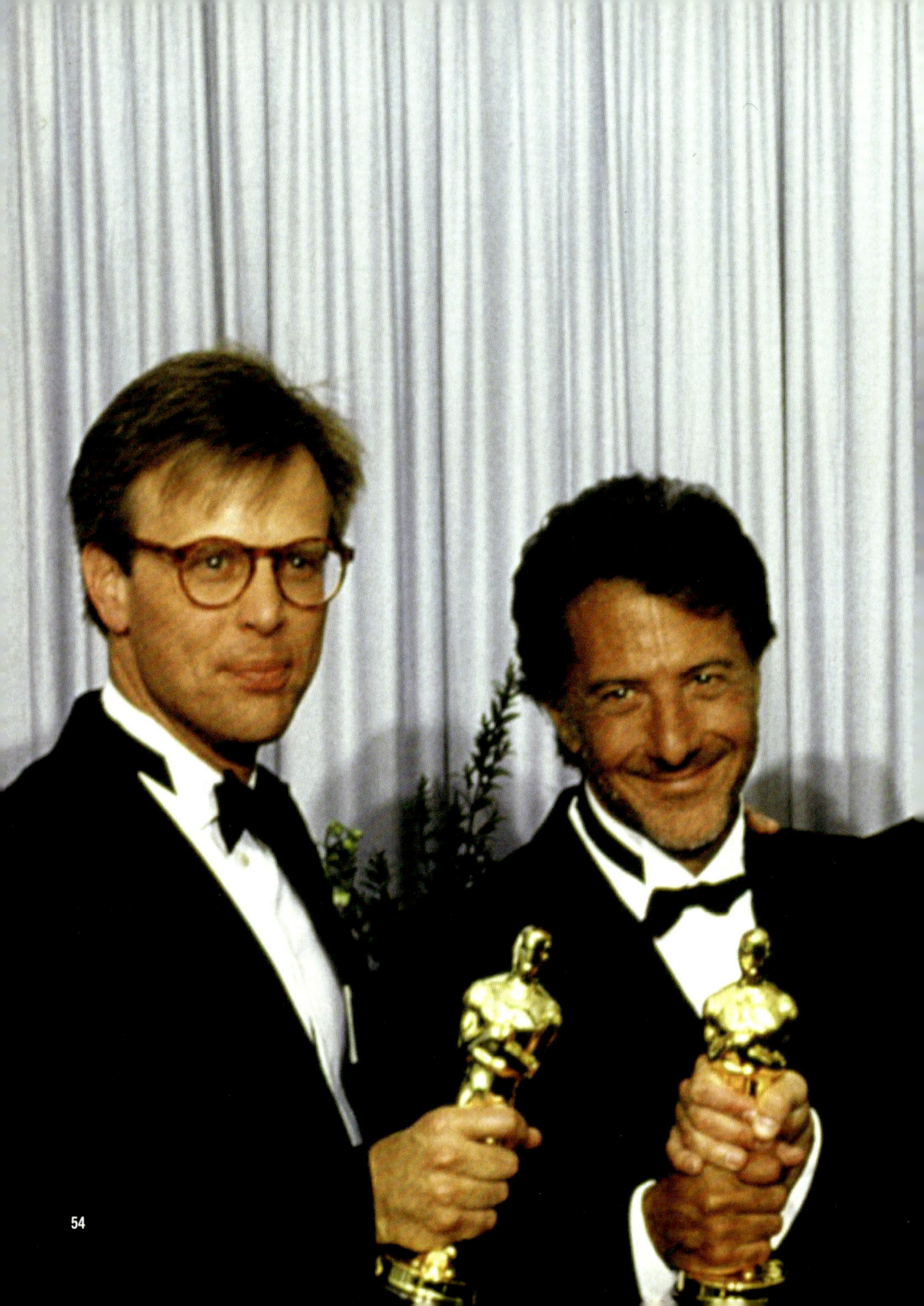

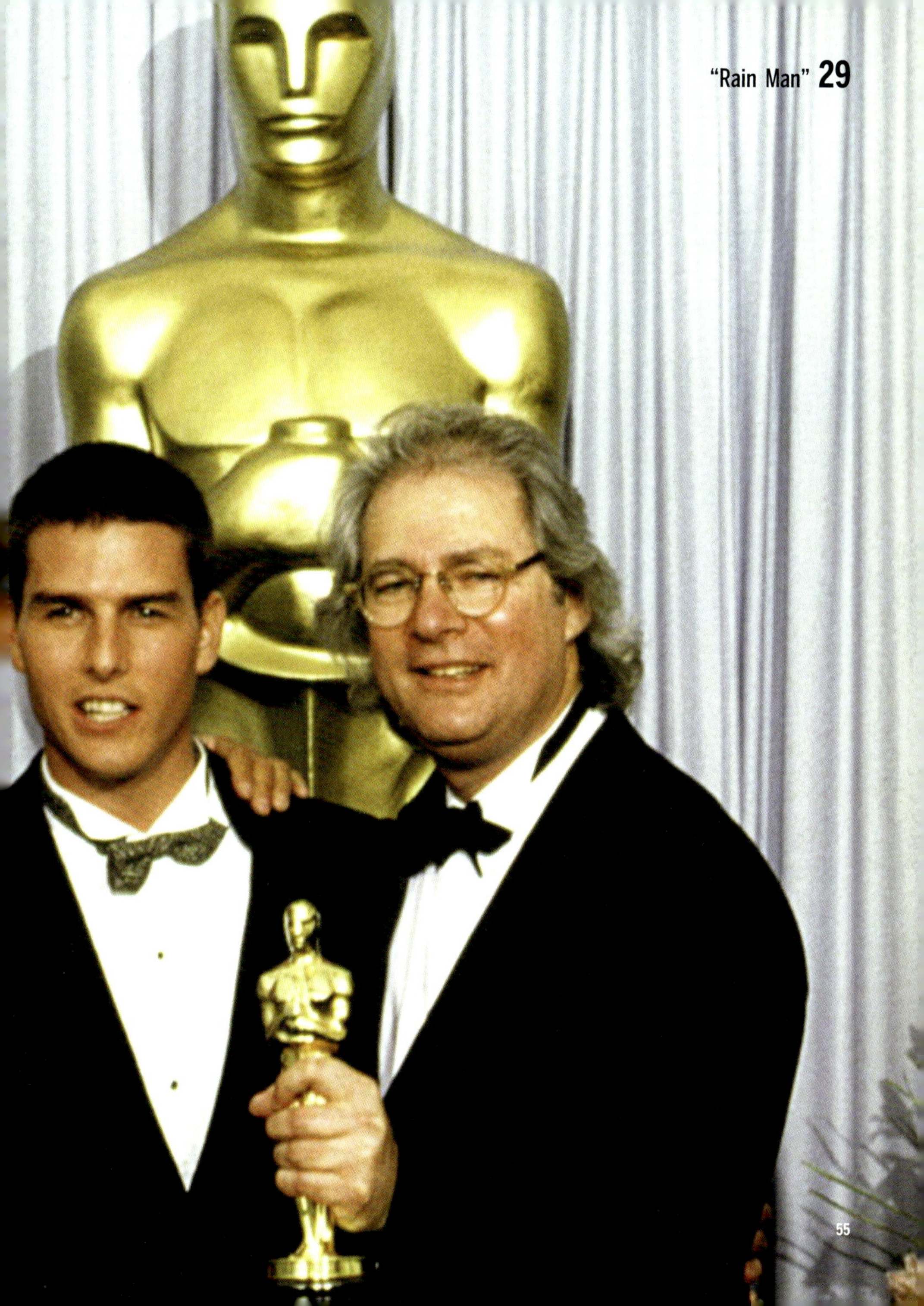

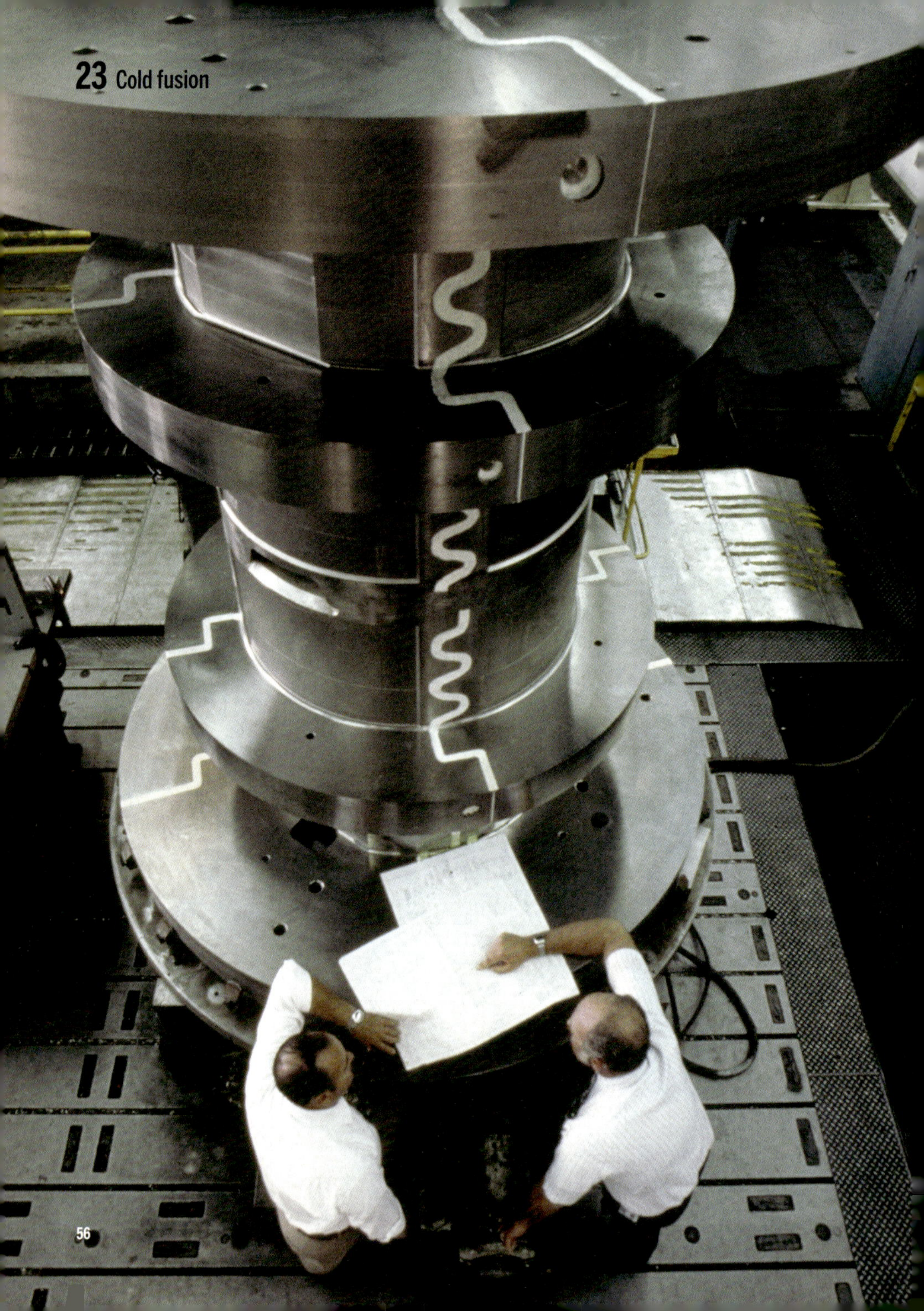

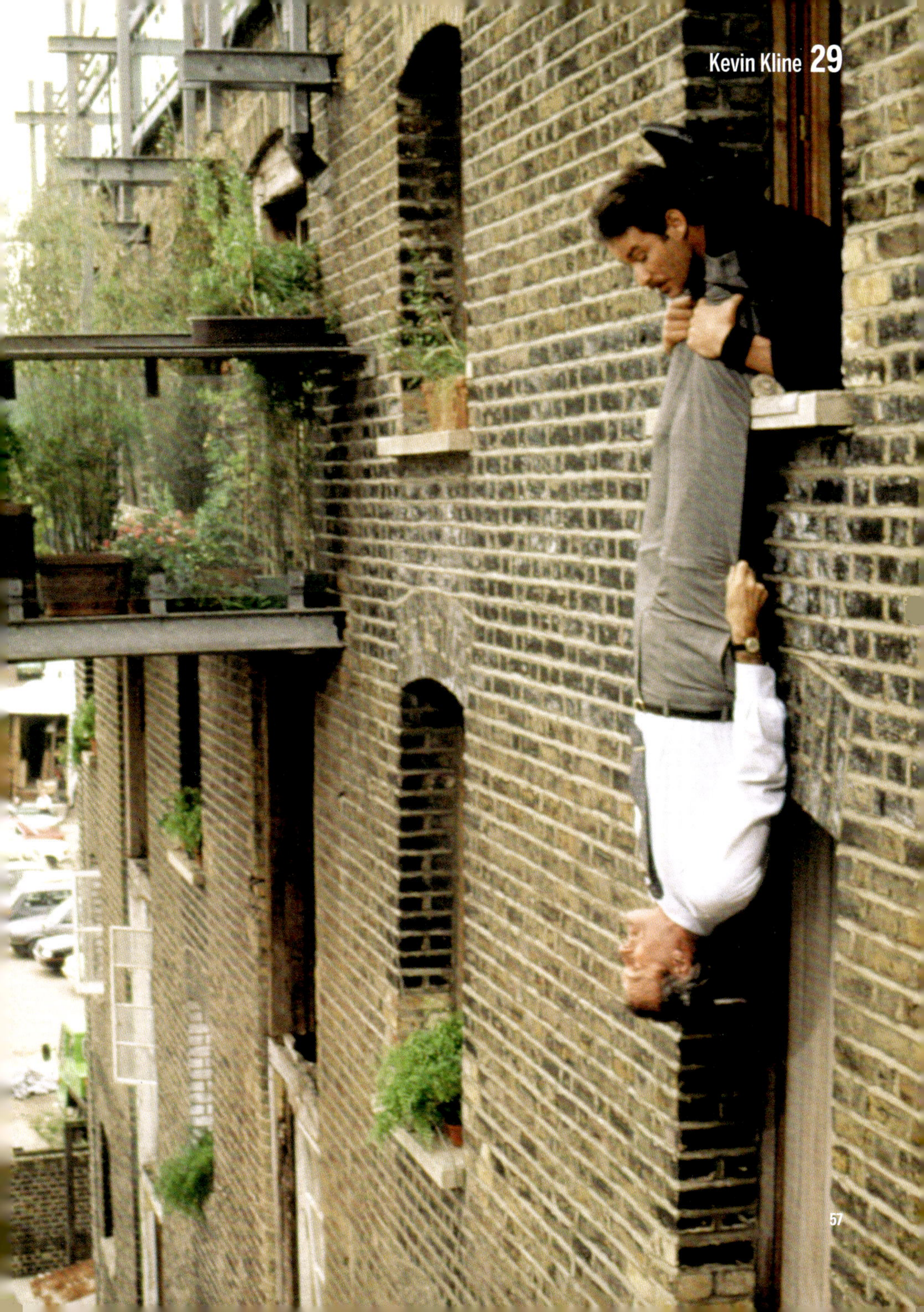

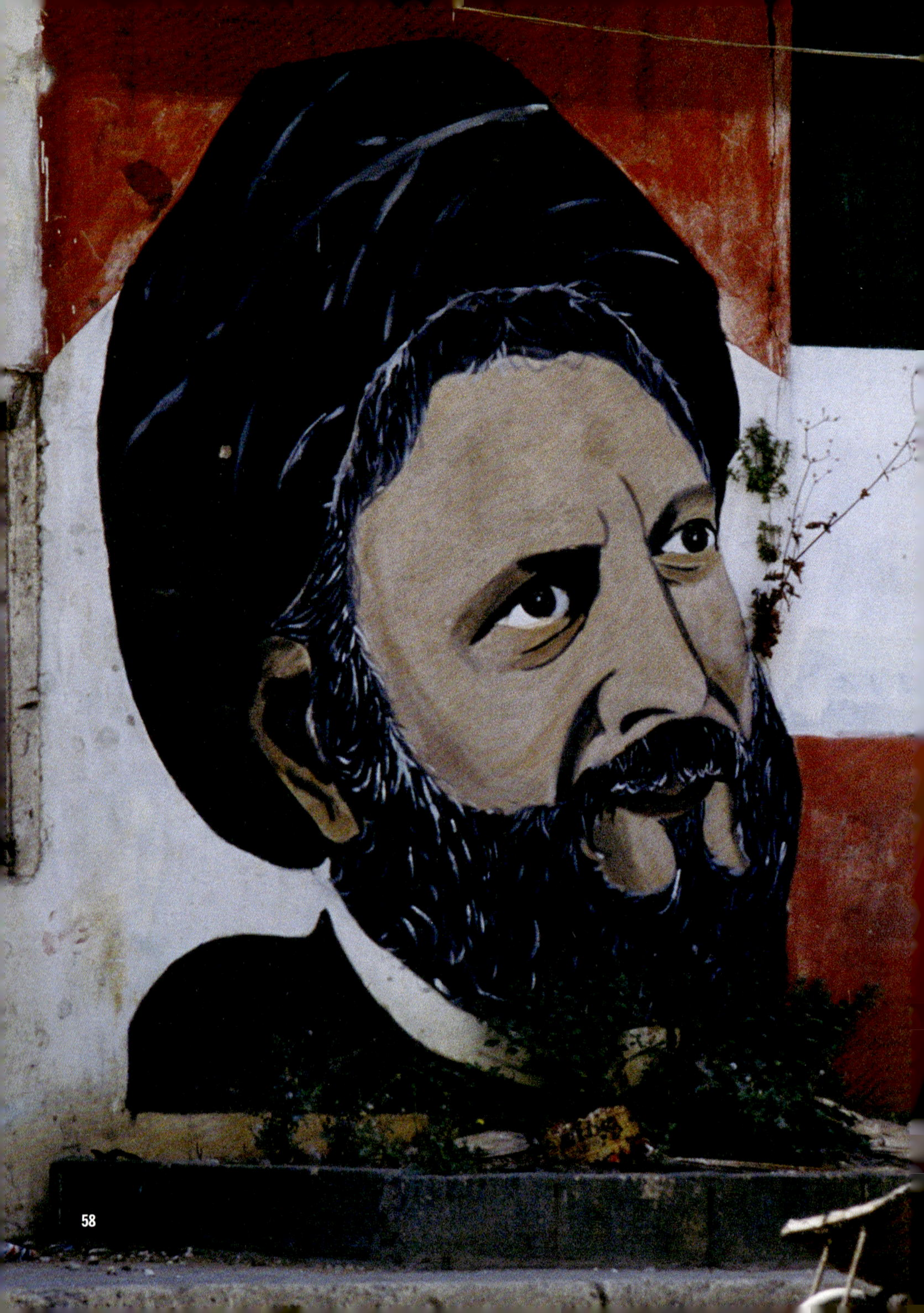

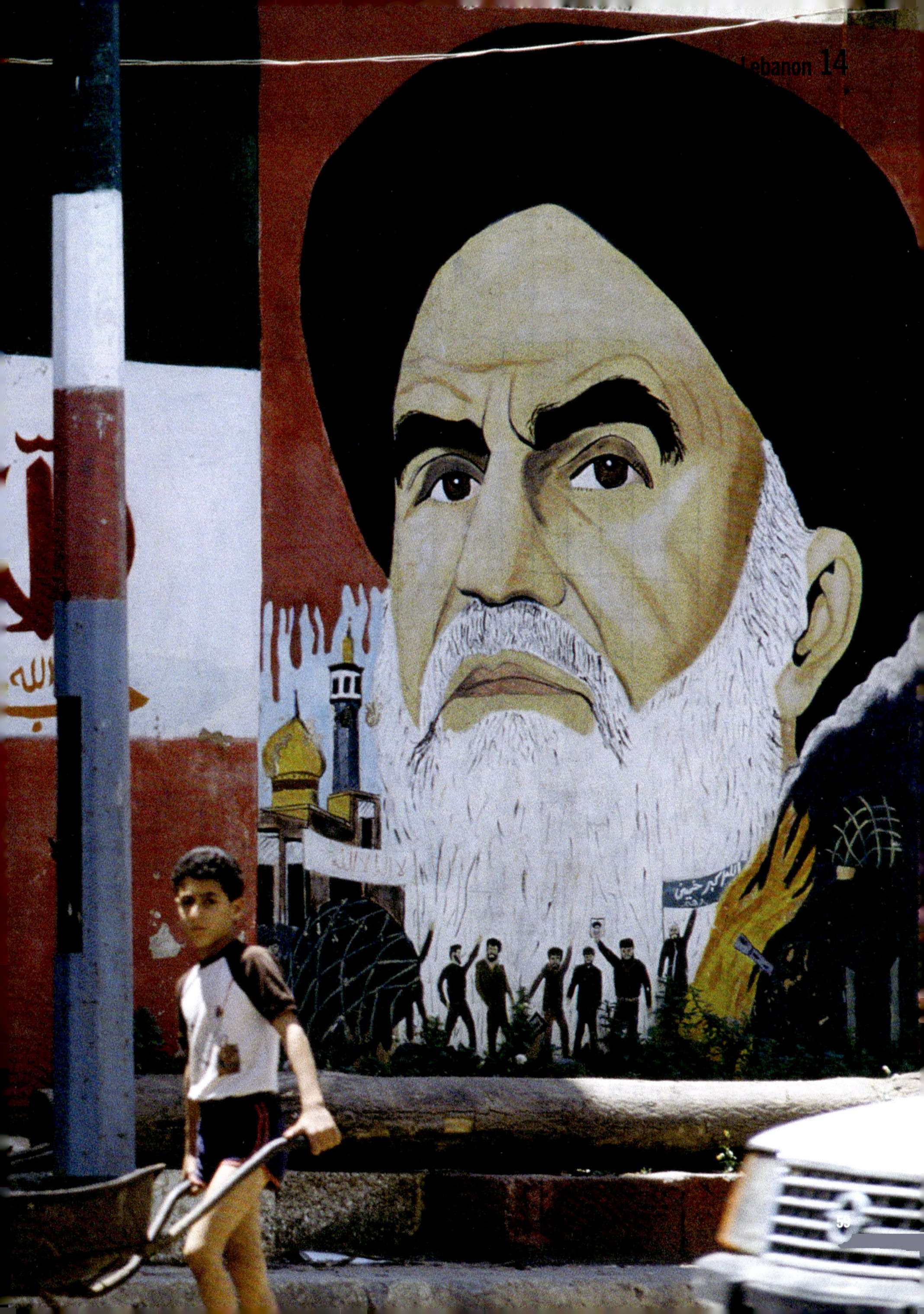

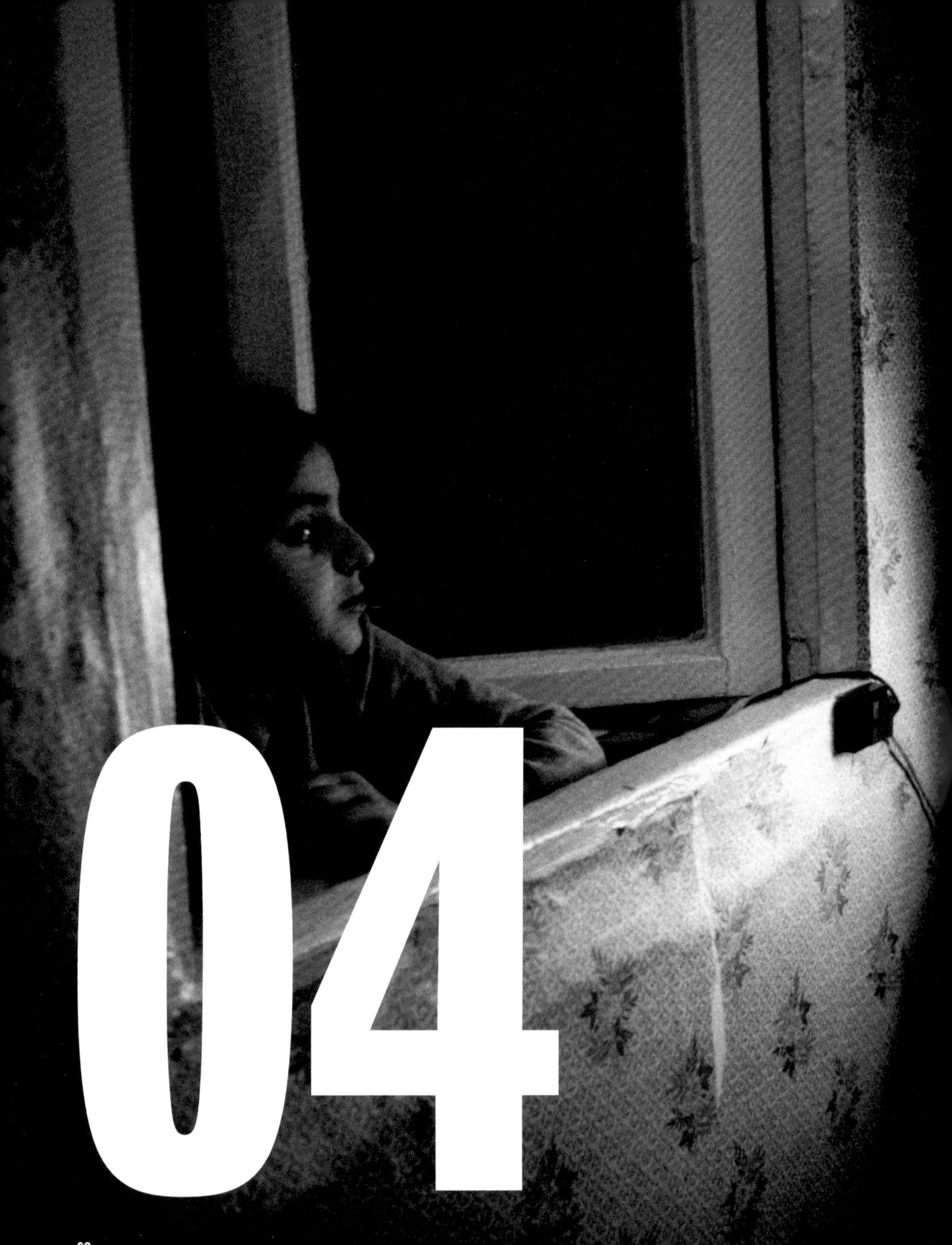

04

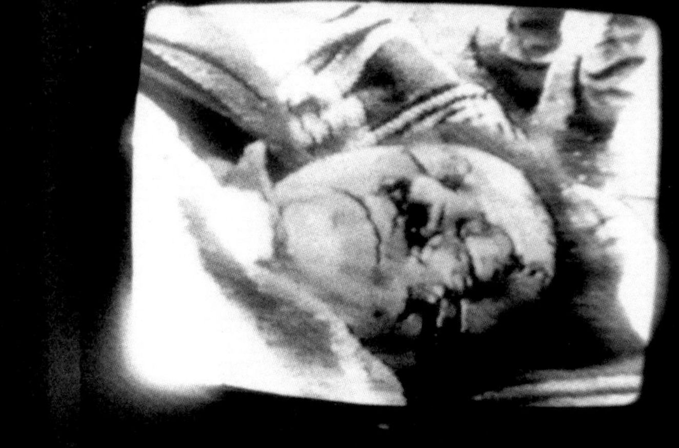

04

Belgium: the 40th anniversary of NATO
is celebrated in Brussels.

07

Barents Sea: the Soviet submarine K-278
Komsomolets sinks killing 41 people.

09

Georgia: the Red Army kills over 20 people
in Tbilisi's main square during a pacifist
demonstration.

12

United States: Sugar Ray Robinson, one of the
world's greatest boxers, dies in Culver City.
He has held the divisional world championship
five times as welterweight, and five times
world champion as middleweight.

15

Great Britain: 96 football supporters lose
their lives at the Hillsborough Stadium in
Sheffield. One of the greatest tragedies in
European football history.

17

United States: release of "Doolittle" by Pixies,
reference song for the entire grunge
movement. At present day it has sold about
one million copies.

21

China: Tian'anmen Square's protest begins.
Students arrive from Beijing, Shanghai, Xian
and Nanjing.

26

United States: actress Lucille Ball dies
in Los Angeles at the age of 77.

30

Italy: Sergio Leone, father of the "Spaghetti
western" genre, and internationally renowned
director, dies in Rome at the age of 60.

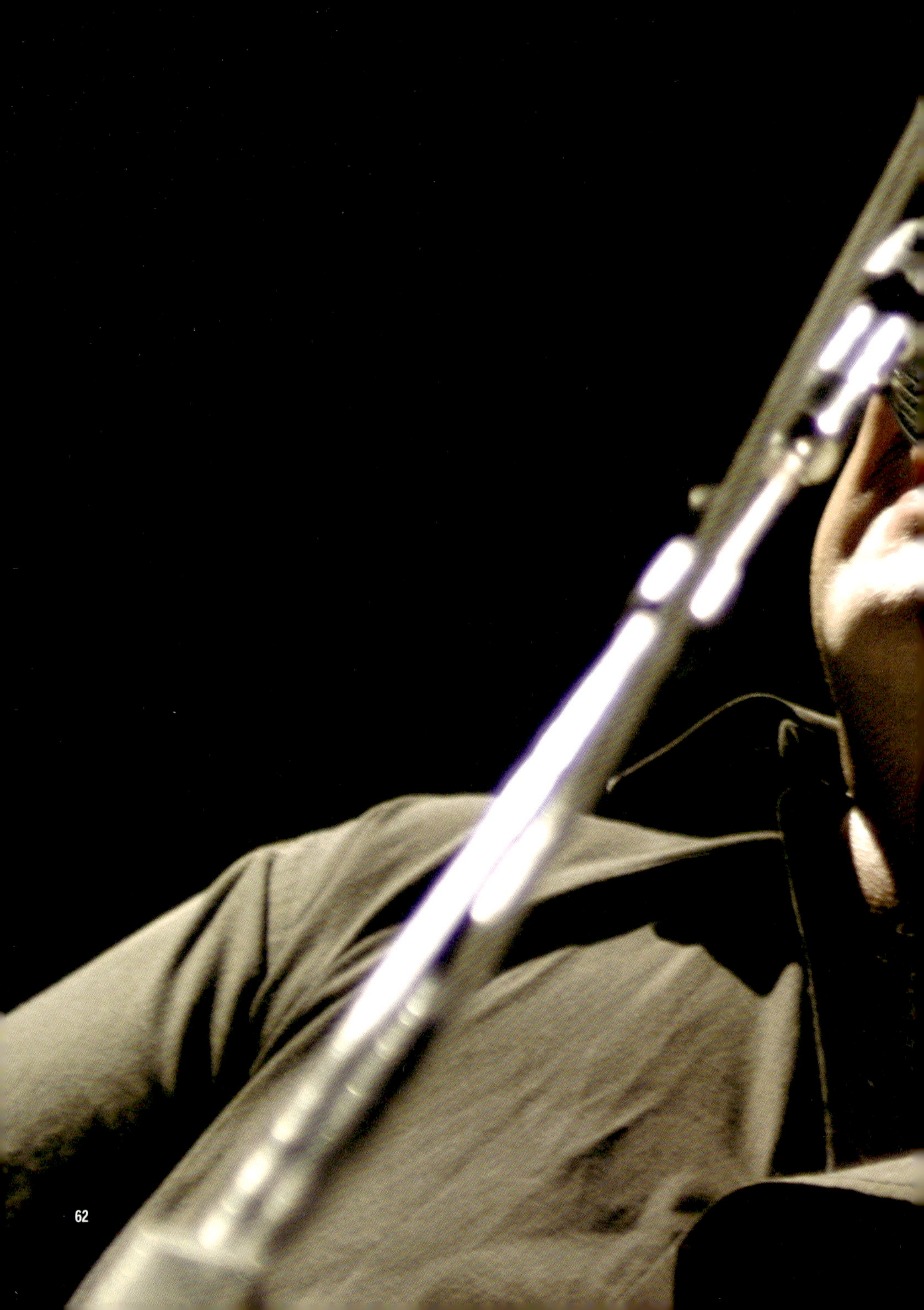

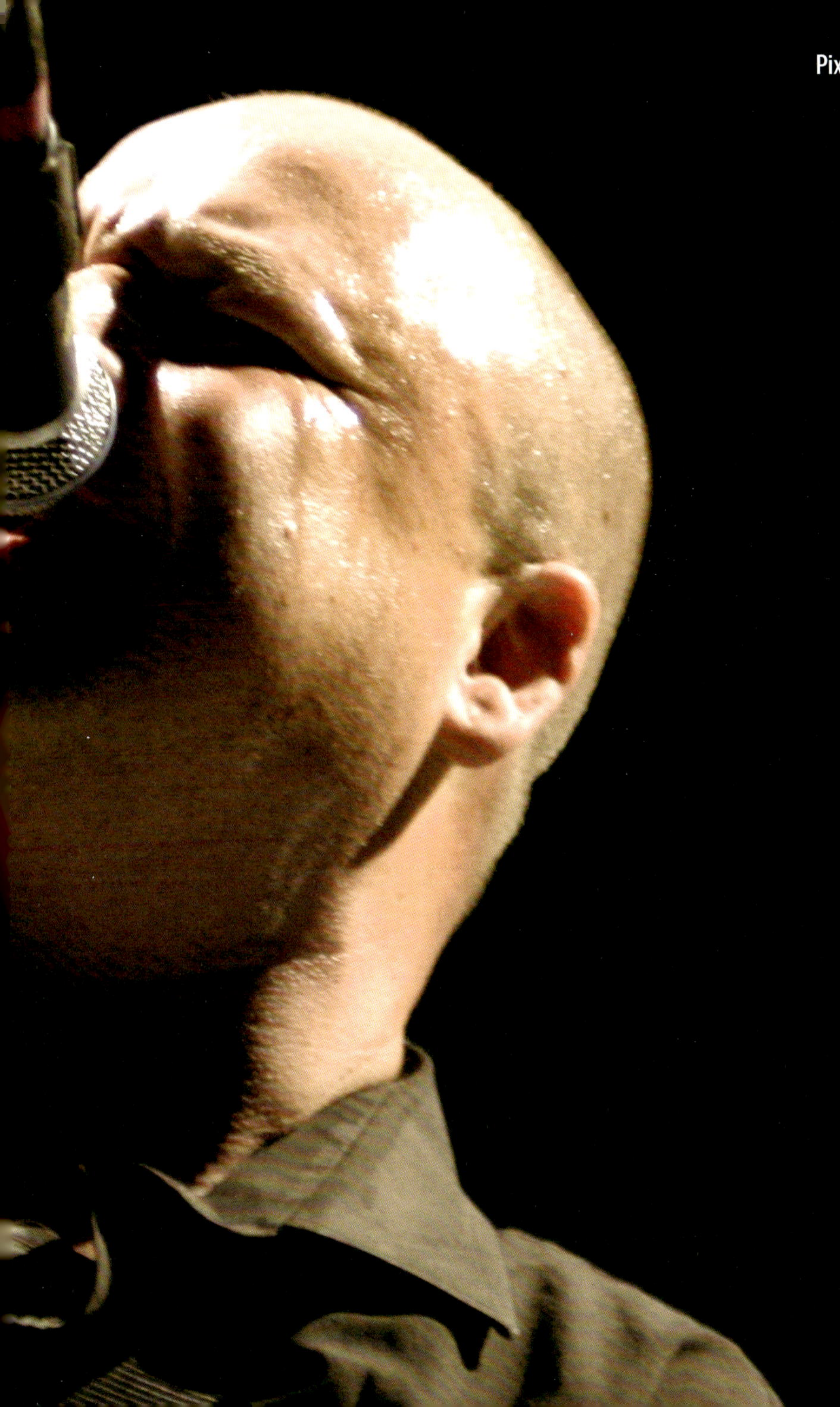

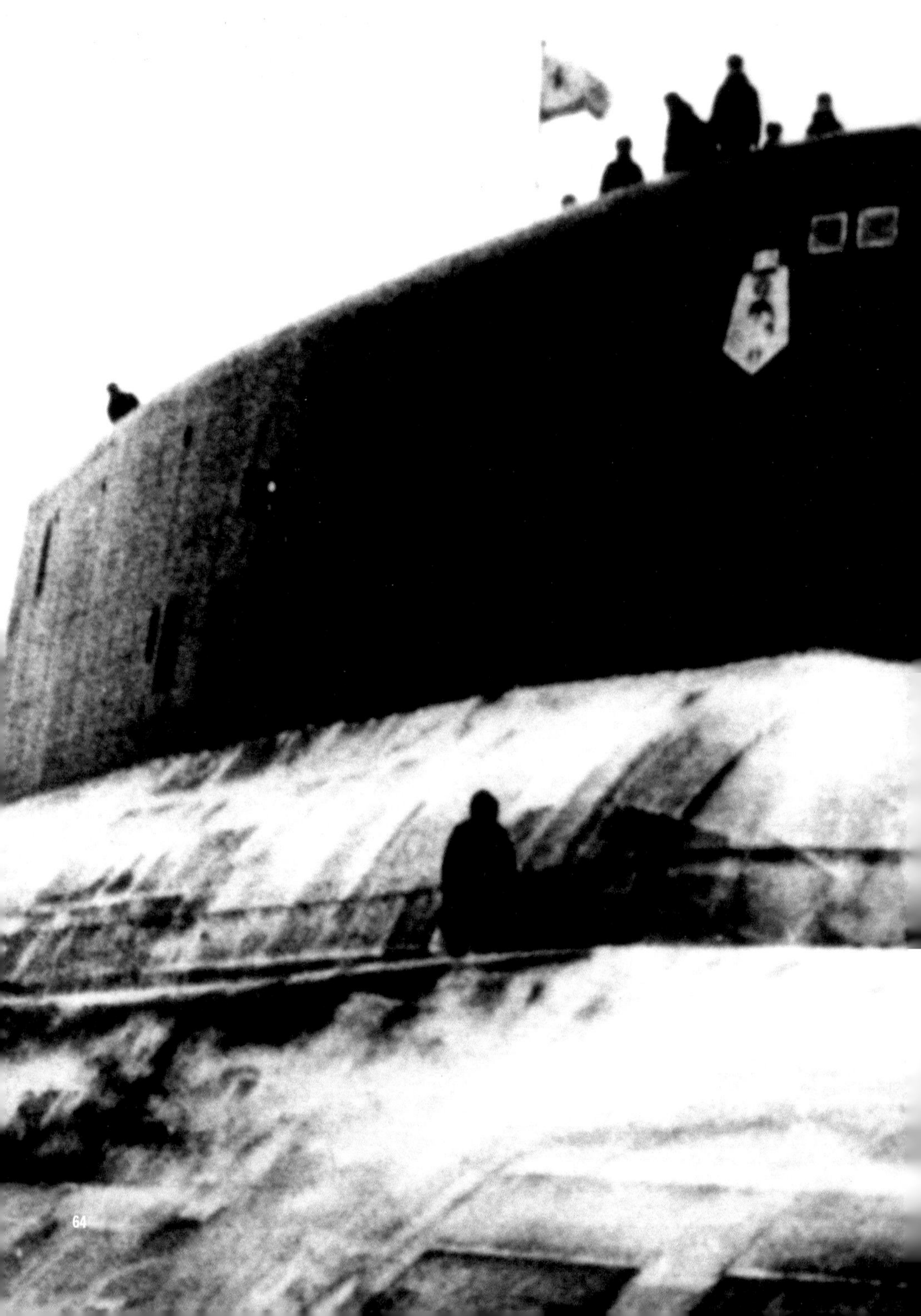

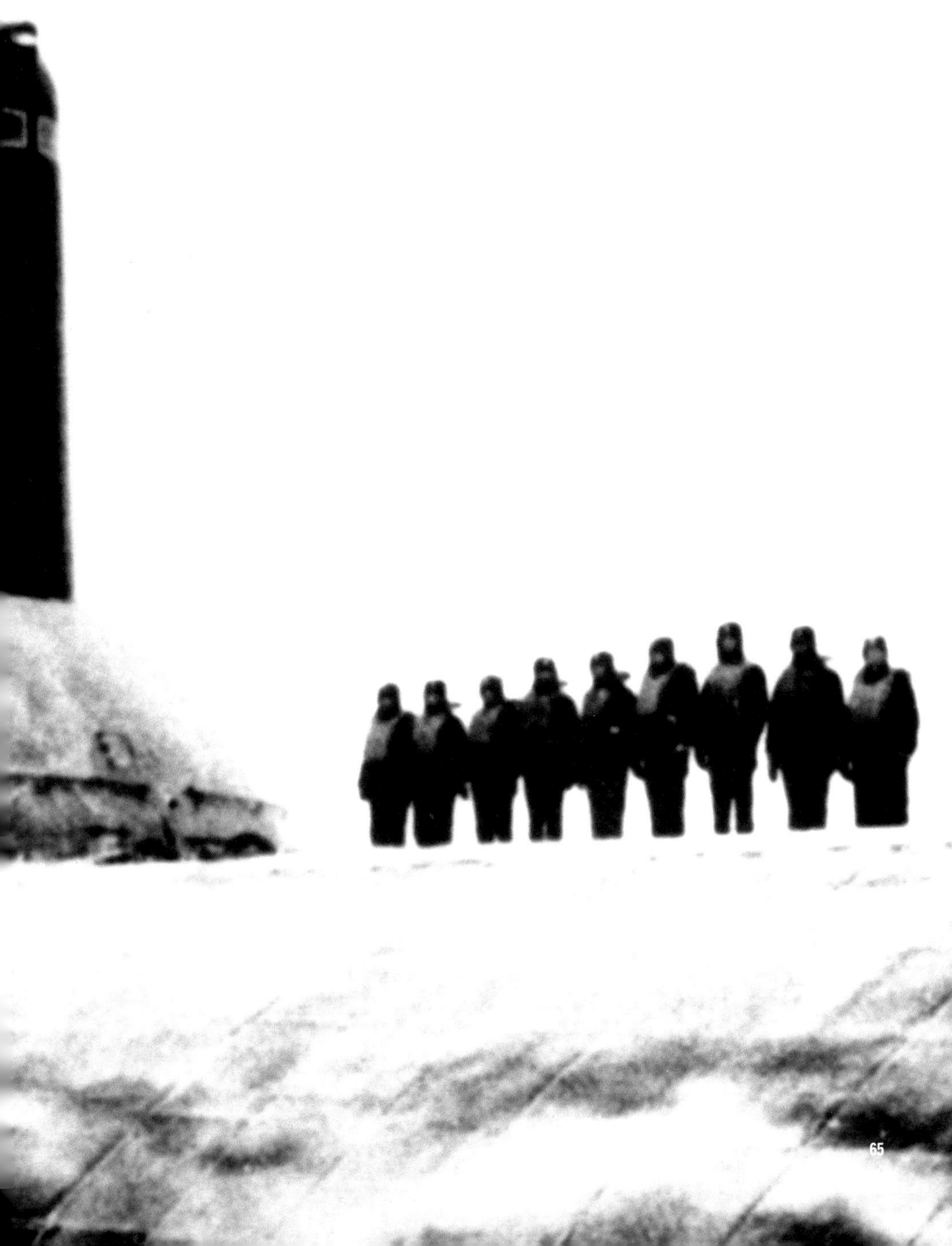

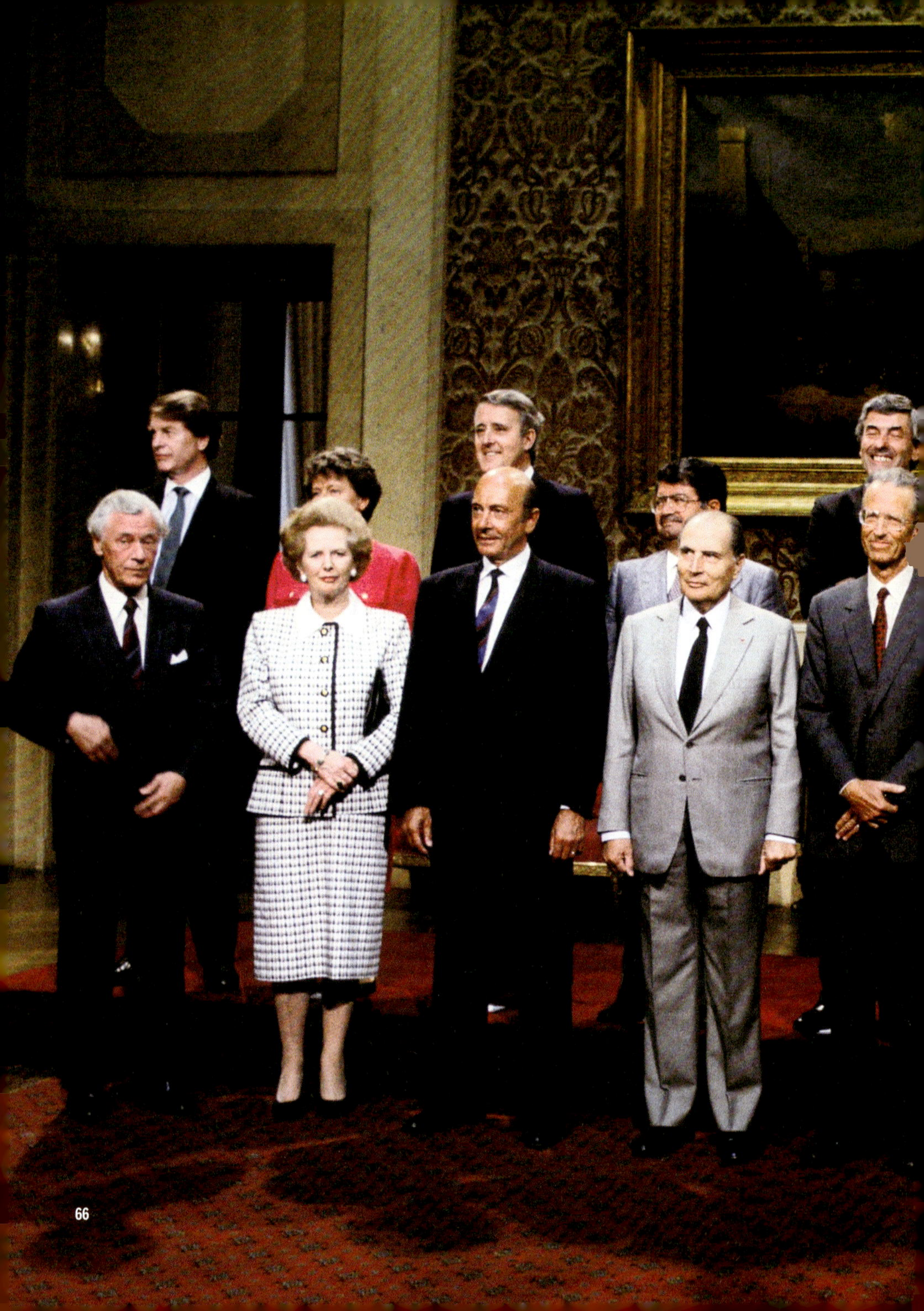

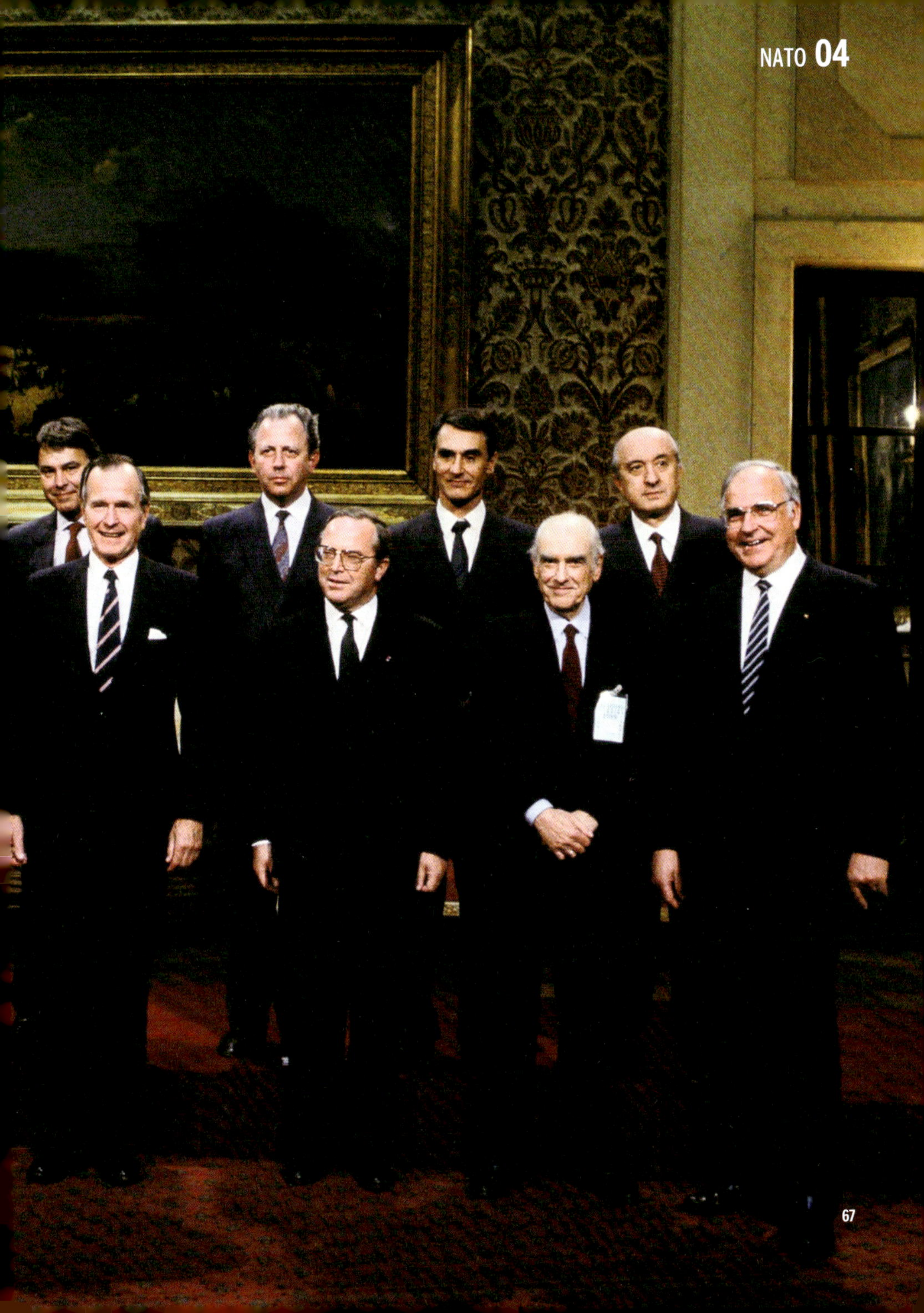

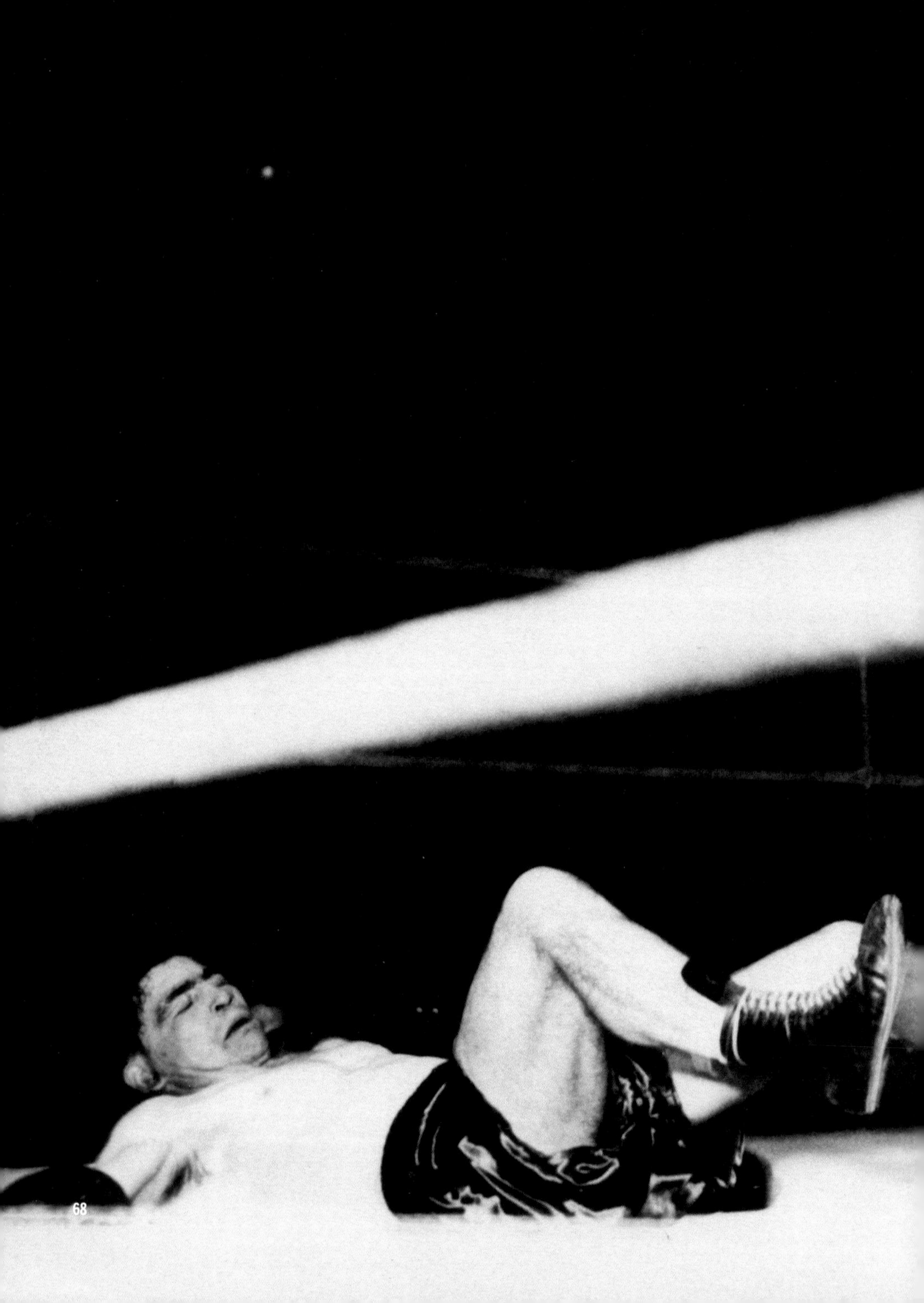

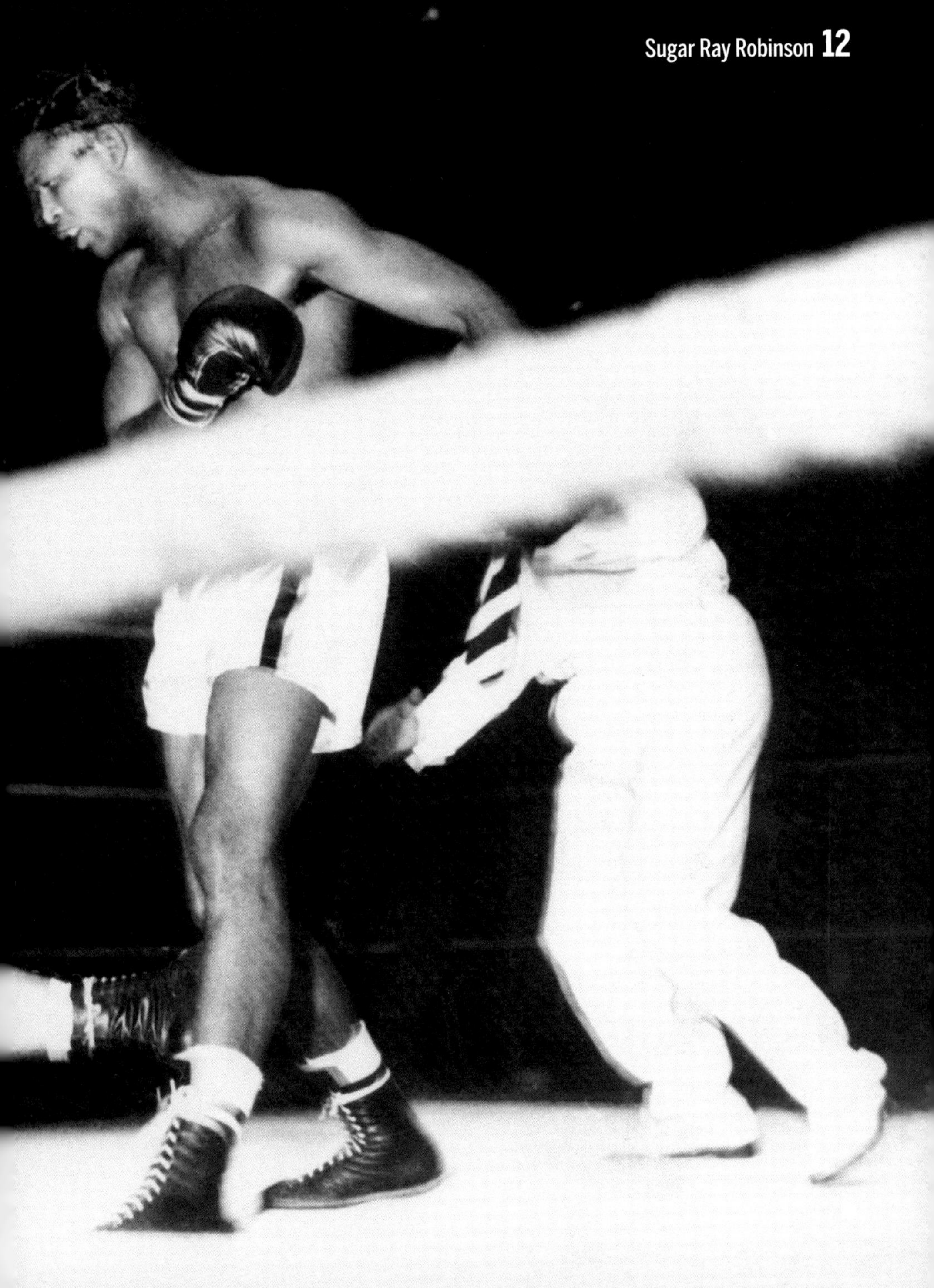

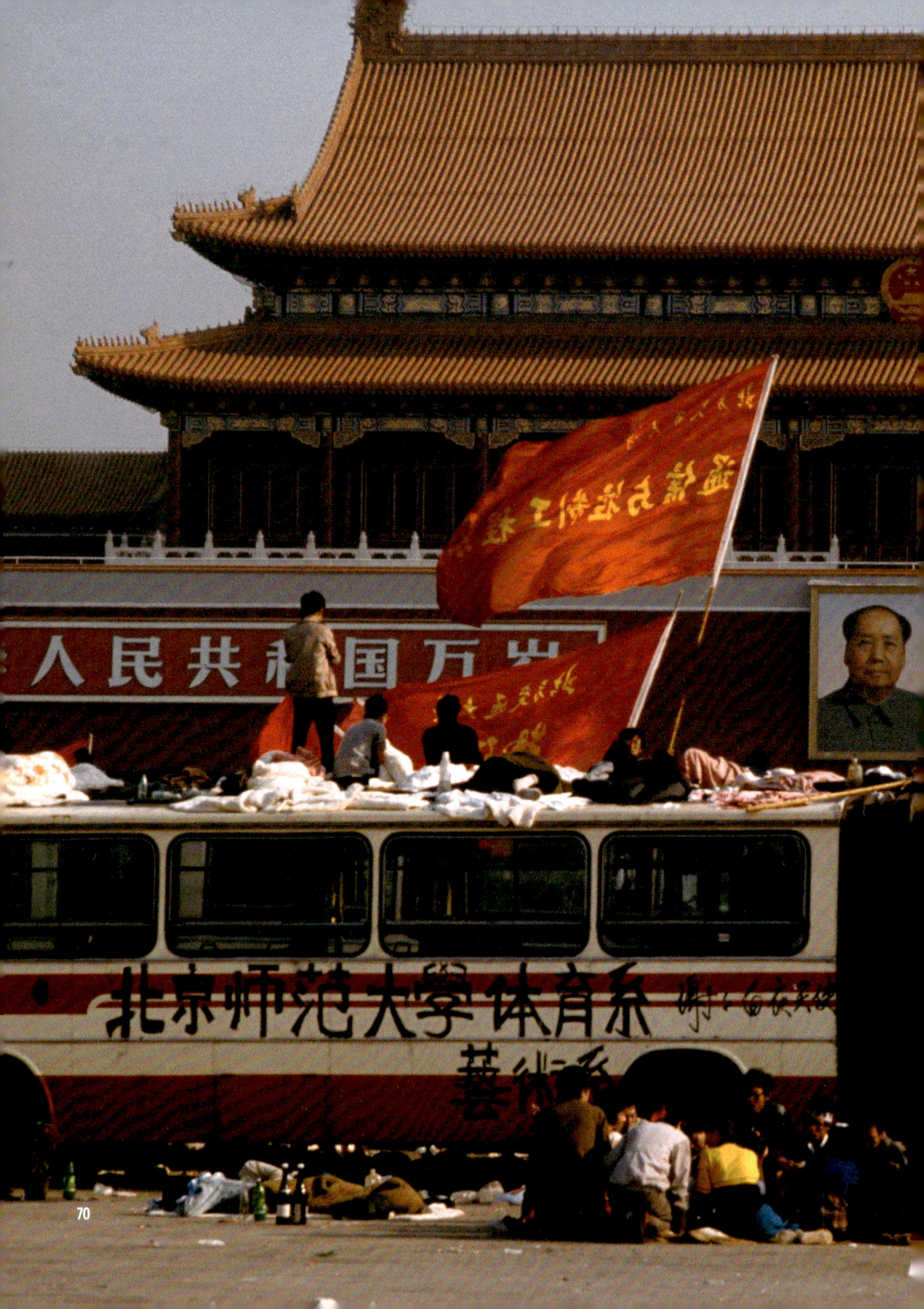
人民共和国万岁
北京师范大学体育系
藝術系

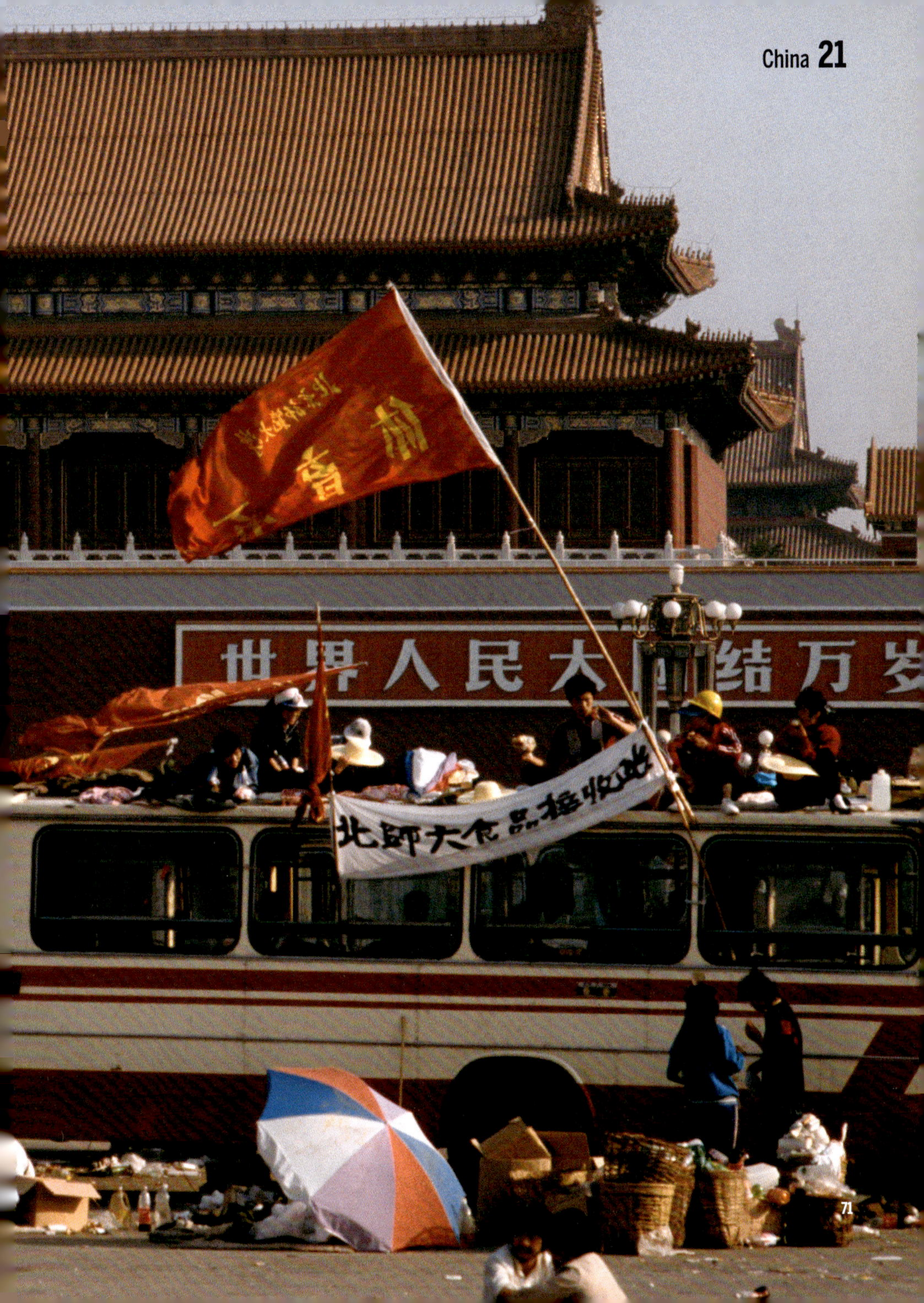
世界人民大□结万岁
北师大食品接收处

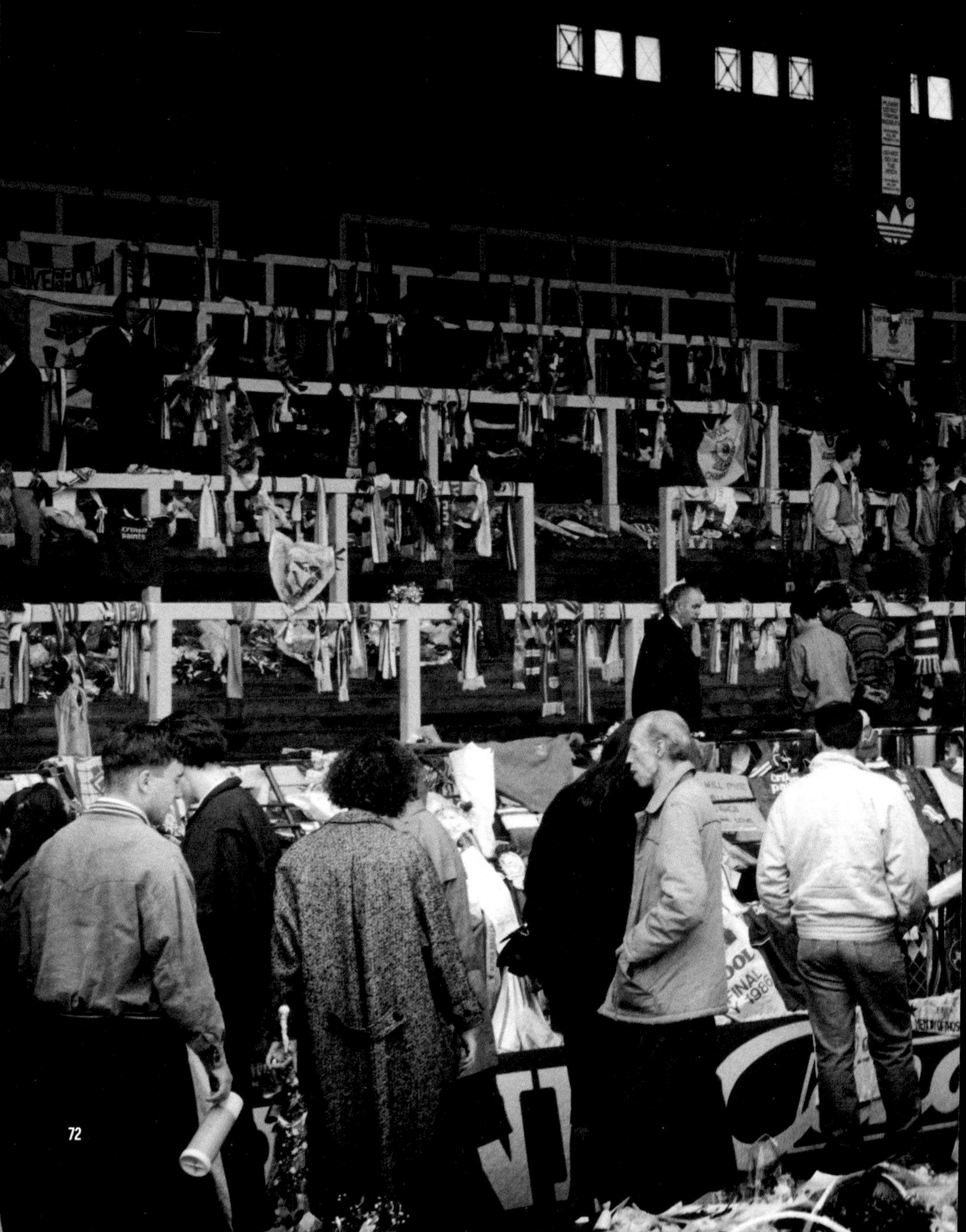

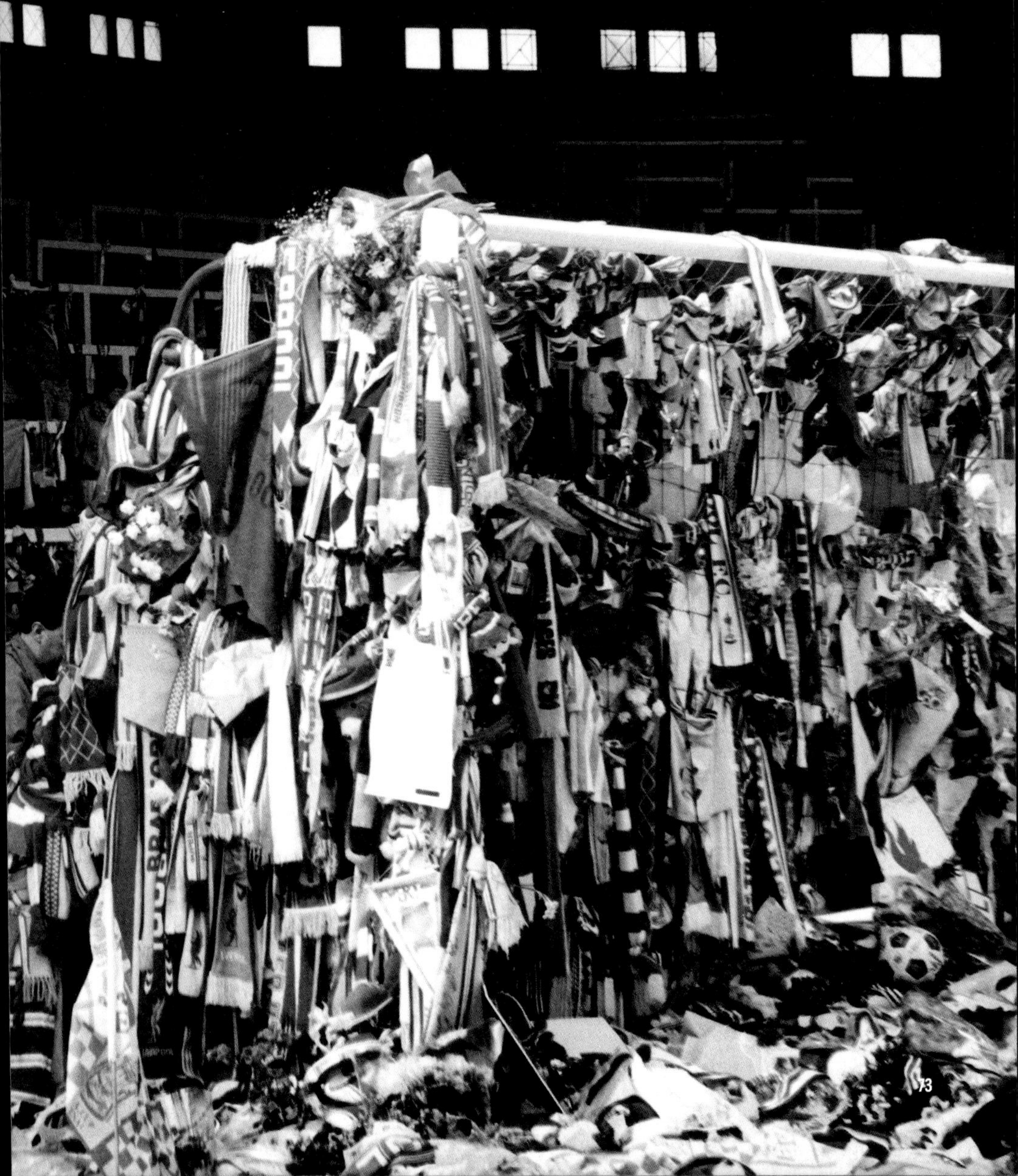

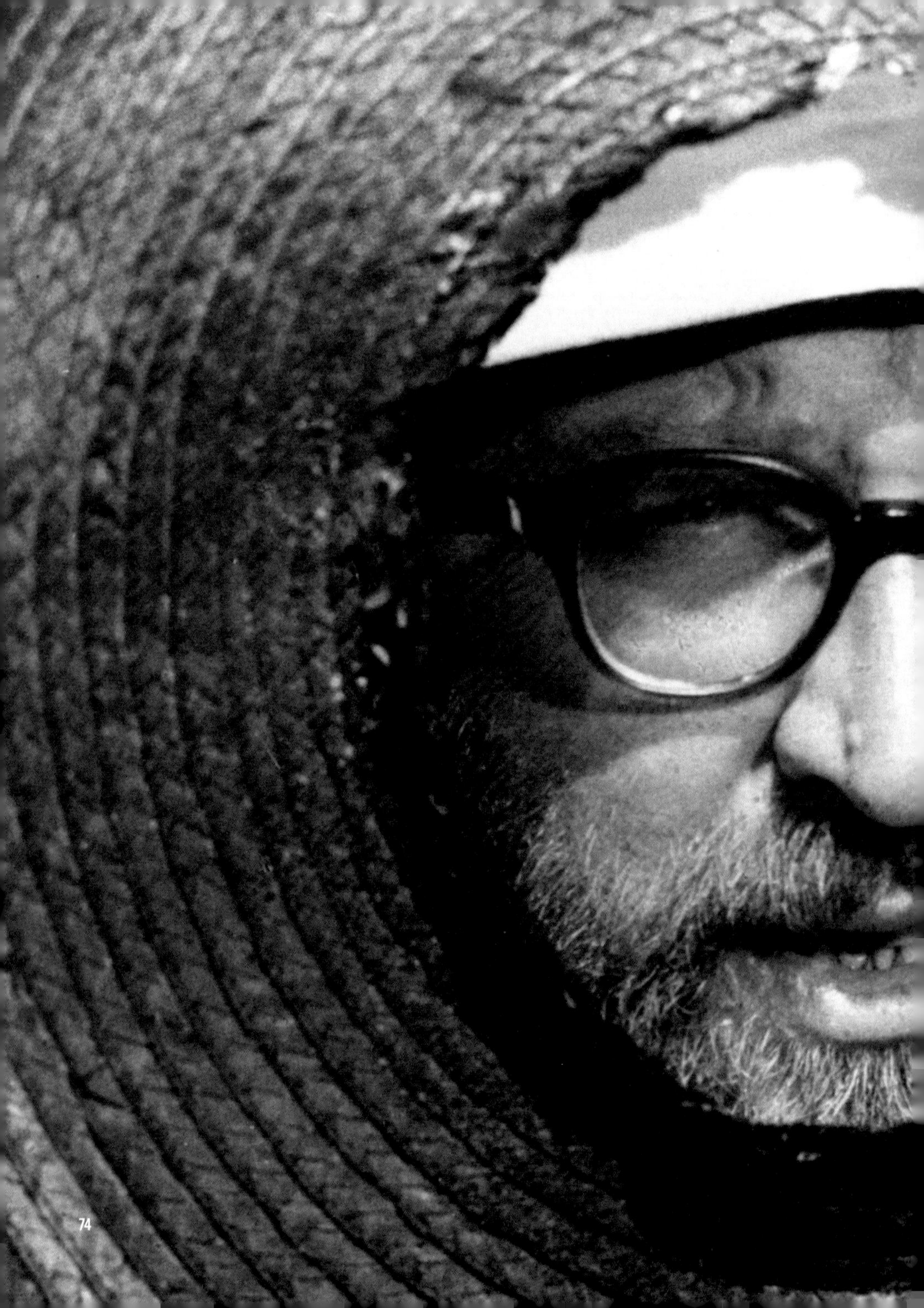

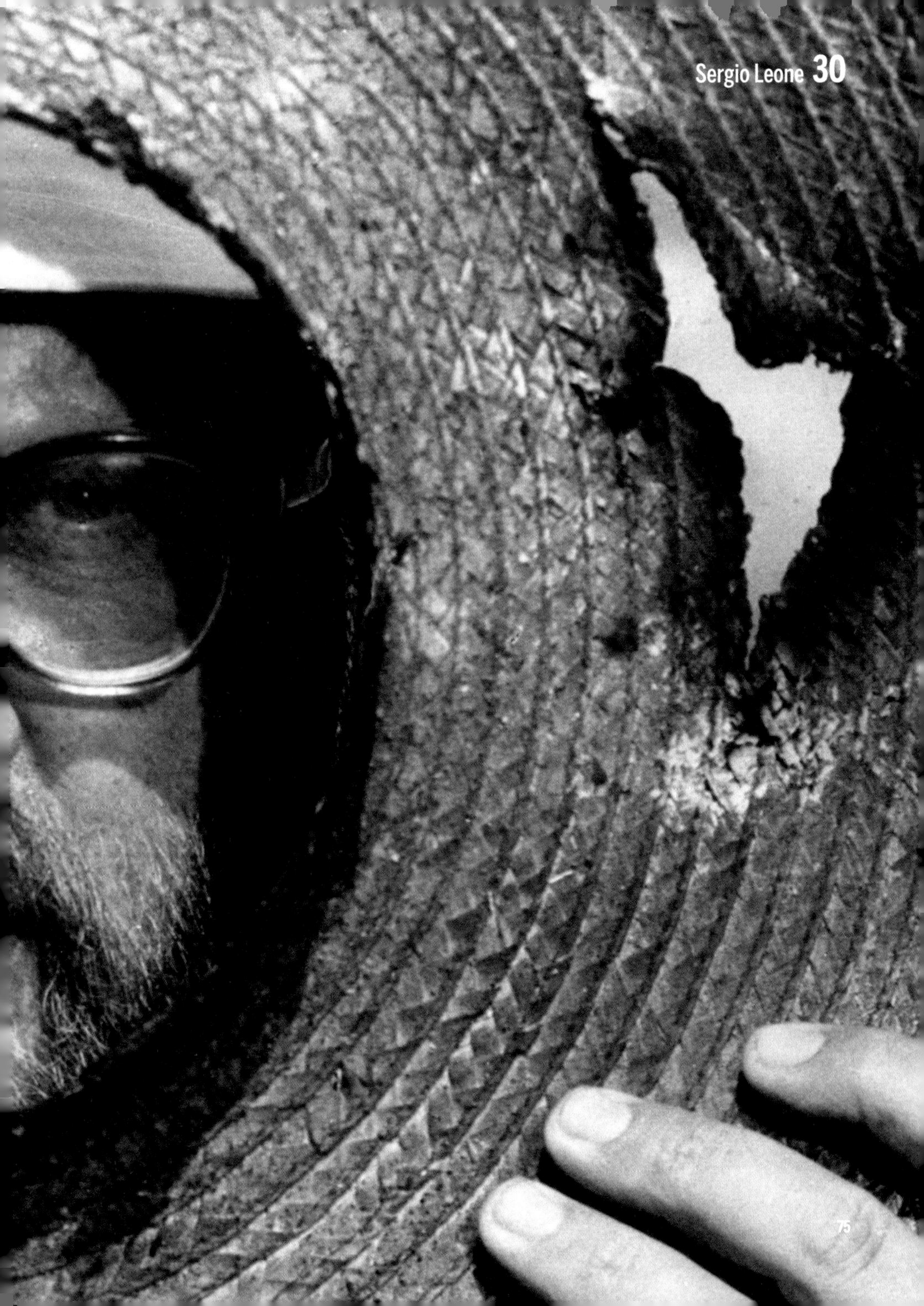

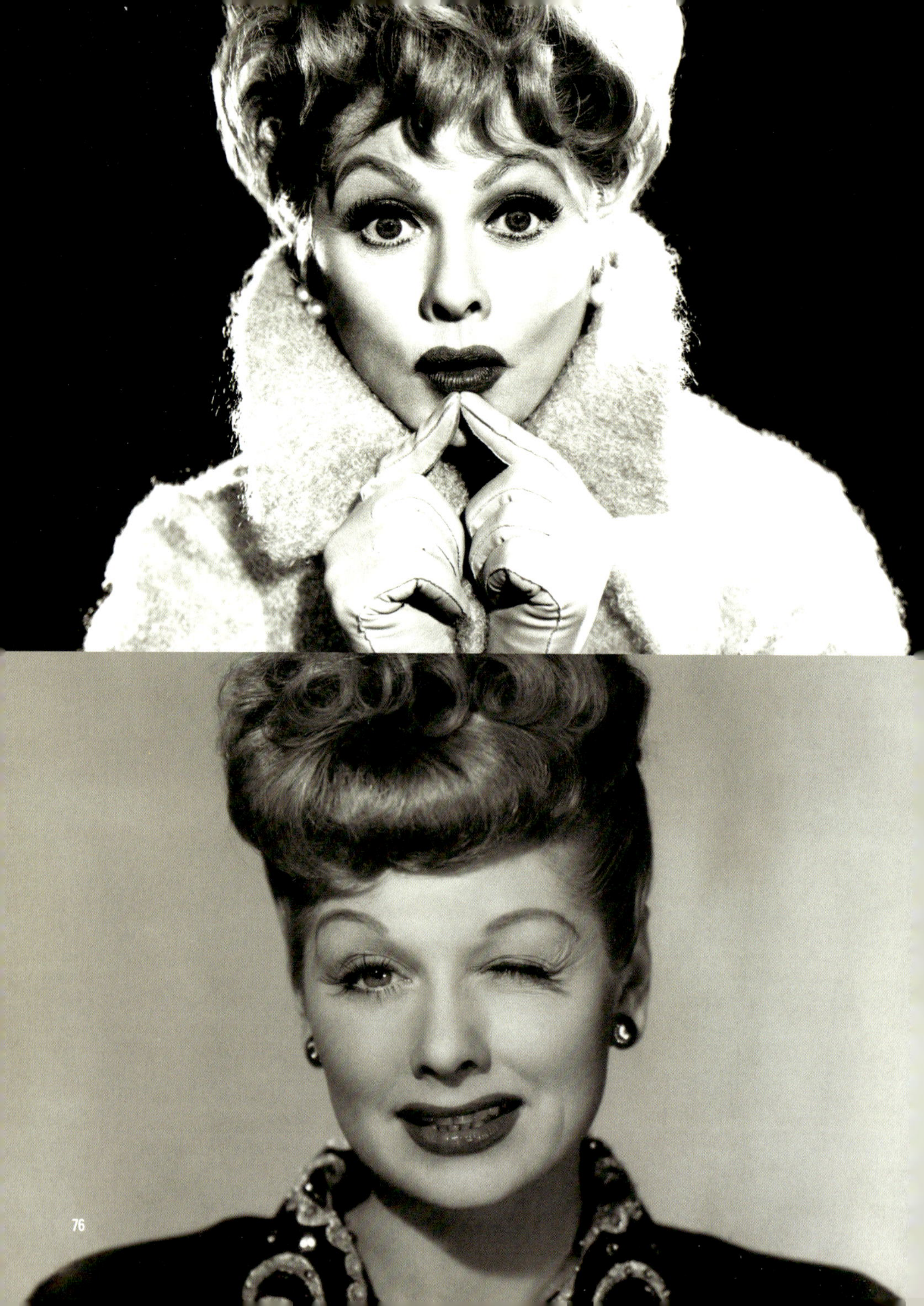

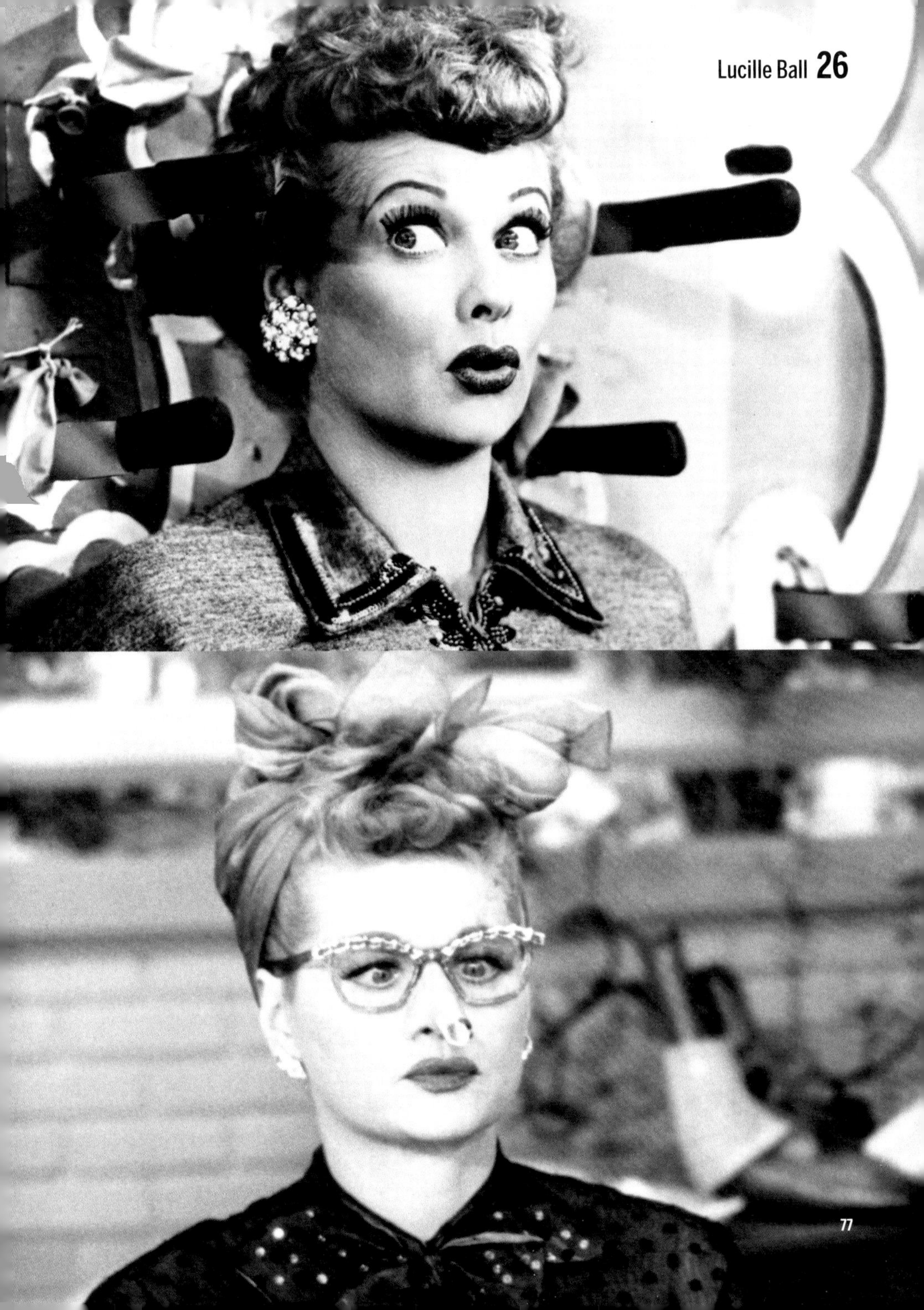

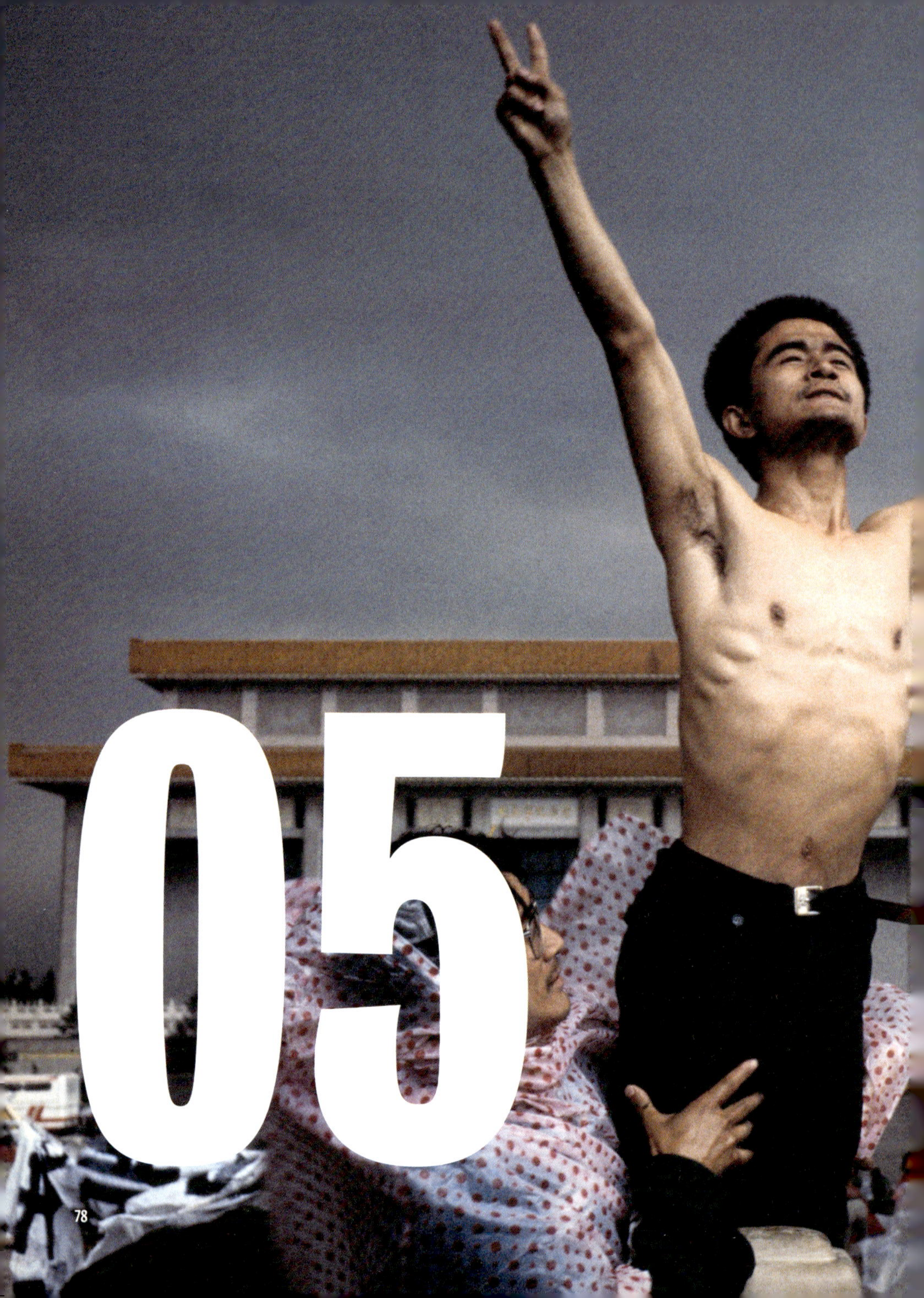

05

01

Great Britain: after 20 years the last episode of "The Benny Hill Show" is broadcast.

Great Britain: "Disintegration" by Cure is released, a commercial success also praised by critics. It still remains the highest selling record of the band with over 3 million copies.

02

Hungary: first breach in the Iron Curtain, 240 km of barbed wire are dismantled along the border with Austria.

10

United States: "Dynasty"'s last episode is broadcast after 8 years.

14

China: Mikhail Gorbachev visits the country. The students' protests and the government's reaction become stronger. The Martial Law is established in the upcoming days.

21

United States: the last episode of "Miami Vice" is broadcast.

23

France: 42nd edition of the Cannes Film Festival. Steven Soderbergh's "Sex, Lies, and Videotape", is awarded with the Golden Palm for Best Picture. The Jury's Special Prize goes ex aequo to Giuseppe Tornatore's "Nuovo cinema Paradiso" and to Bertrand Blier's "Too Beautiful for You" ("Trop belle pour toi").

24

United States: the third episode of Indiana Jones's saga "Indiana Jones and the Last Crusade" by Steven Spielberg with Harrison Ford and Sean Connery. It is an international blockbuster.

Spain: at the Camp Nou stadium in Barcelona, A.C. Milan beats Steaua Bucarest 4-0 and wins the European Cup, with two goals each by Ruud Gullit and Marco Van Basten.

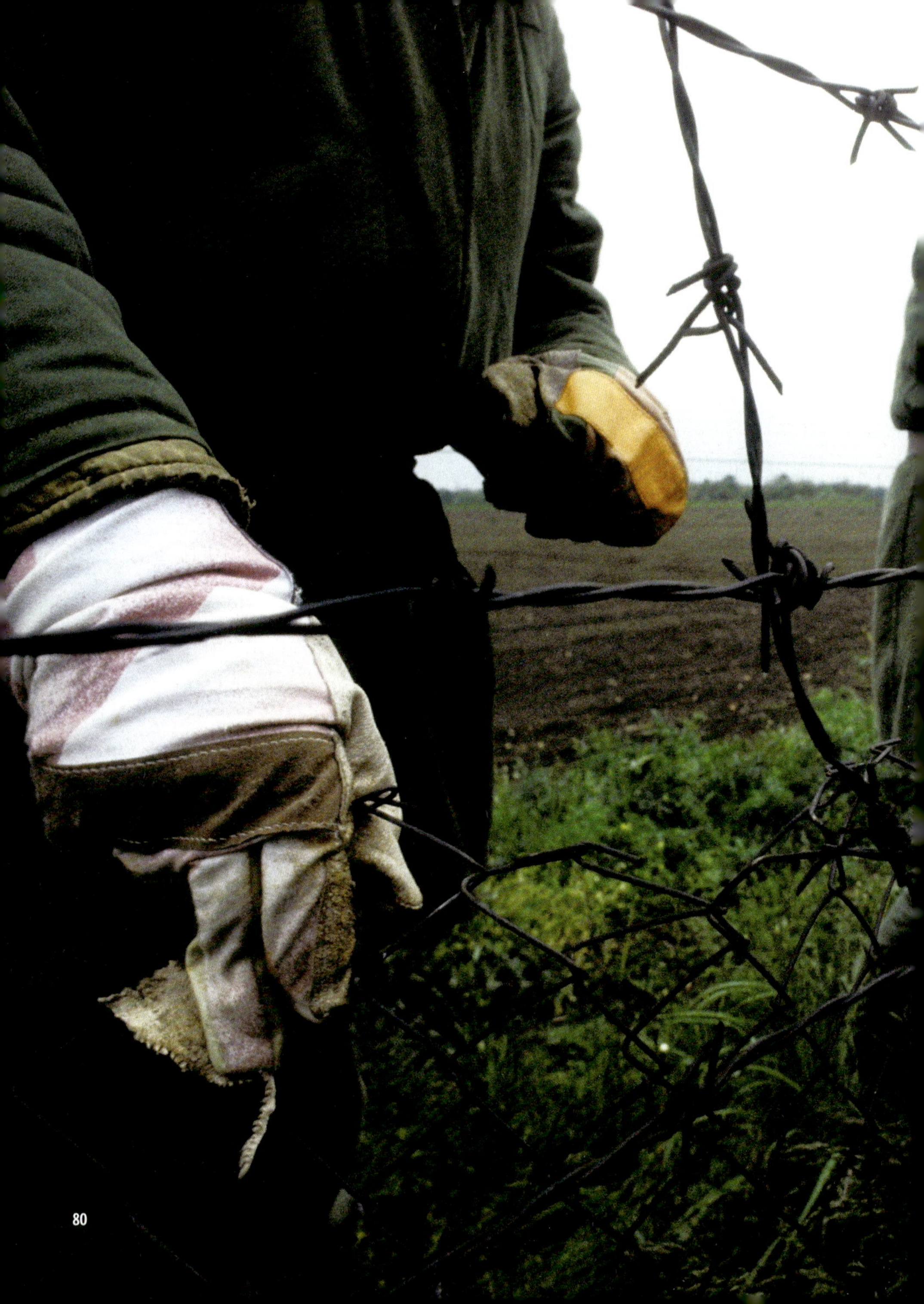

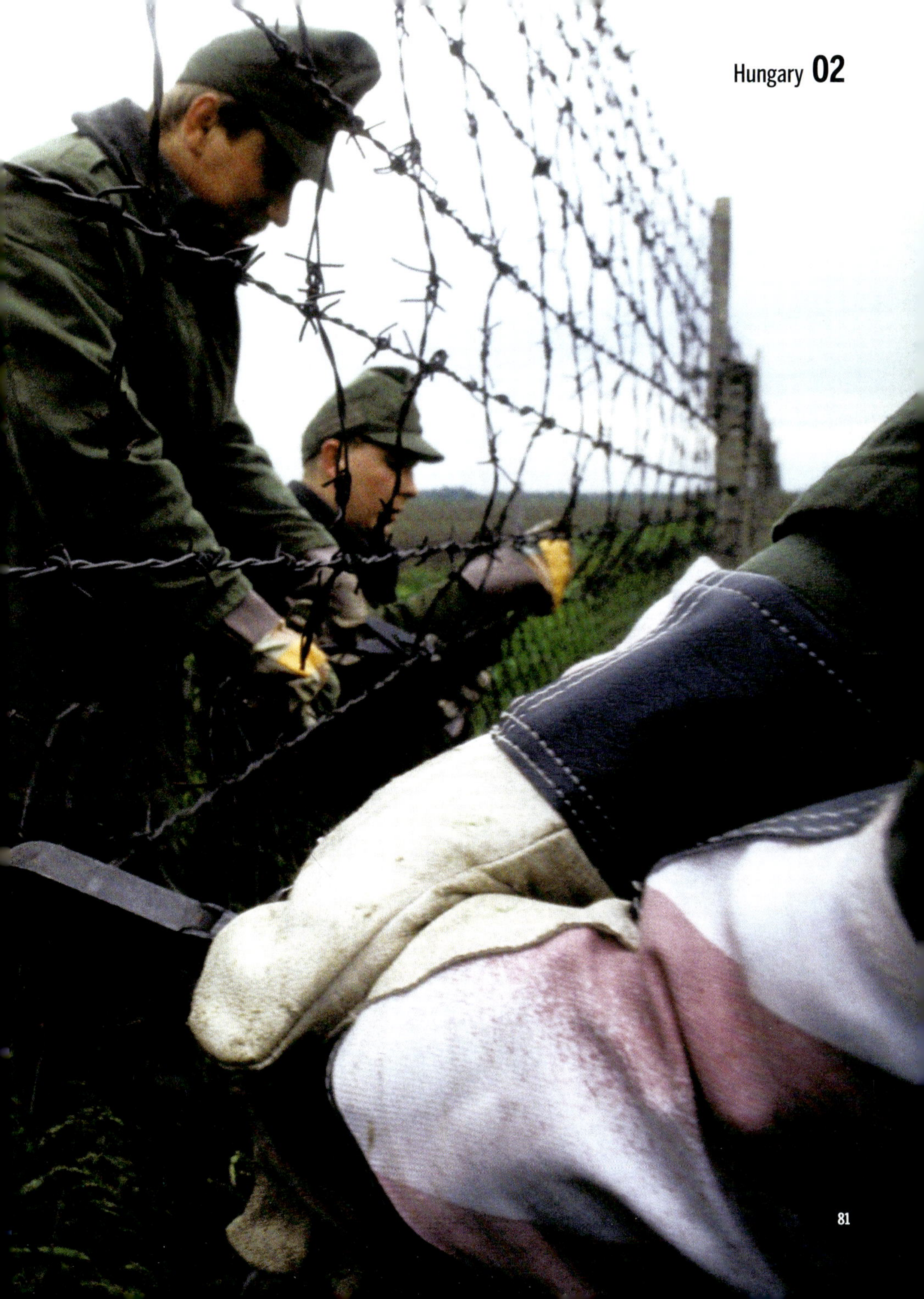

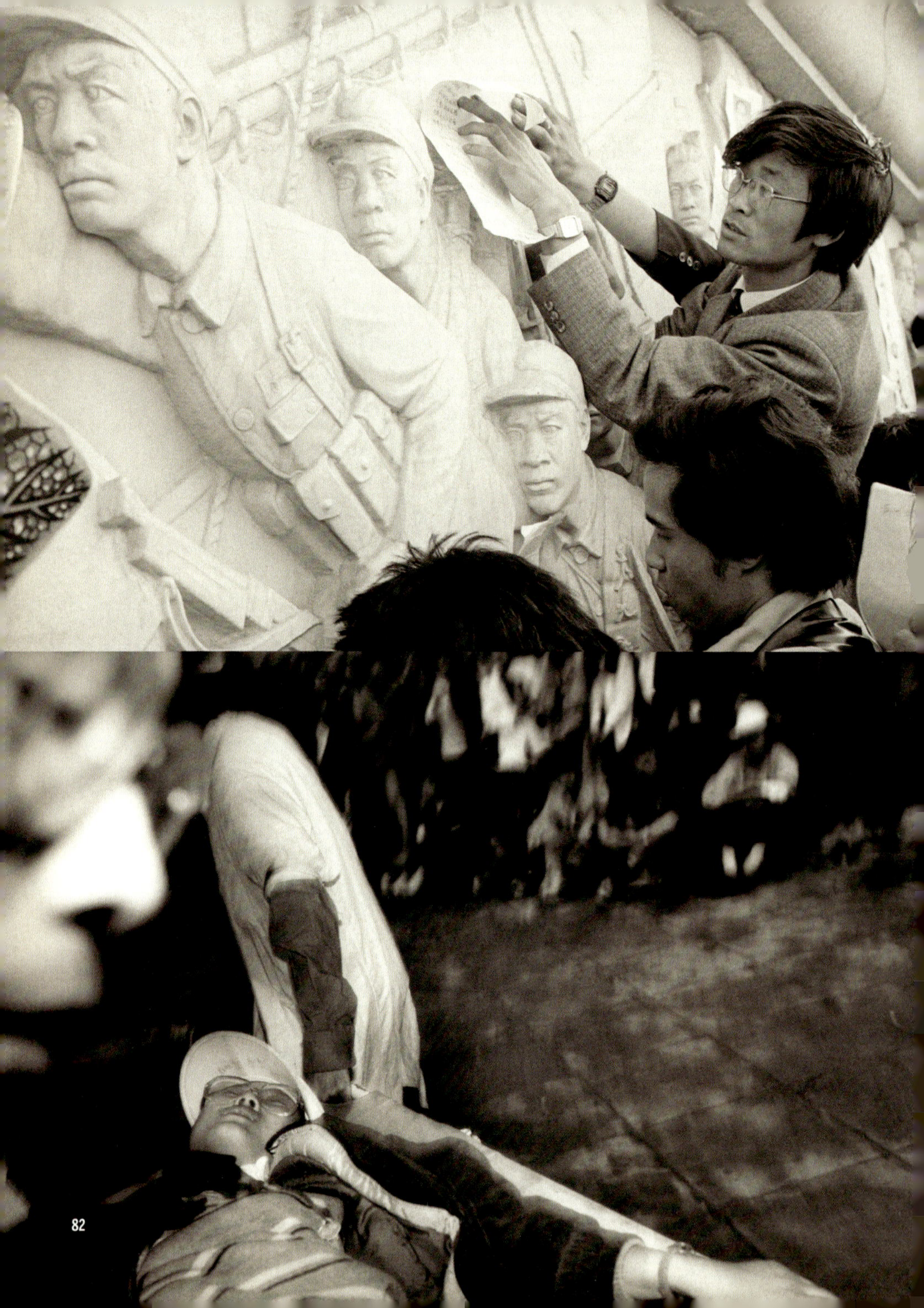

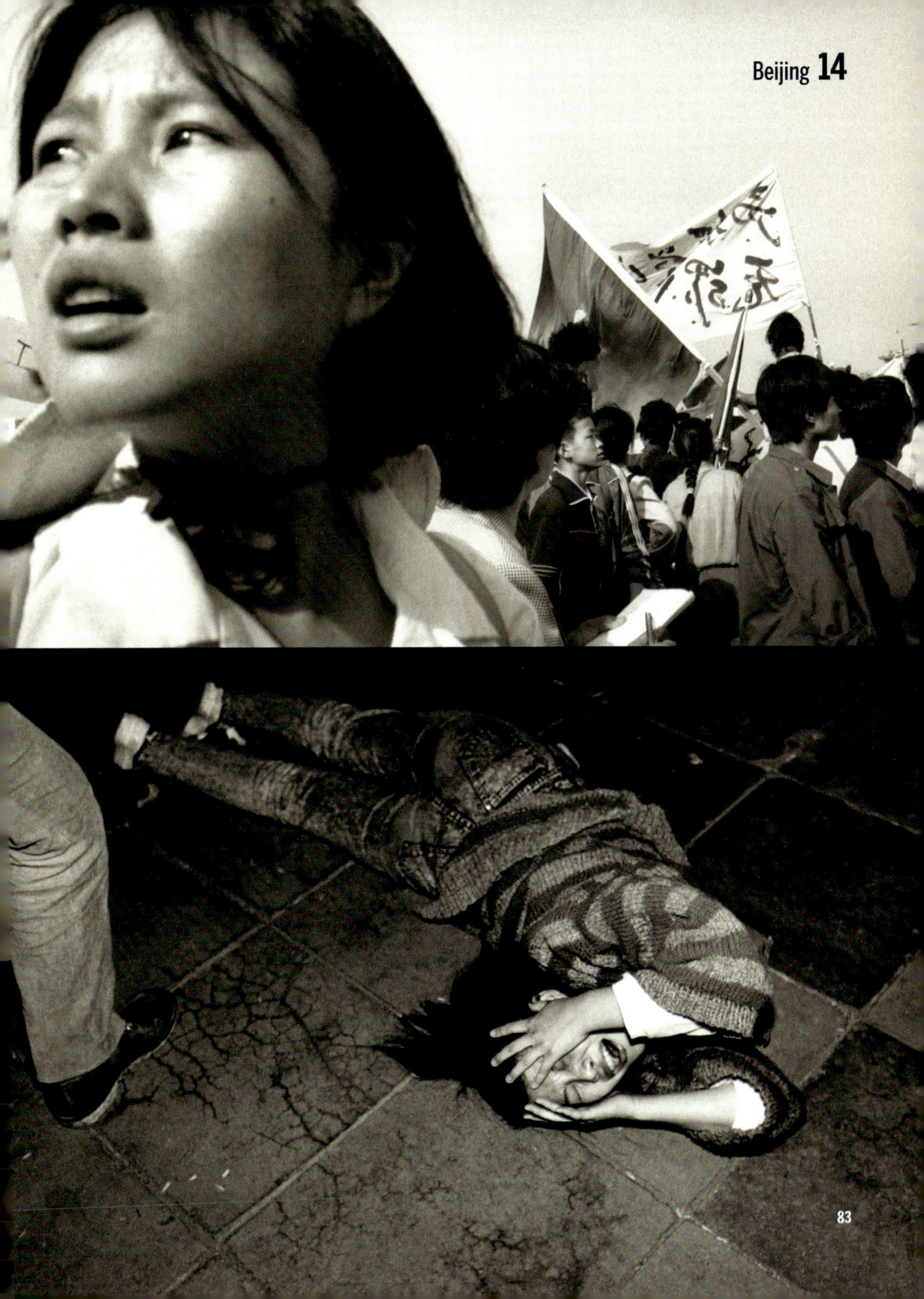

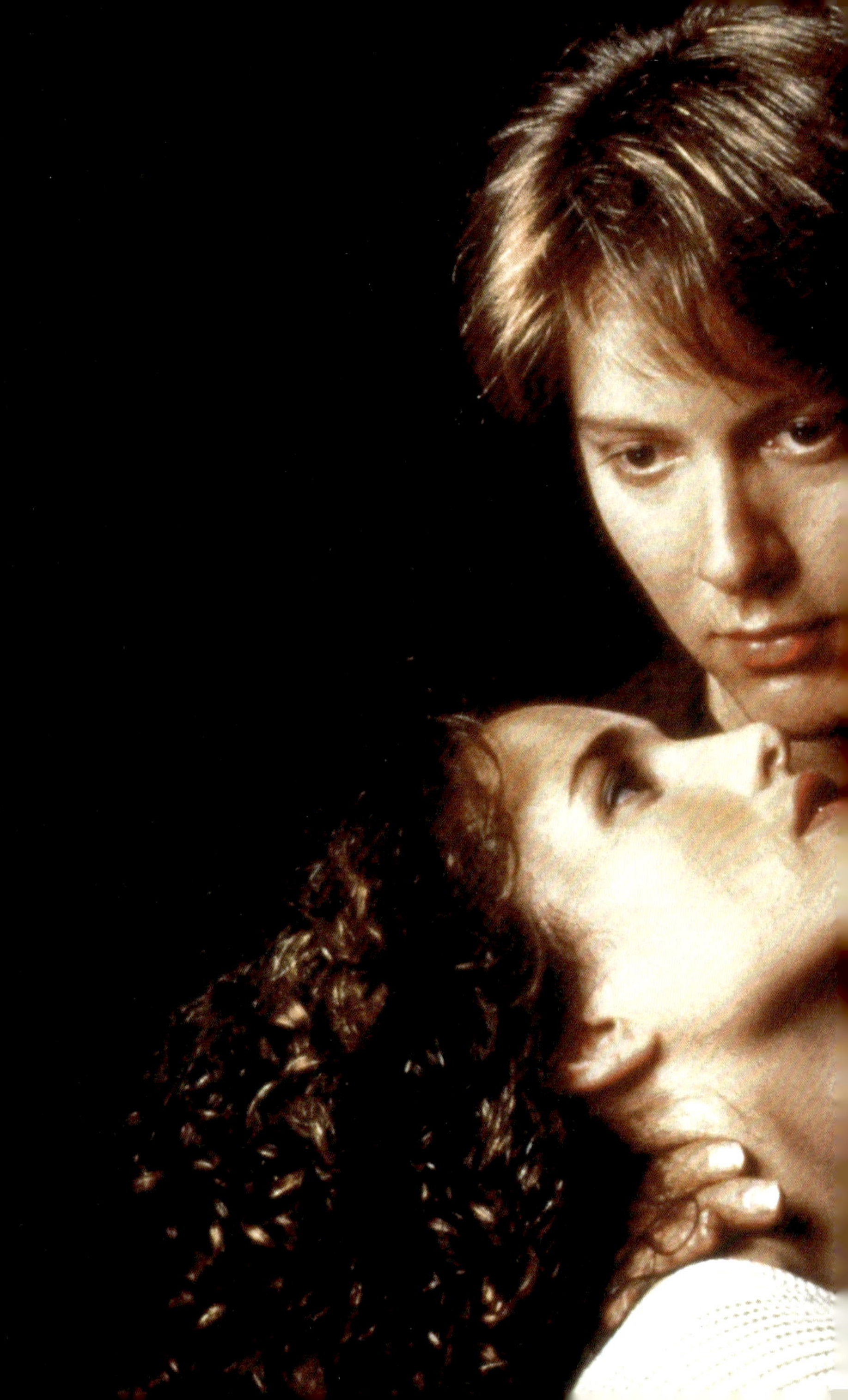

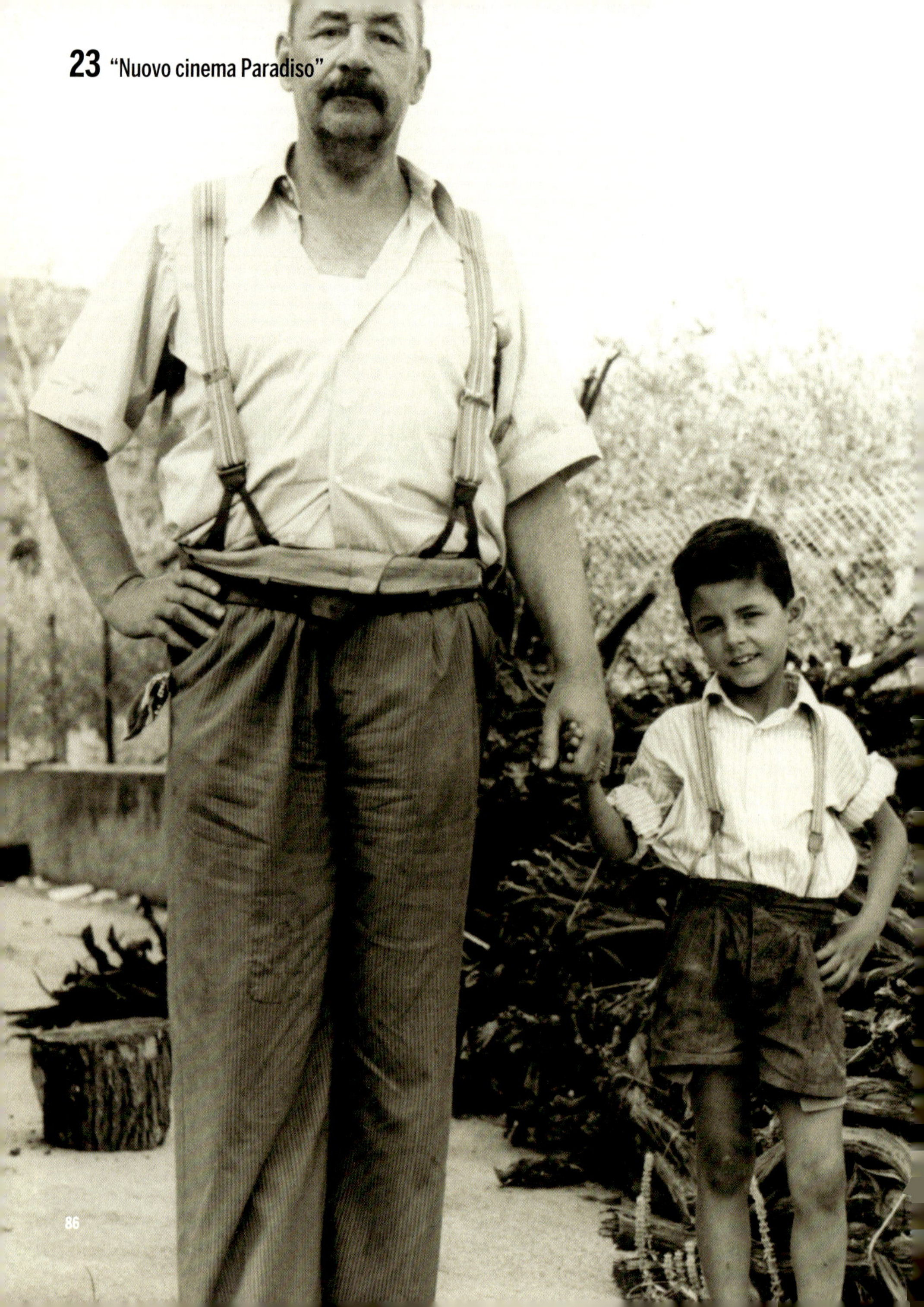

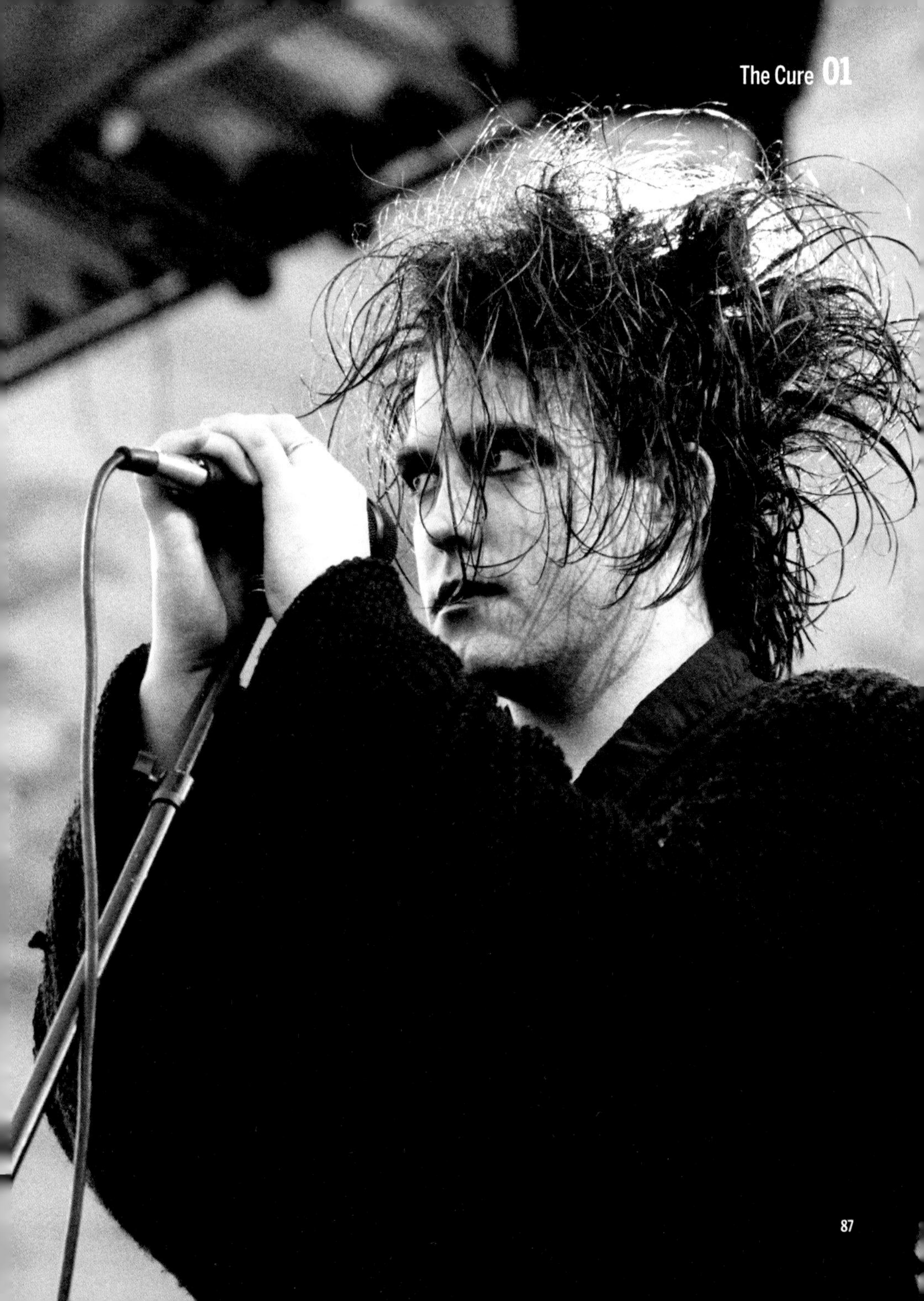

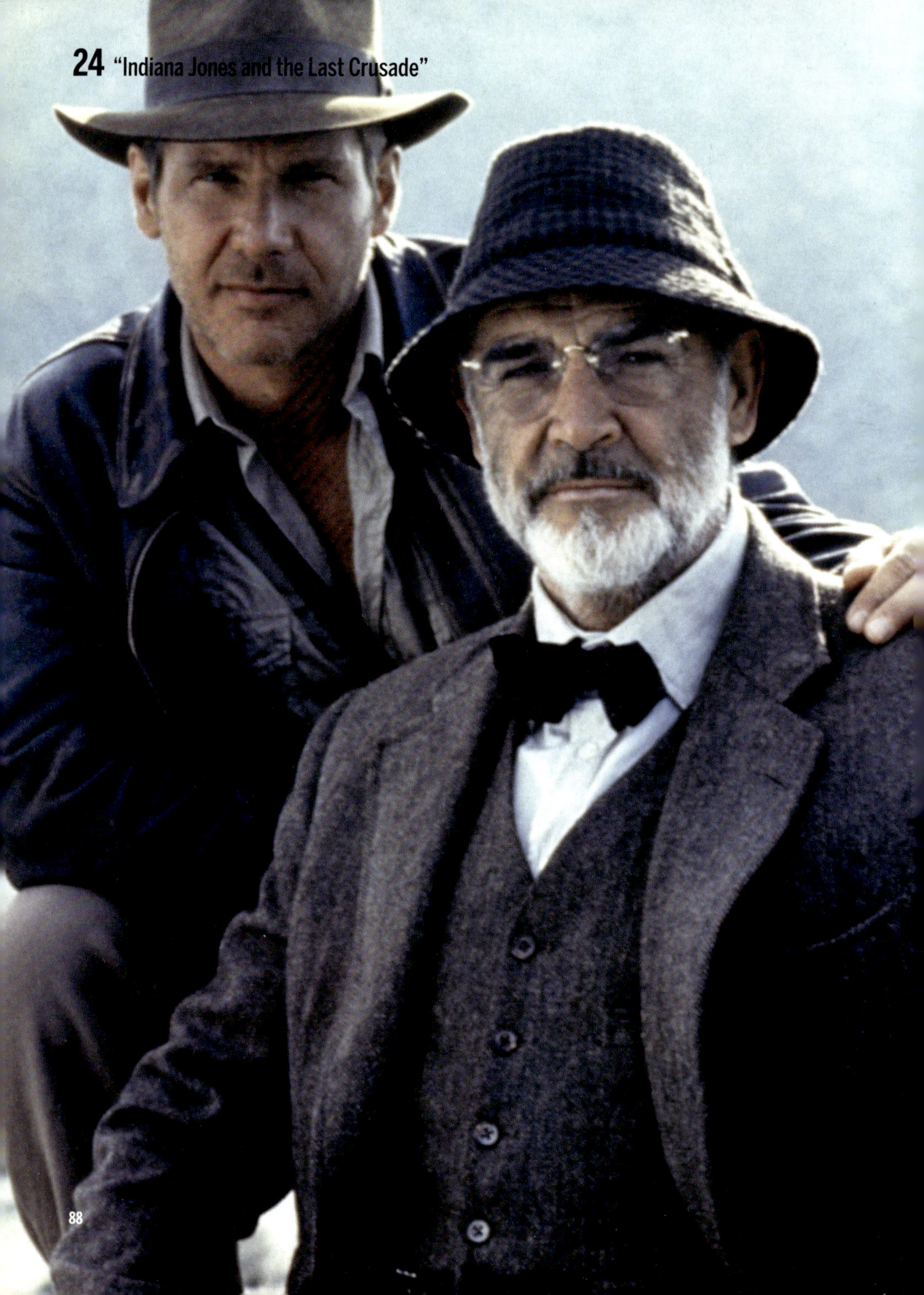

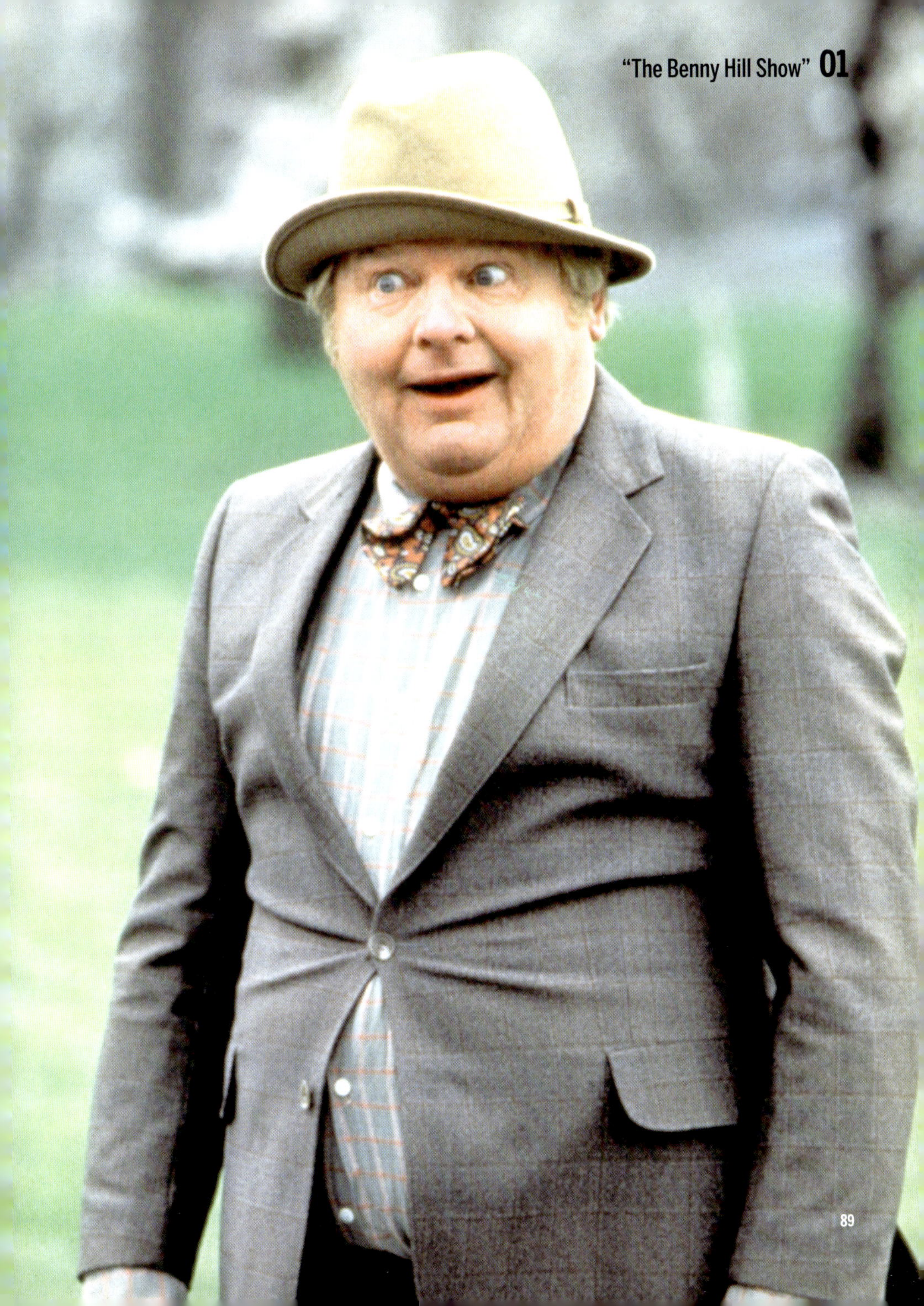

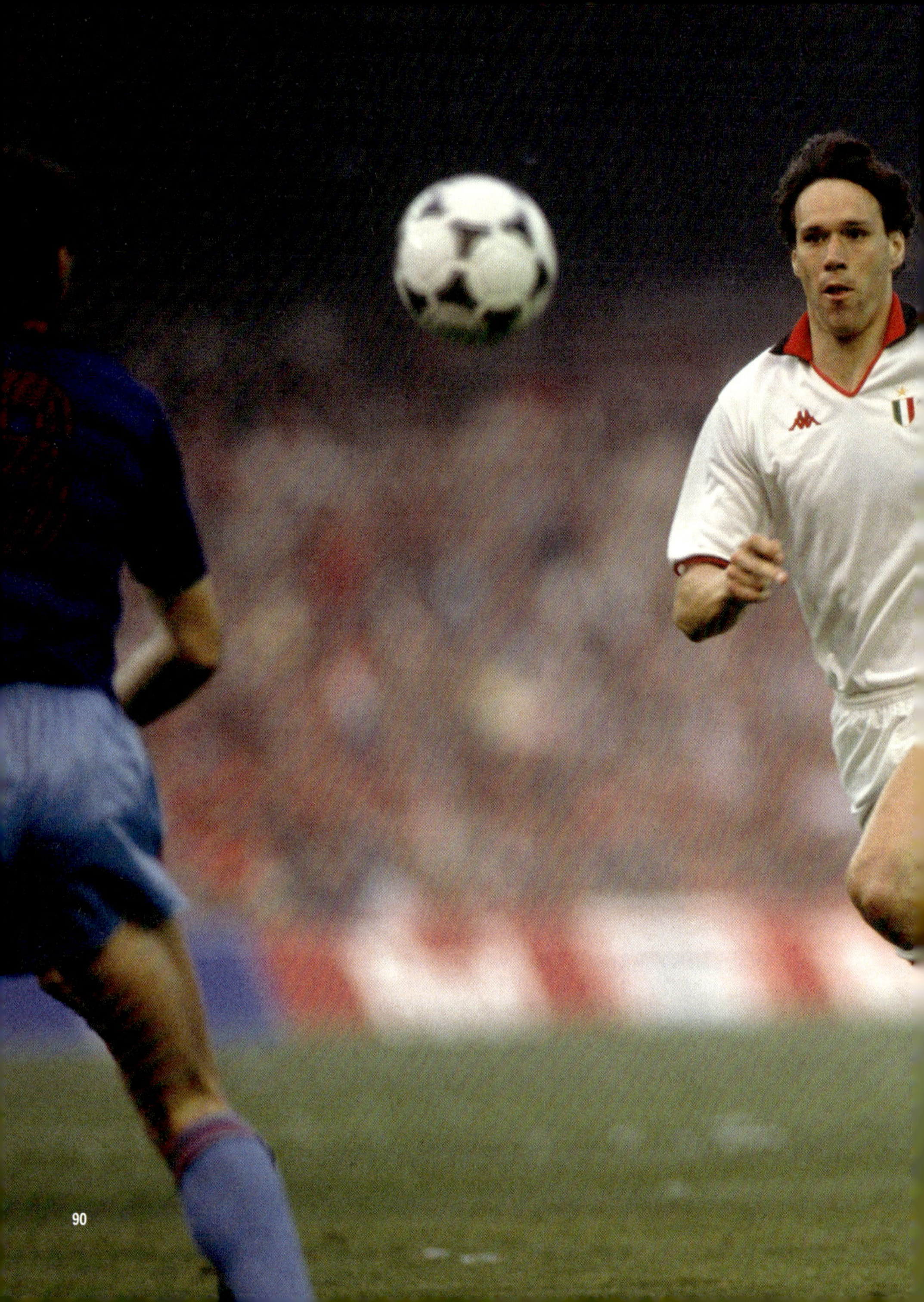

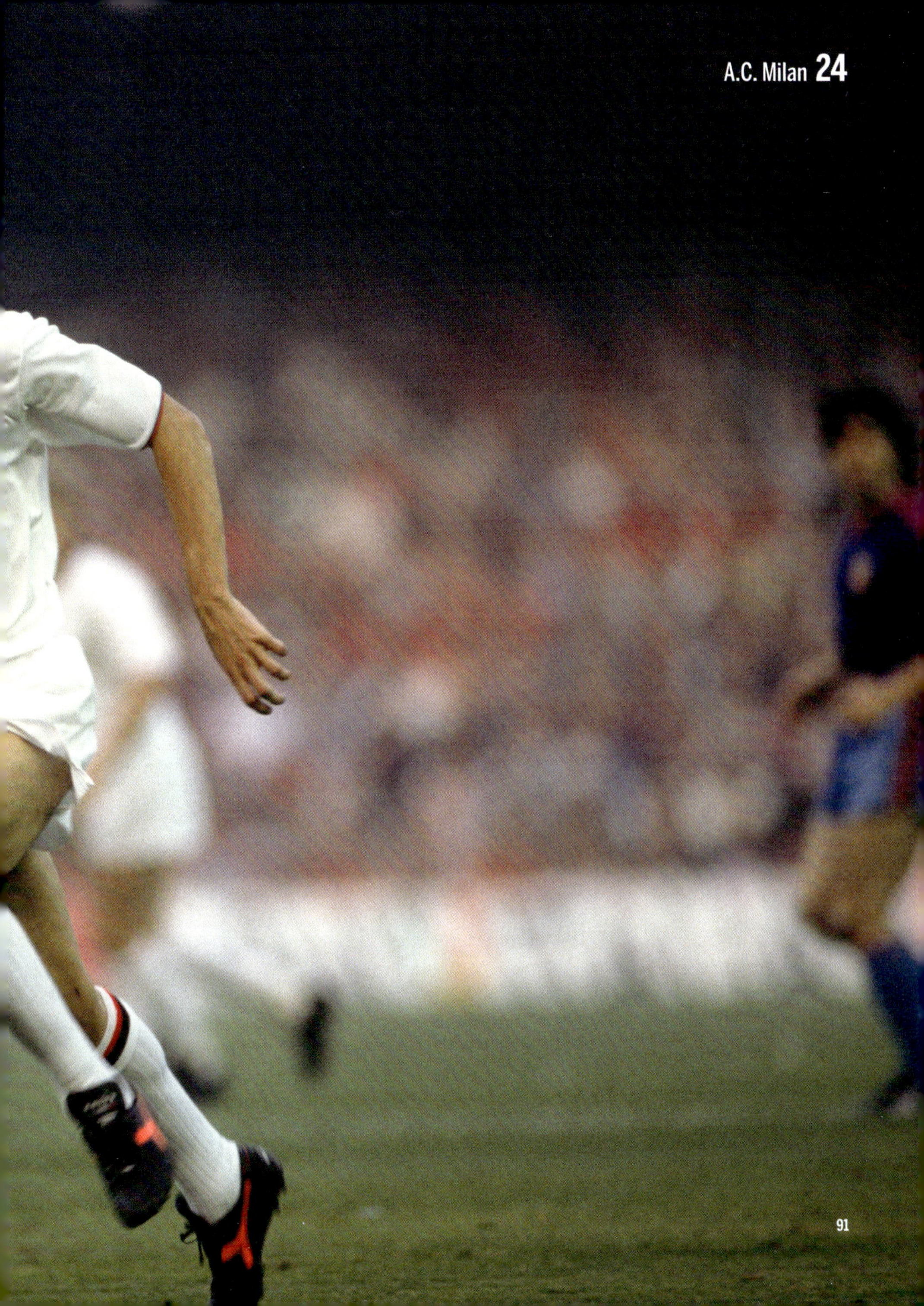

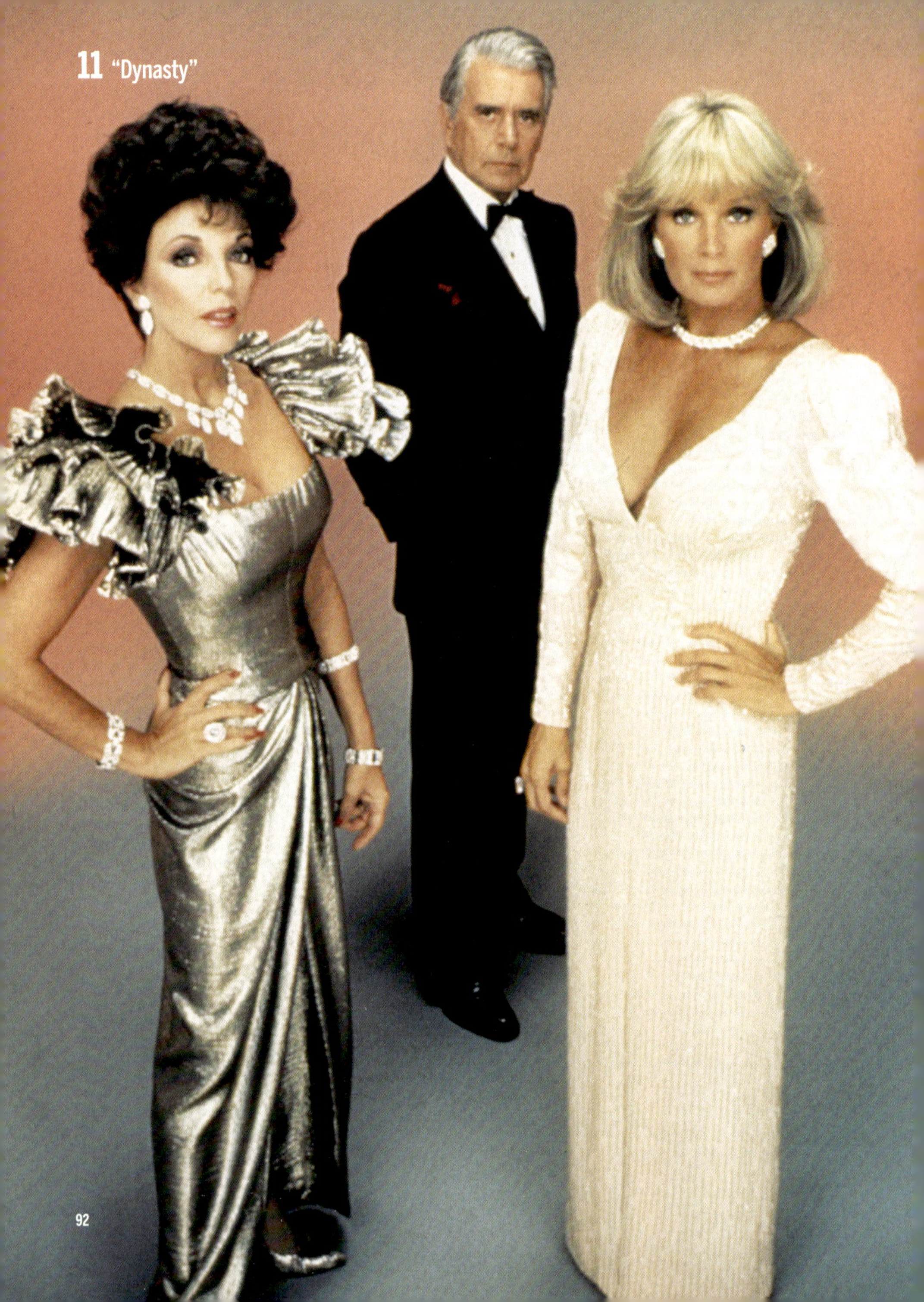

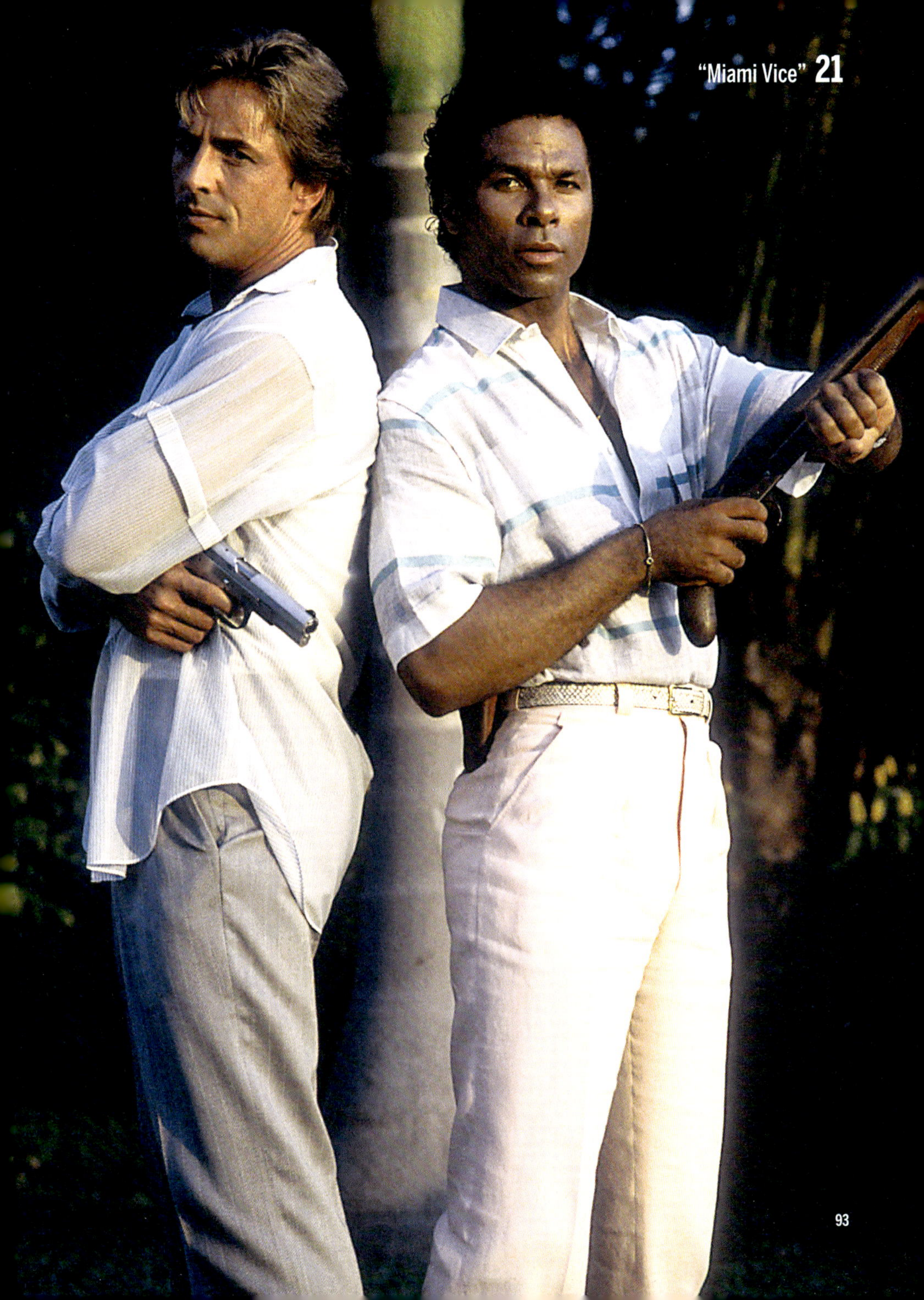

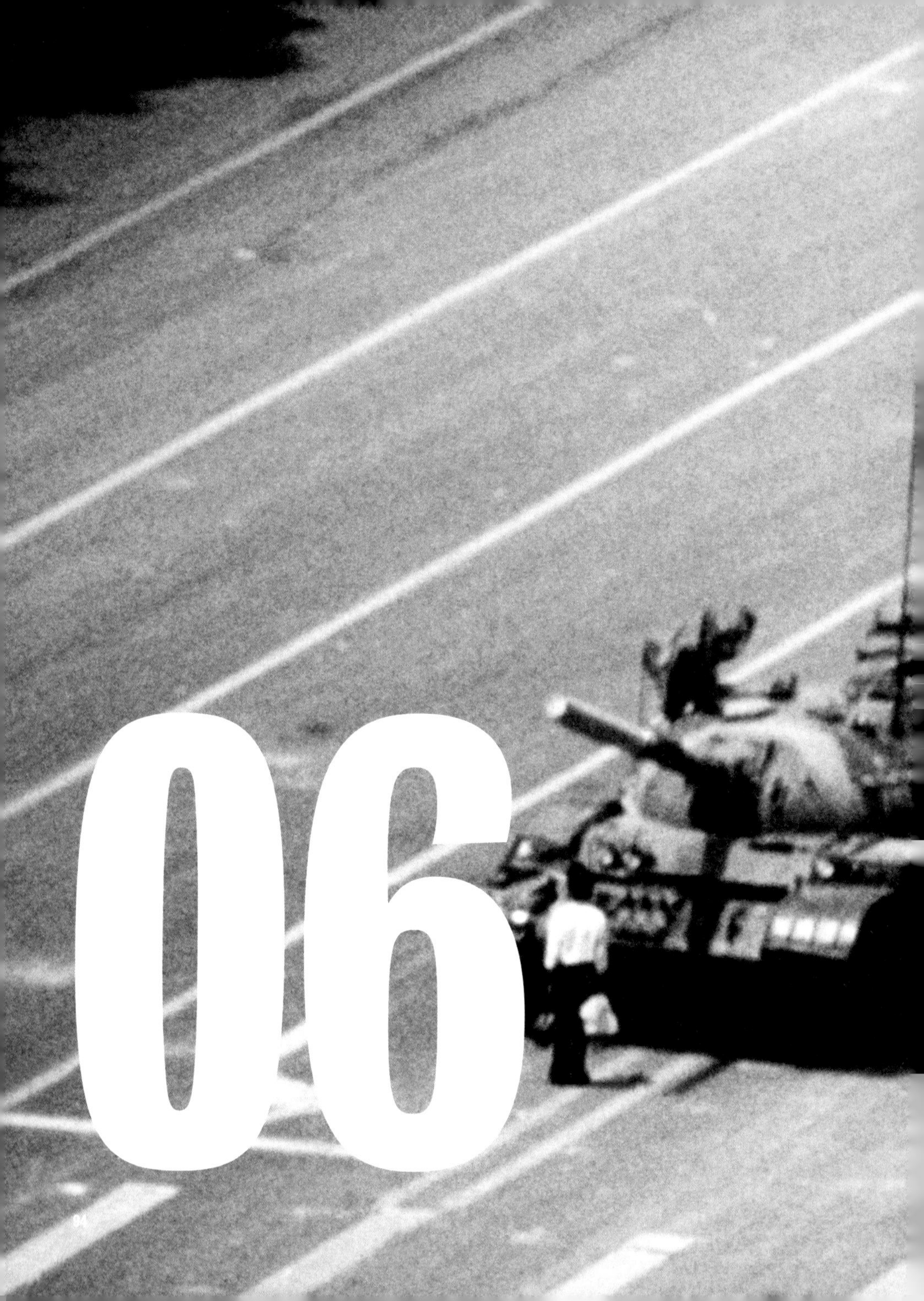

06

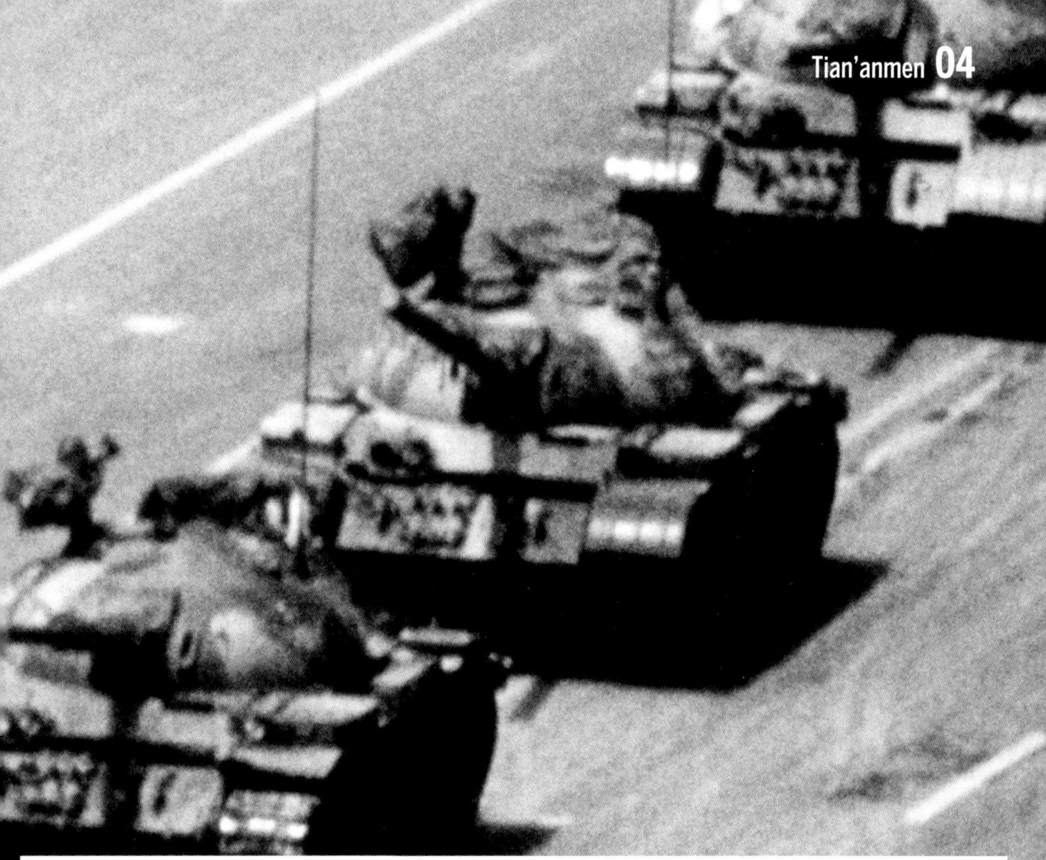

02

United States: the "Dead Poets Society" by Peter Weir with Robin Williams is released.

03

Iran: religious and political leader ayatollah Khomeini since 1979, dies in Teheran. Millions of followers gather to honour his remains. Eight people die crushed by the crowd and 500 are wounded.

04

China: the army approaches Tian'anmen Square. Confronted with the protesters' resistance they open fire and reach the square. Television networks broadcast live the tanks' entrance.

Poland: Solidarność wins the elections, it is the firsti anti-communist movement to impose itself in Eastern Europe.

16

Hungary: 250.000 people crowd Heroes' Square in Budapest for the commemoration of Imre Nagy, the prime minister executed in 1958.

Austria: Herbert von Karajan one of the most prominent post-war conductors, dies in Anif, aged 81.

21

Great Britain: British police arrest 250 people celebrating the Summer solstice at Stonehenge.

23

United States: release of "Batman" by Tim Burton with Michael Keaton, Kim Basinger and Jack Nicholson, both financially successful and praised by critics, it was the top-grossing movie based on a DC Comics novel.

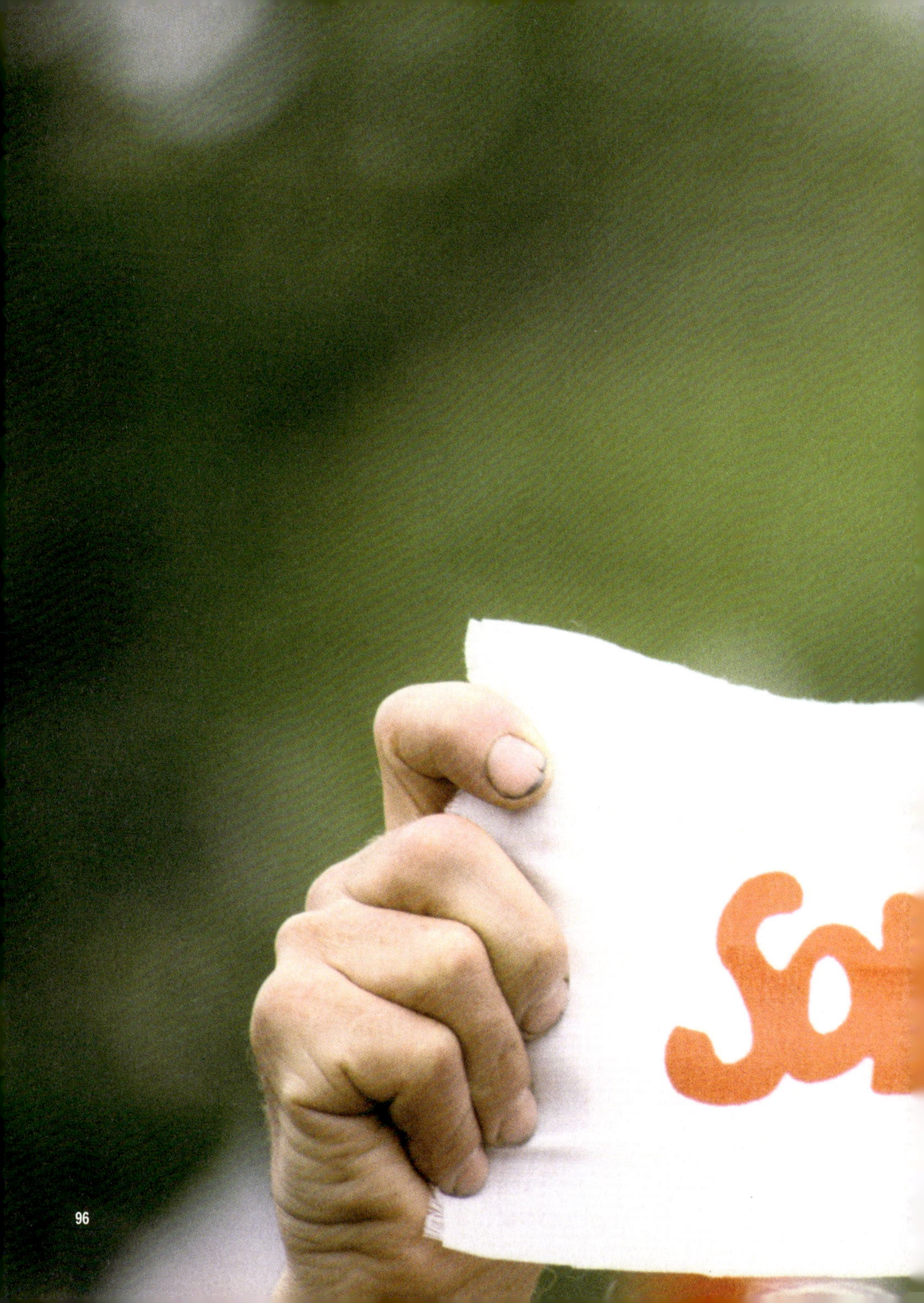
So

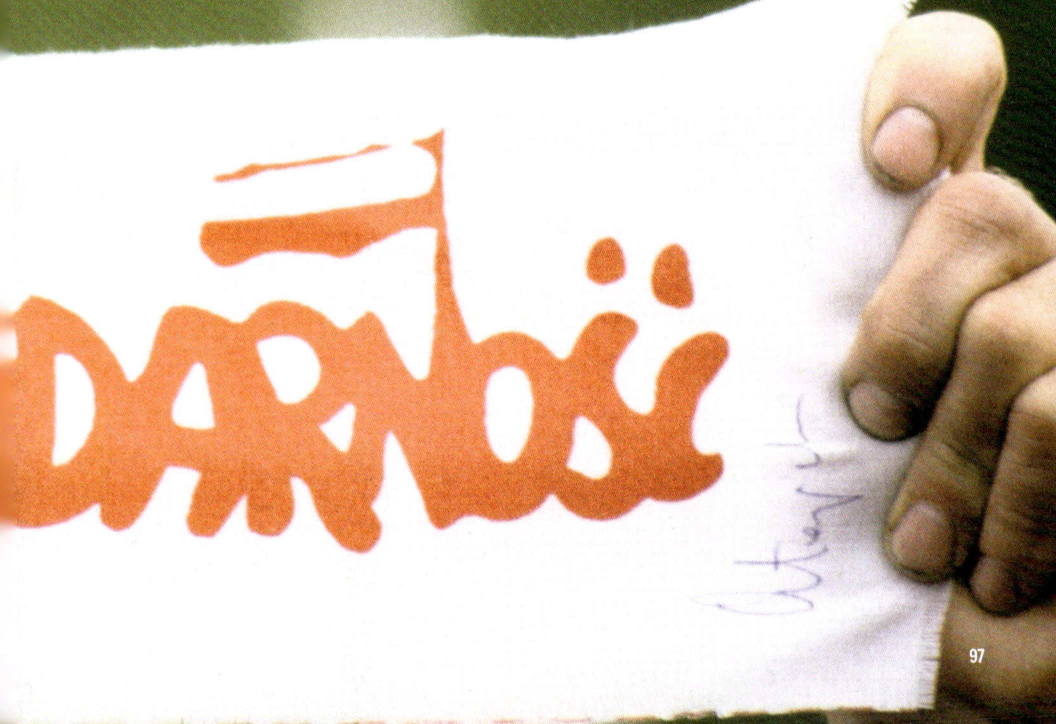

DARIši

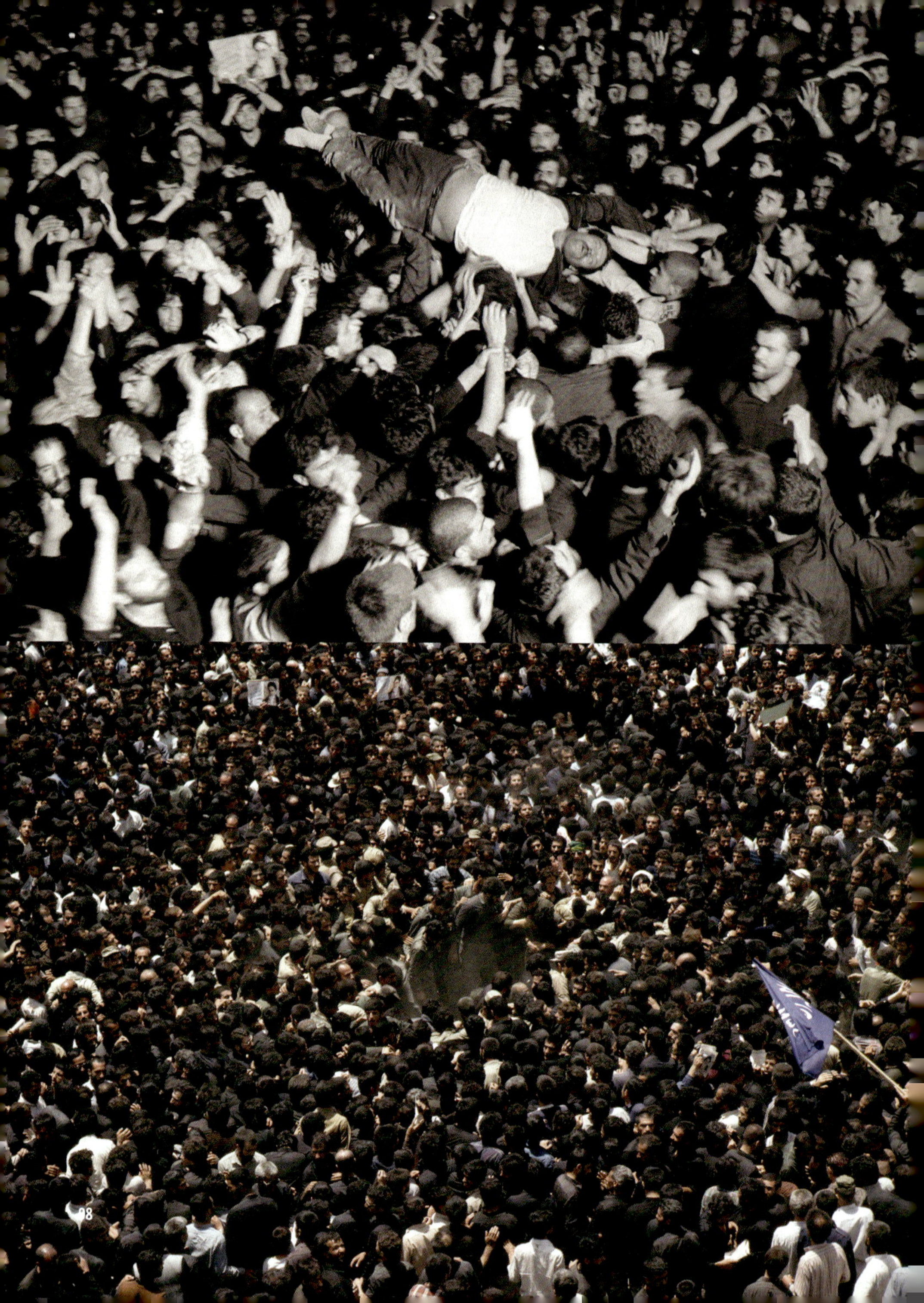

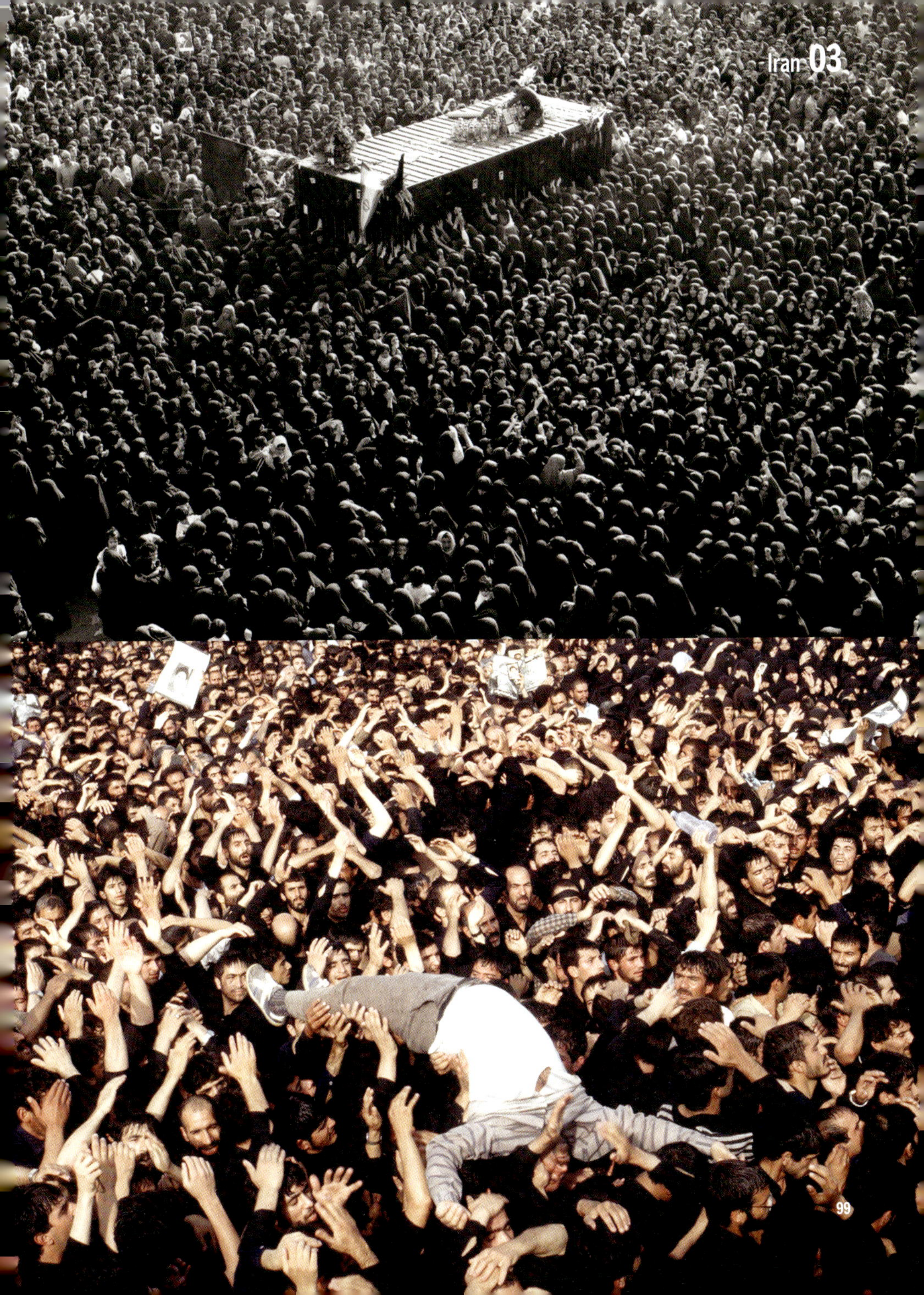

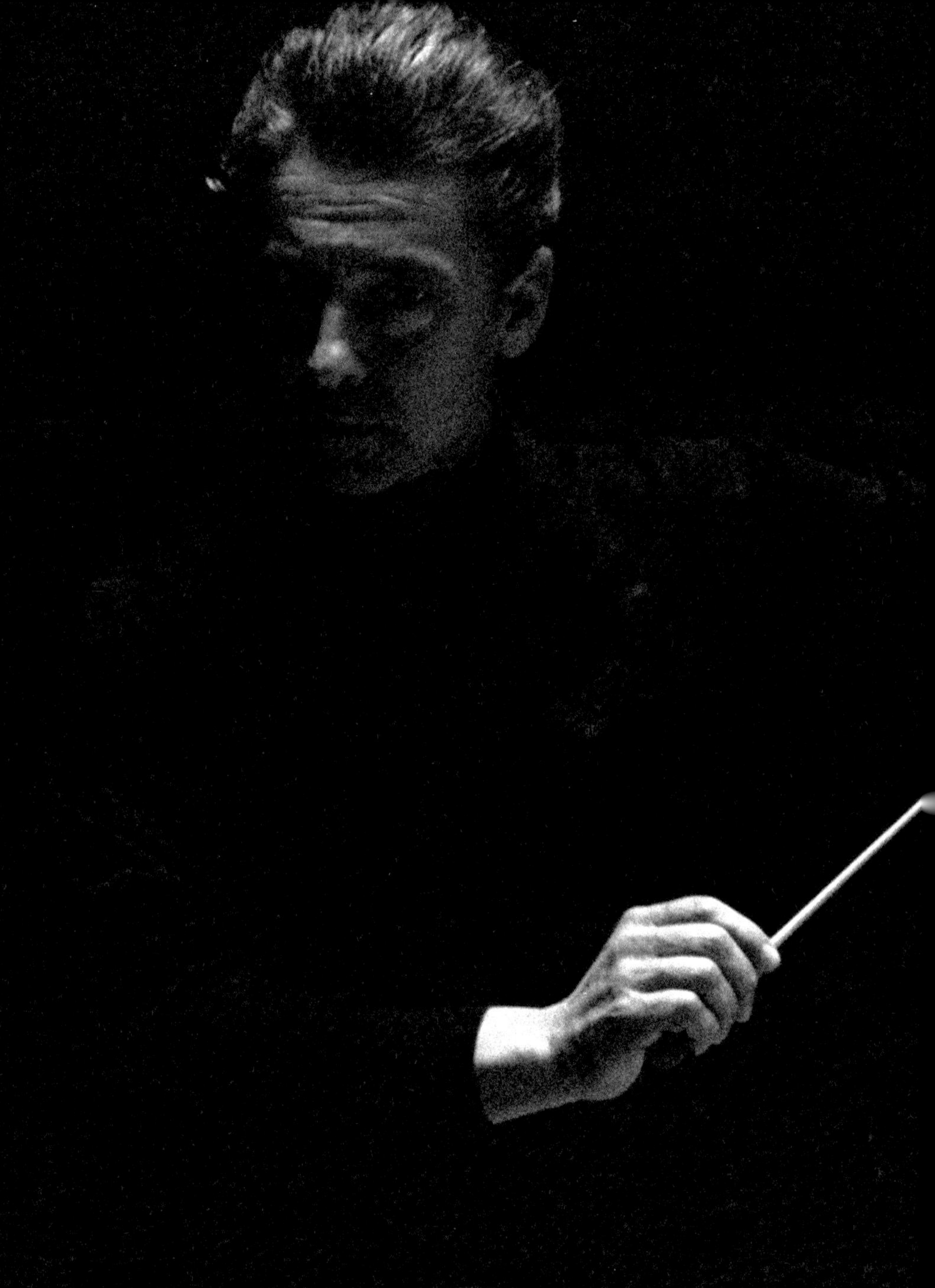

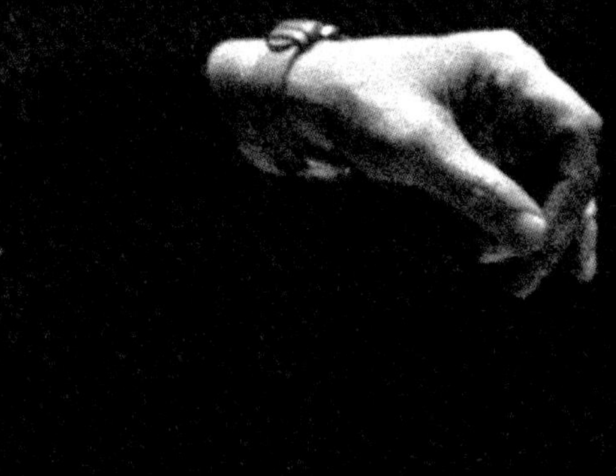

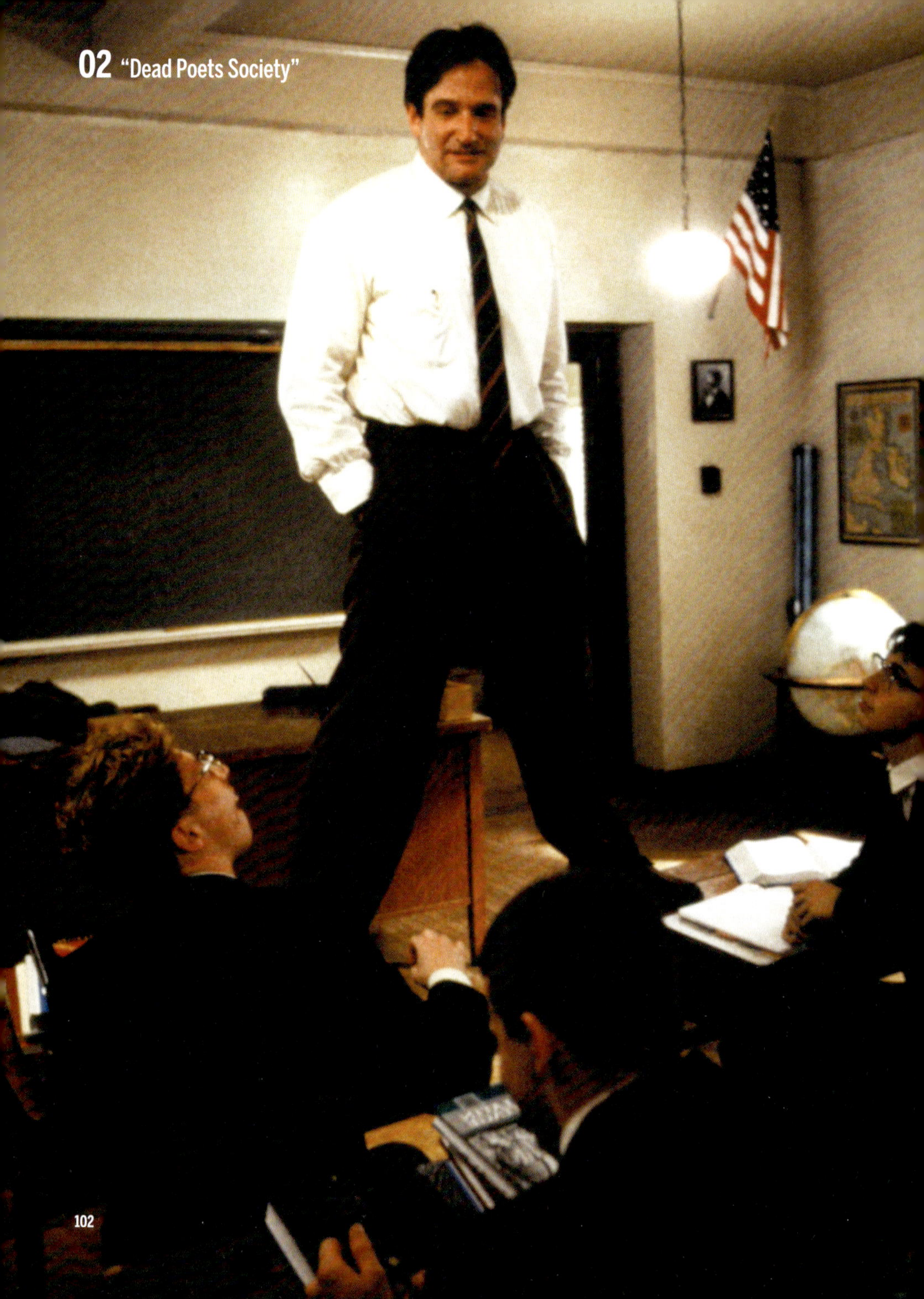

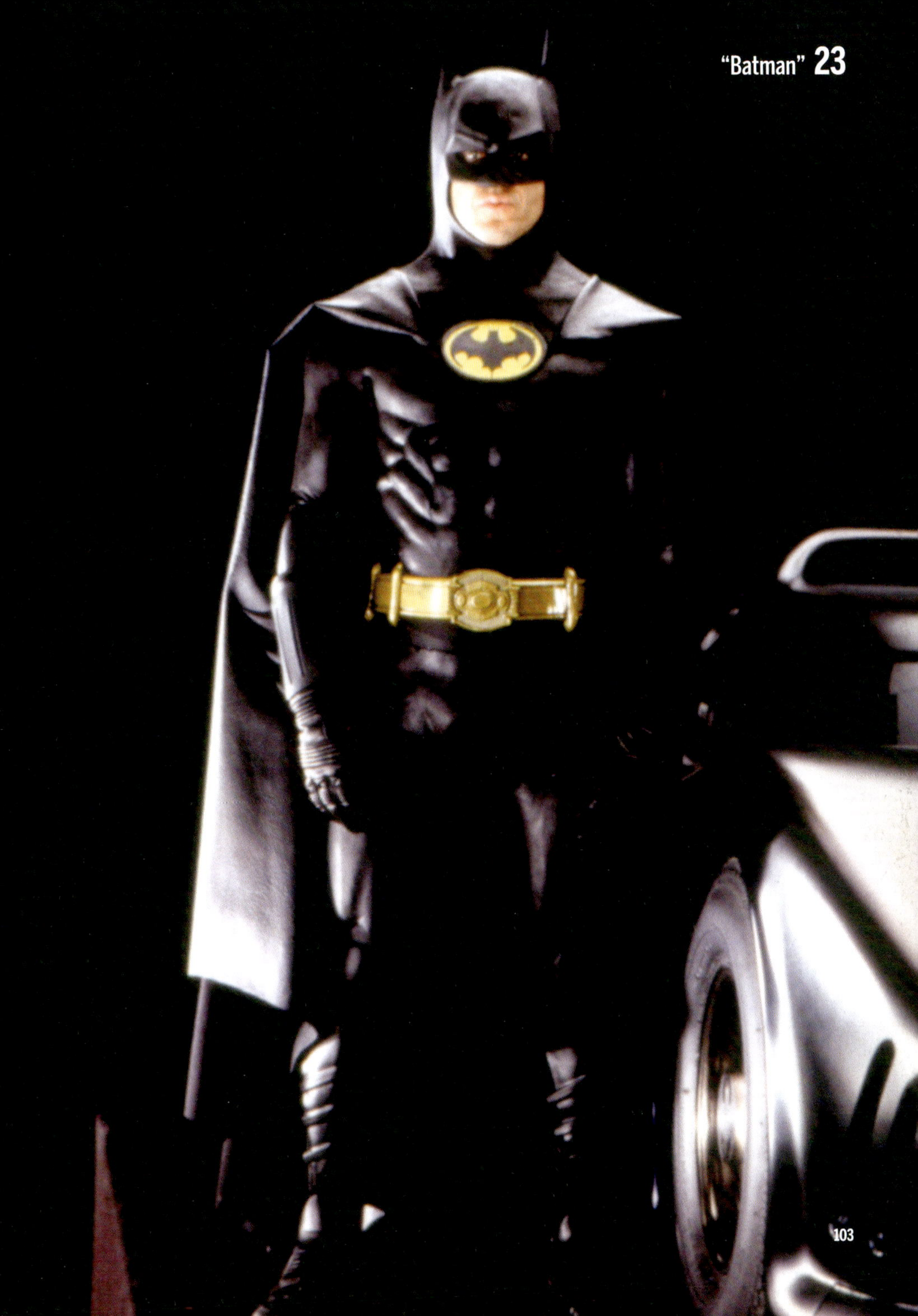

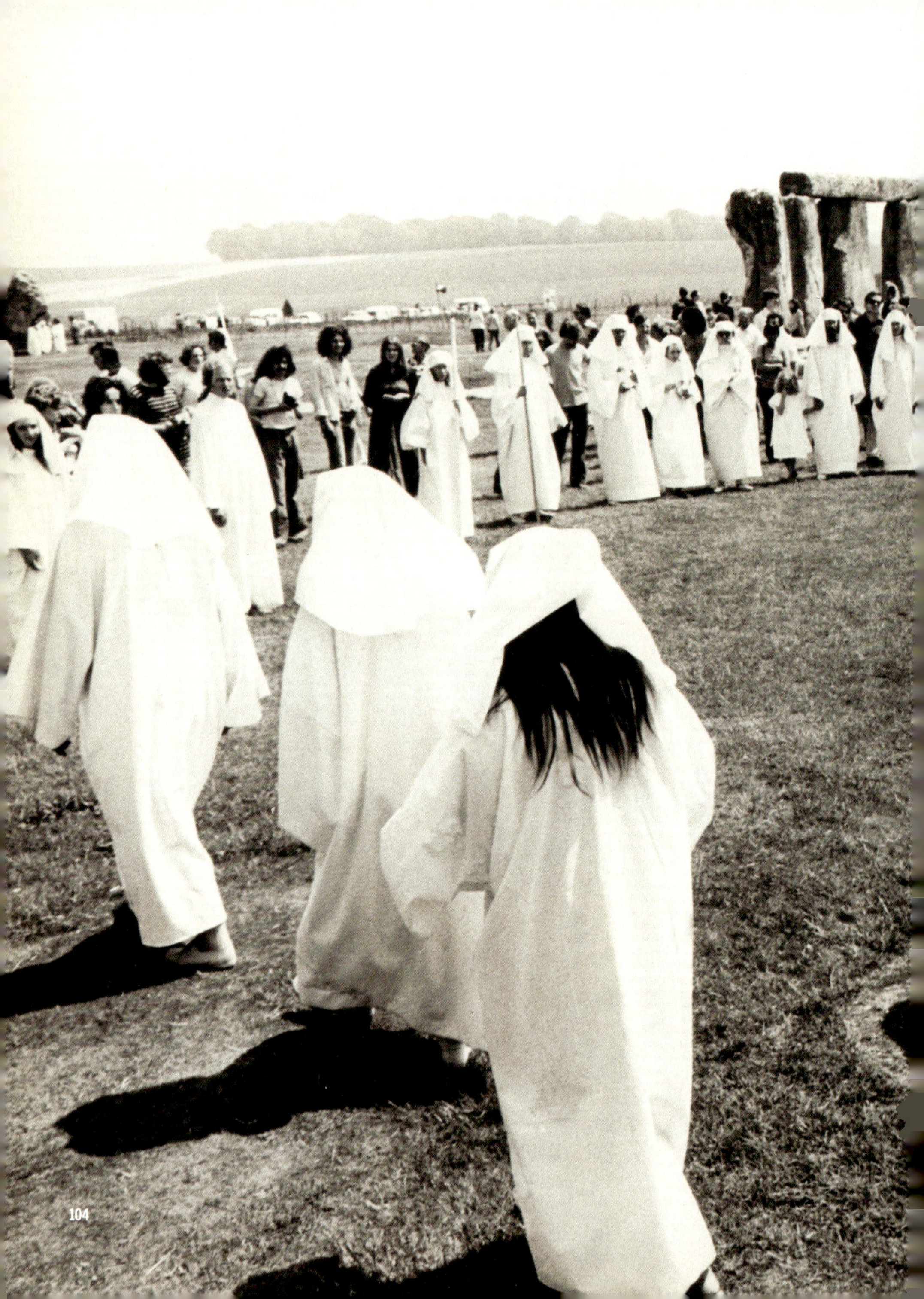

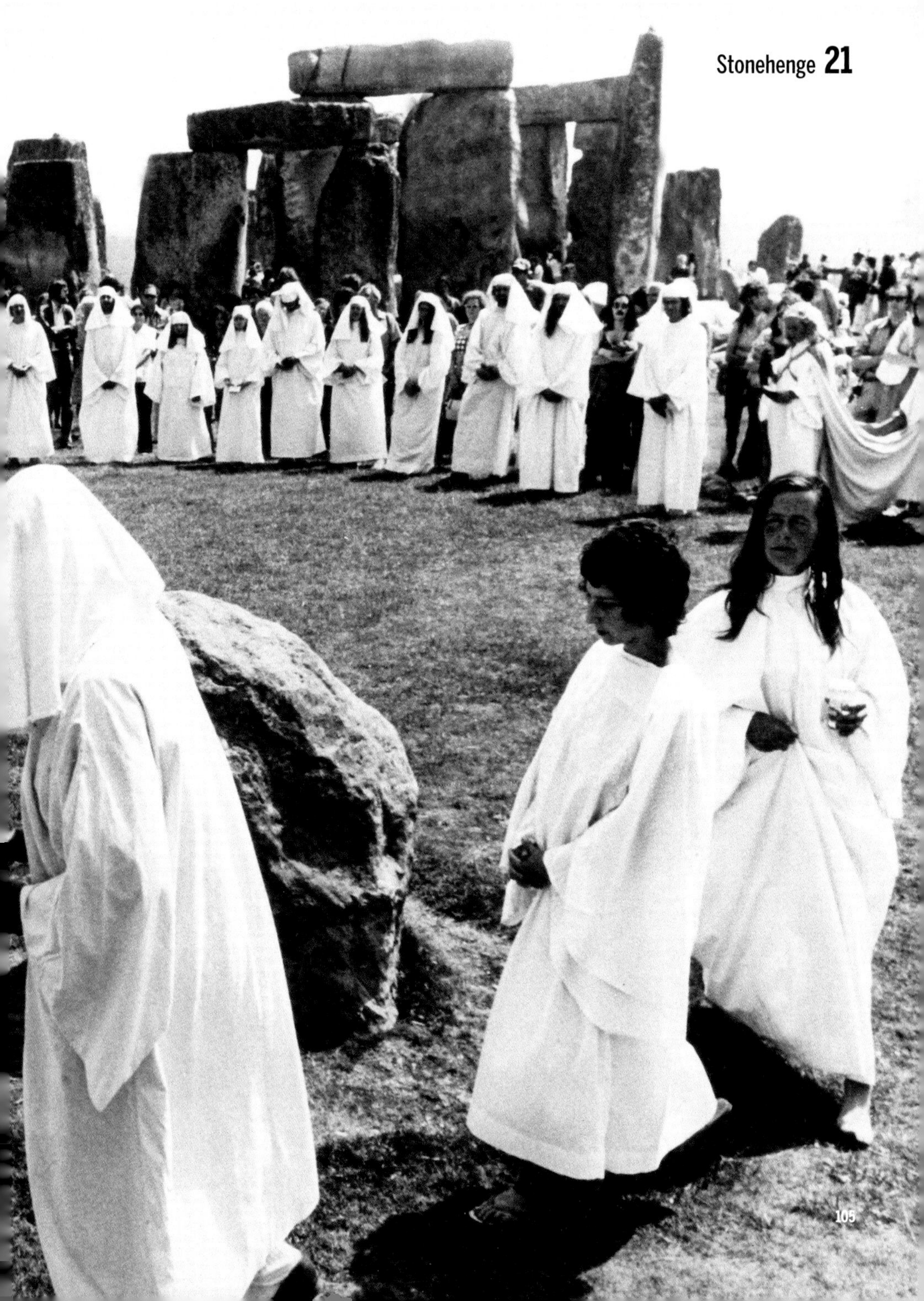

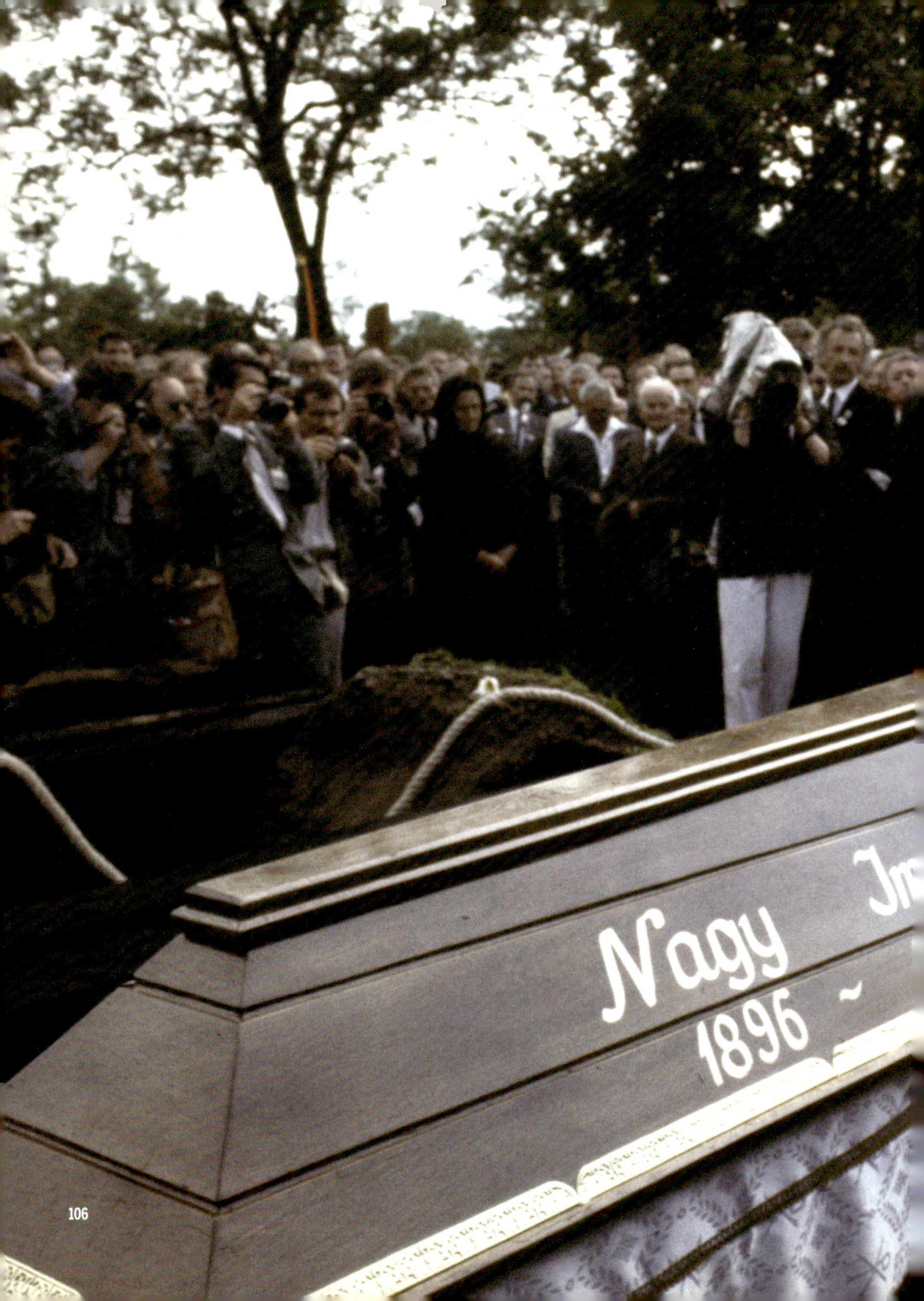
Nagy
1896 –

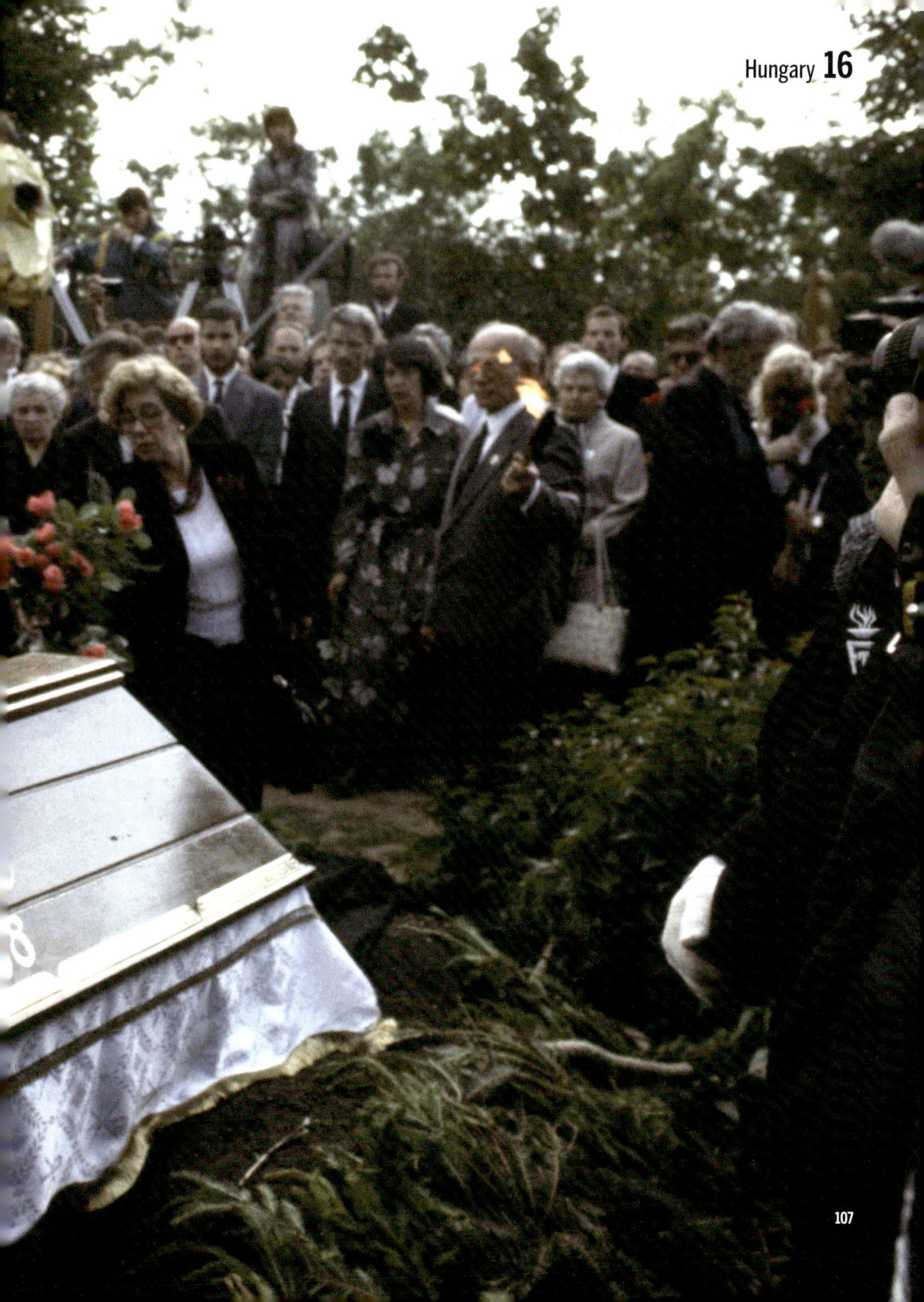

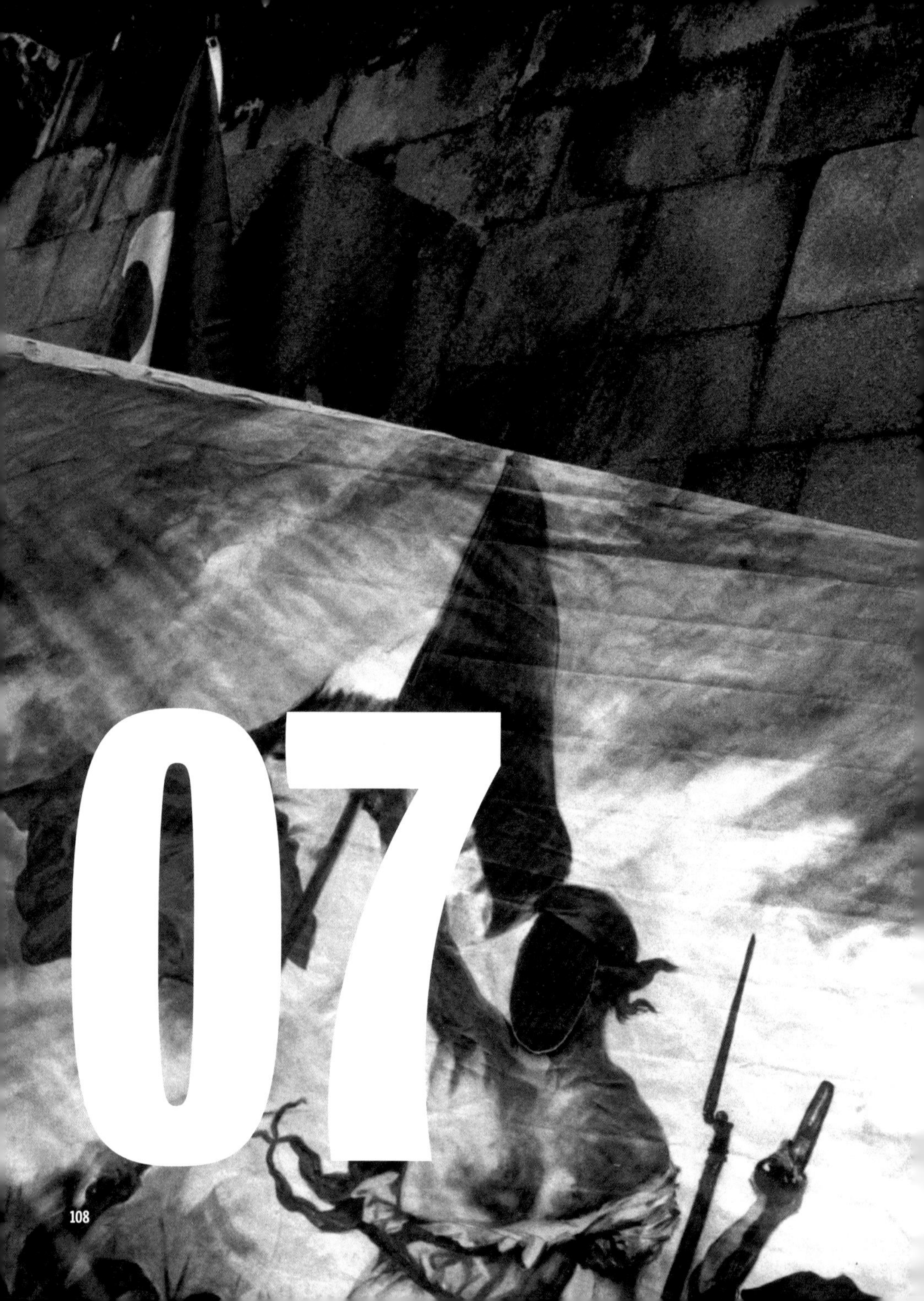

07

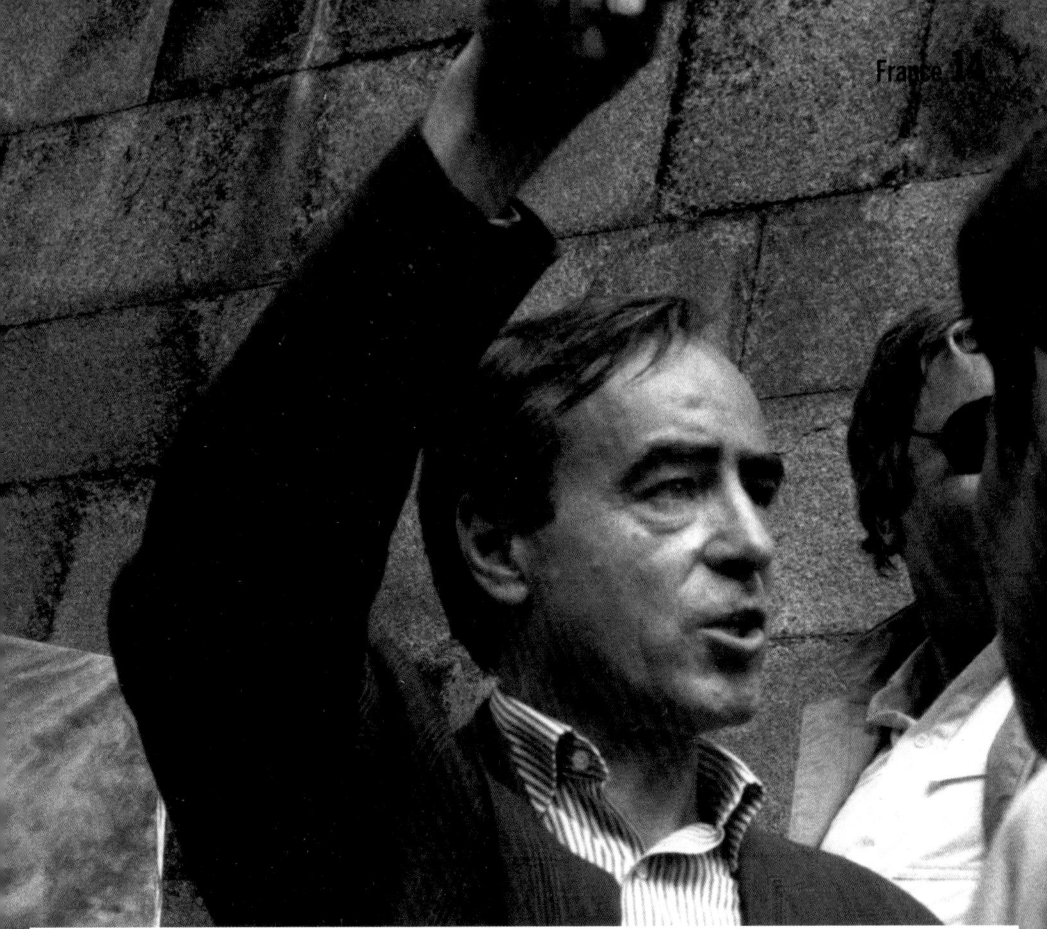

07

United States: release of "Lethal Weapon 2" by Richard Donner with Mel Gibson and Danny Glover.

11

Great Britain: actor Laurence Olivier dies in Steyning, aged 82.

14

France: celebrations for the bicentenary of the Revolution.

United States: release of "When Harry met Sally..." by Rob Reiner with Billy Crystal and Meg Ryan.

15

Italy: a floating platform in Venice's Canal Grande, it is Pink Floyd's stage. The concert is broadcasted worldwide for the first time seen by approximately 100 million spectators.

20

Myanmar: opposition leader Aung San Suu Kyi is kept under house arrest.

23

Great Britain: Daniel Radcliffe aka Harry Potter in J.K. Rowling's saga movie version is born in London.

Greg LeMond wins the Tour de France. He crossed the finishing line only 8 seconds before the French Laurent Fignon. The following month he wins the Road Cycling World Championship and is elected sportsman of the year by "Sports Illustrated", first time for a cyclist. He has been the first American to win the Tour in 1986.

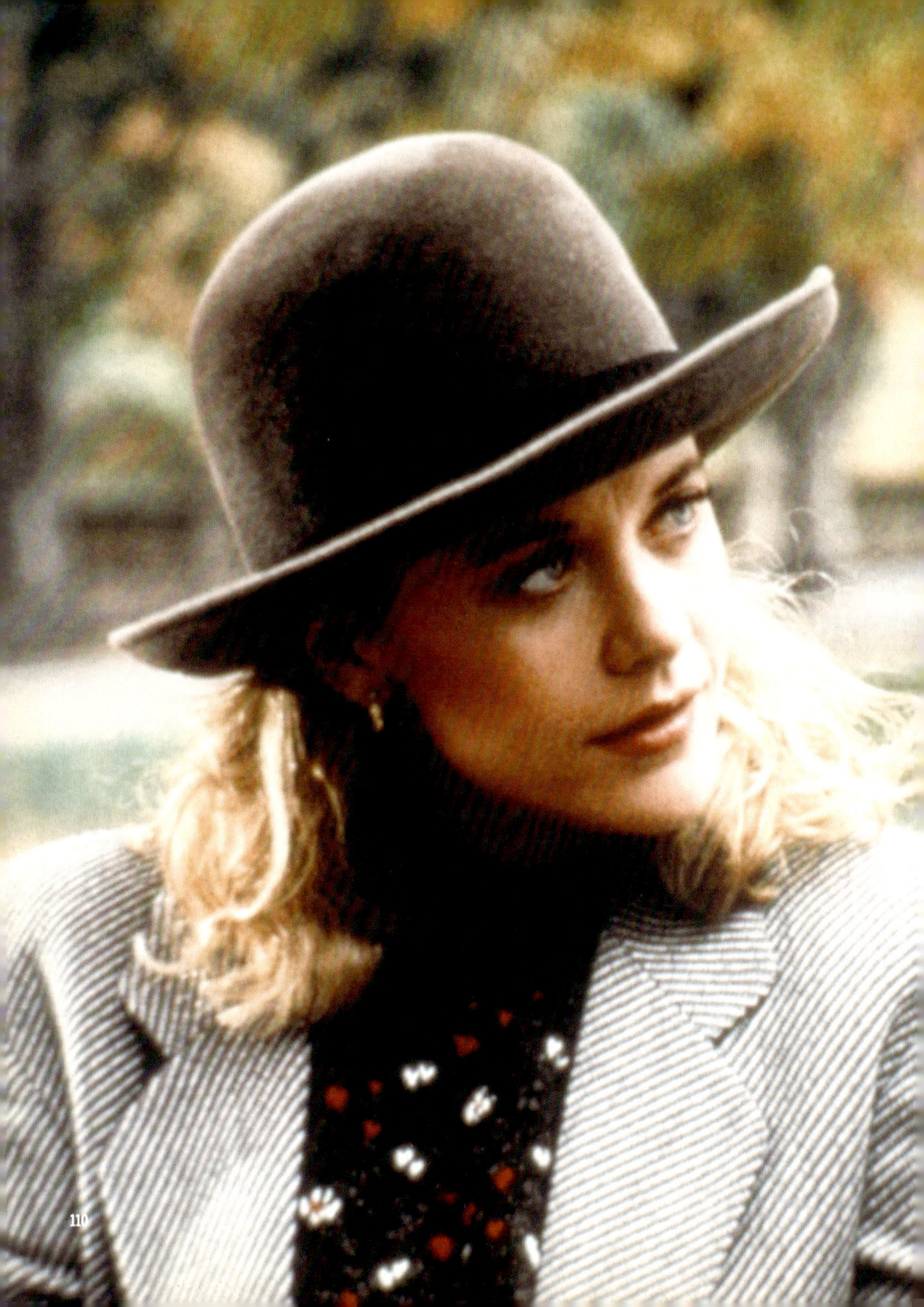

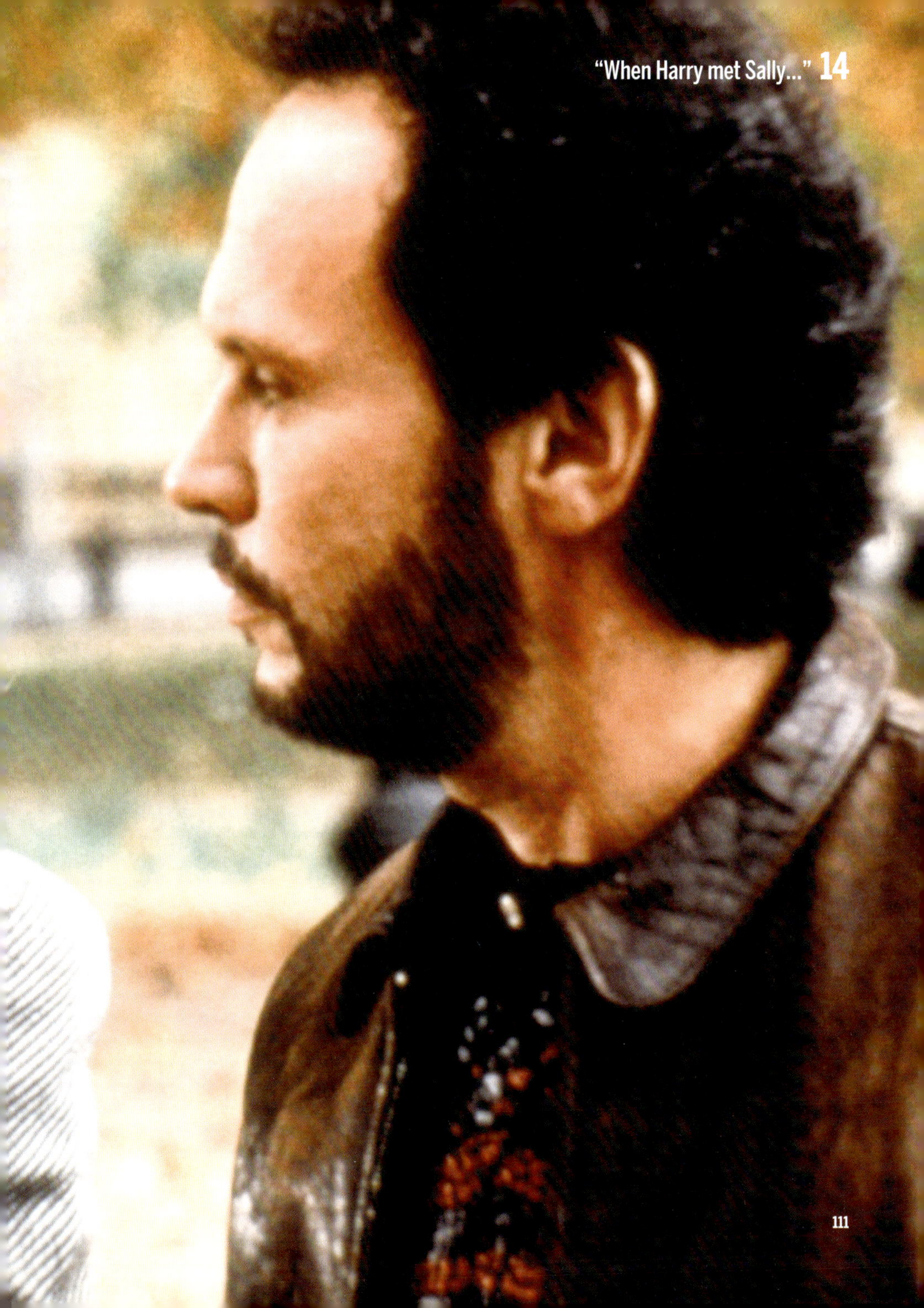

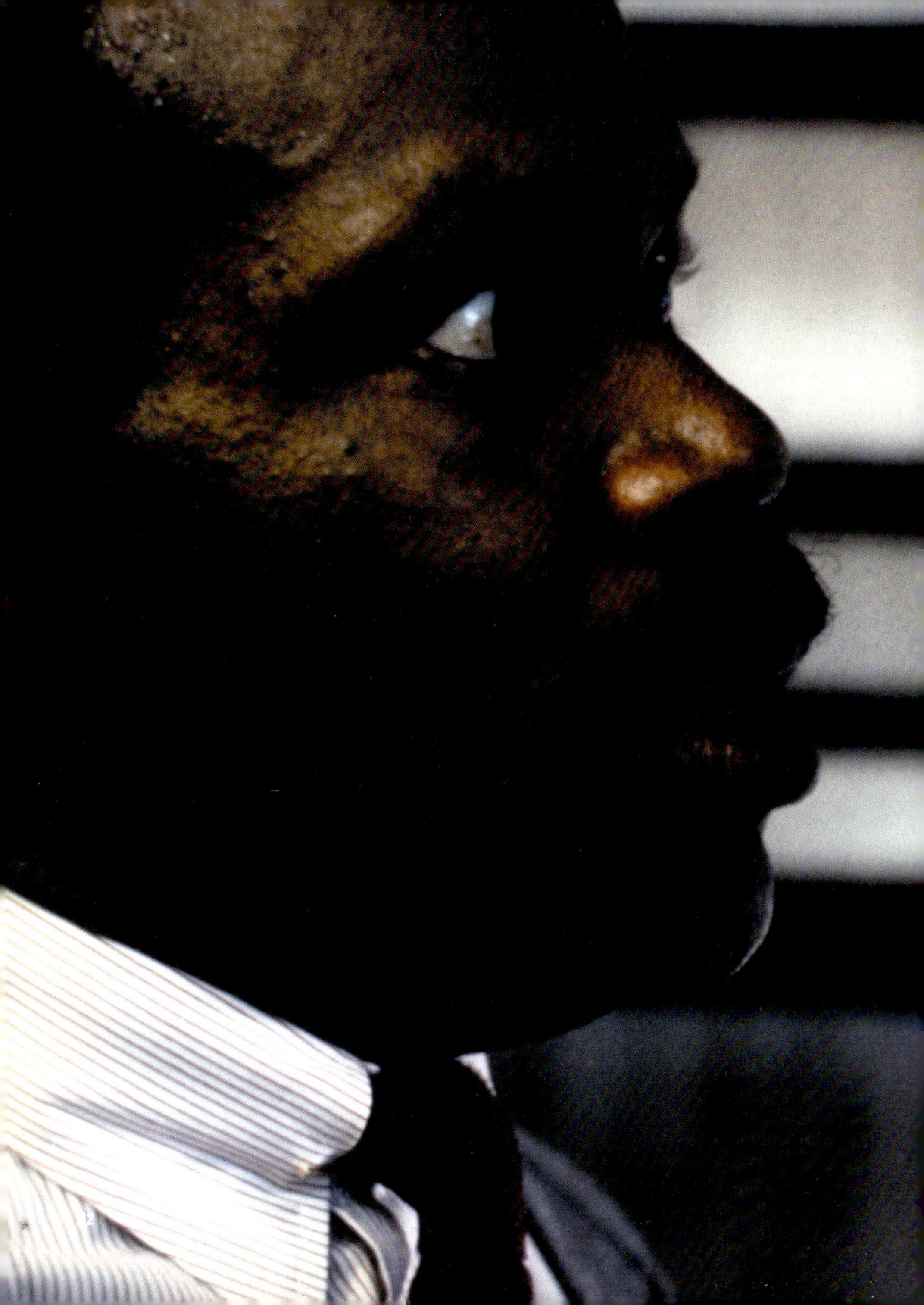

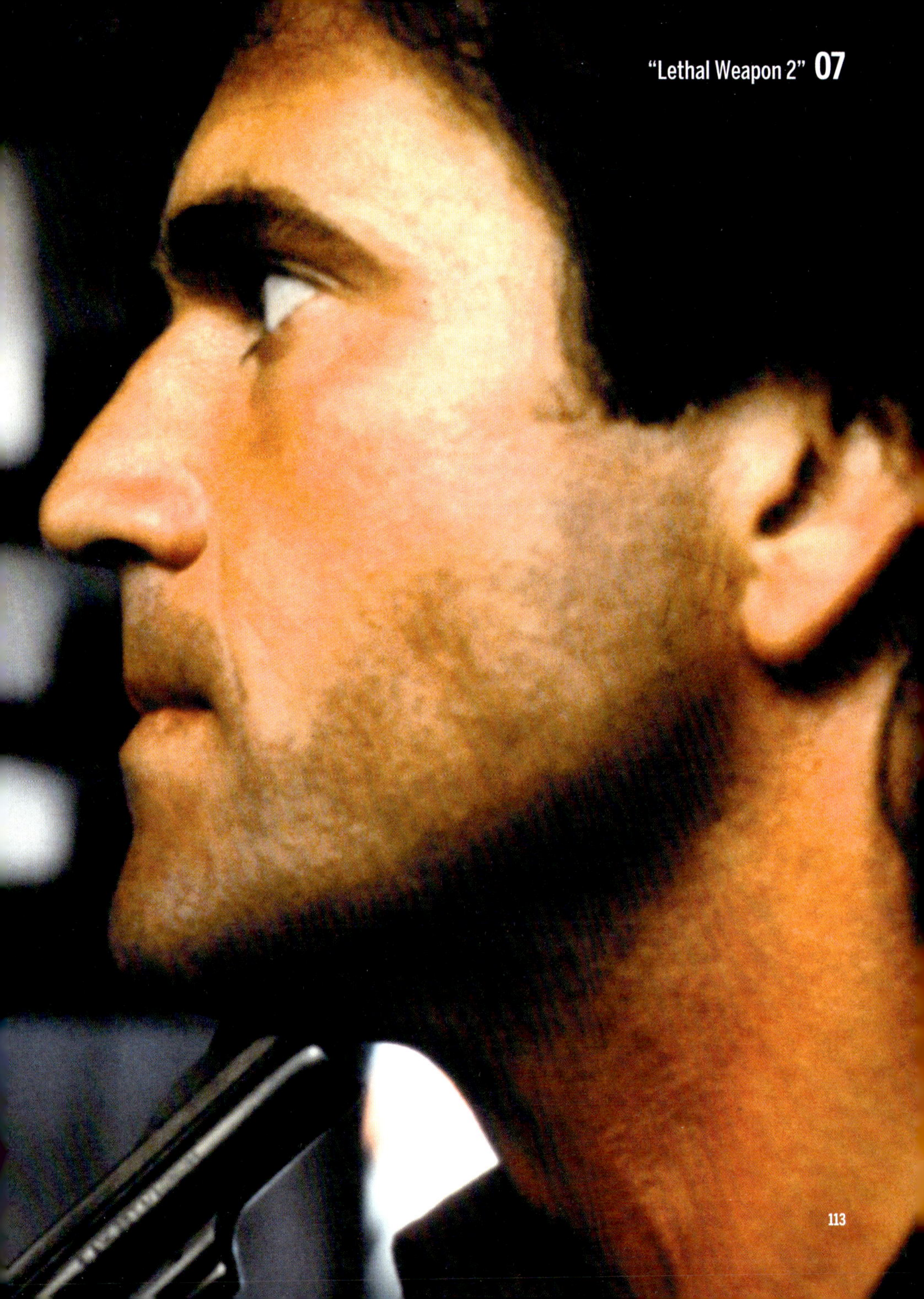

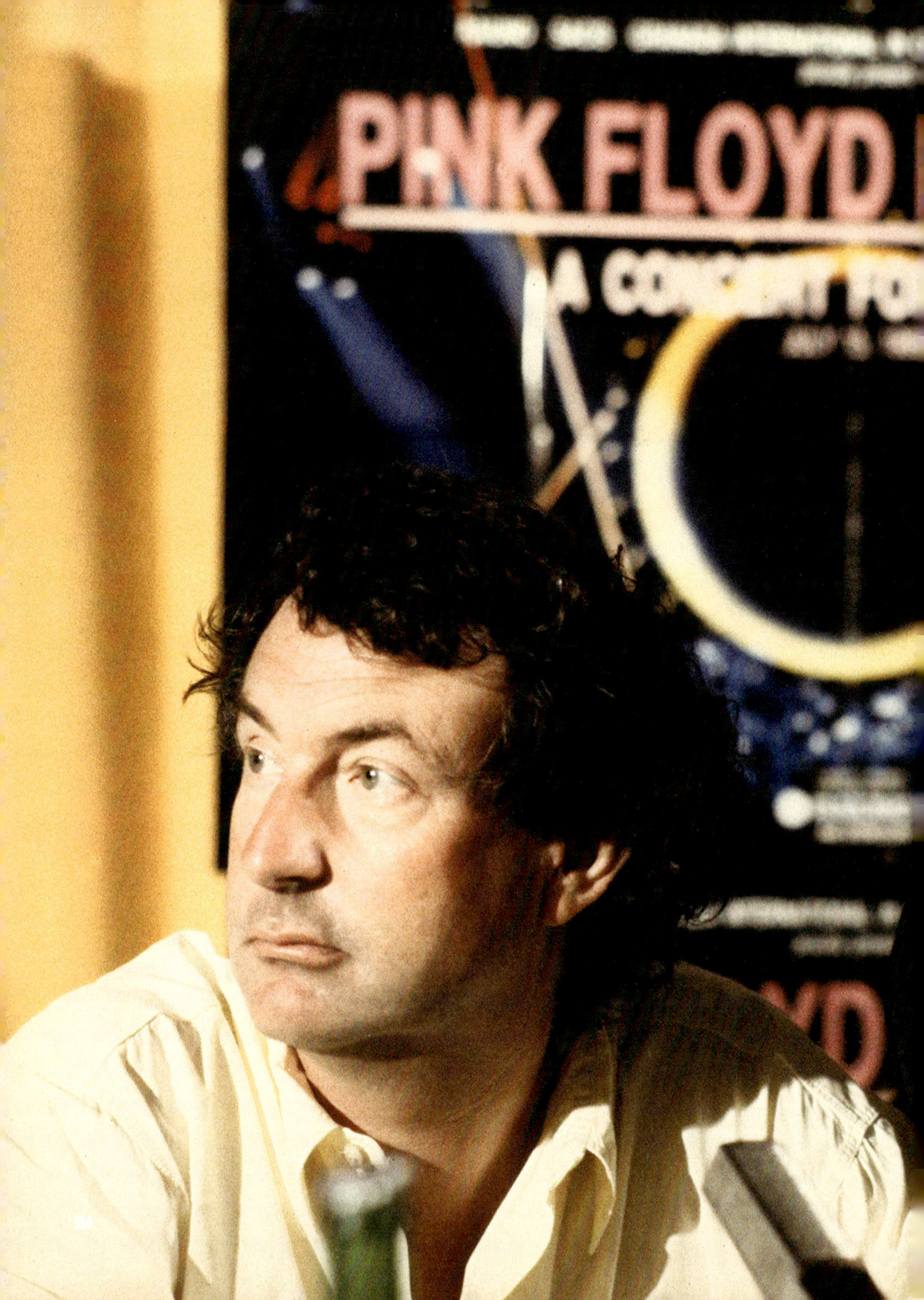
PINK FLOYD
A CONCERT

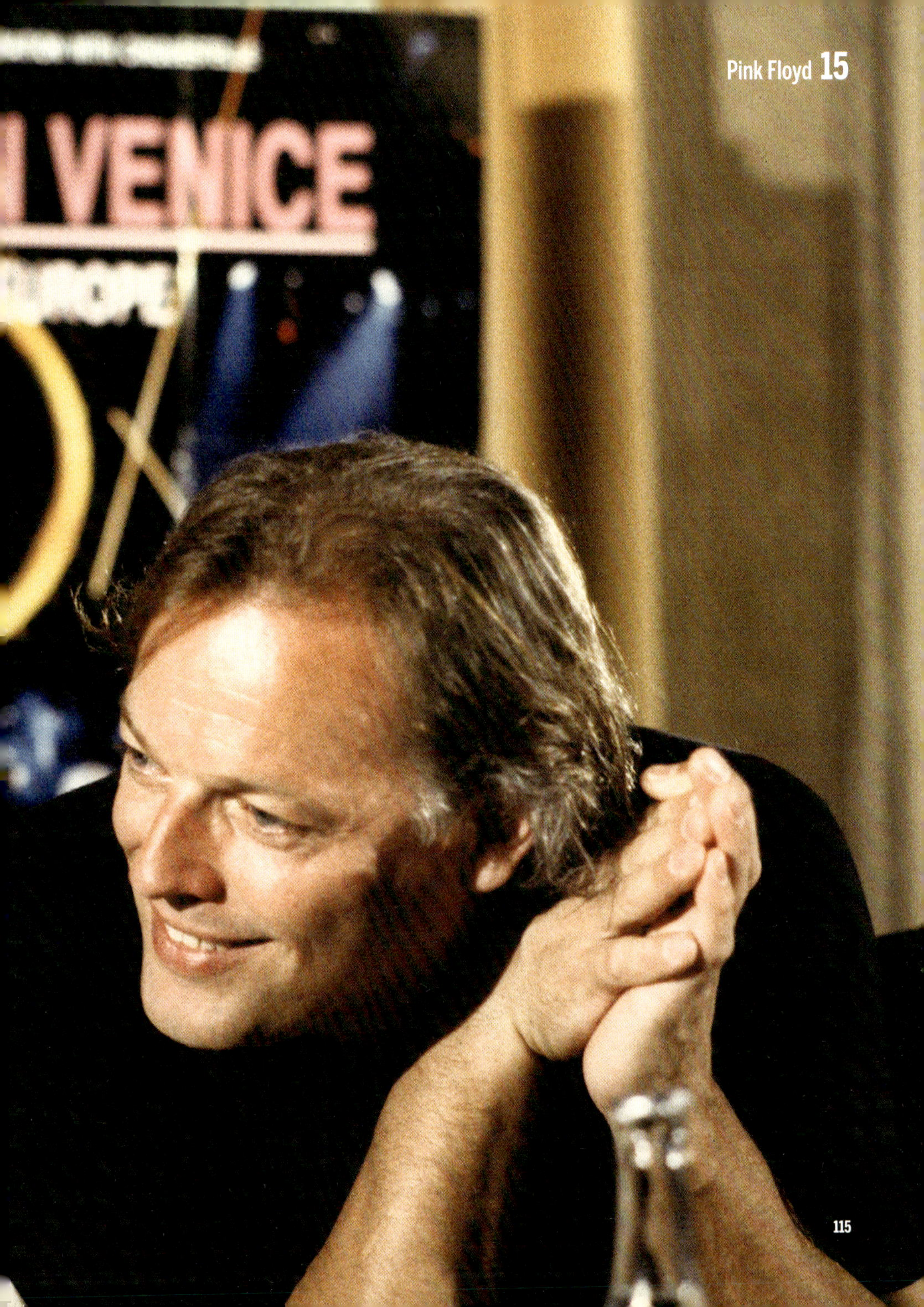

VENICE

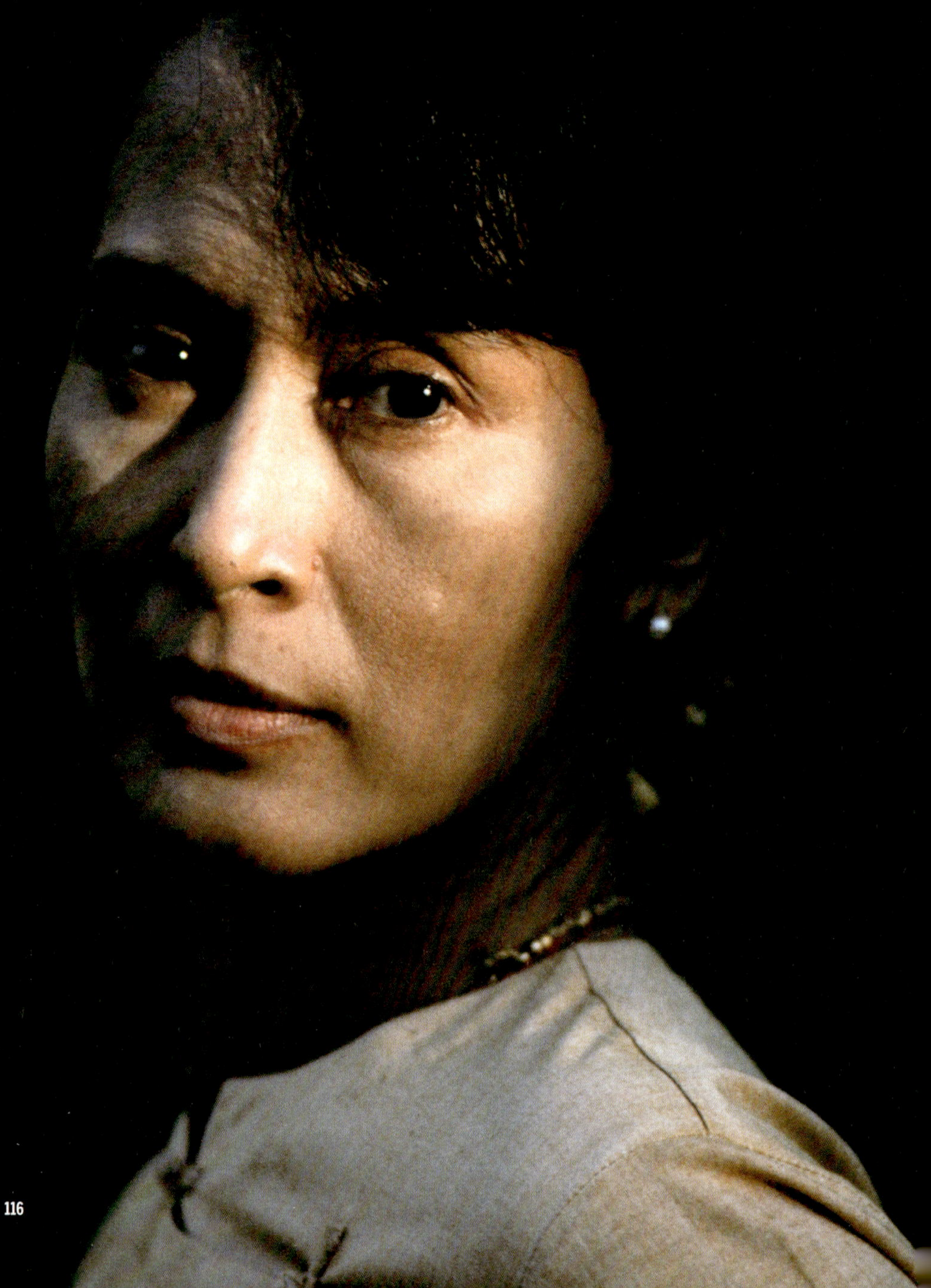

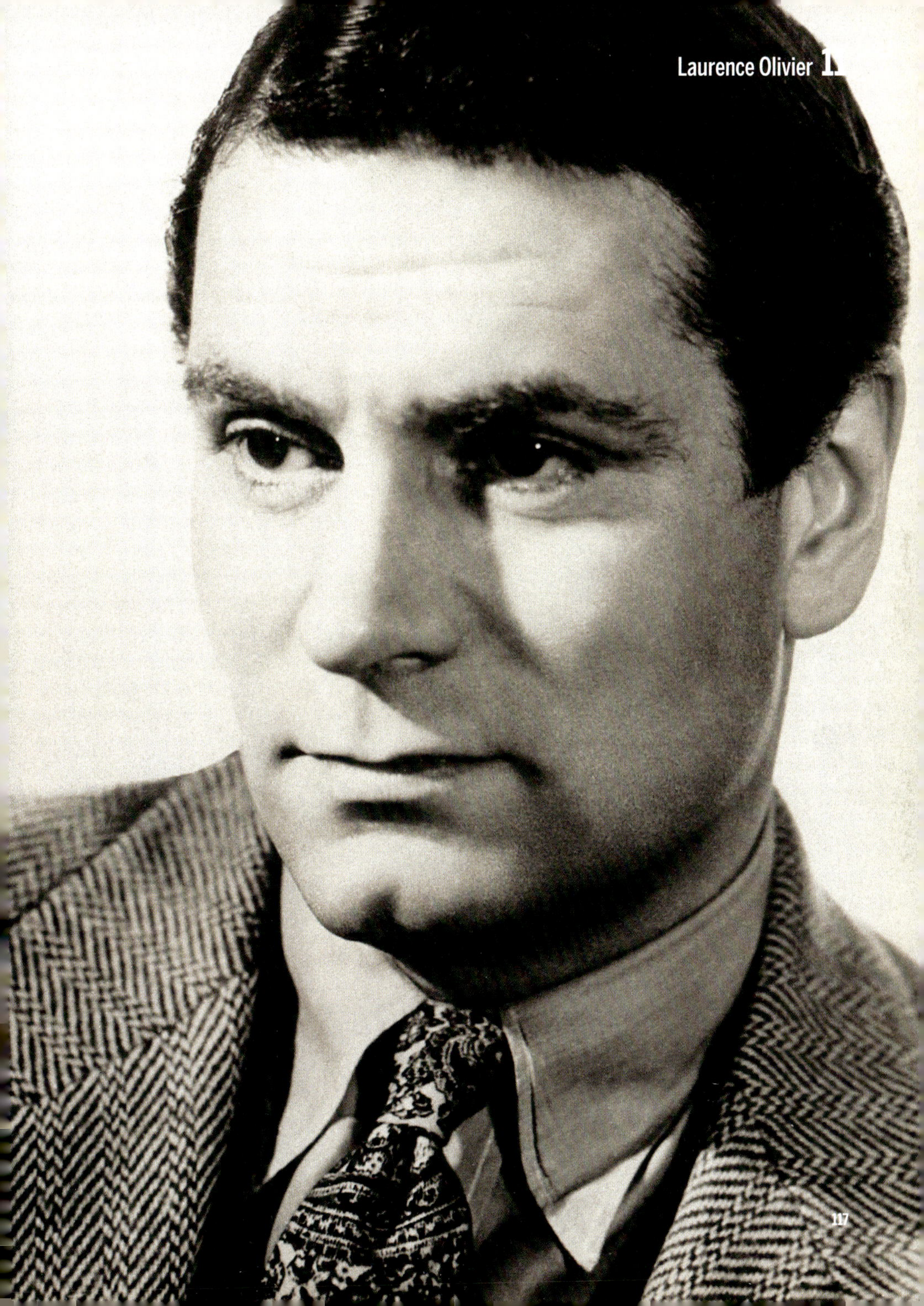

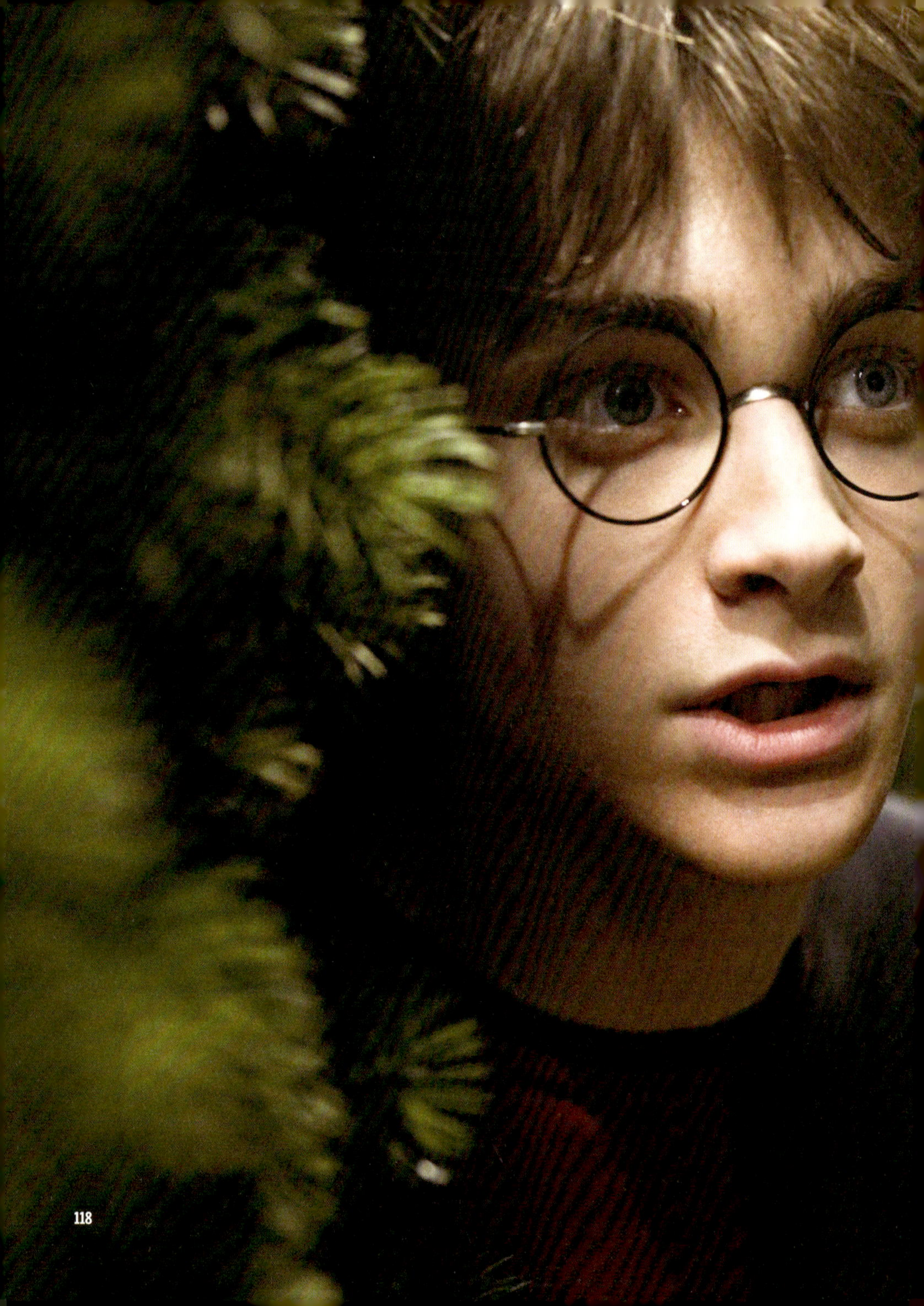

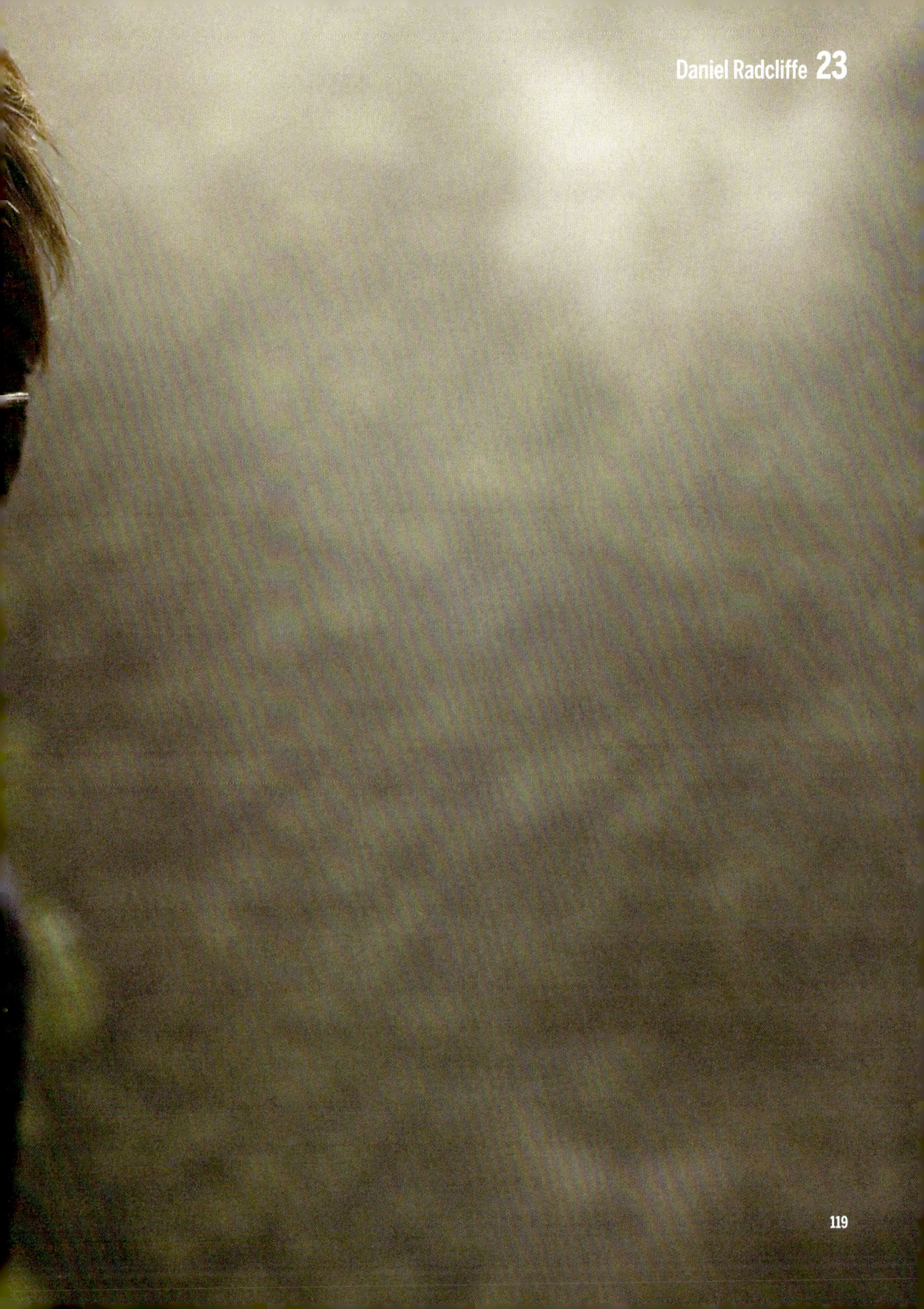

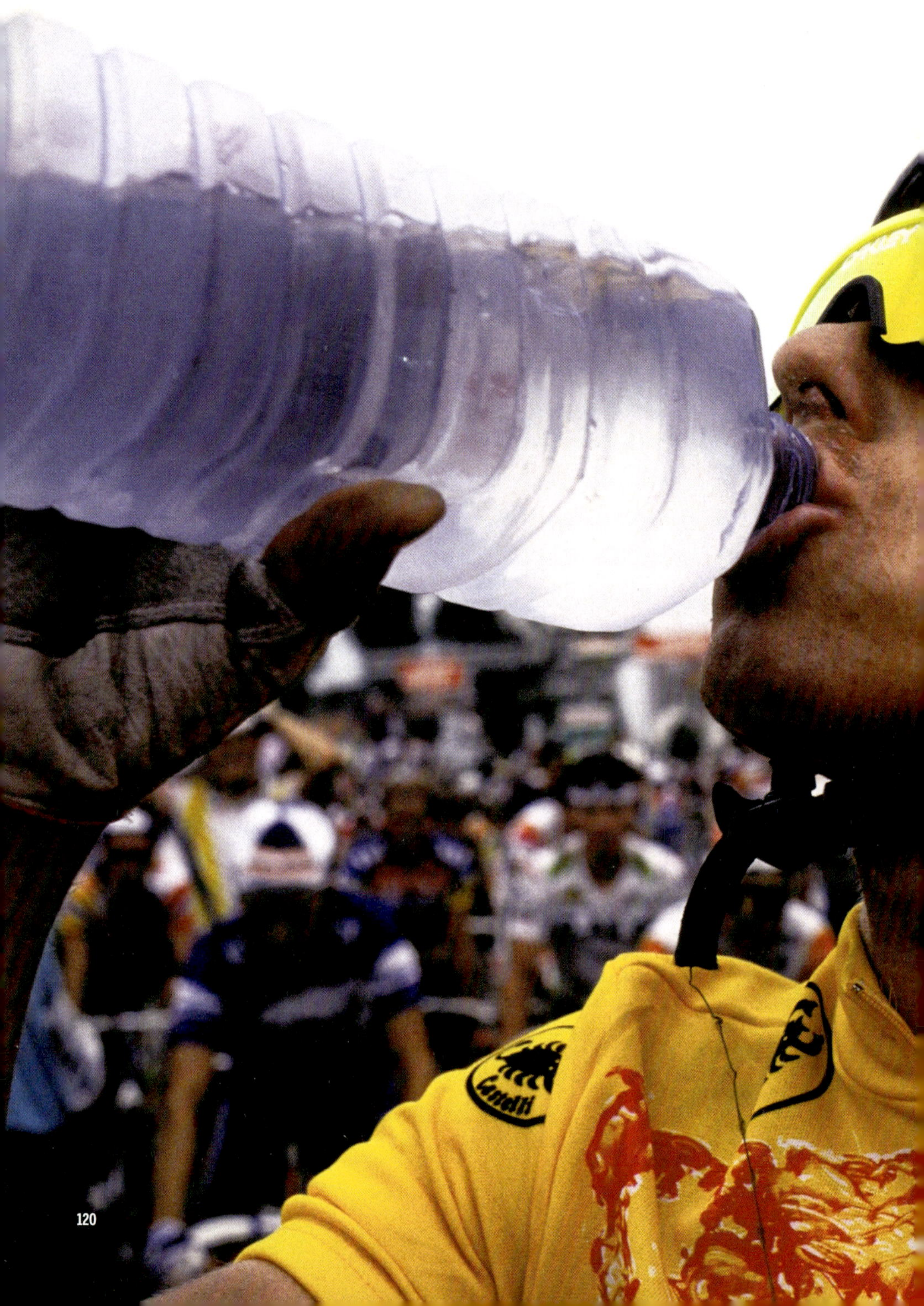

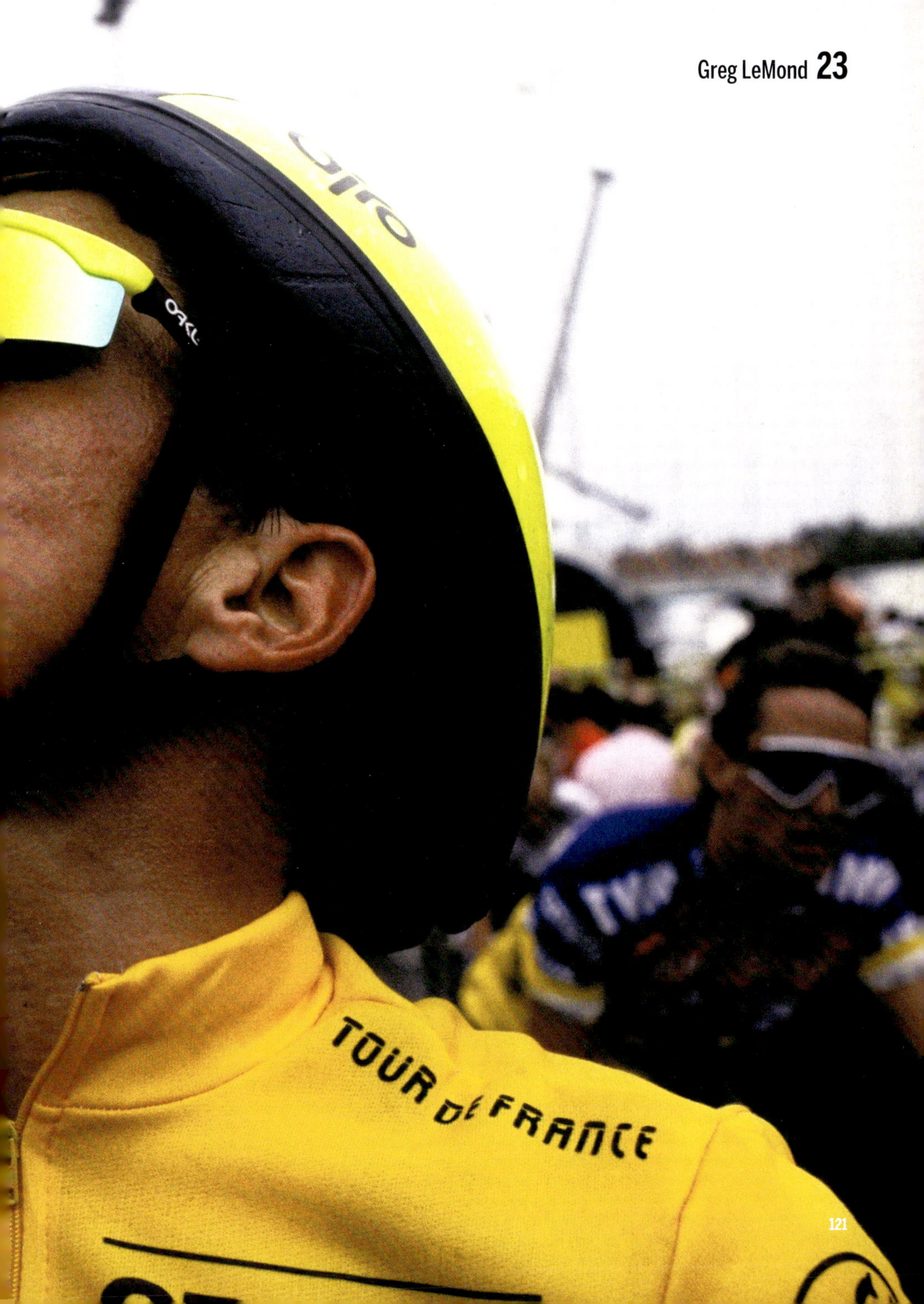
TOUR DE FRANCE

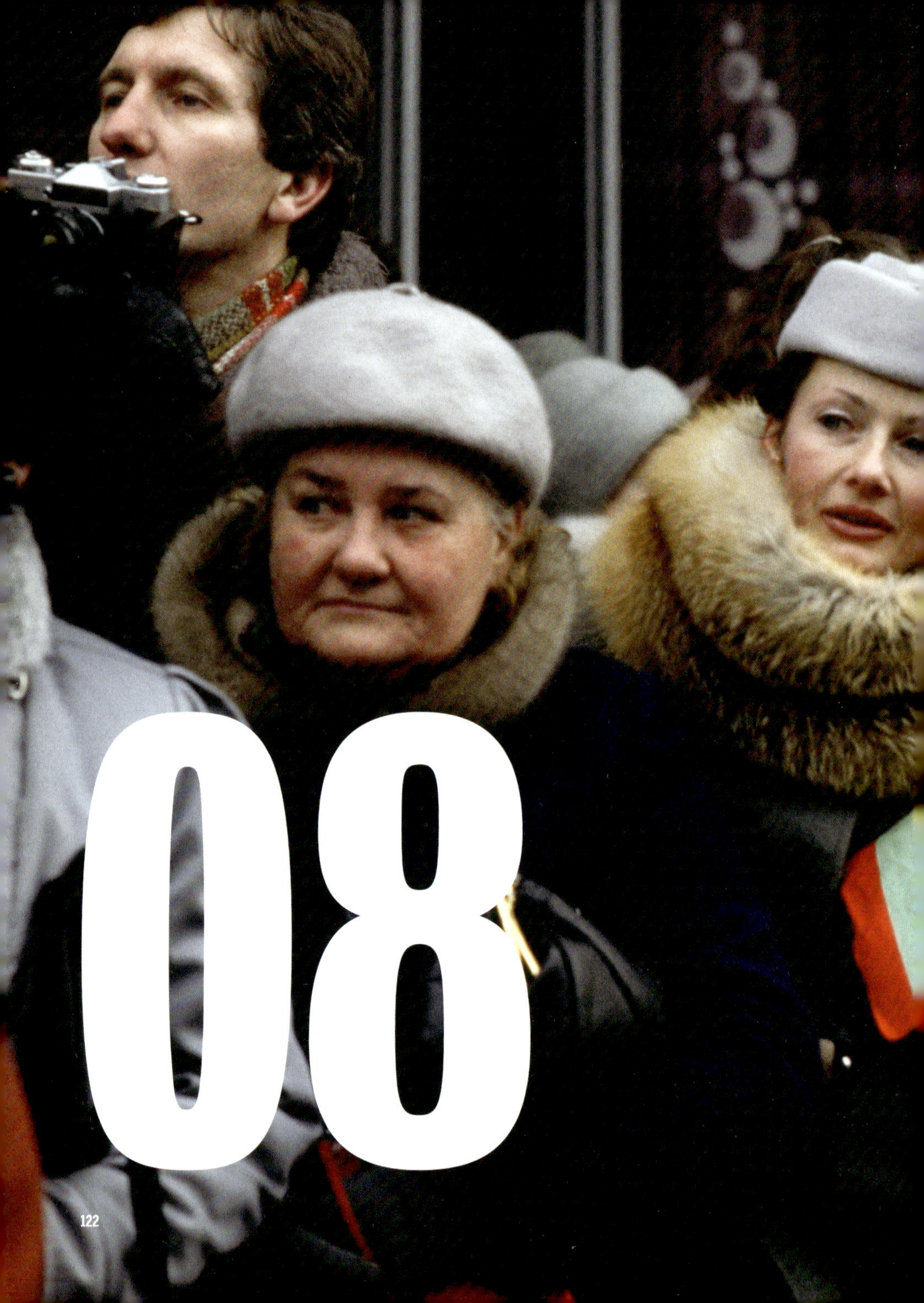

08

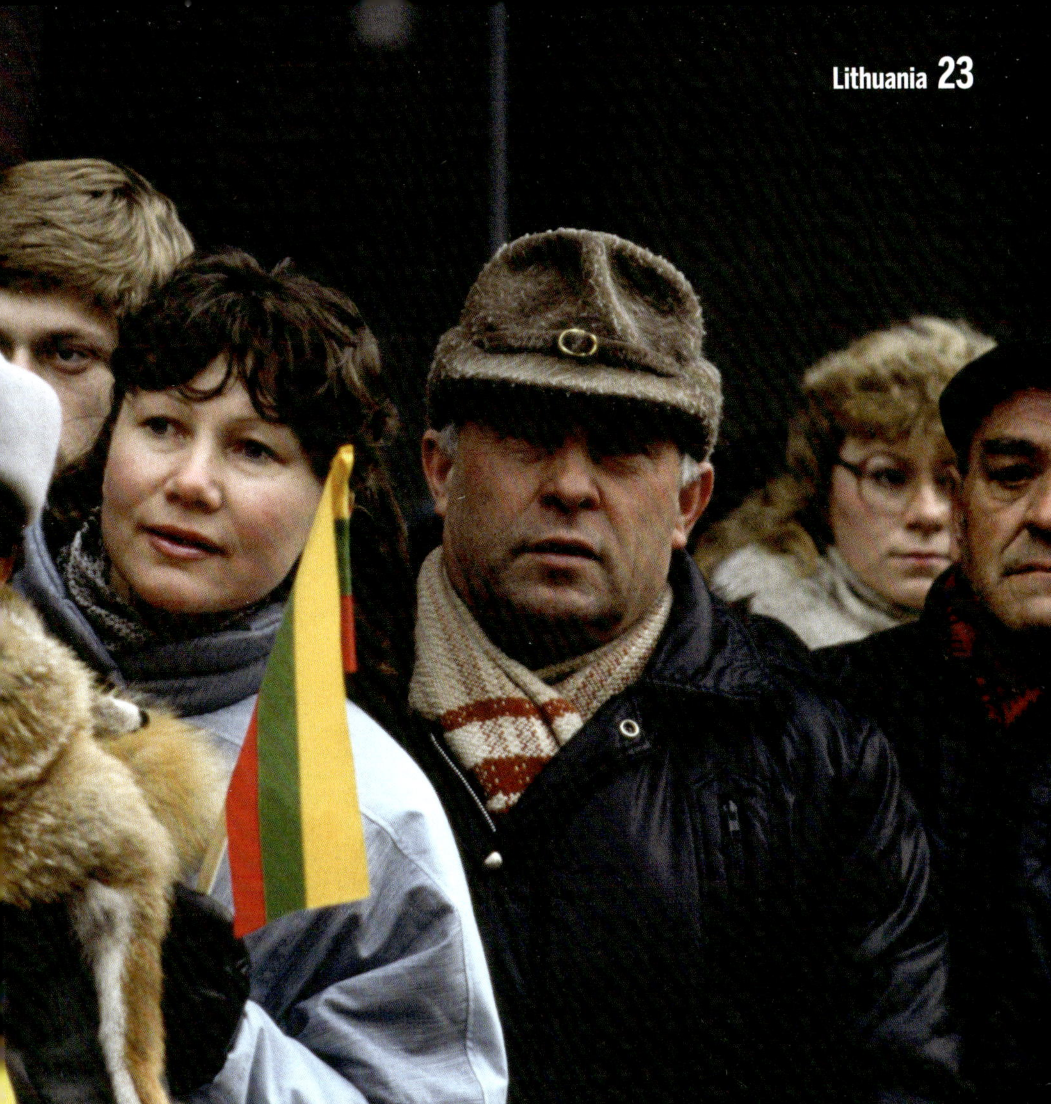

19

Poland: President Wojciech Jaruzelski appoints Tadeusz Mazowiecki, of Solidarność, as Prime Minister, the first non-communist in 42 years.

23

Baltic States: 2 million people in Estonia, Latvia and Lithuania join hands and form a human chain 600 km long, subsequently called the "Baltic Way". They protest against Soviet occupation and ask for freedom and independence.

25

Solar System: space probe Voyager II reaches Neptune.

29

Great Britain: release of "Personal Jesus" by Depeche Mode.

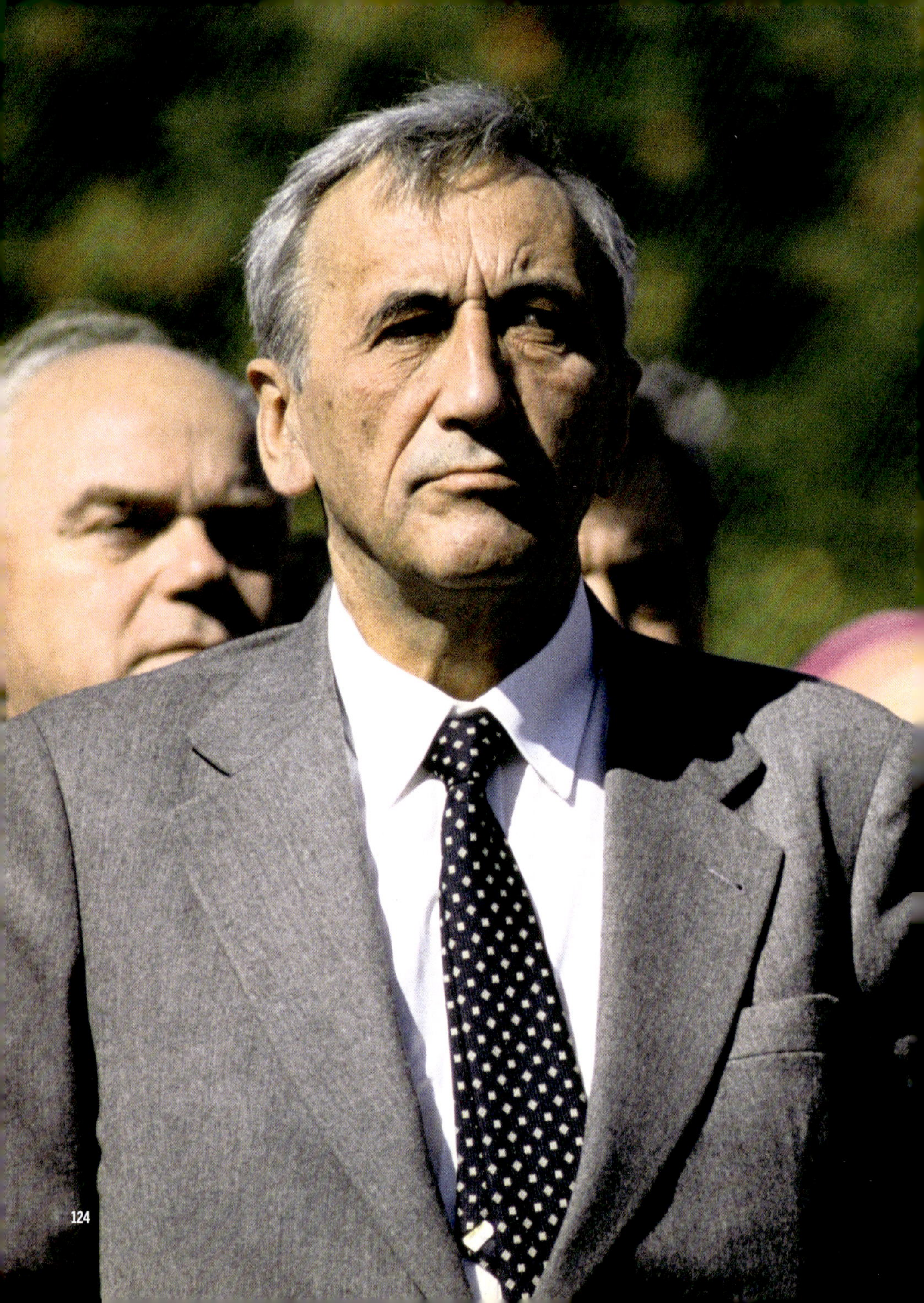

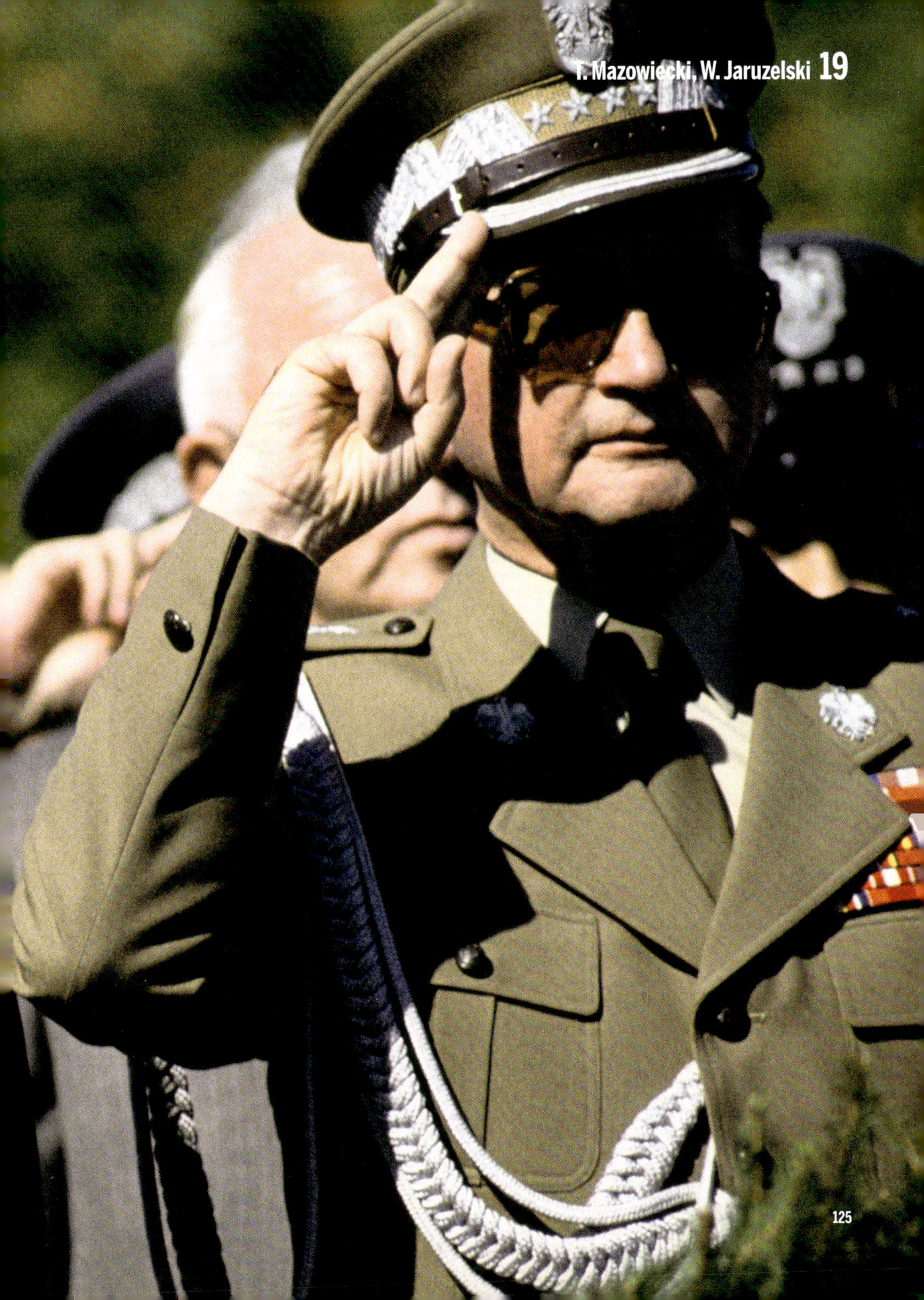

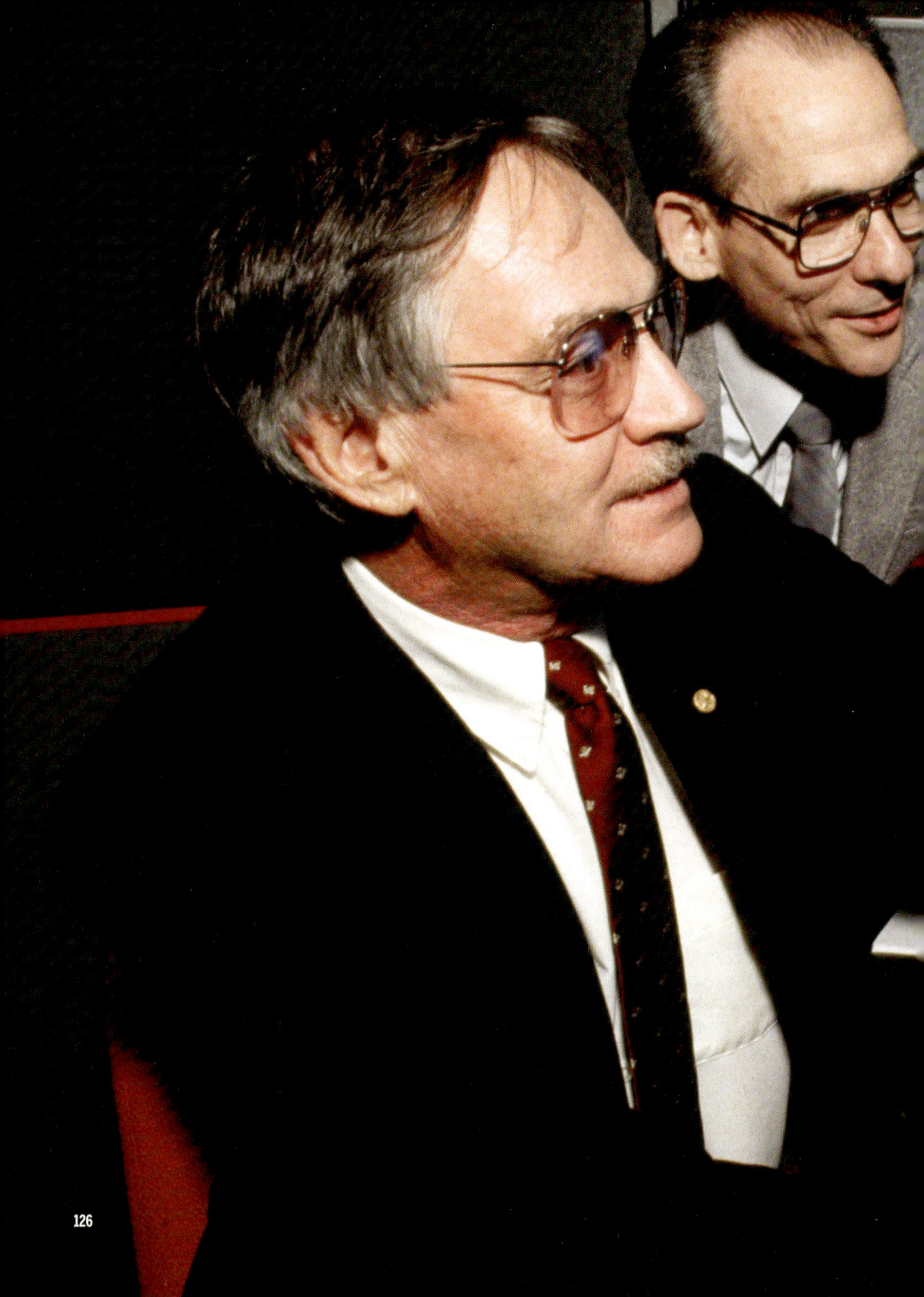

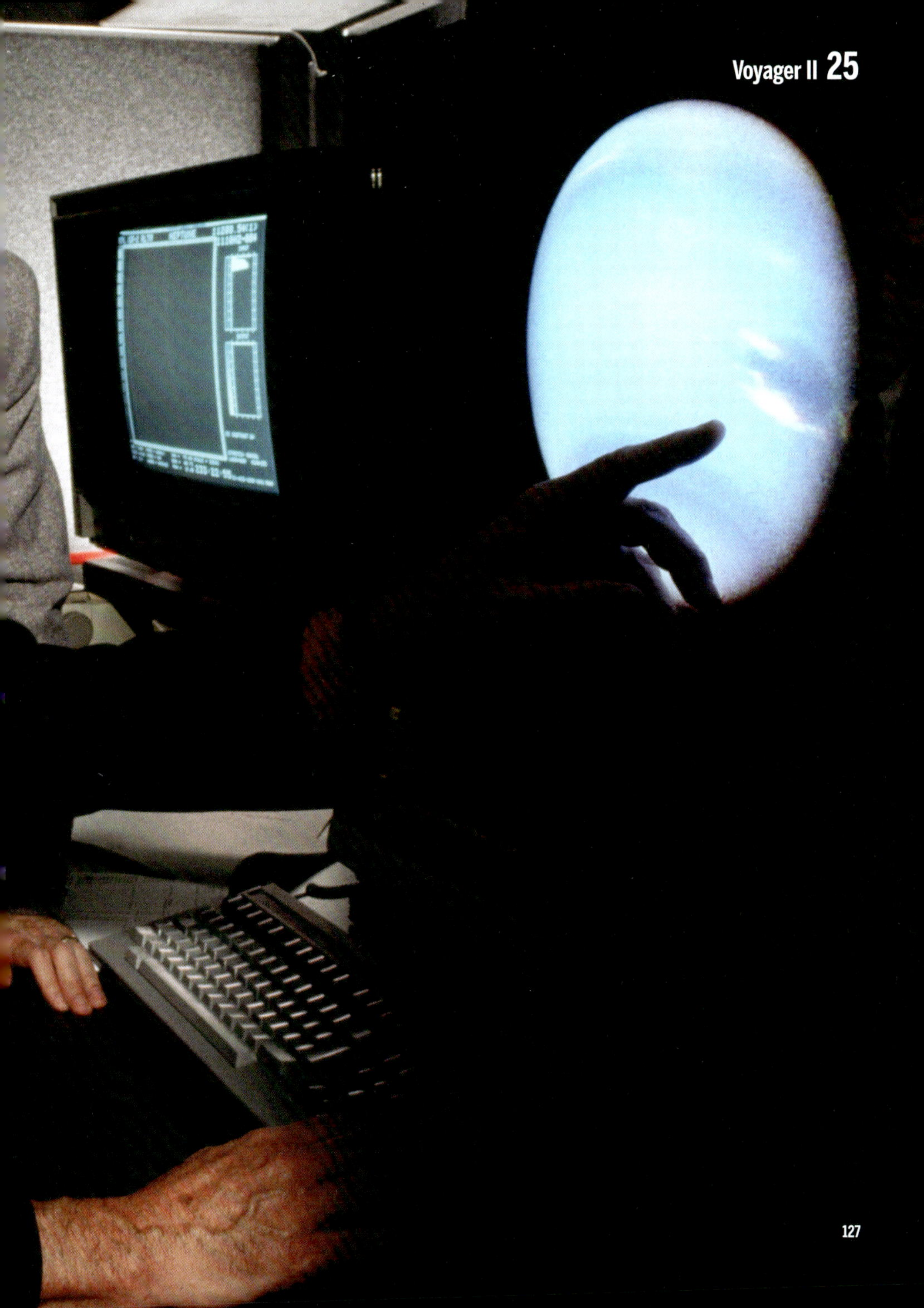

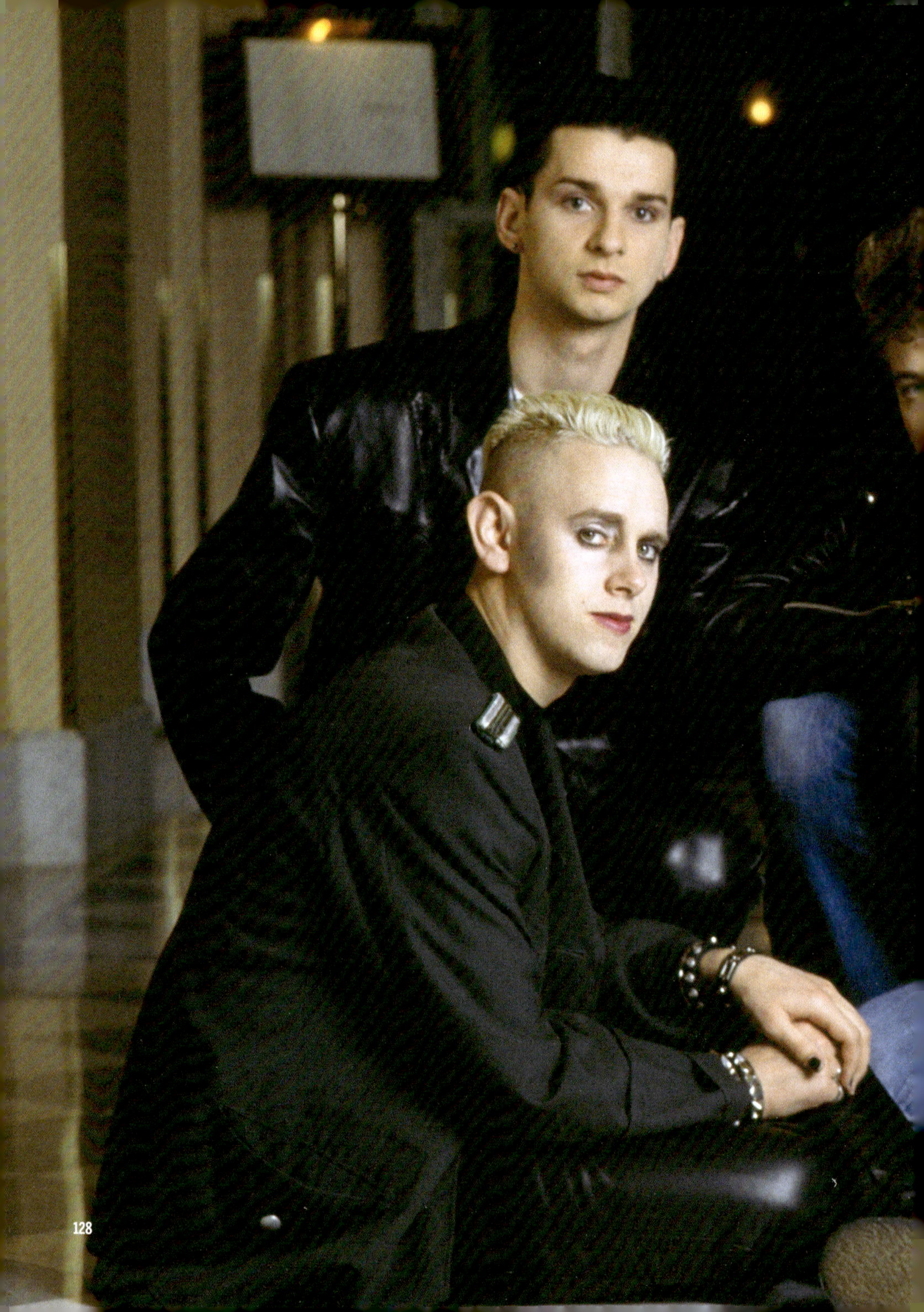

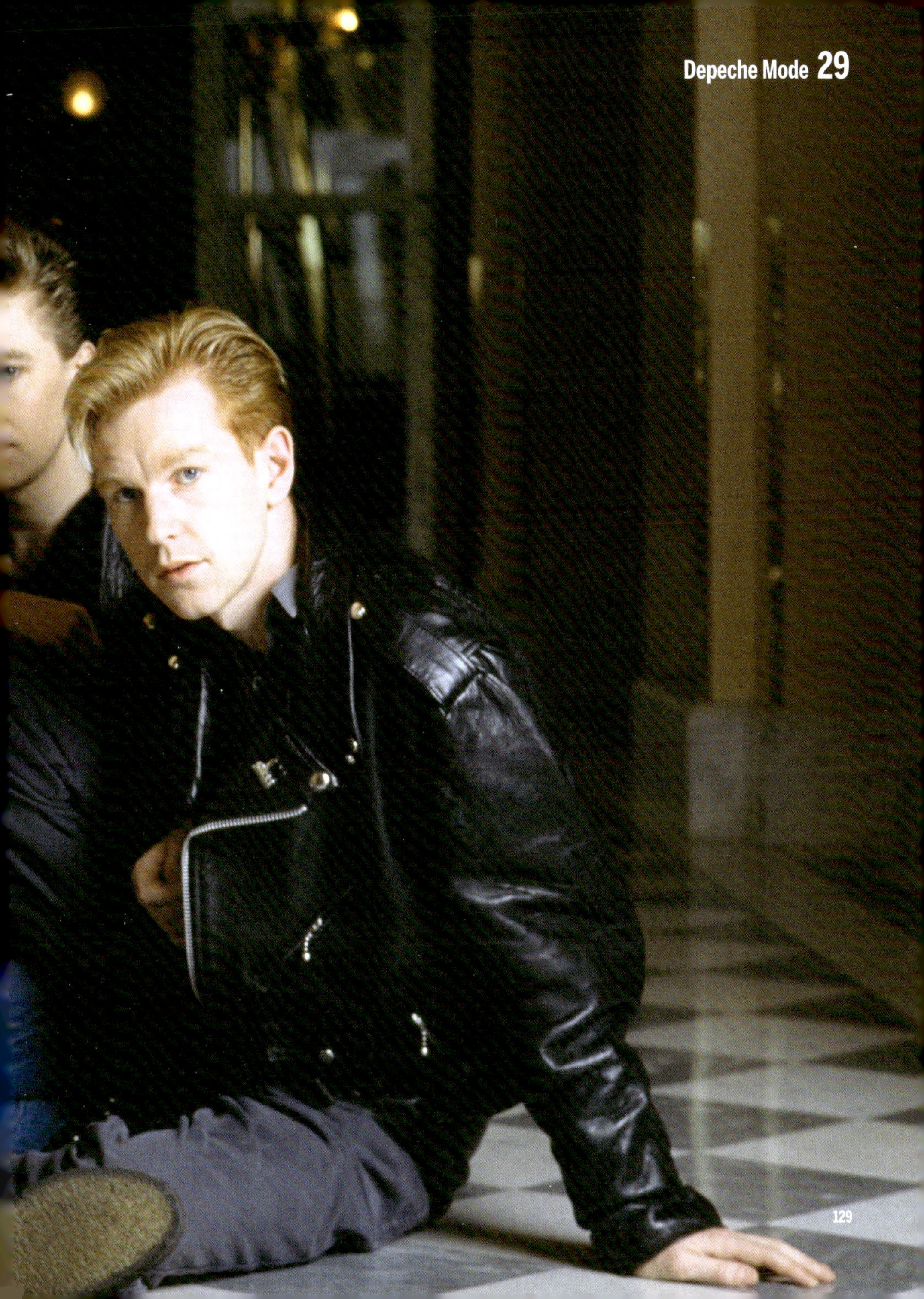

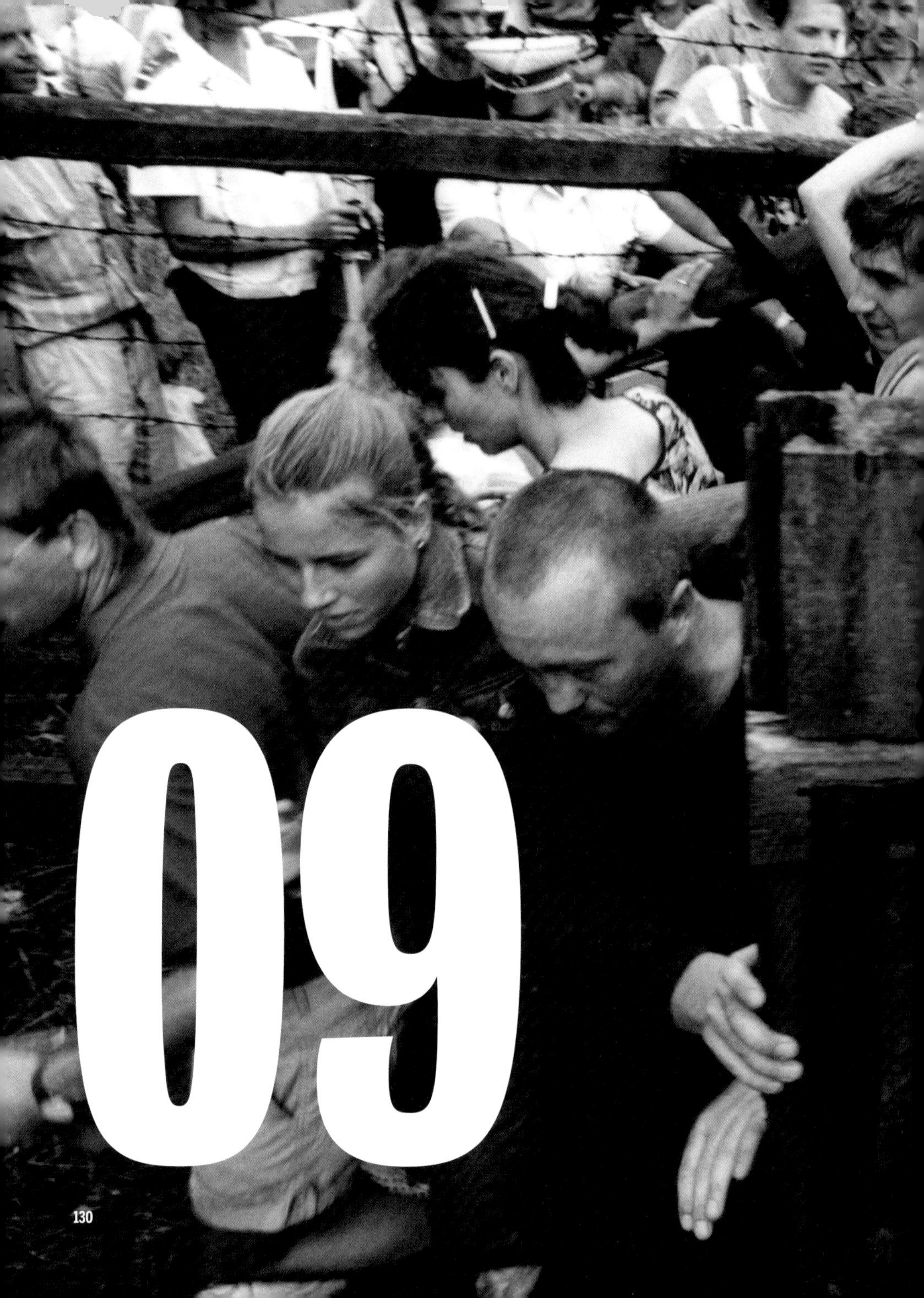
09

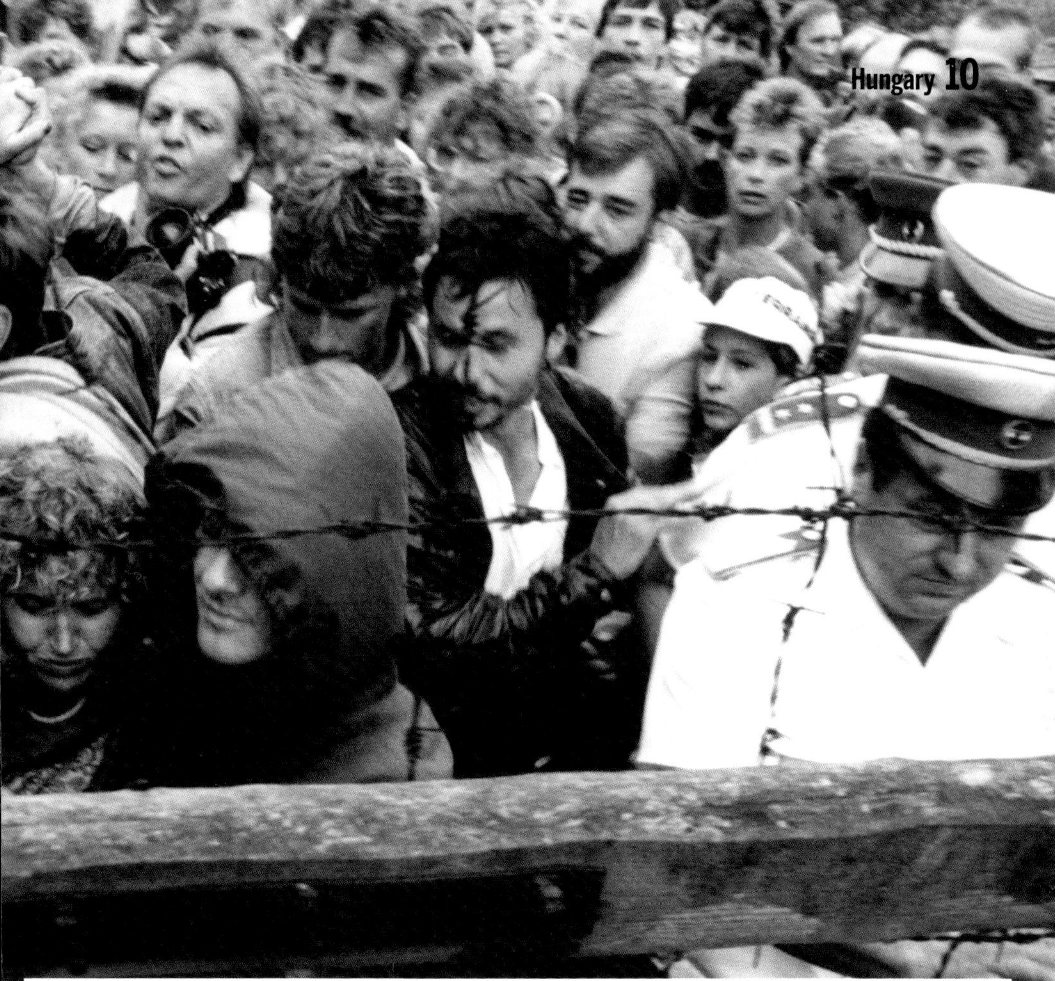

01

Germany: Bill and Tom Kaulitz singer and guitarist of music band Tokio Hotel, are born in Liepzig.

02

United States: release of "The best" by Tina Turner.

04

Switzerland: Georges Simenon, one of the most fecund writers of the 20th century and "father" of inspector Maigret, dies in Lausanne, aged 86.

10

Hungary: the government opens the borders with Austria, thus creating the first passage in the Iron Curtain, through which many DDR refugees entered the country.

15

Italy: 46th edition of the Venice Film Festival. The Golden Lion goes to "A City of Sadness" by Hou Hsiao-Hsien, but the true protagonist of the Festival is Krzysztof Kieślowski with his "Decalogue".

20

South Africa: Frederik Willem de Klerk is the new President who opens the path to the abolishment of apartheid.

22

United States: the first episode of "Baywatch" is broadcast on NBC.

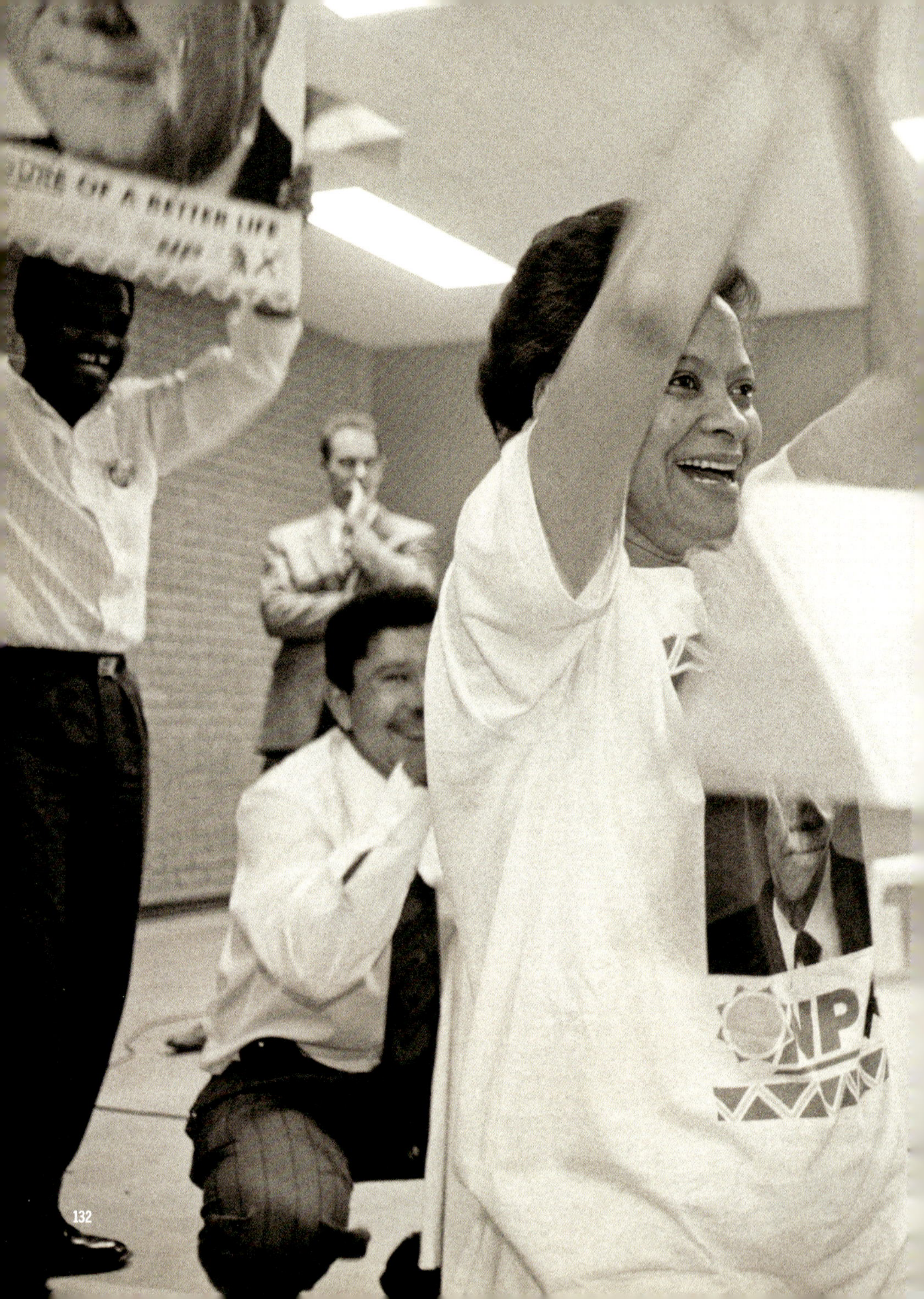

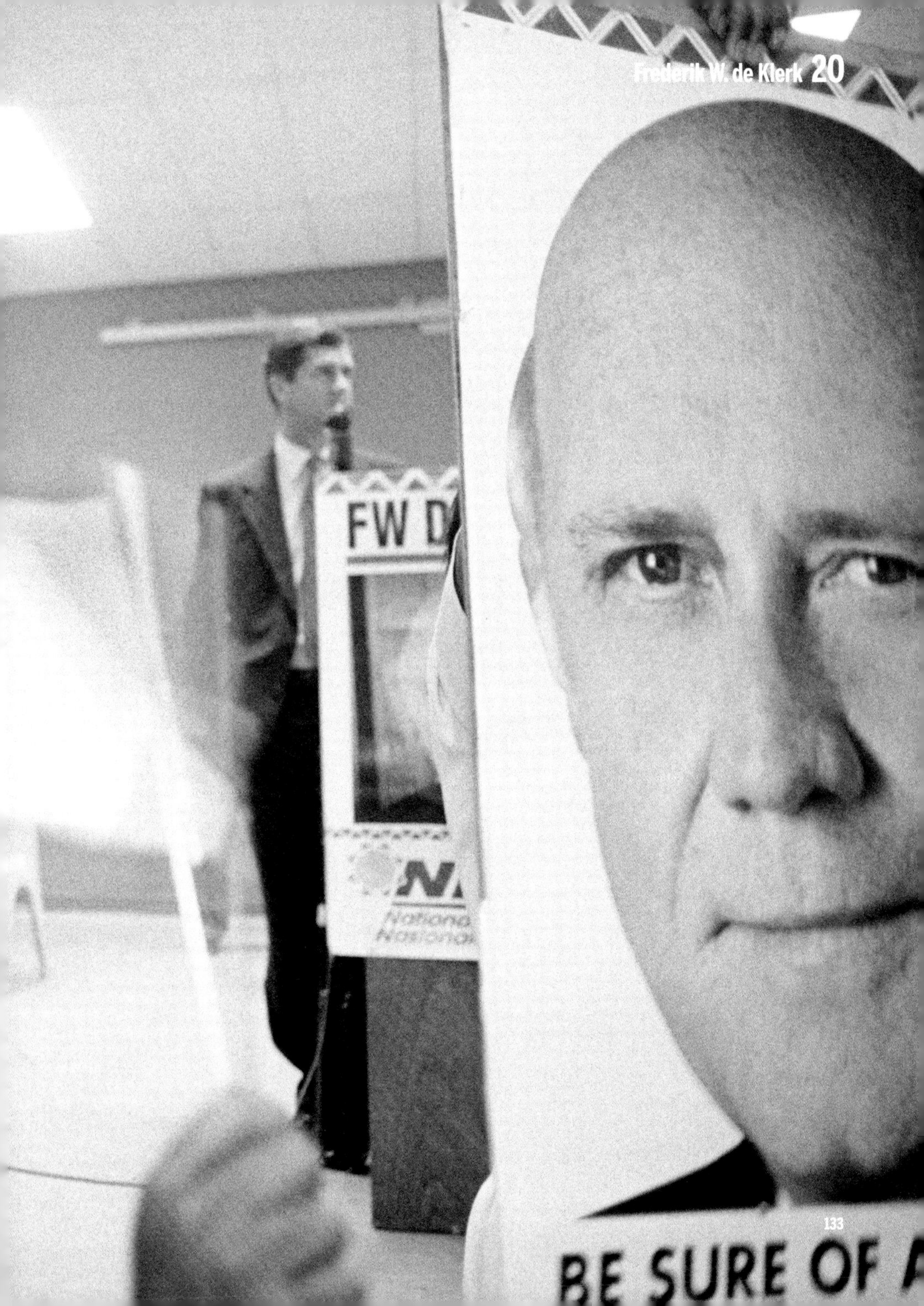

FW D
N
Nationa
Nationa
BE SURE OF

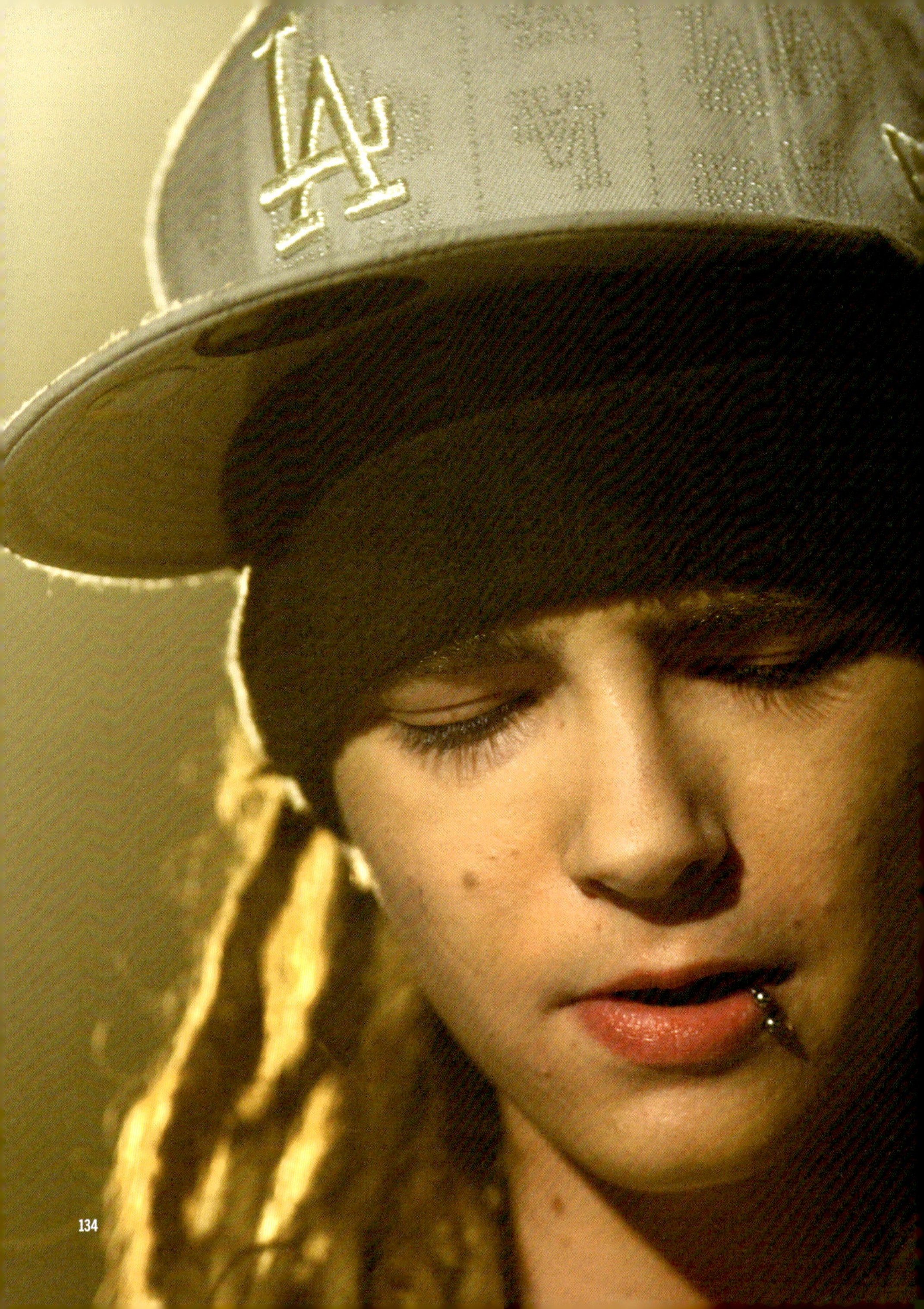

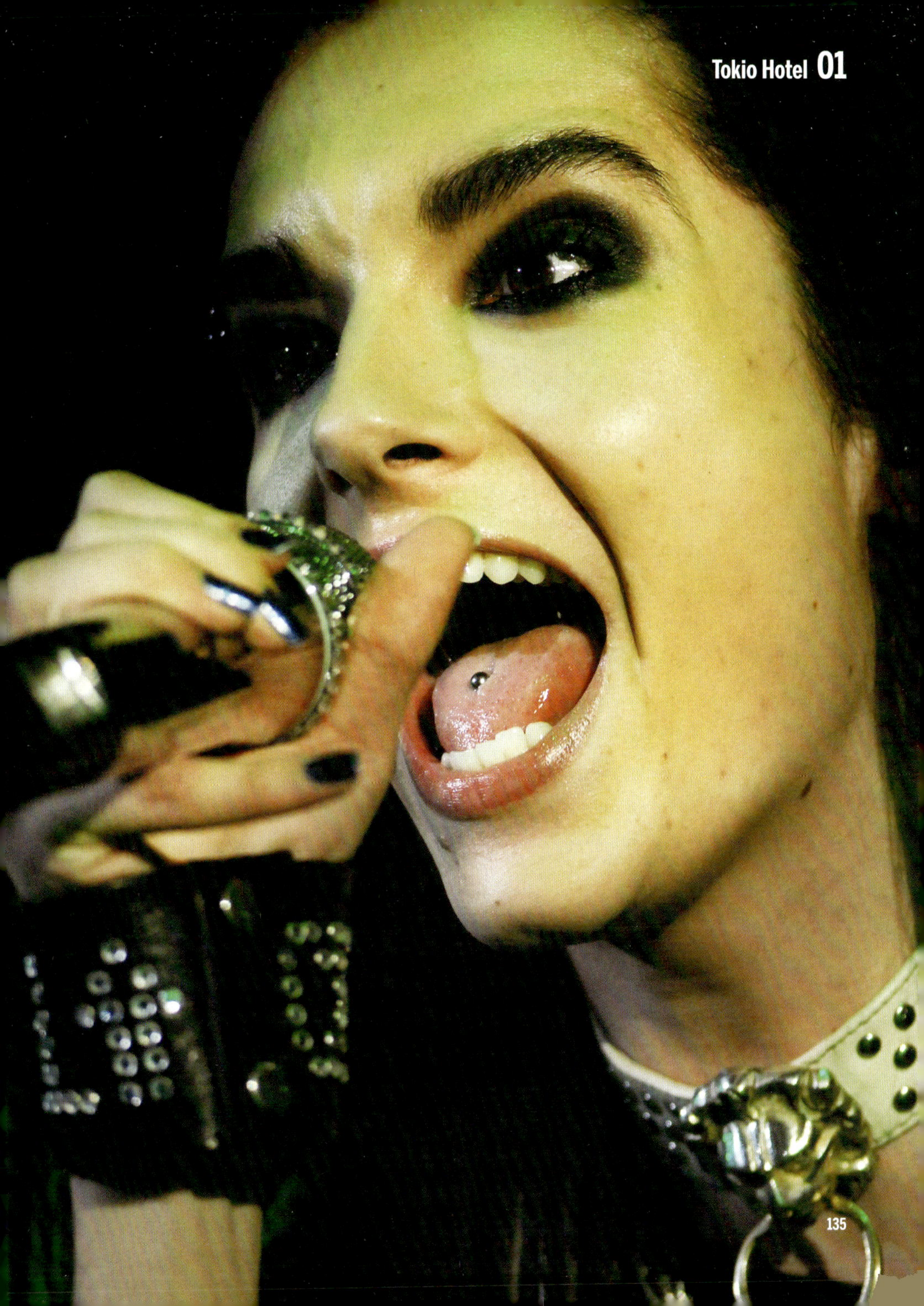

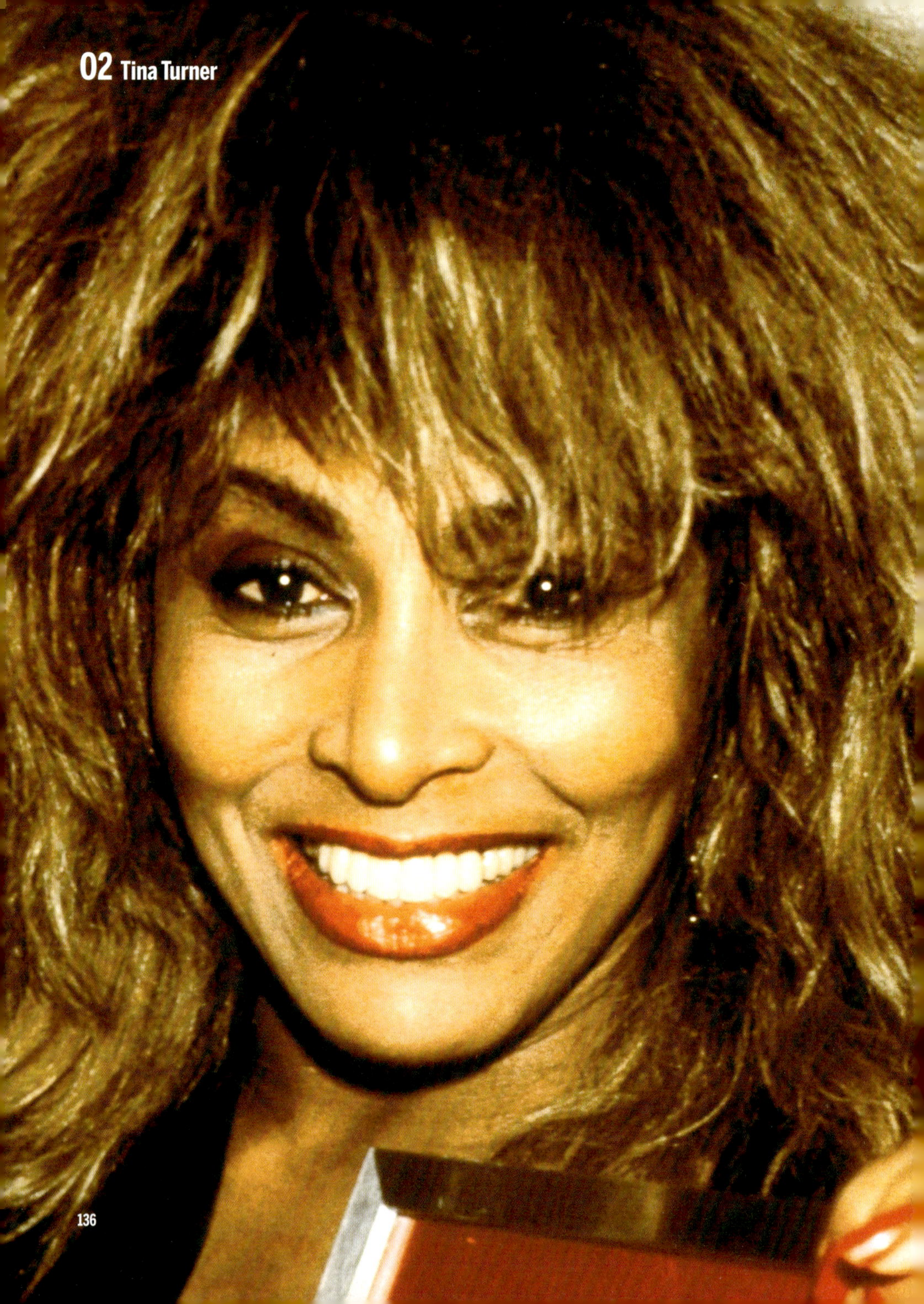

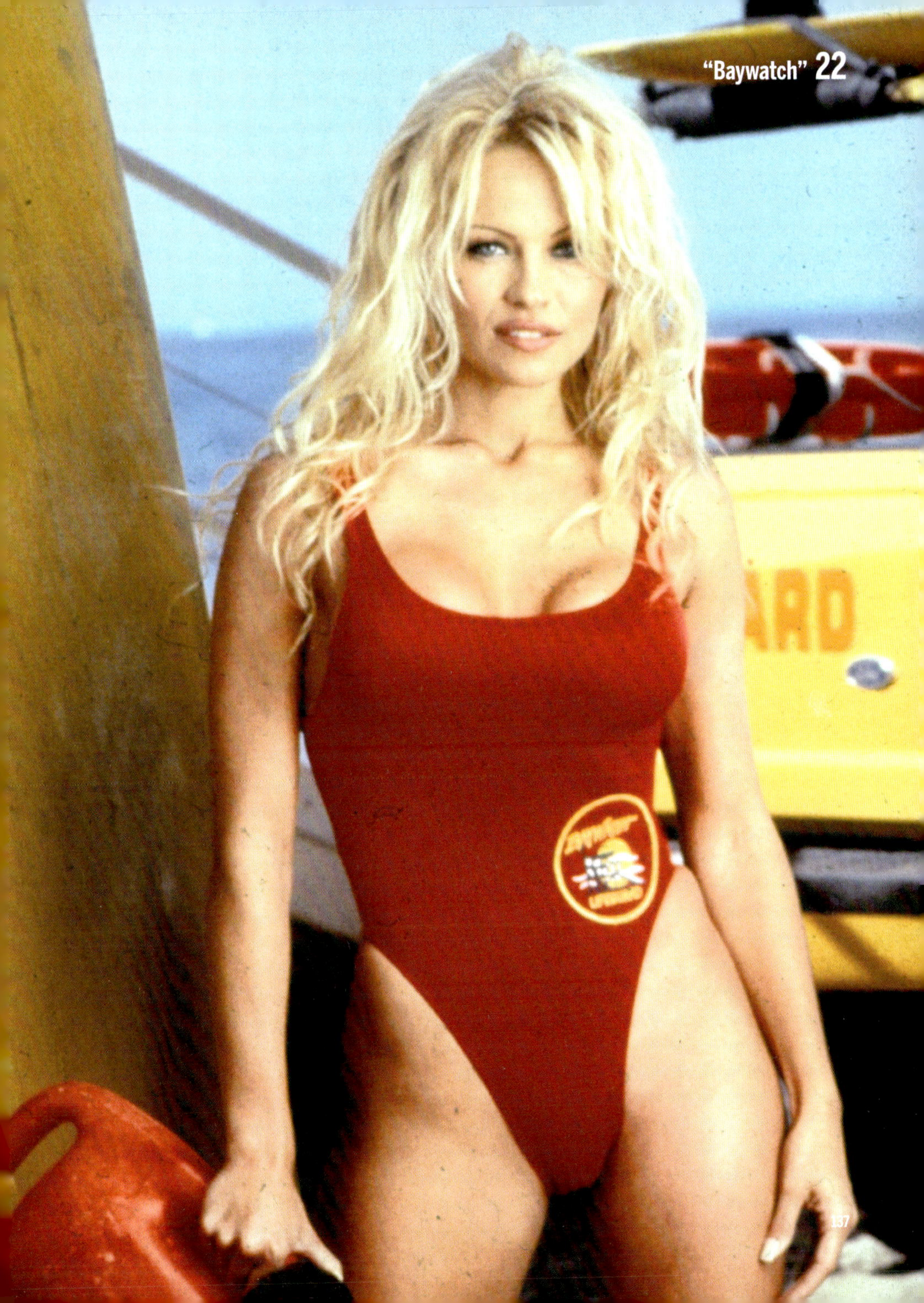
"Baywatch" 22
ARD
137

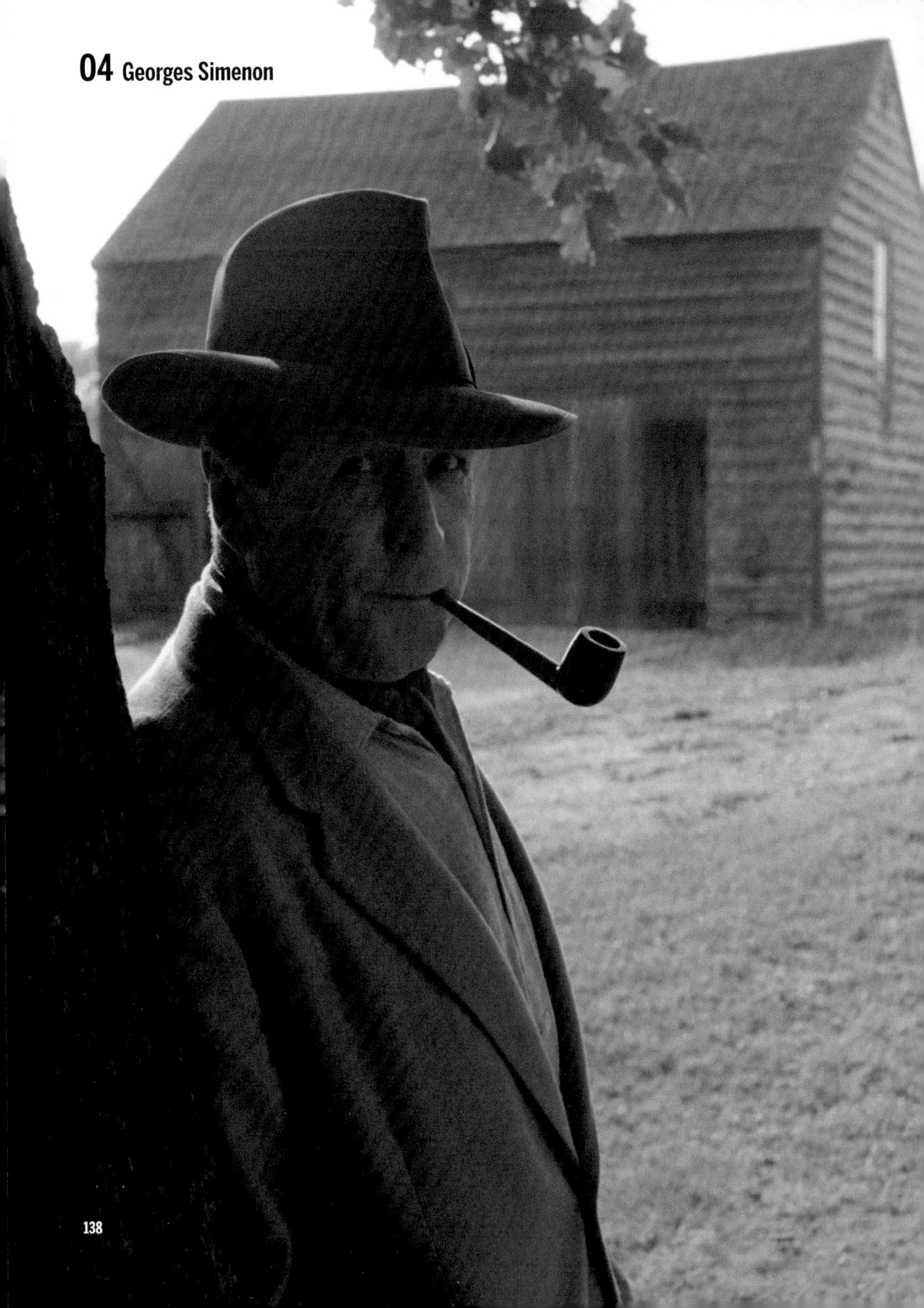

04 Georges Simenon

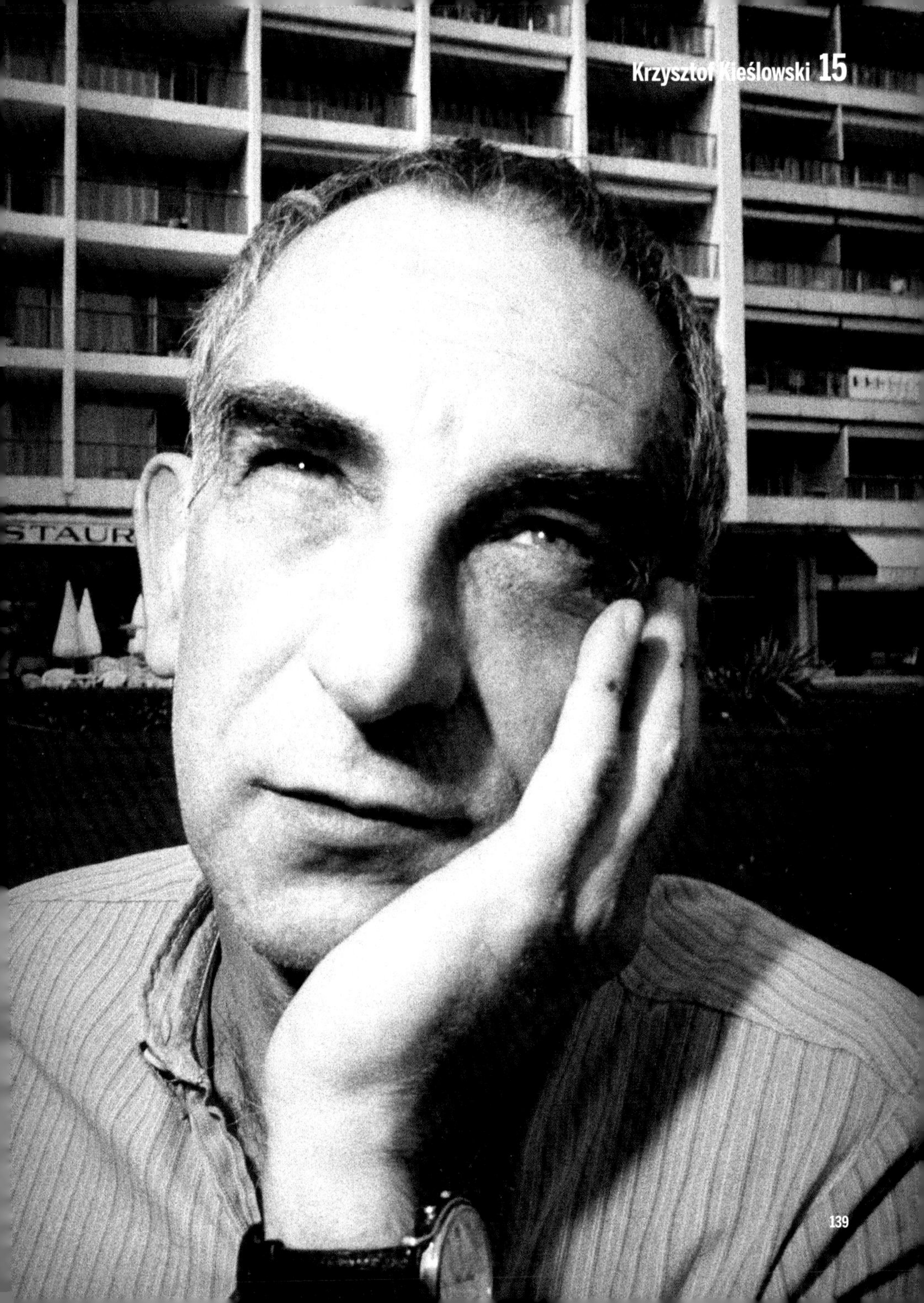

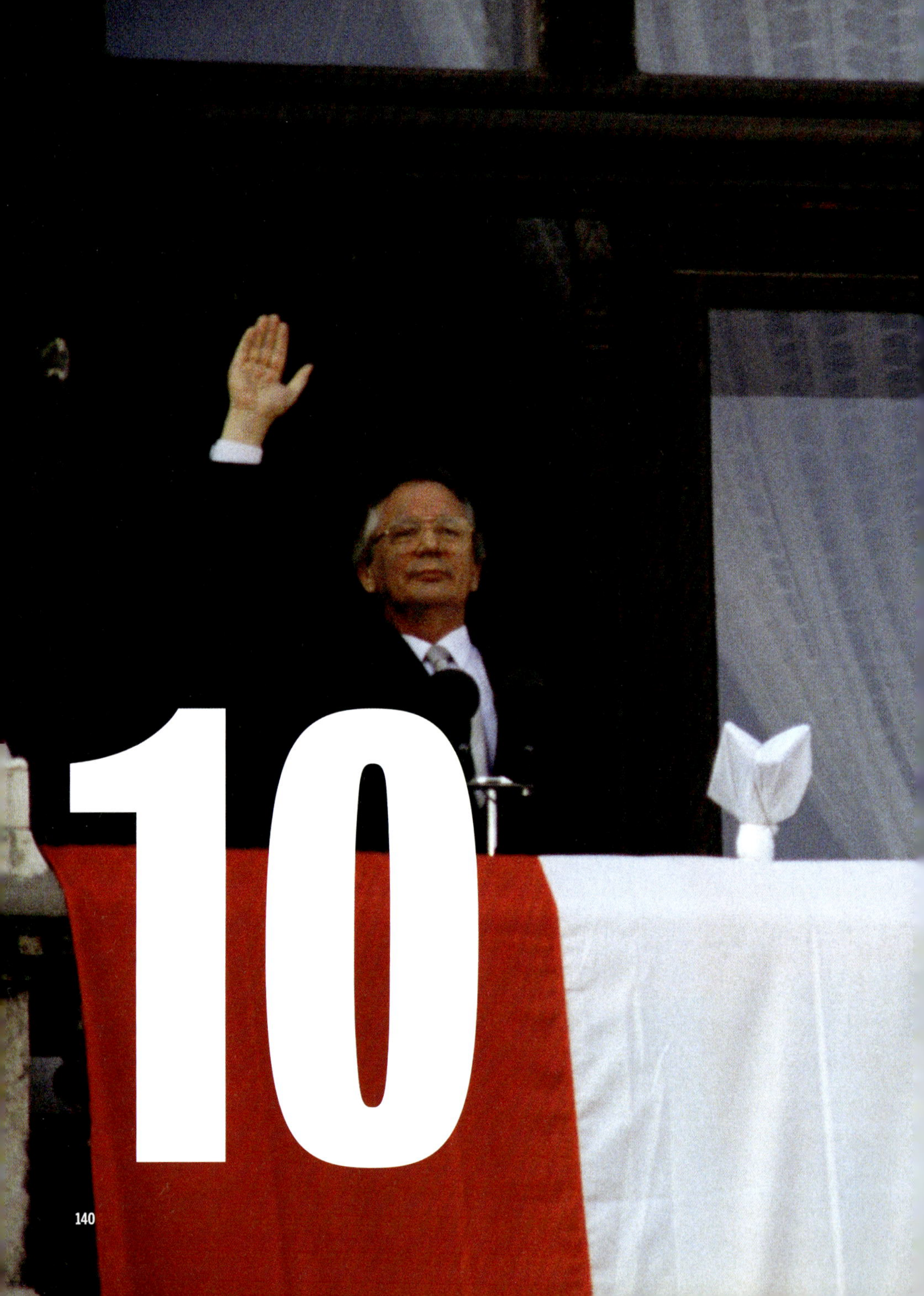

10

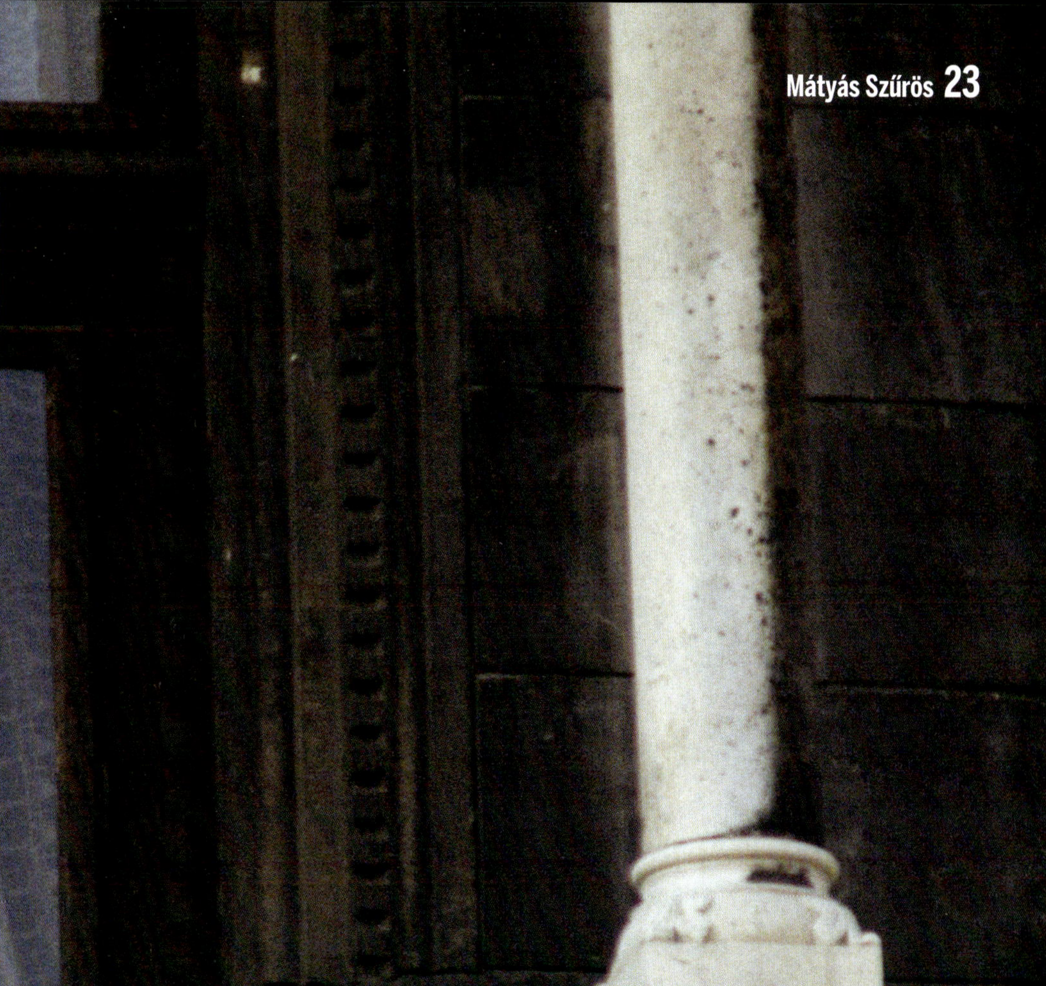

05

Sweden: Nobel Peace Prize goes to the 14th Dalai Lama, Tenzin Gyatso "for having always refused violence in his struggle for Tibet's freedom".

06

France: actress Bette Davis dies in Neuilly-sur-Seine at the age of 81.

13

United States: black Friday in Wall Street and the end of a long favourable period in Stock Exchange. The crash will influence all stock markets in the world.

United States: release of "Look Who's Talking" by Amy Heckerling with John Travolta and Kirstie Alley.

17

United States: earthquake in Loma Prieta, 7.1 degrees on the Richter Scale, hits the San Francisco Bay, 63 people die.

18

Germany: Erich Honecker, President of the DDR, discharges for health reasons.

23

Hungary: President Mátyás Szűrös officially declares the birth of the Republic of Hungary and the end of the People's Republic of Hungary.

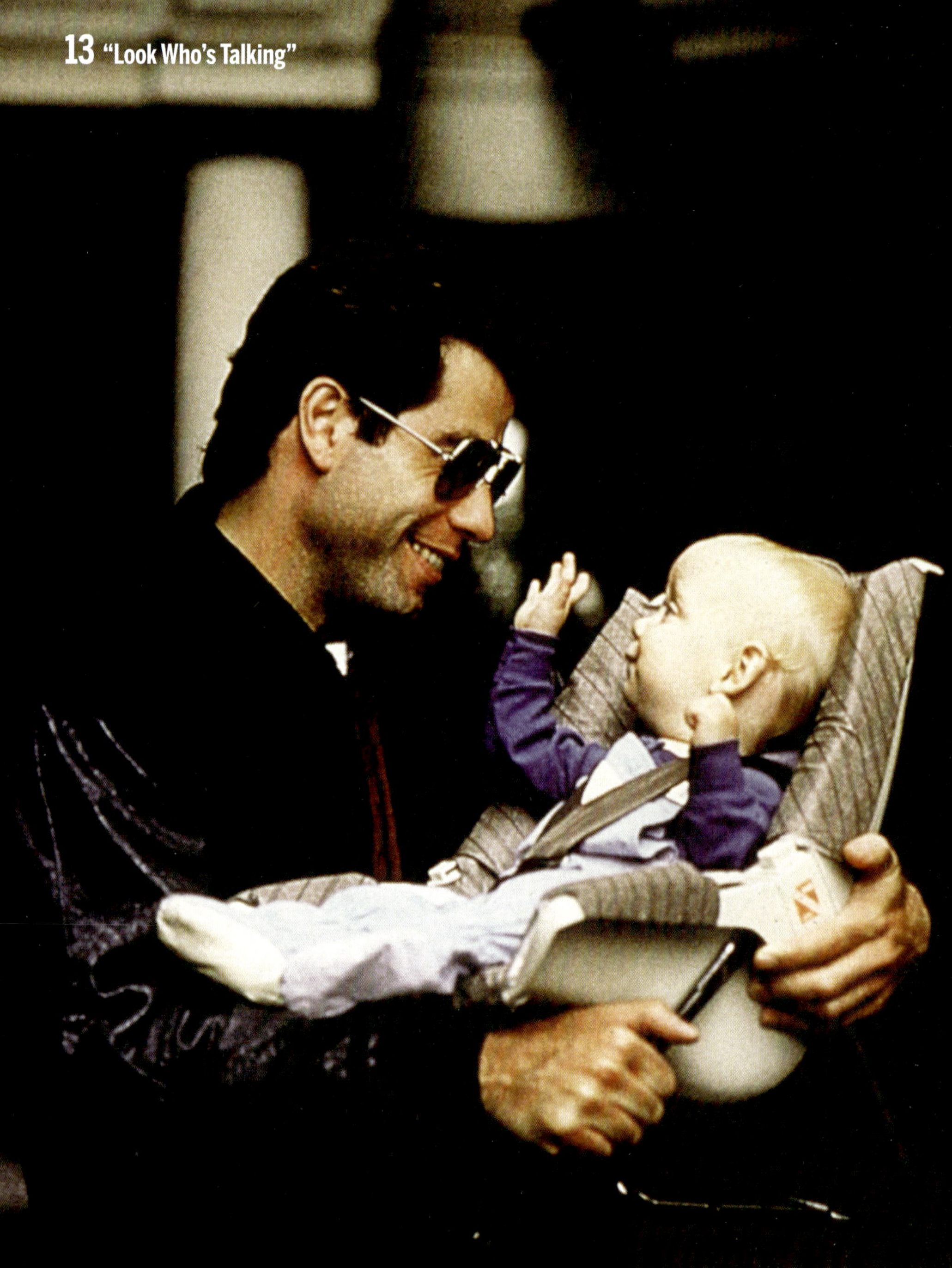

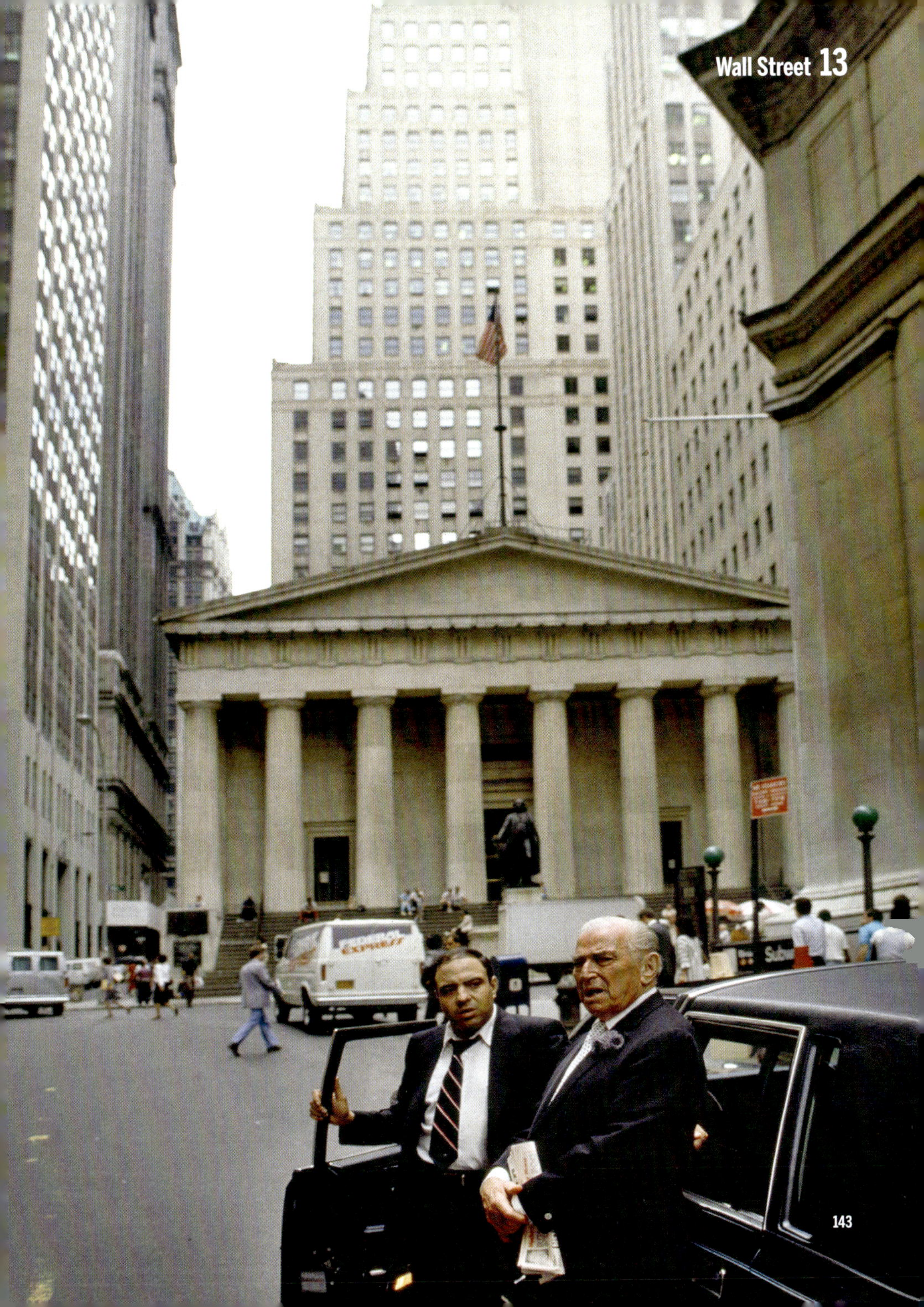

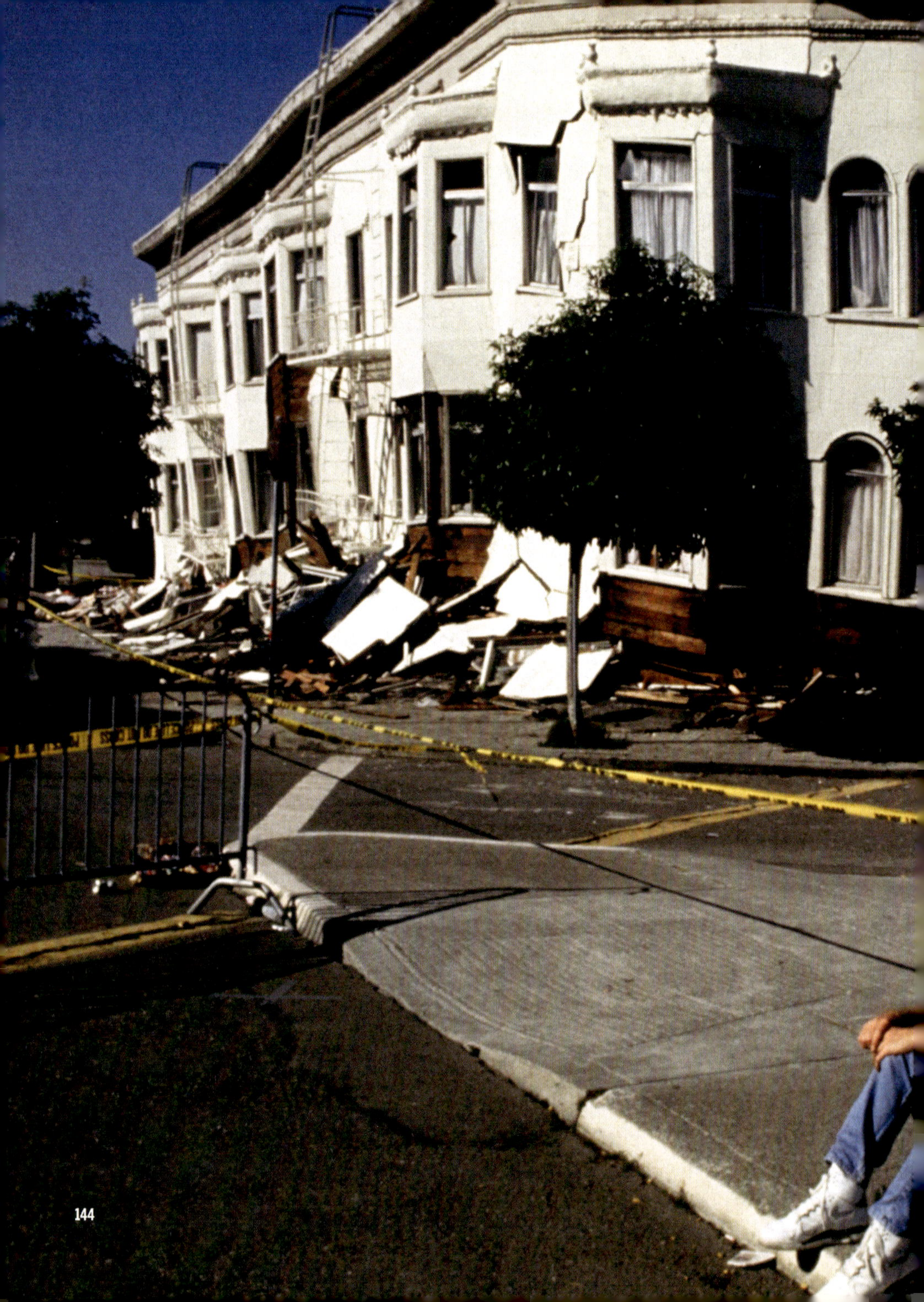

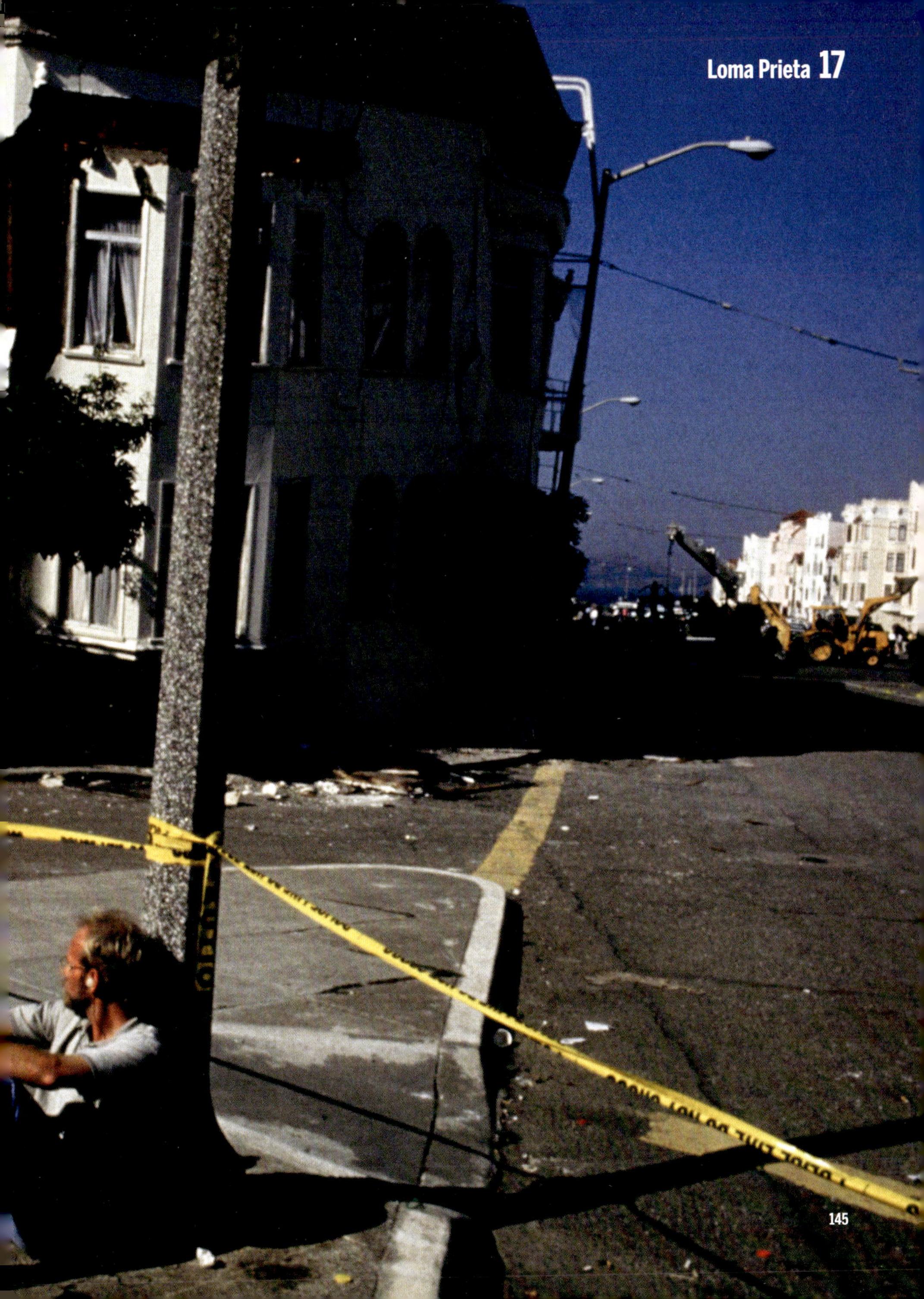

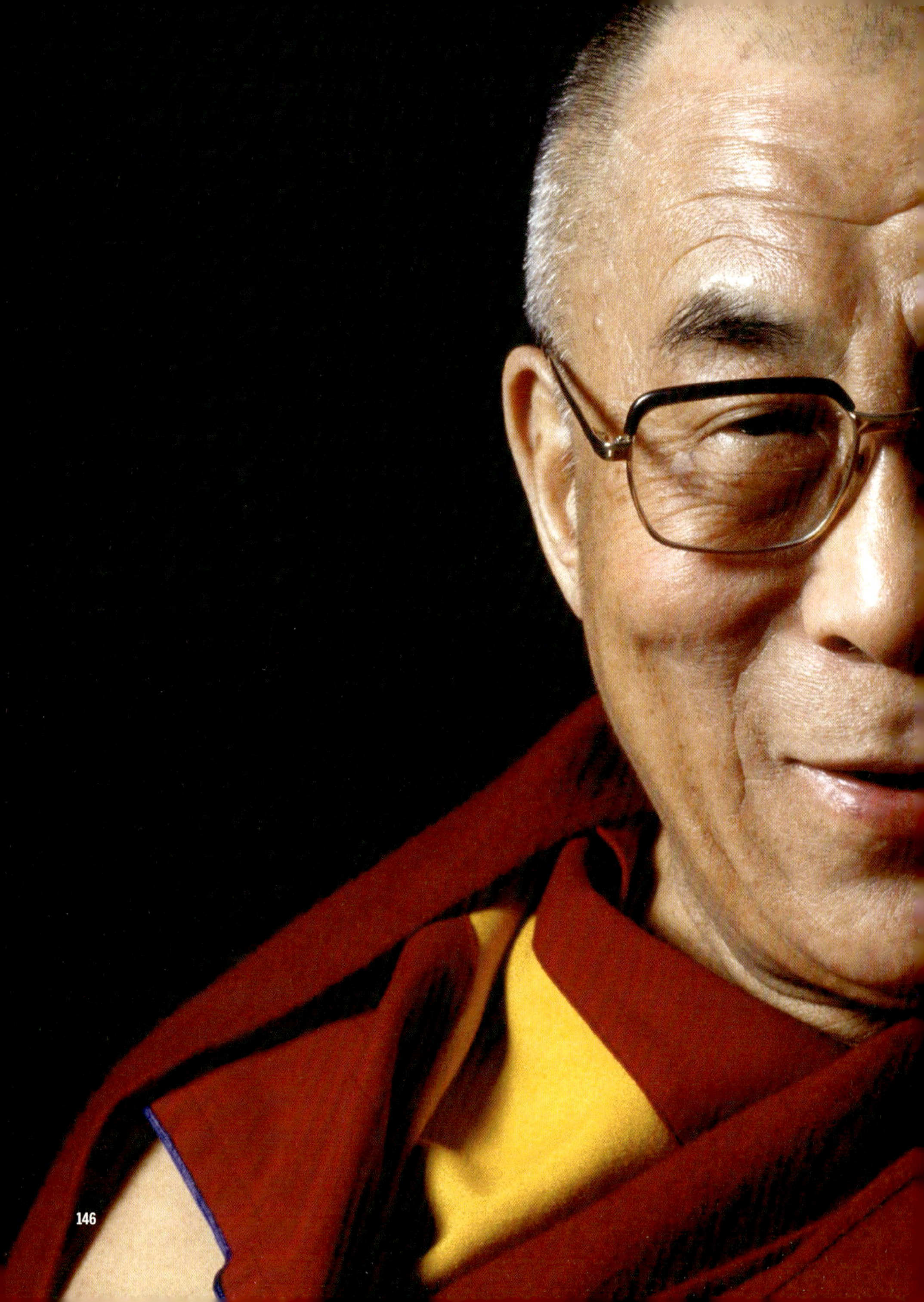

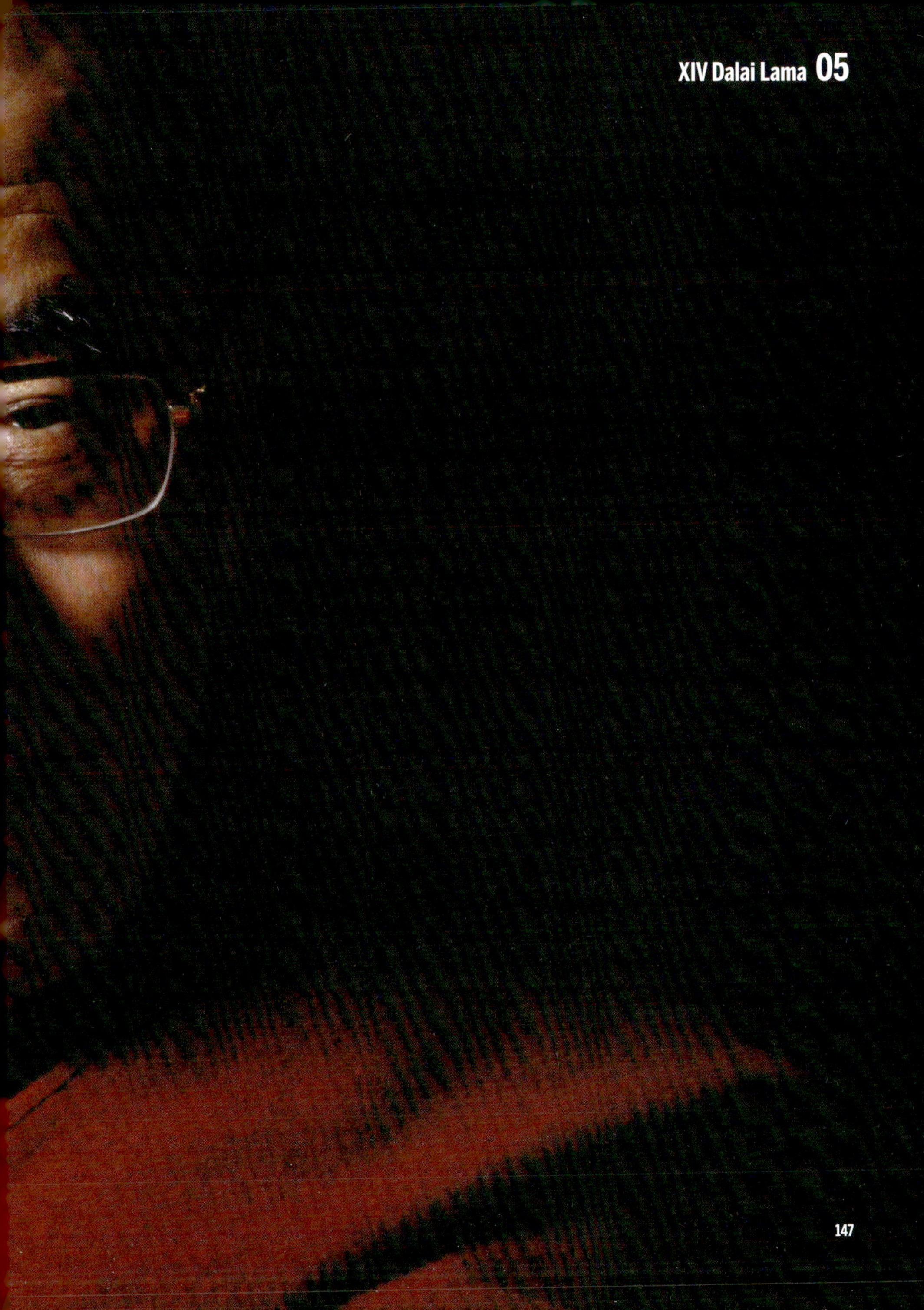

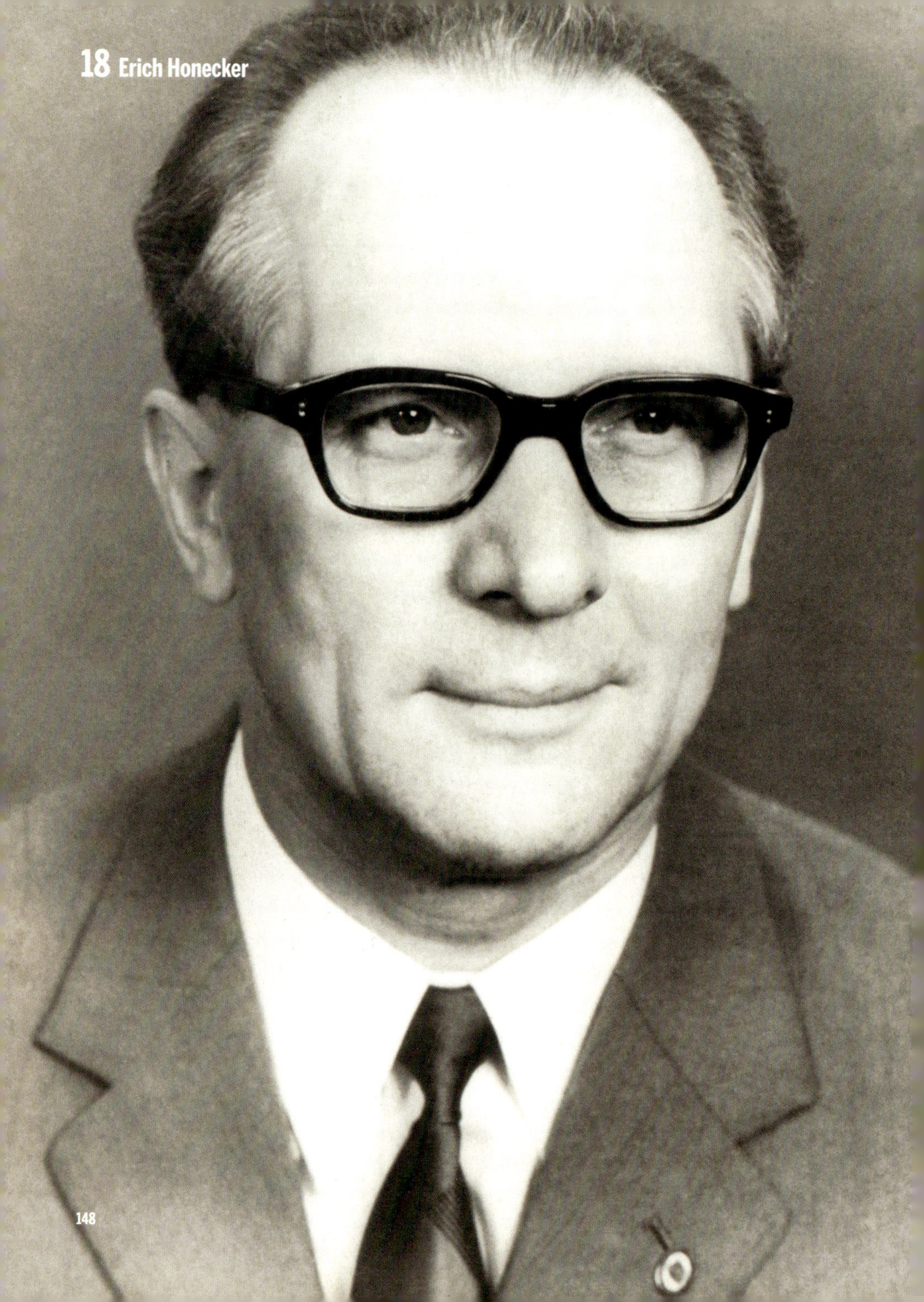

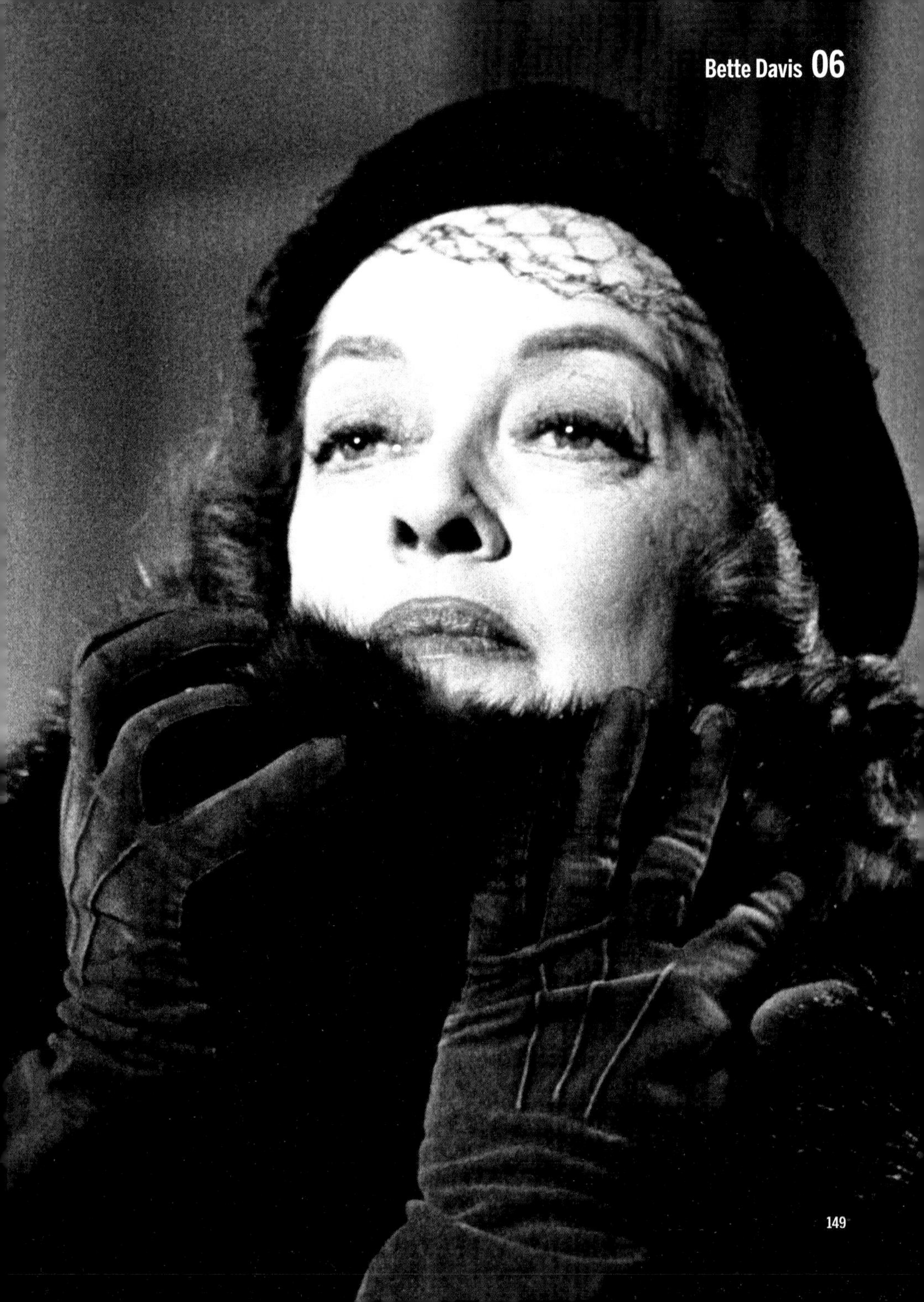

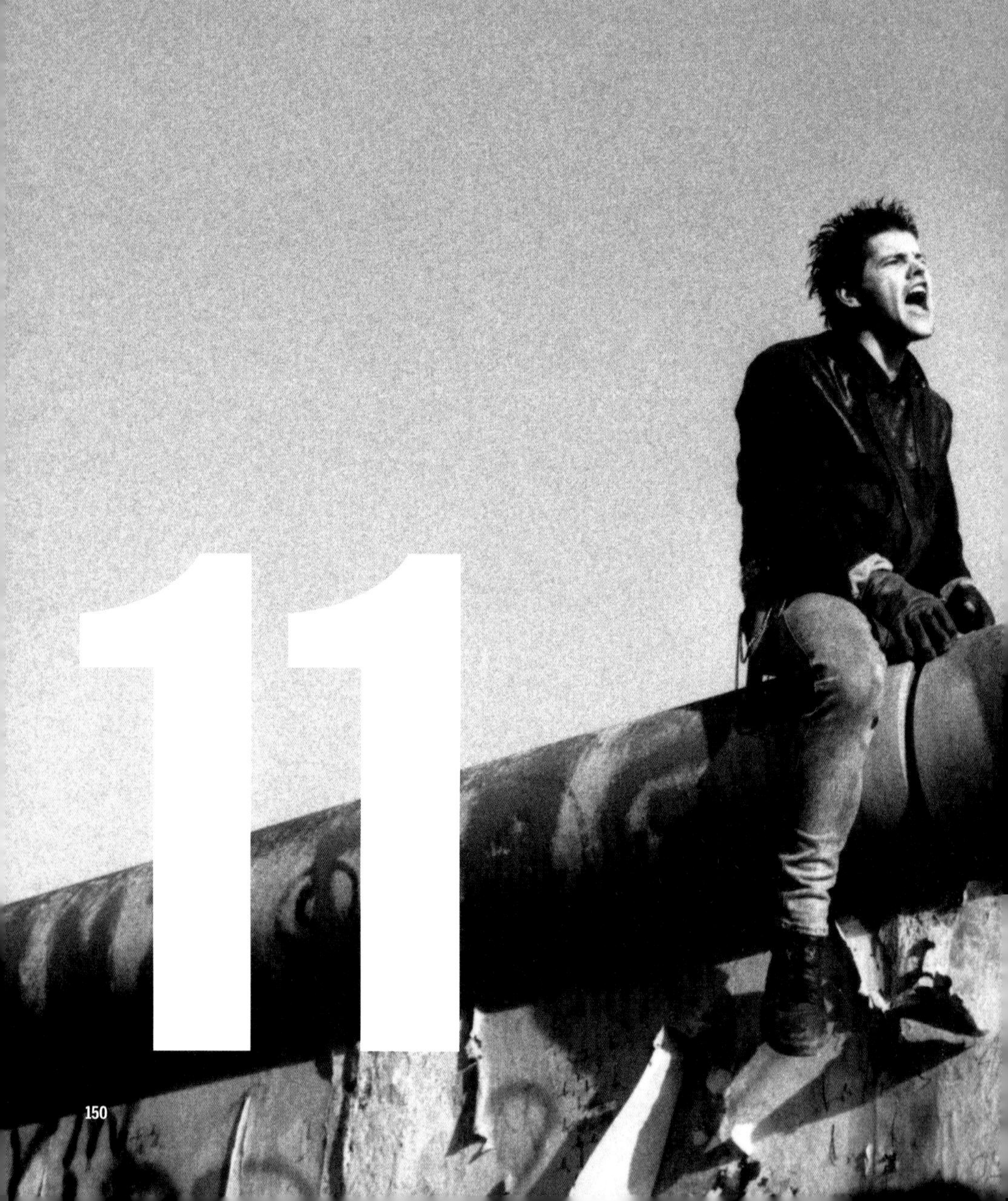

11

05

Australia: Alain Prost wins the Formula One Championship n Adelaide, after the historic dispute in Japan with his team mate, Ayrton Senna. It is his last year with McLaren.

United States: Vladimir Samoylovich Horowitz, considered one the 20th century major pianists dies in New York, aged 86.

09

Germany: after 28 years East Germany's government declares that visitors are allowed to enter West Germany and Berlin; after this announcement, a huge multitude of East Germans starts to joyfully climb over the top of the Wall to reach the West Germans on the other side.

12

Brazil: first democratic elections after 25 years of dictatorship. Ignazio Lula Da Silva also runs for President with the Labour Party. But electoral frauds and the strong opposition of banks and enterprises lead Fernando Collor de Mello, head of the National Reconstruction Party, to victory.

17

Bulgaria: Communist leader Todor Zhivkov is replaced by the Minister of Foreign Affairs Petar Mladenov, who changes the party's name into Bulgarian Socialist Party.

17-28

Czechoslovakia: the "Velvet Revolution" begins with a pacifist student protest in Bratislava. The day after, riot police suppresses a peaceful student demonstration in Prague. By November 20th the number of peaceful protesters in Prague swells from 200.000 to an estimated half-million. The protest led by Havel and Dubček, brought the entire leadership of the Czech communist party to resign and to call for free elections in December.

22

Lebanon: a bomb explodes in the western part of Beirut at the passage of President René Moawad's parade, killing him and other 63 people.

United States: release of "Back to the Future Part II" by Robert Zemeckis with Michael J. Fox and Christopher Lloyd

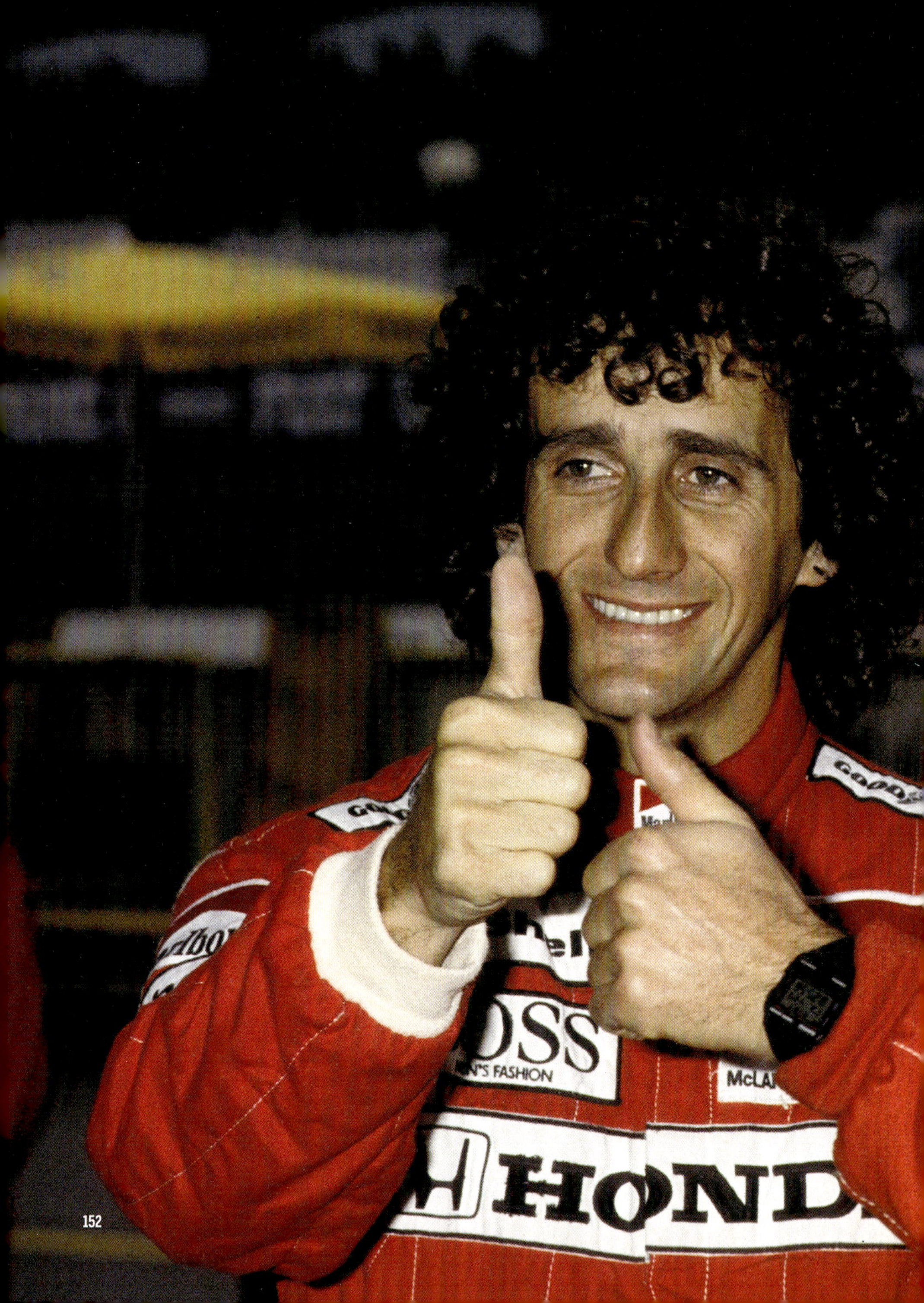

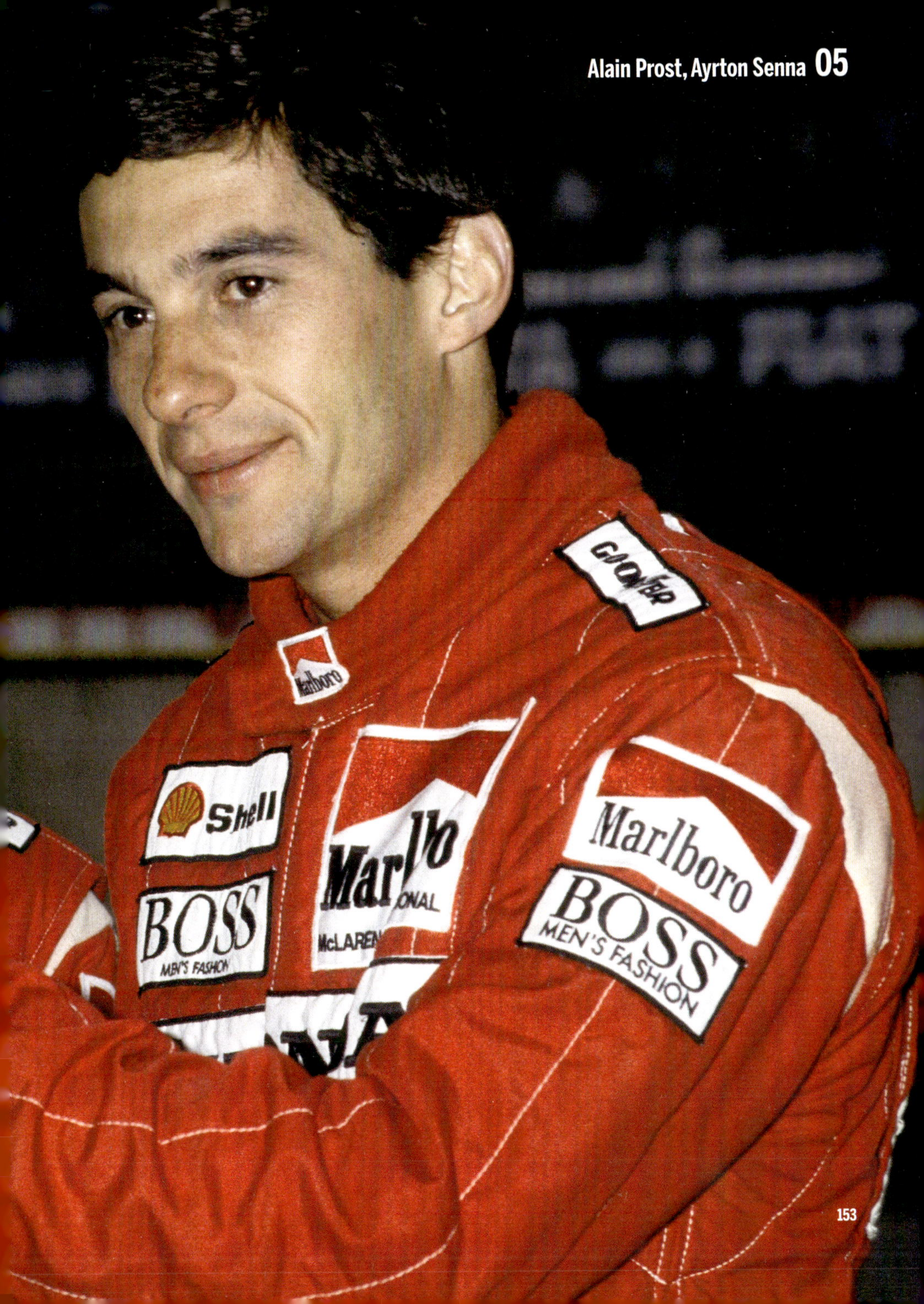

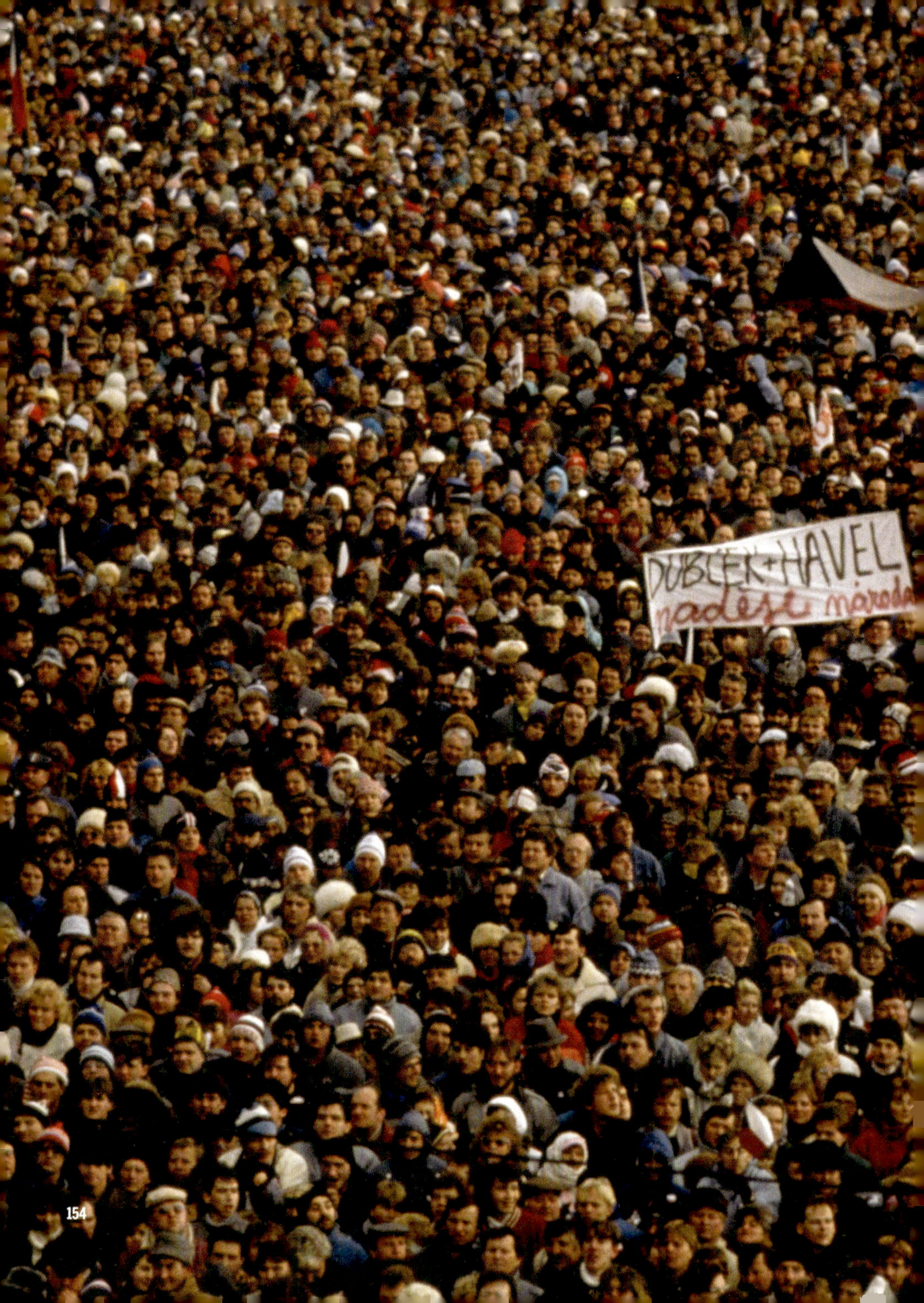

DUBČEK+HAVEL
naděje národa

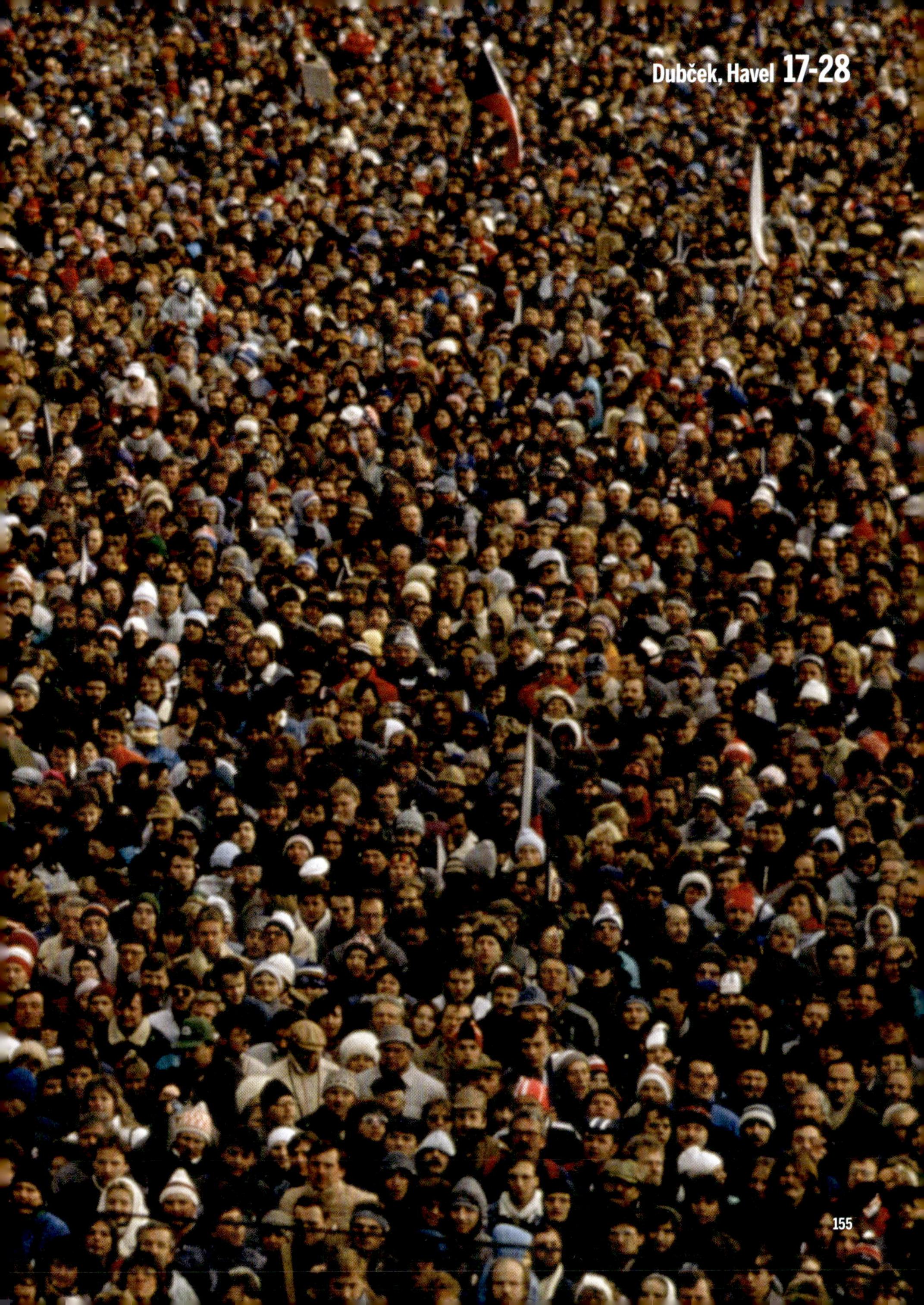

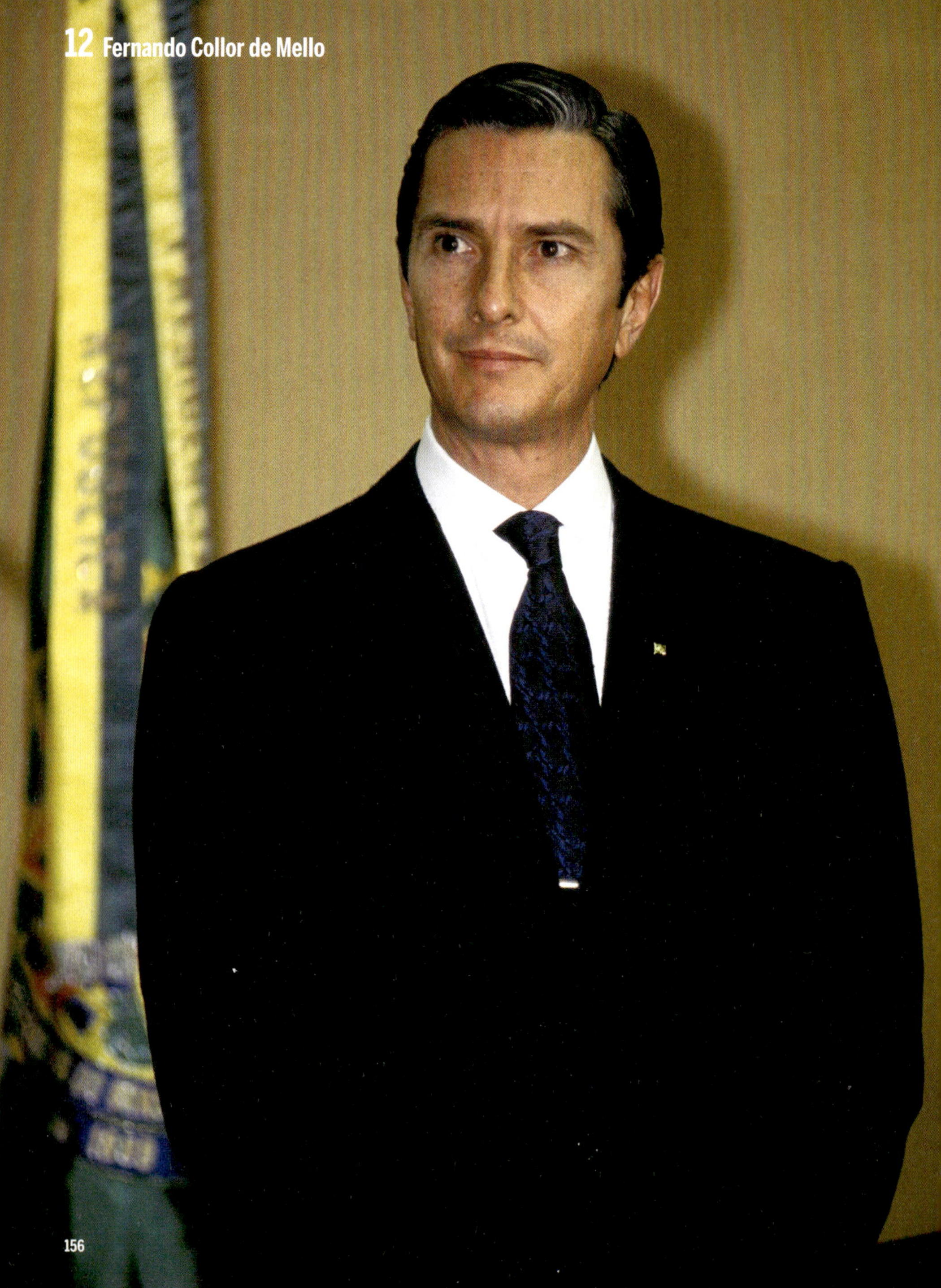

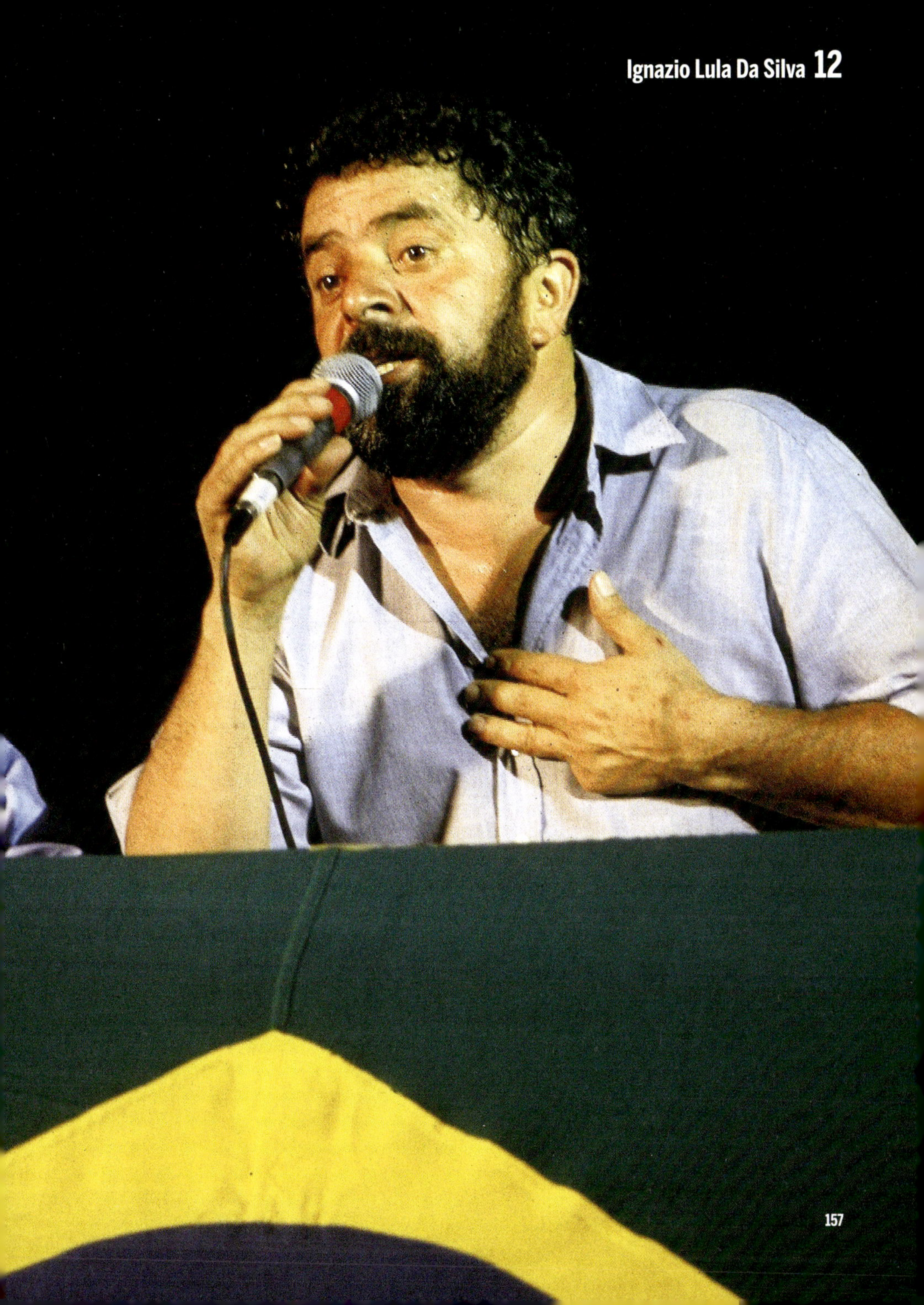

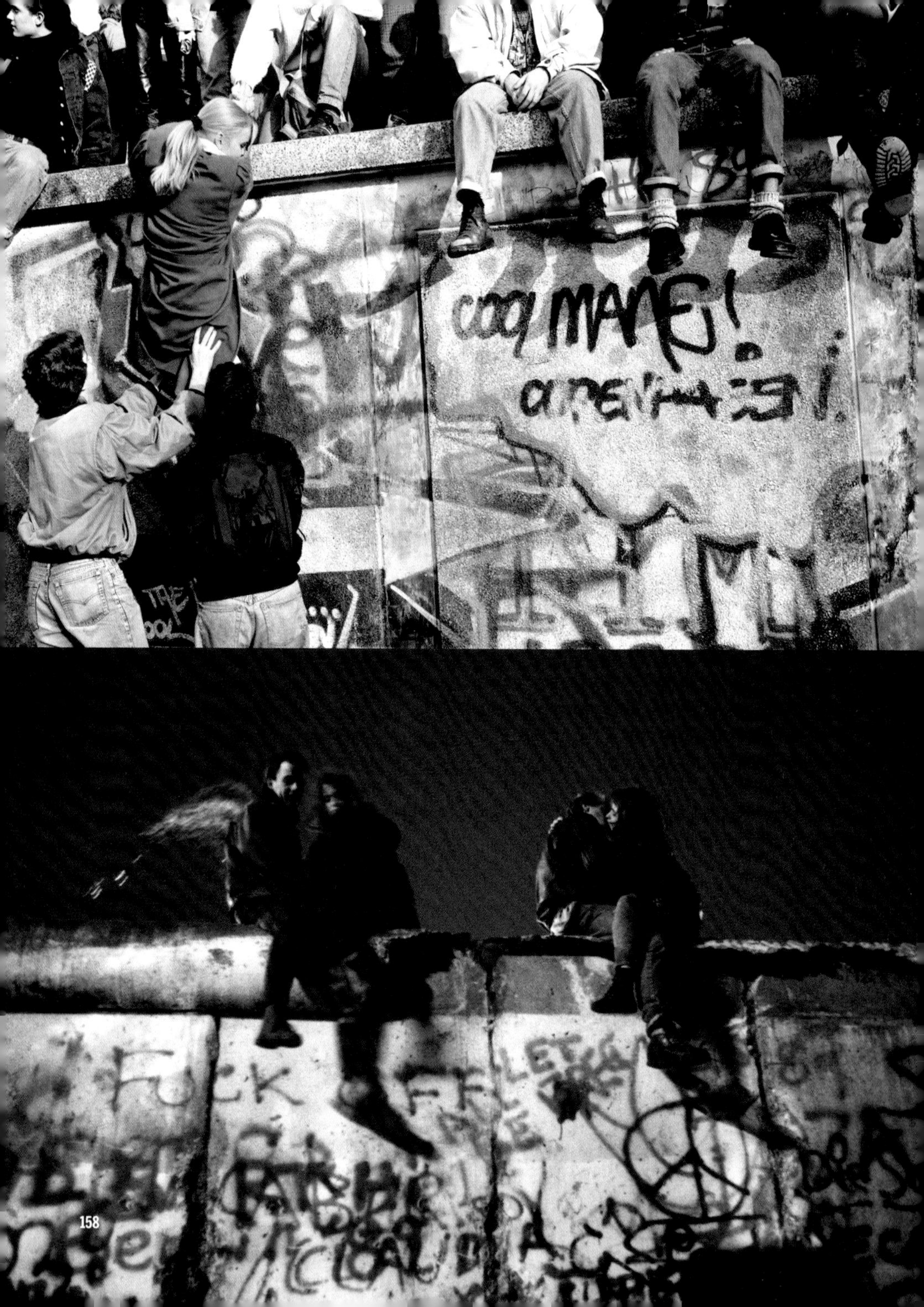

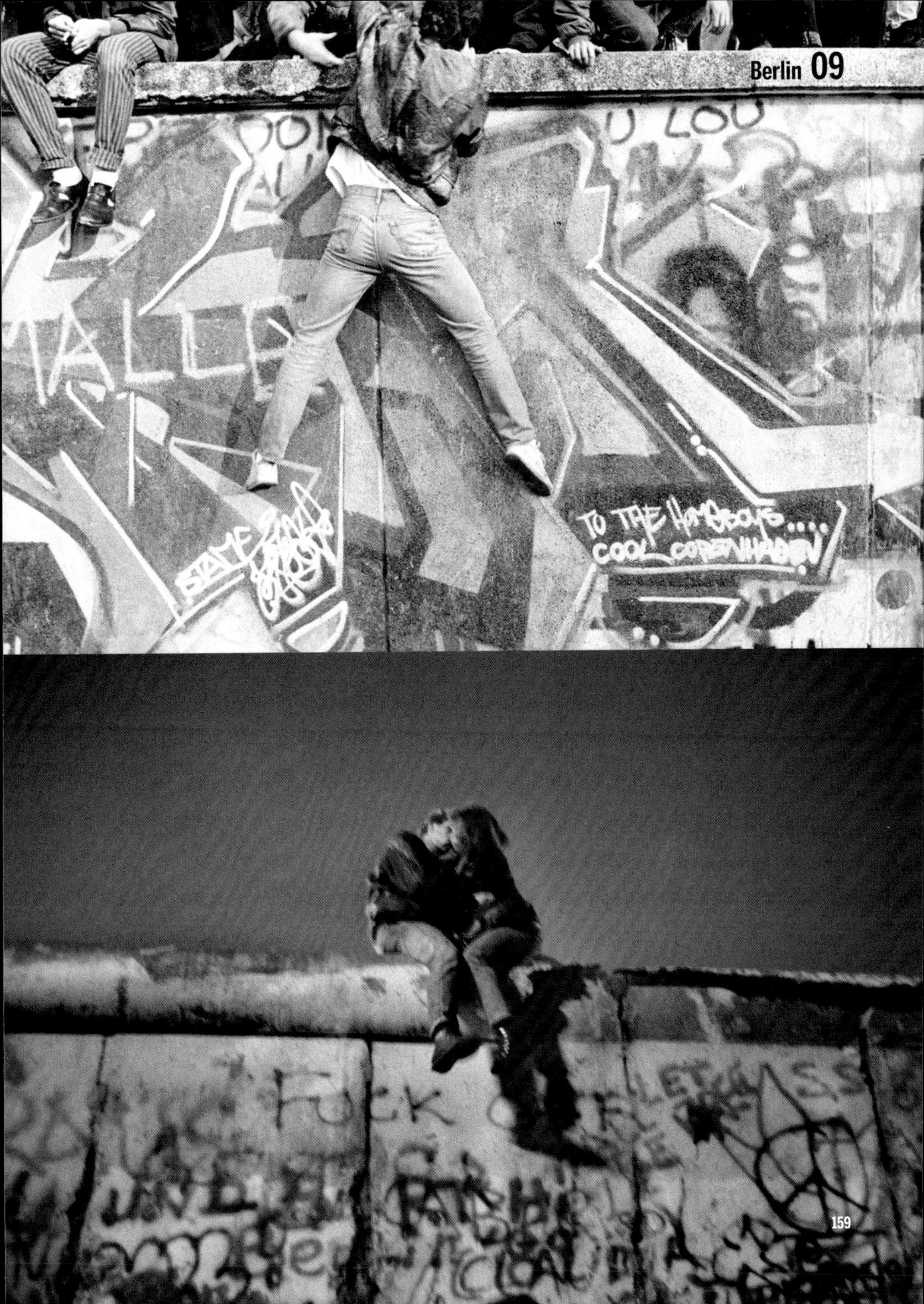

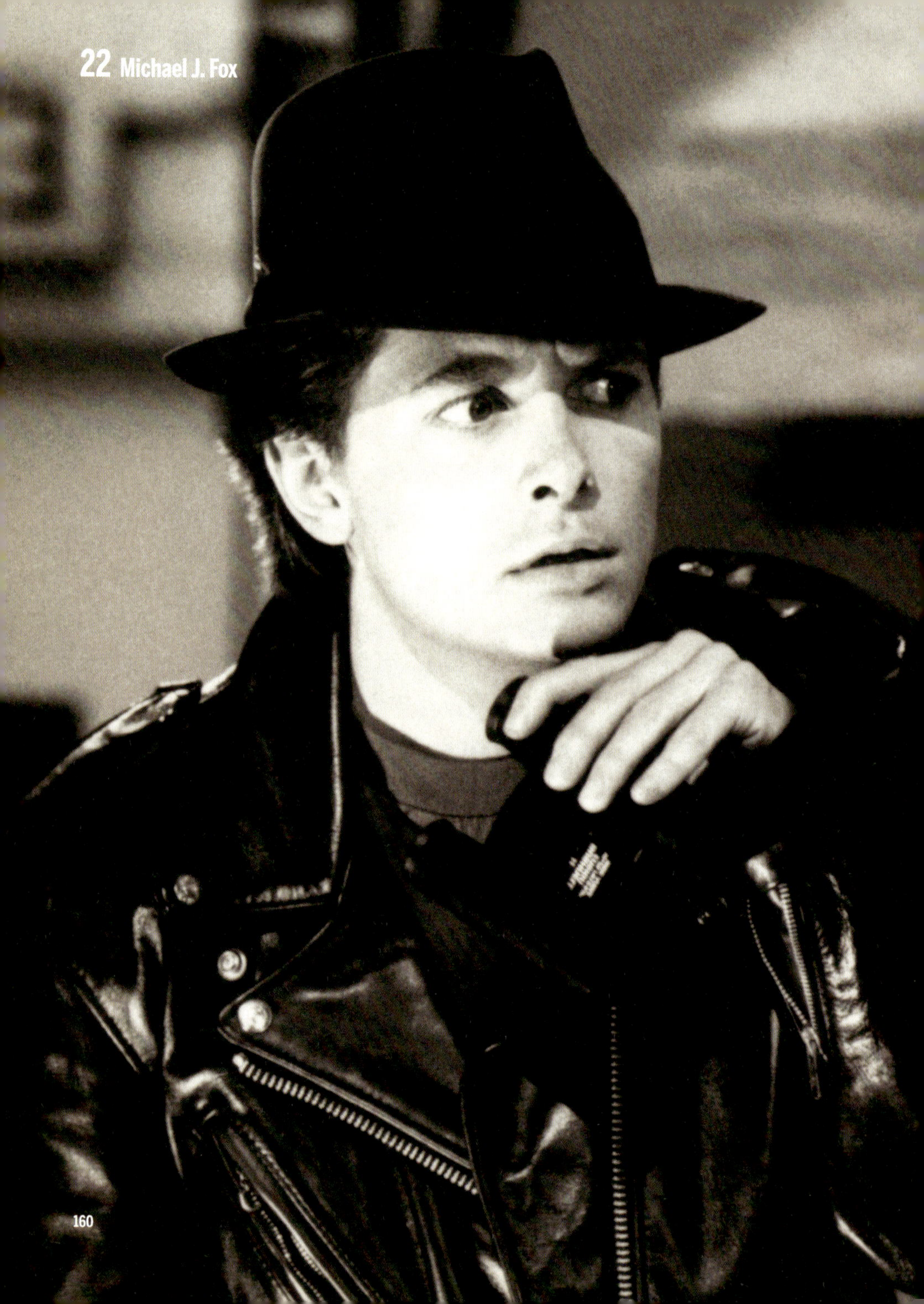

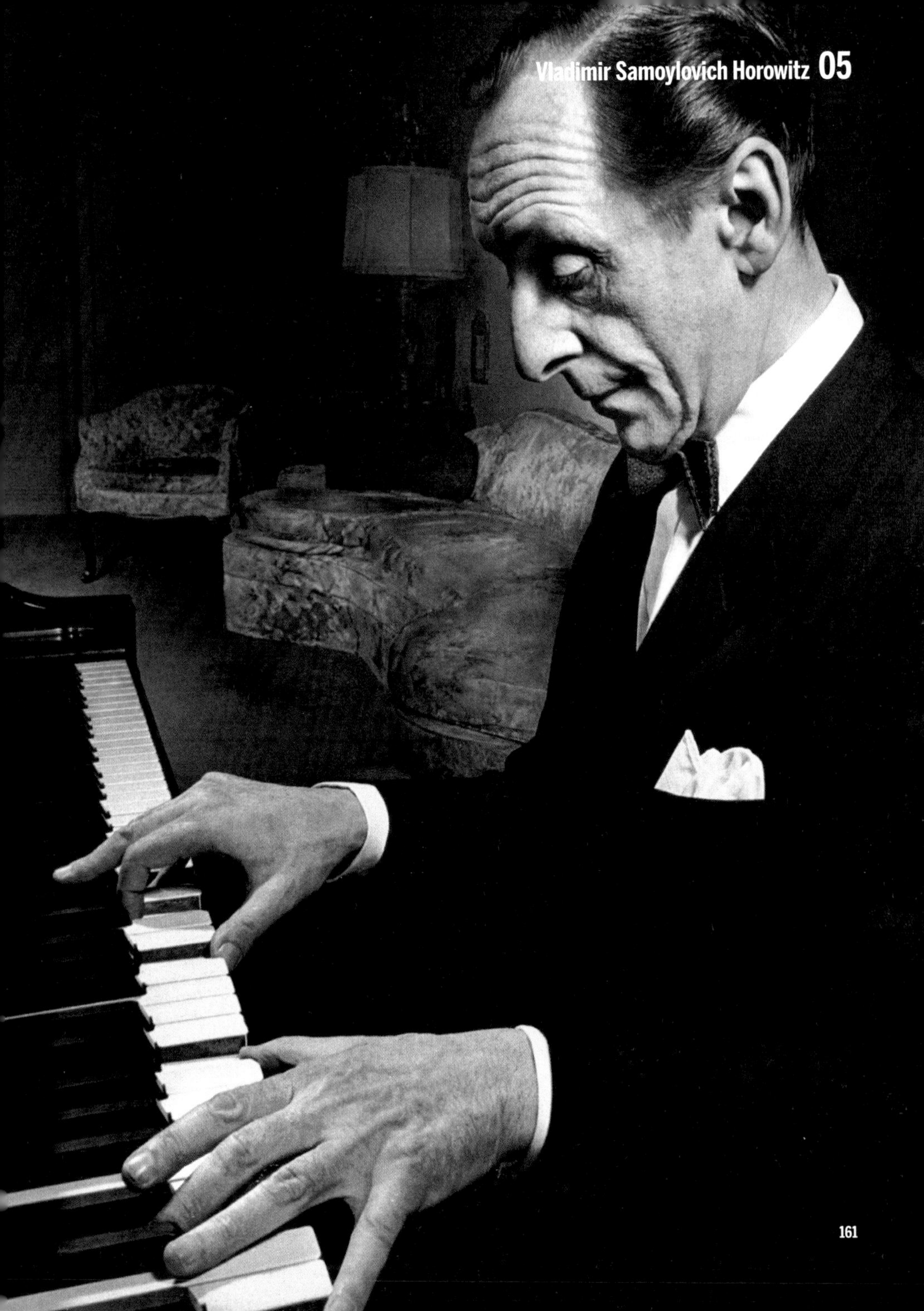
Vladimir Samoylovich Horowitz 05

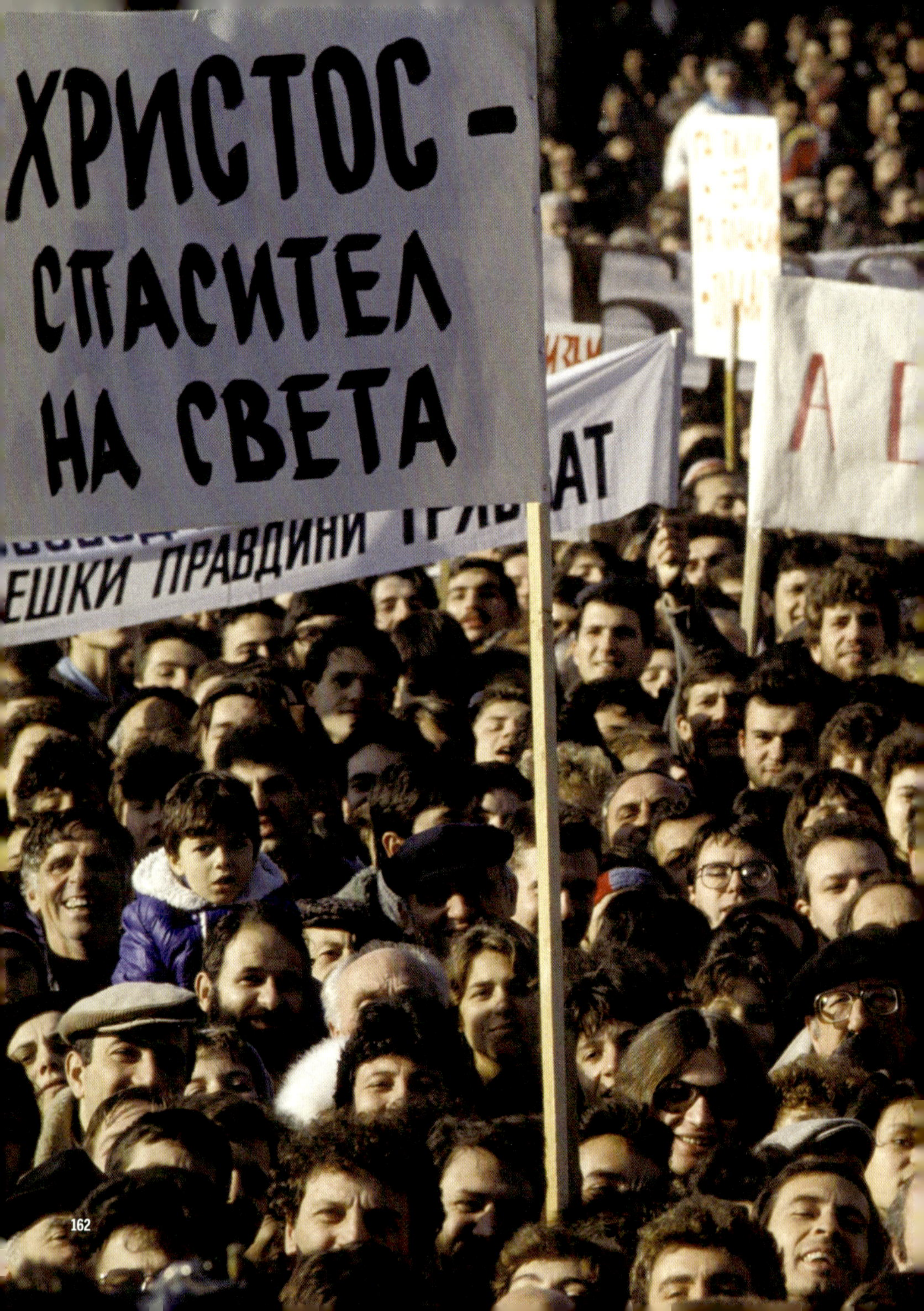

ХРИСТОС –
СПАСИТЕЛ
НА СВЕТА

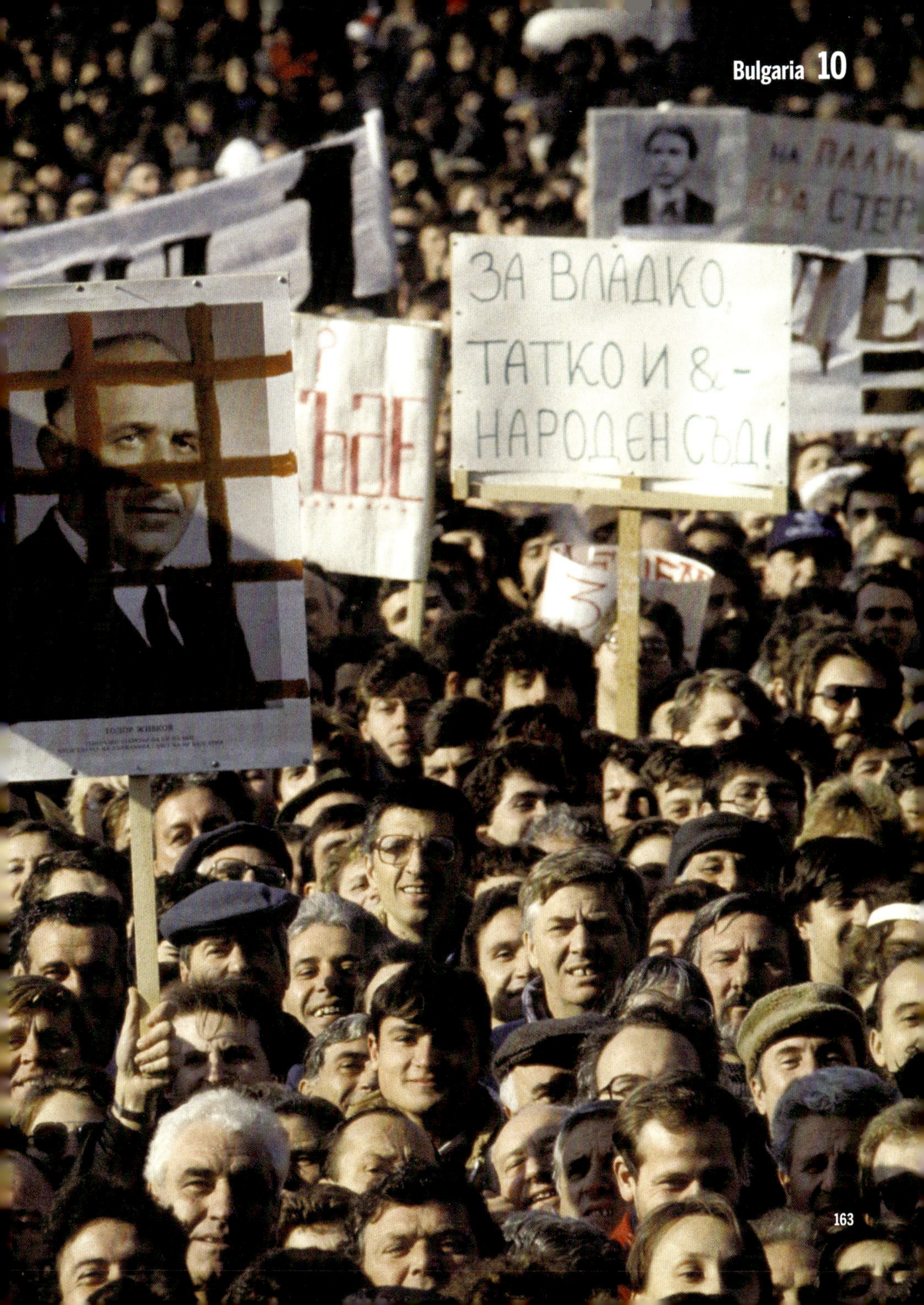
ЗА ВЛАДКО,
ТАТКО И & -
НАРОДЕН СЪД!
ТОДОР ЖИВКОВ

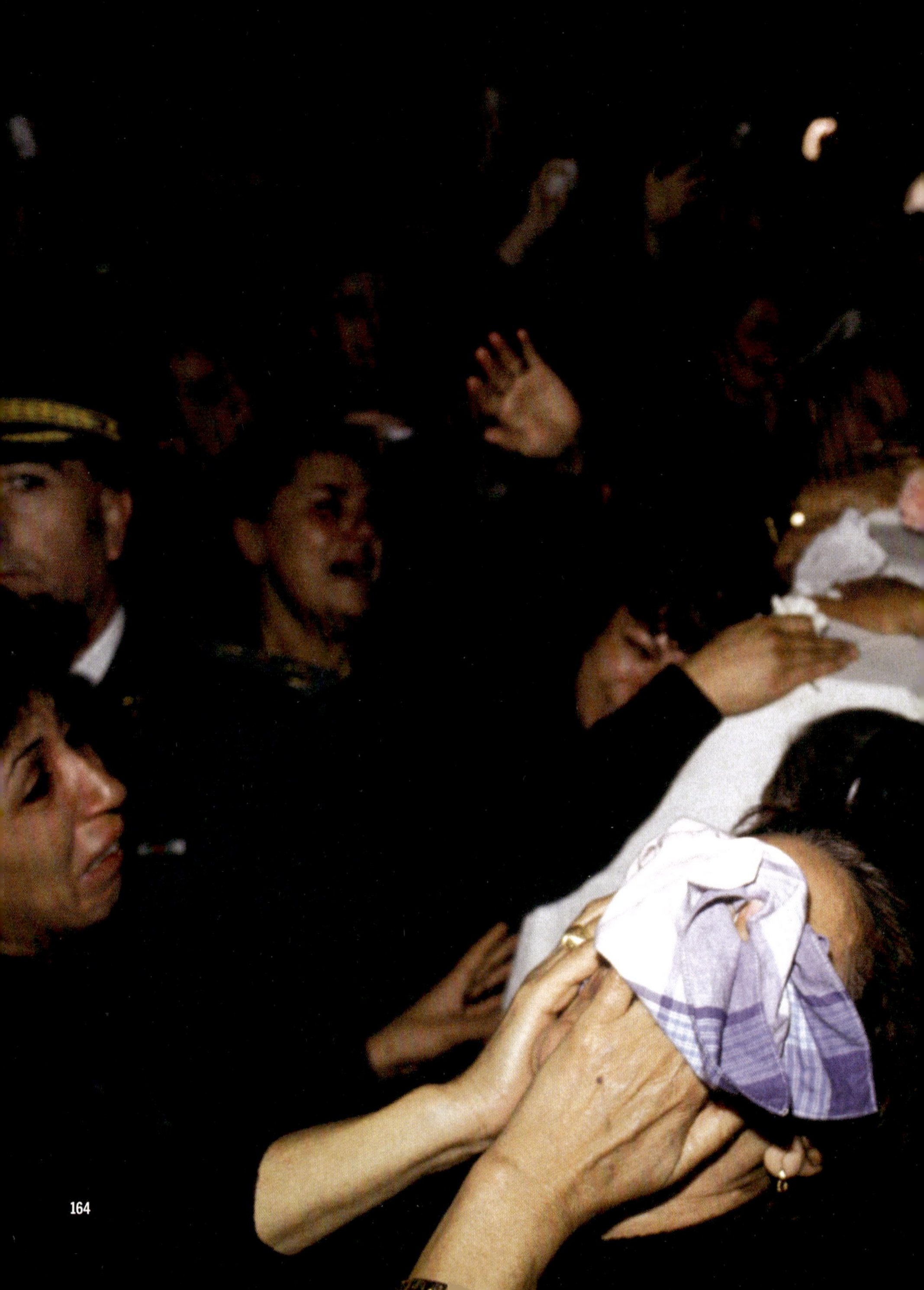

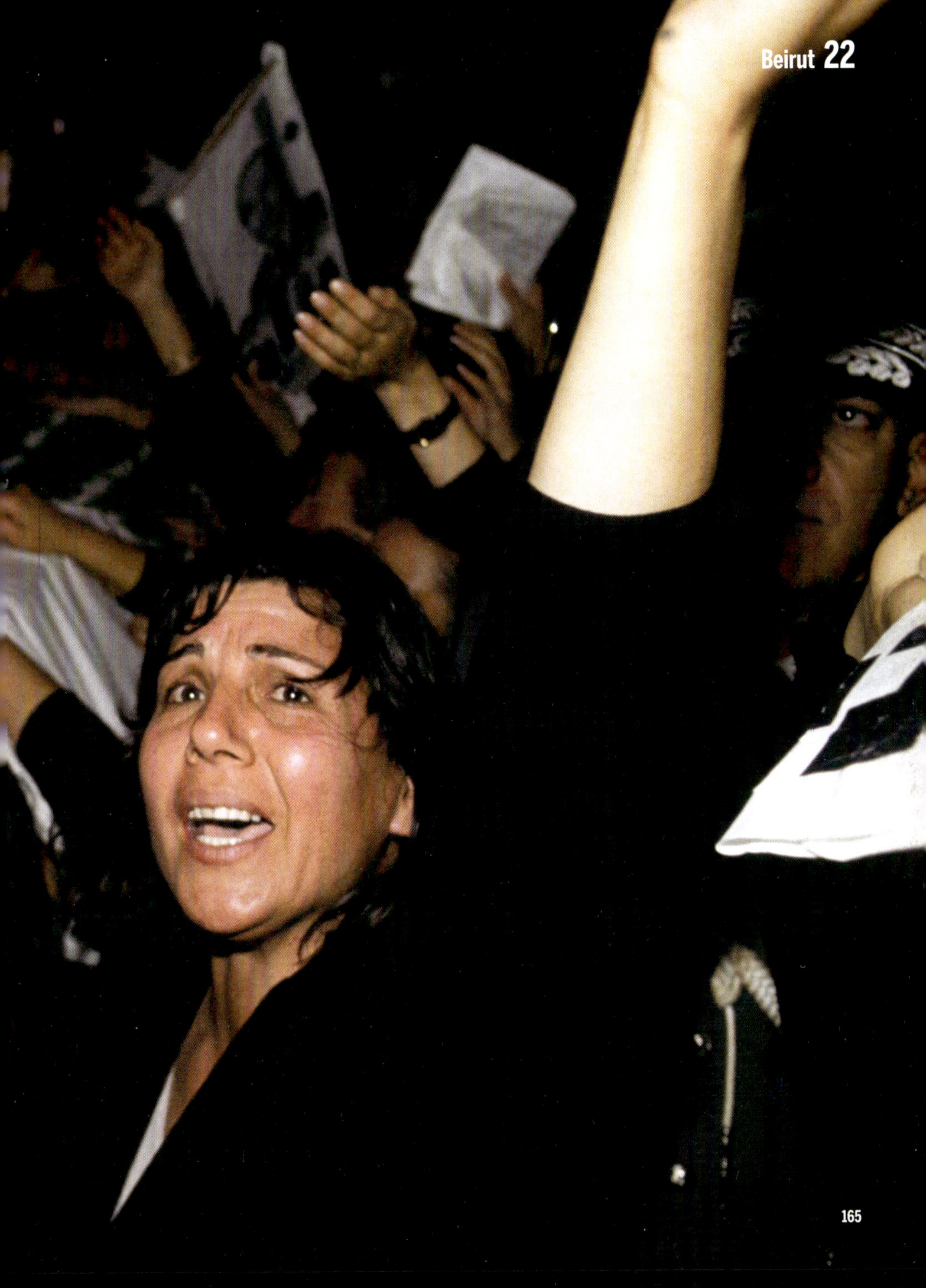

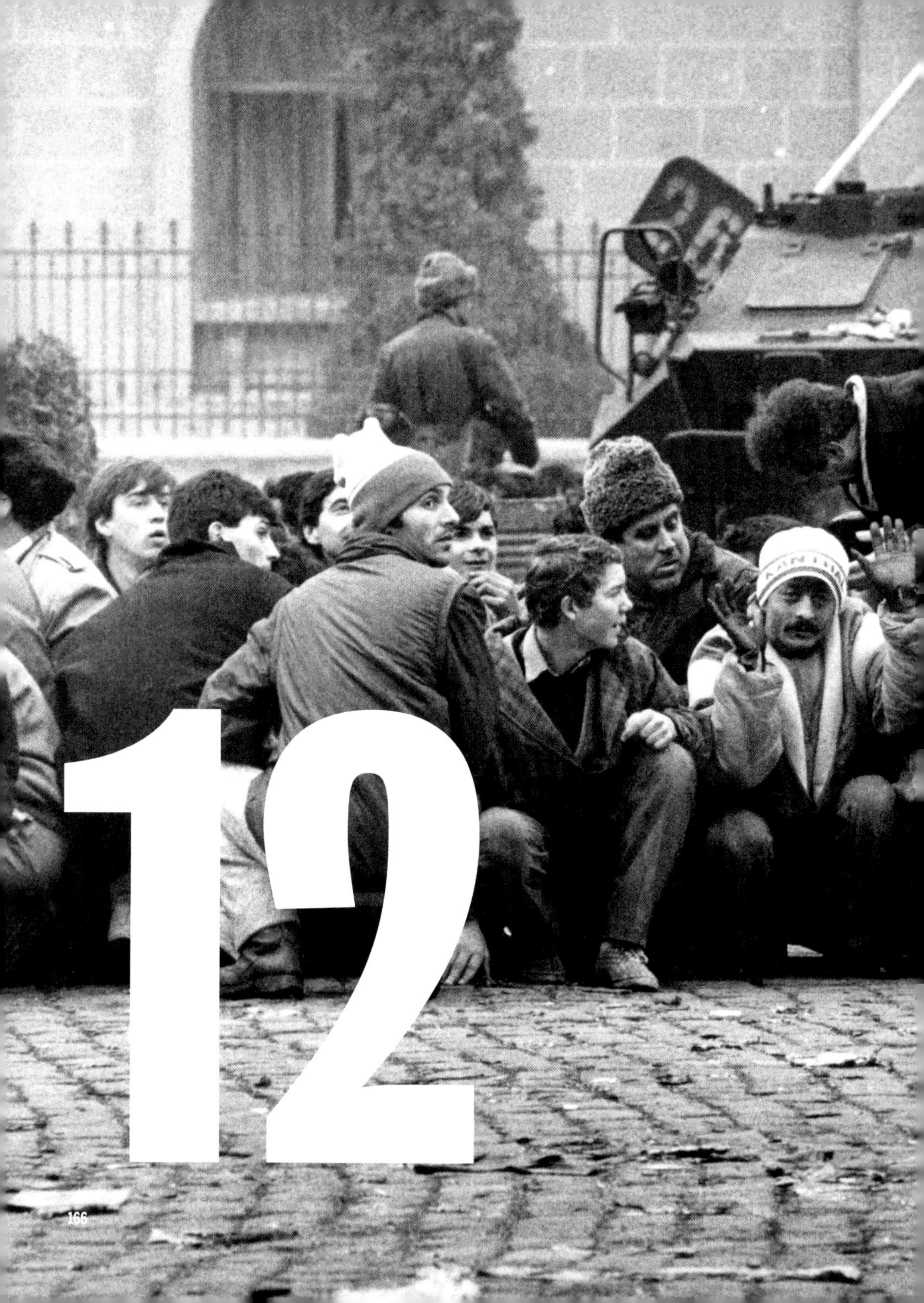

12

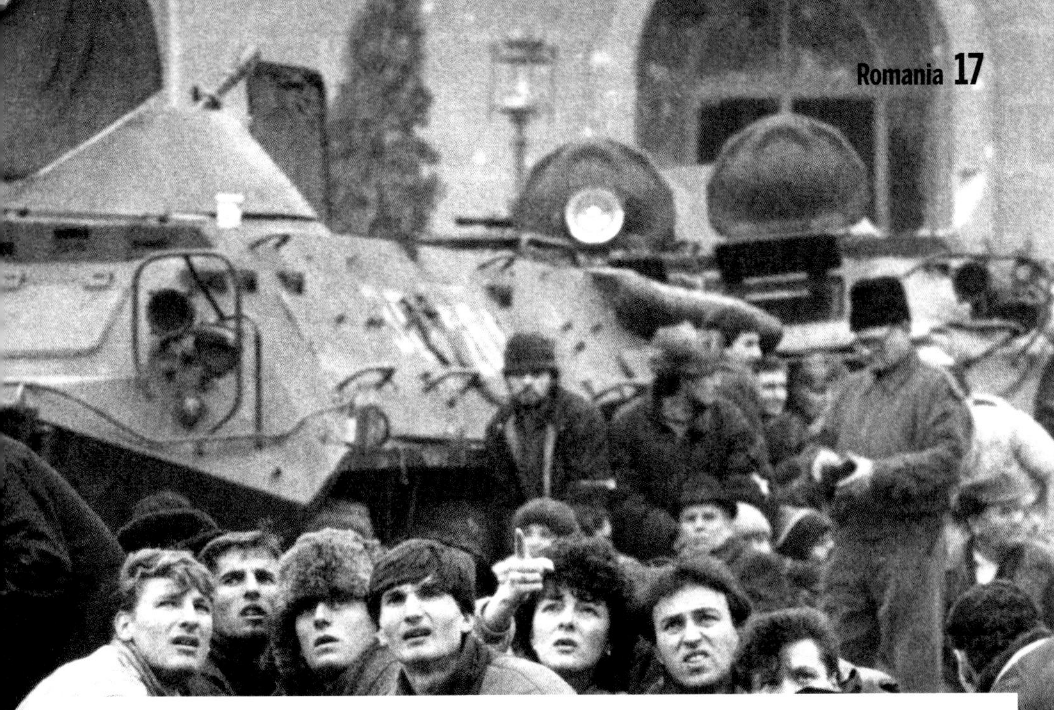

03

Malta: George H. W. Bush and Mikhail Gorbachev sign an agreement to limit military presence in Europe. It is the beginning of the end of the Cold War.

06

Great Britain: the serial "Doctor Who" ends after 26 seasons.

07

Great Britain: Nicholas Hoult, co-star with Hugh Grant in "About a boy" and star in "Skins", is born in Wokingham.

08

United States: release of "The War of the Roses" by Danny De Vito with Michael Douglas, Kathleen Turner and Danny De Vito.

14

Chile: after 16 years the first democratic elections are held following the 1988 referendum which prevented the renewal of dictator Pinochet's presidential mandate.

15

Russia: nuclear physicist and Nobel Peace Prize Andrej Dmitrievič Sakharov dies in Moscow at the age of 68.

United States: release of "Driving Miss Daisy" by Bruce Beresford with Morgan Freeman, Jessica Tandy, Dan Aykroyd and Esther Rolle.

16

Spain: actress Silvana Mangano dies in Madrid, aged 59.

United States: actor Lee Van Cleef dies in Oxnard, California, aged 64.

17

Romania: a wide protest explodes in Timişoara to stop communist authorities from dismissing Calvinist preacher László Tőkés. The protest soon turns into revolt thanks to the help of part of the regime with the aim to eliminate Ceauşescu.

20

Panama: US troops invade the country and overthrow Manuel Noriega's dictatorship.

United States: release of "Born on the Fourth of July" by Oliver Stone with Tom Cruise.

22

France: playwriter and Nobel Prize Samuel Beckett dies in Paris, aged 83.

Romania: during Ceauşescu's speech in a rally in Bucarest, some gunshots trigger the Revolution against the dictator. In a week, the clashes in the country have caused 1,550 people to die. Ion Iliescu becomes President of the National Salvation Front.

25

Romania: Nicolae and Elena Ceauşescu are executed after their attempted flight.

29

Czechoslovakia: Václav Havel is elected President.

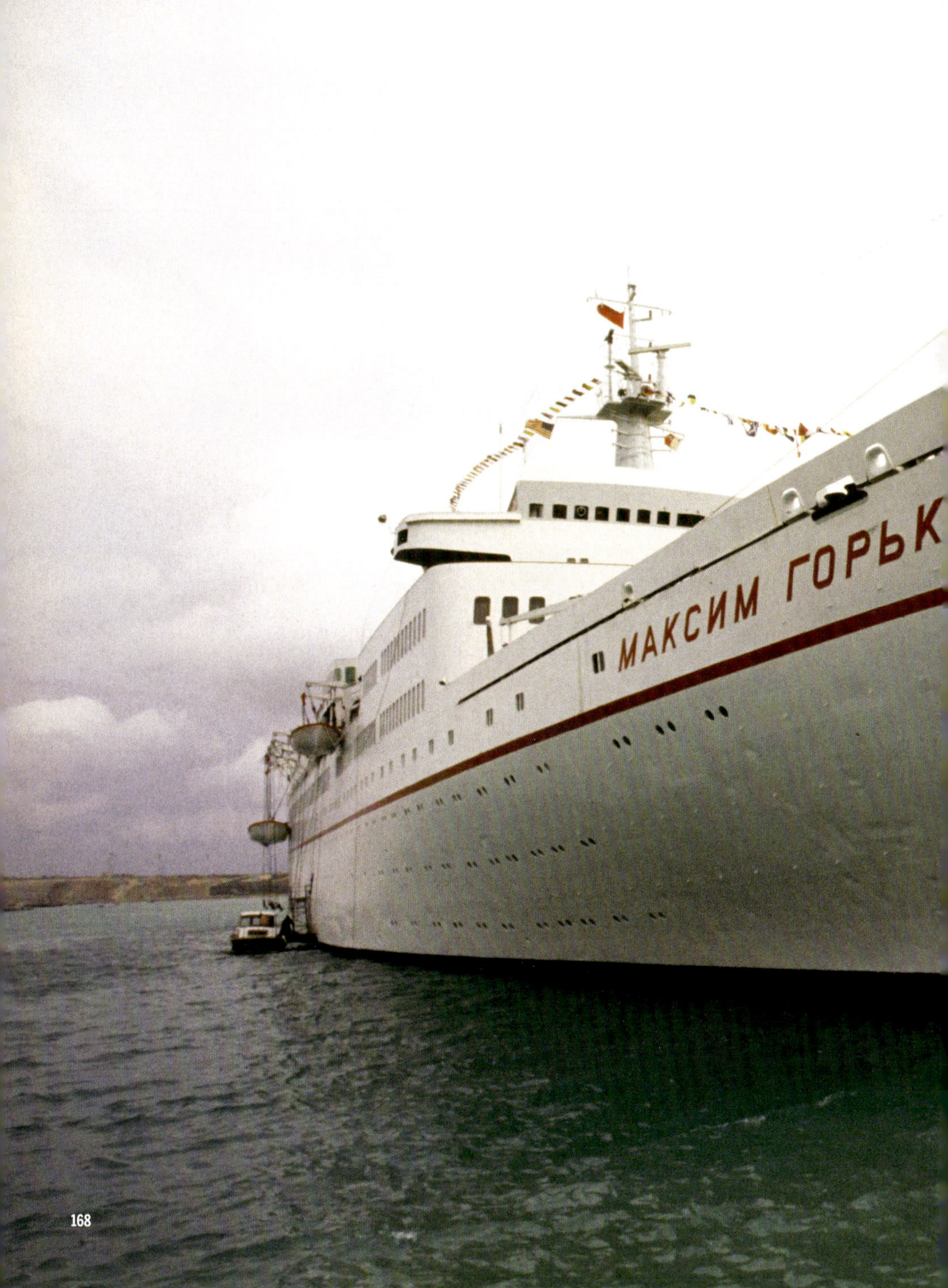

МАКСИМ ГОРЬК

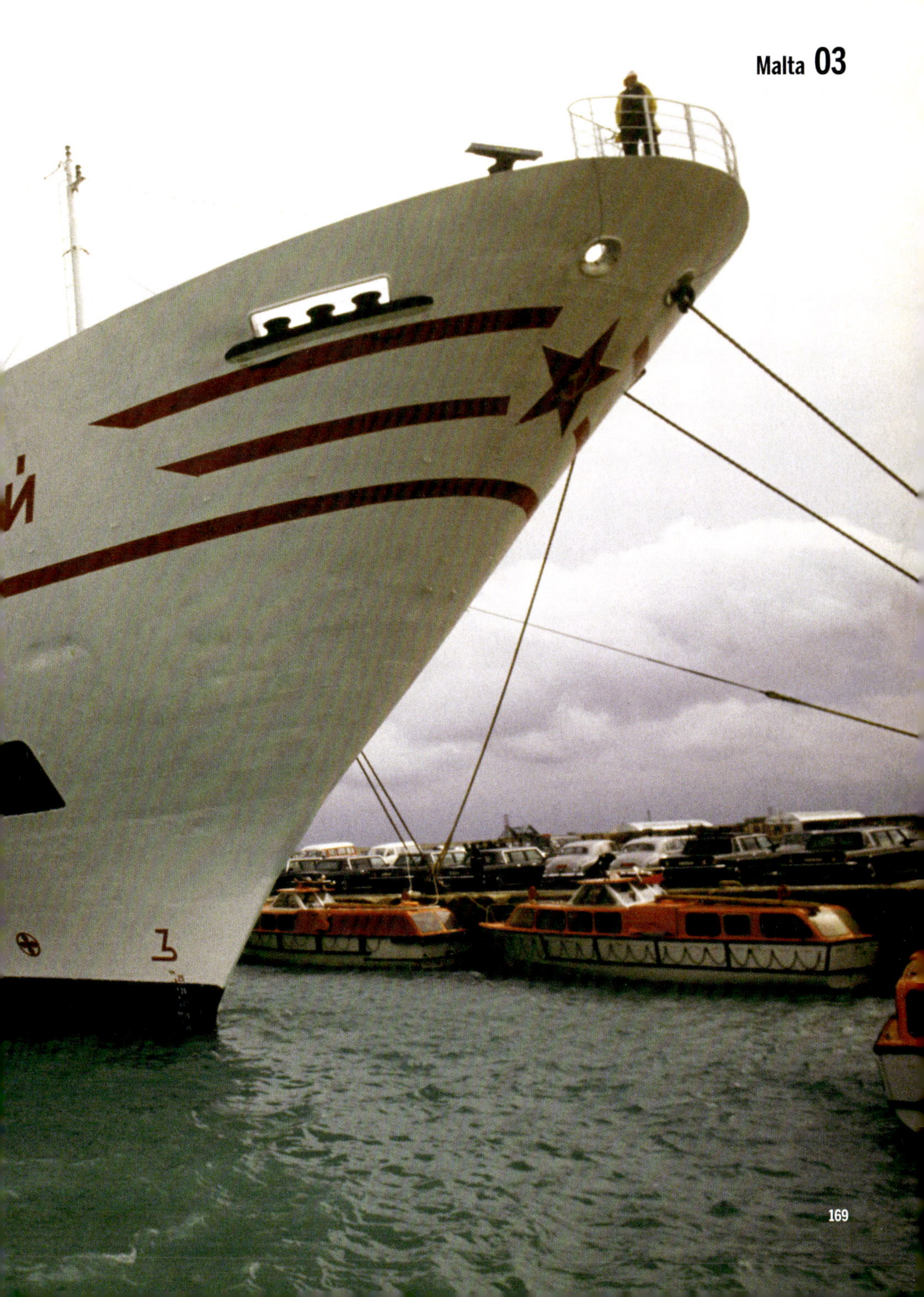

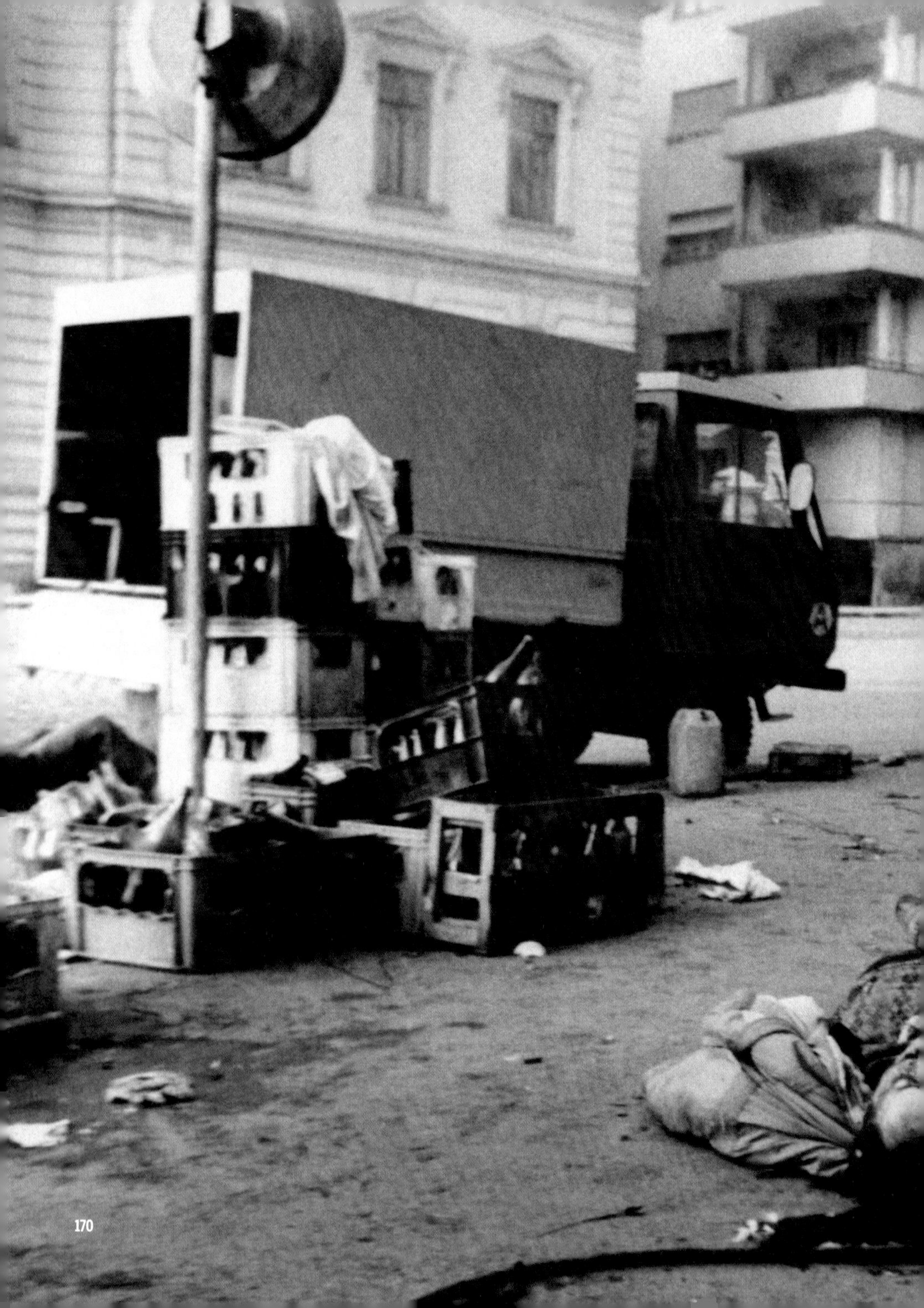

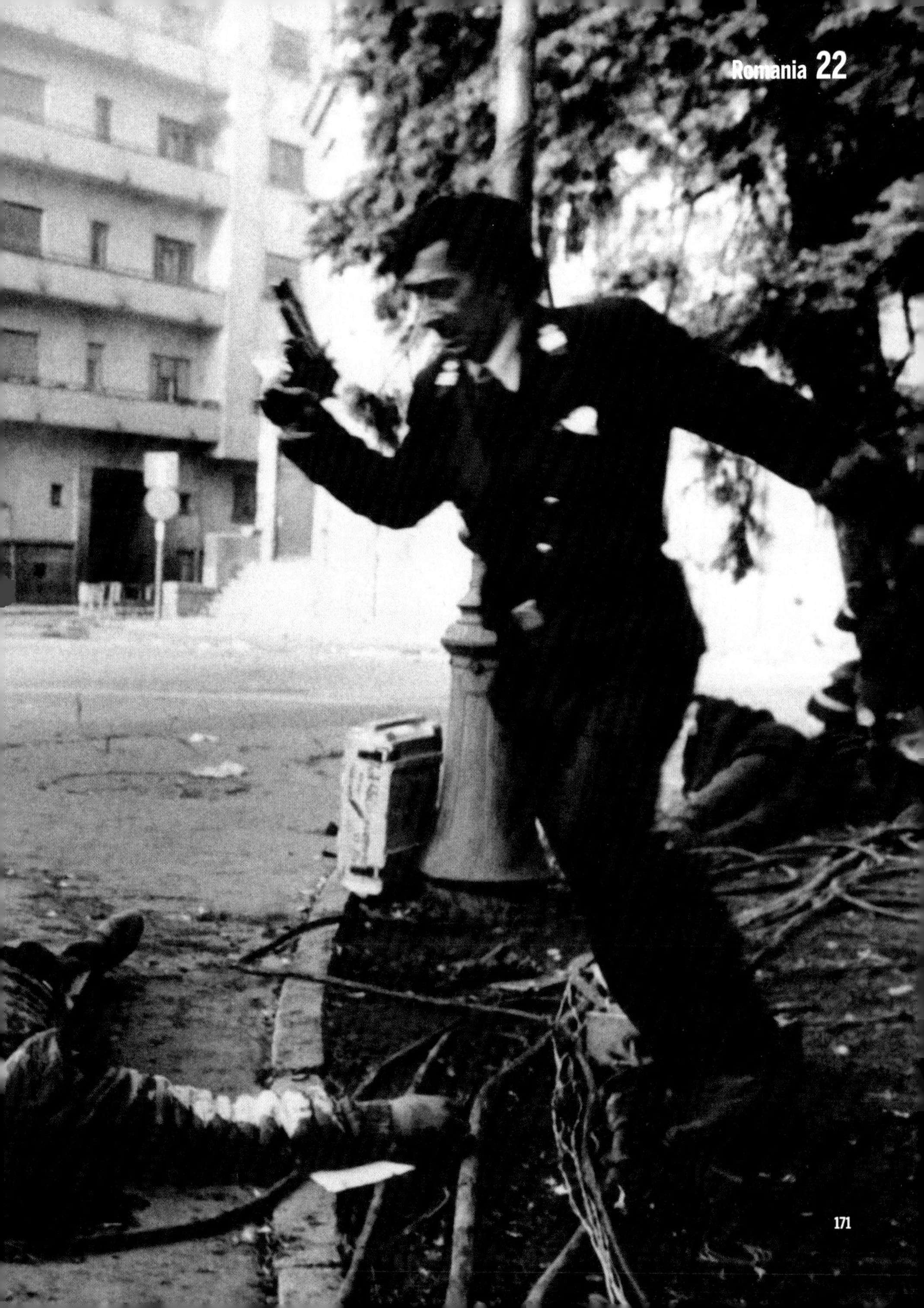

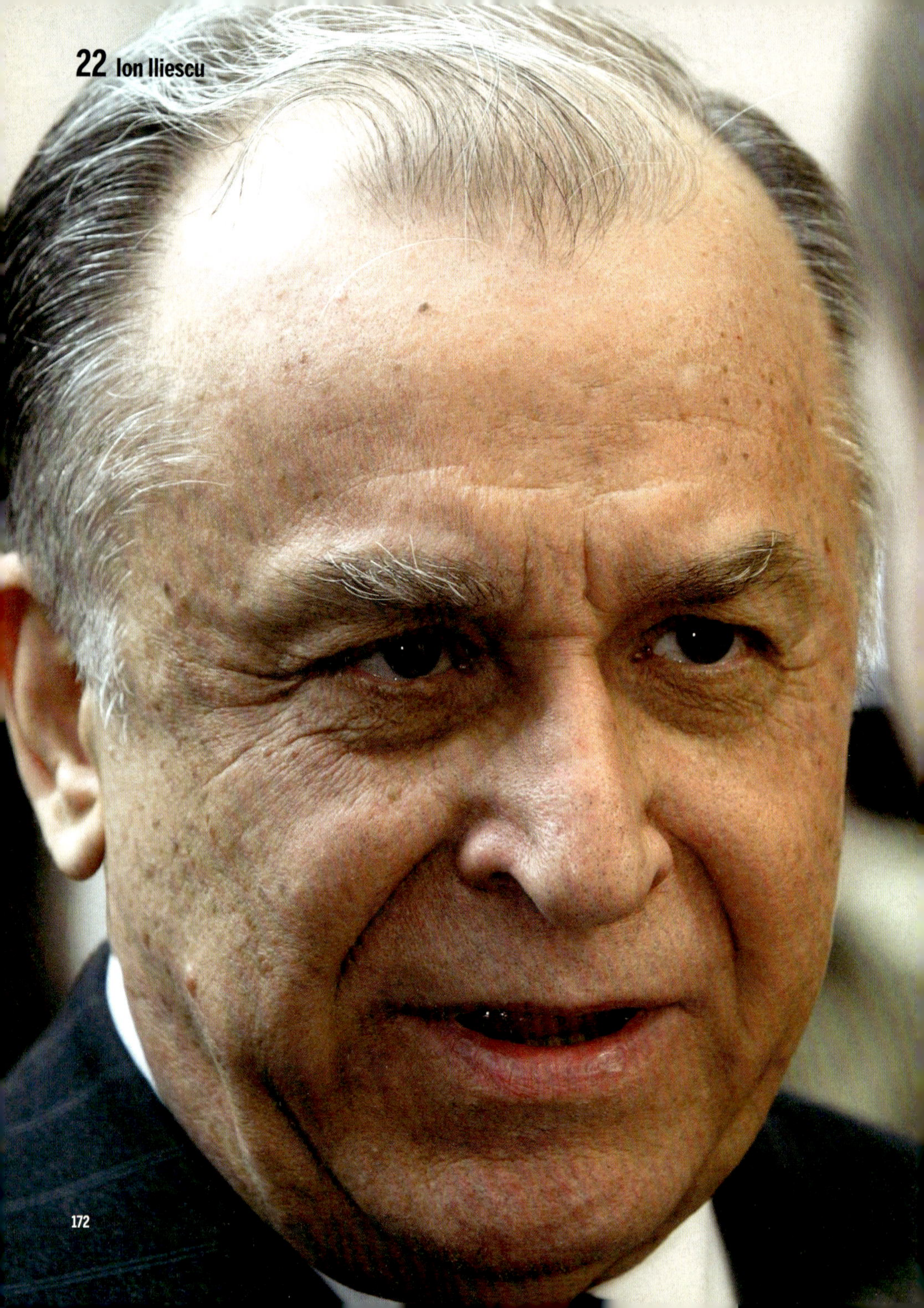

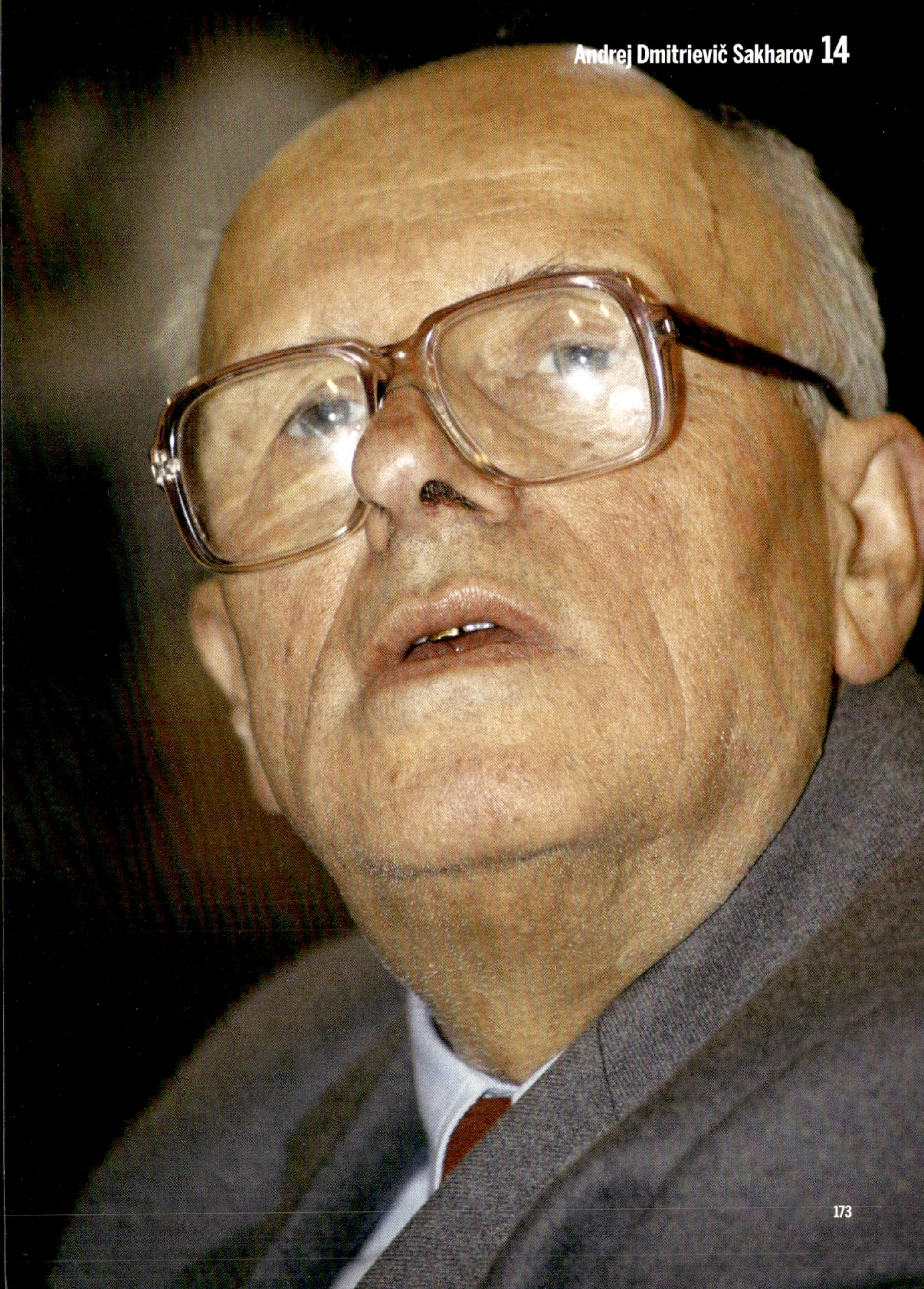

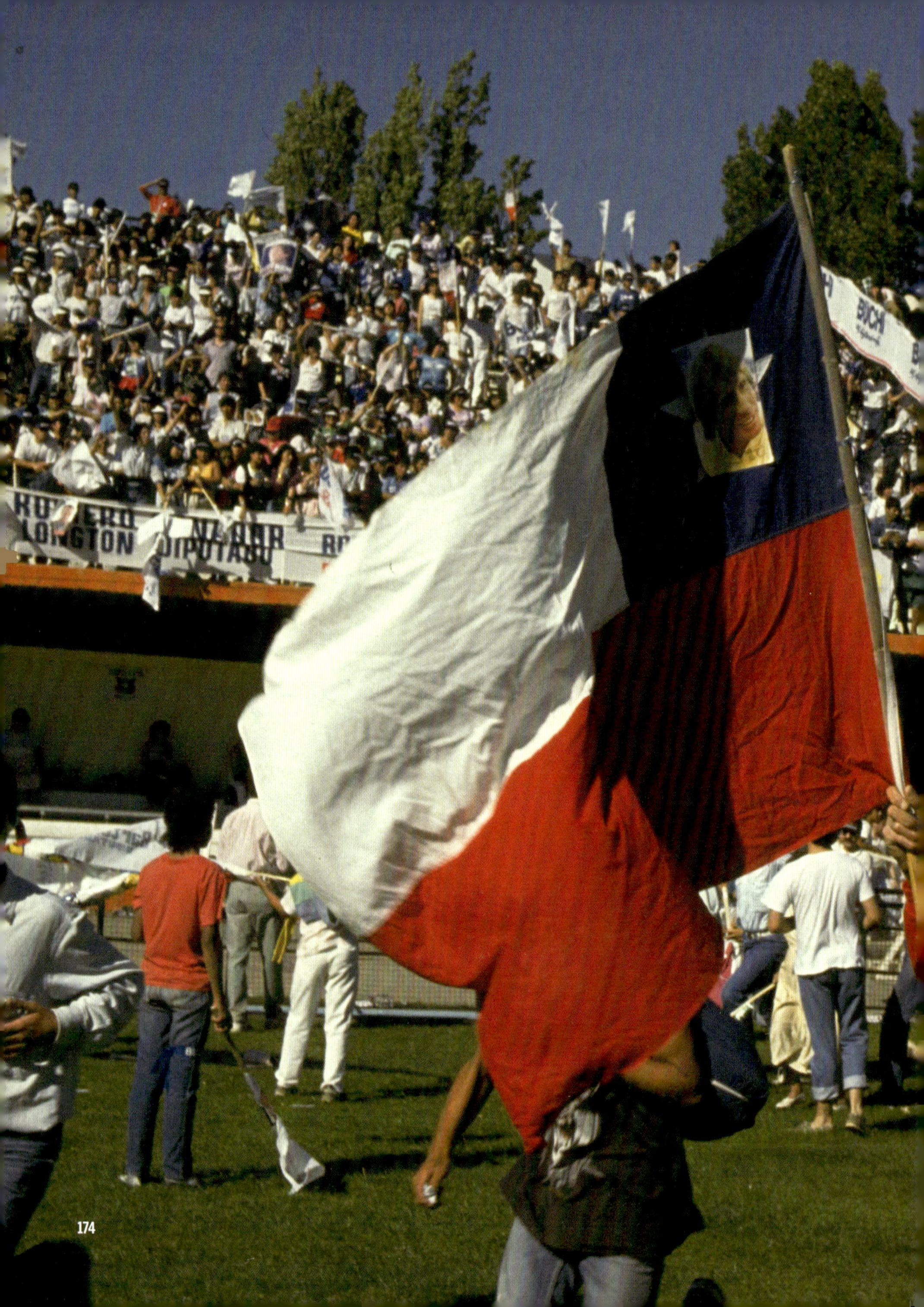

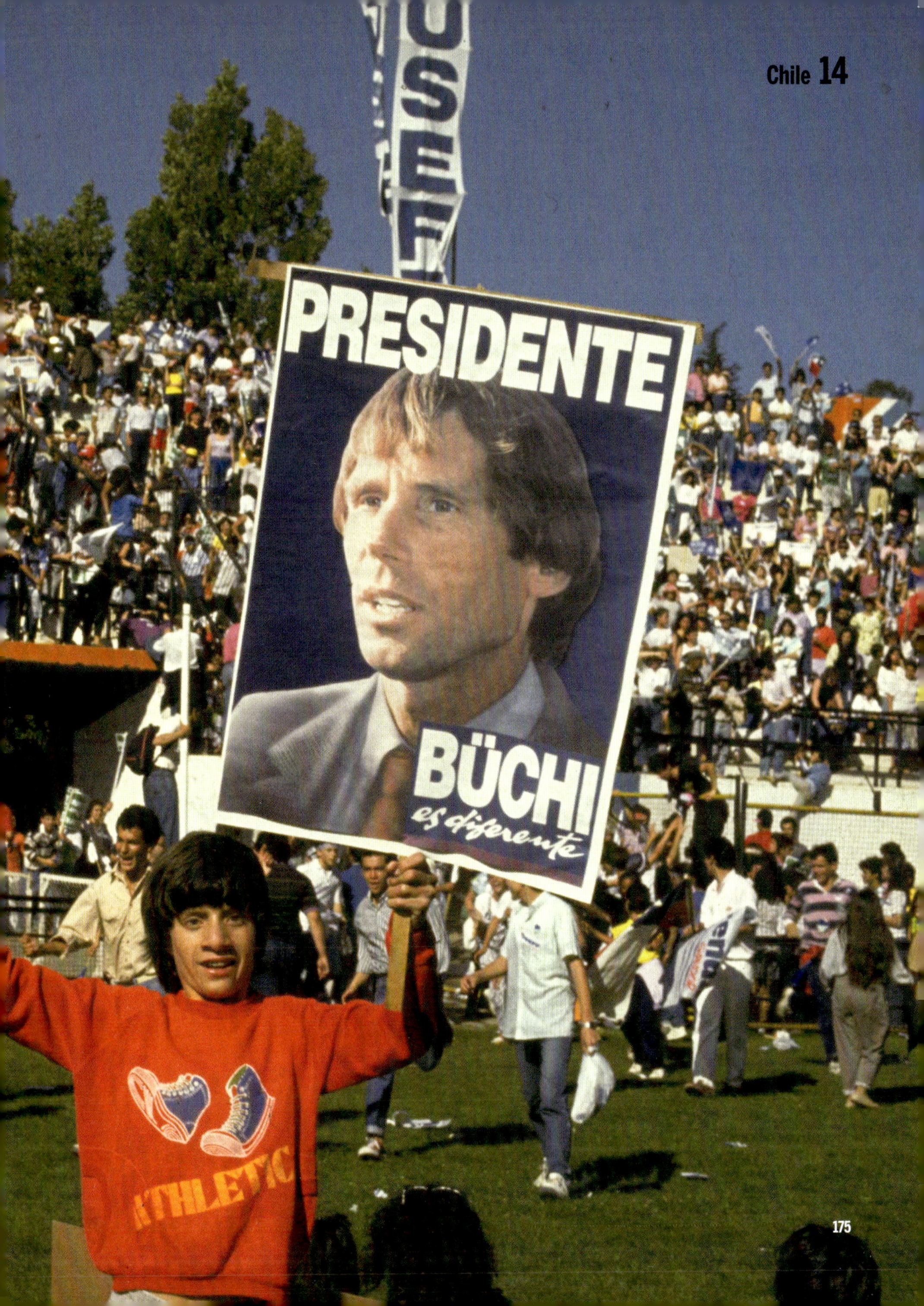
PRESIDENTE
BÜCHI
es diferente

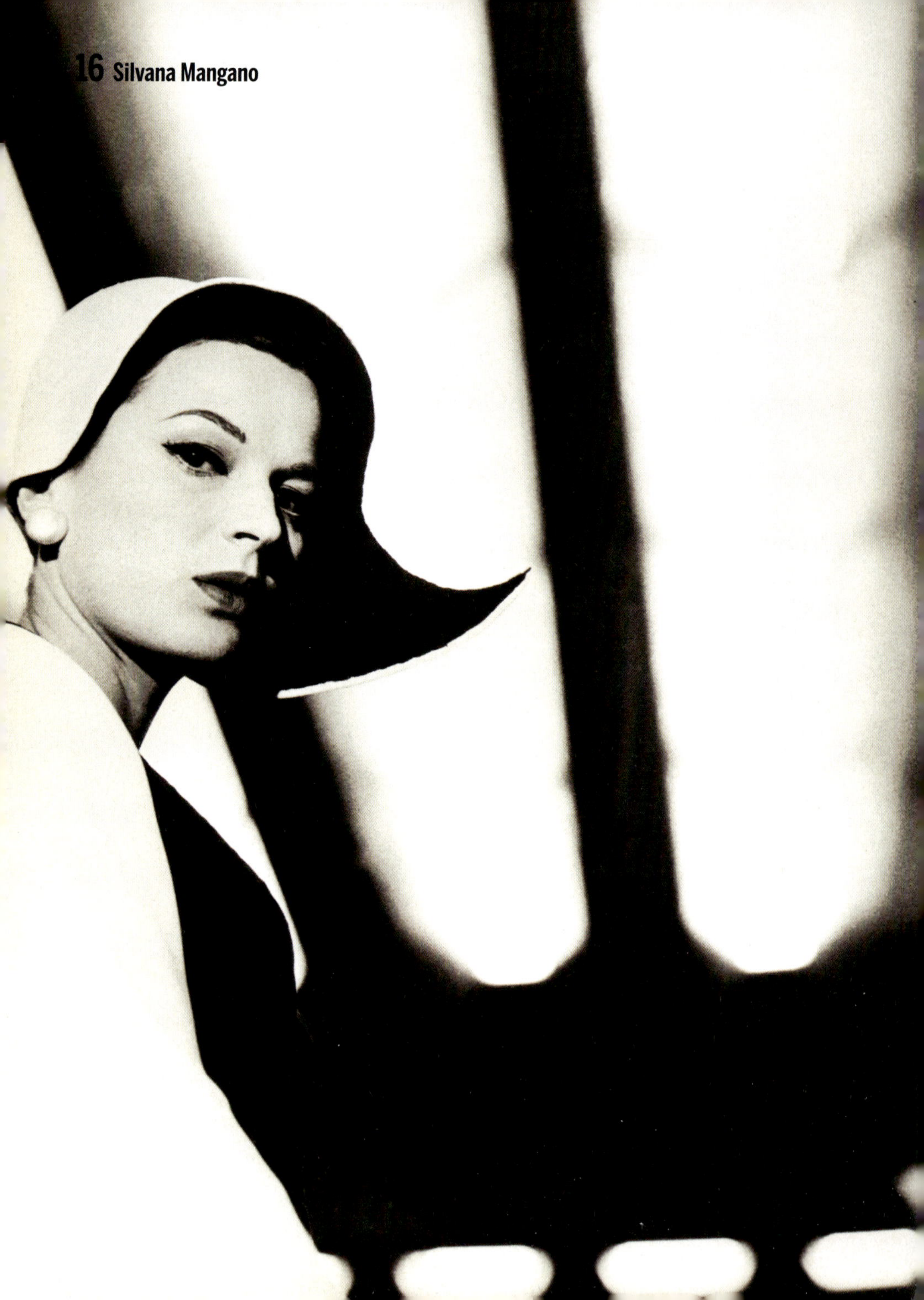

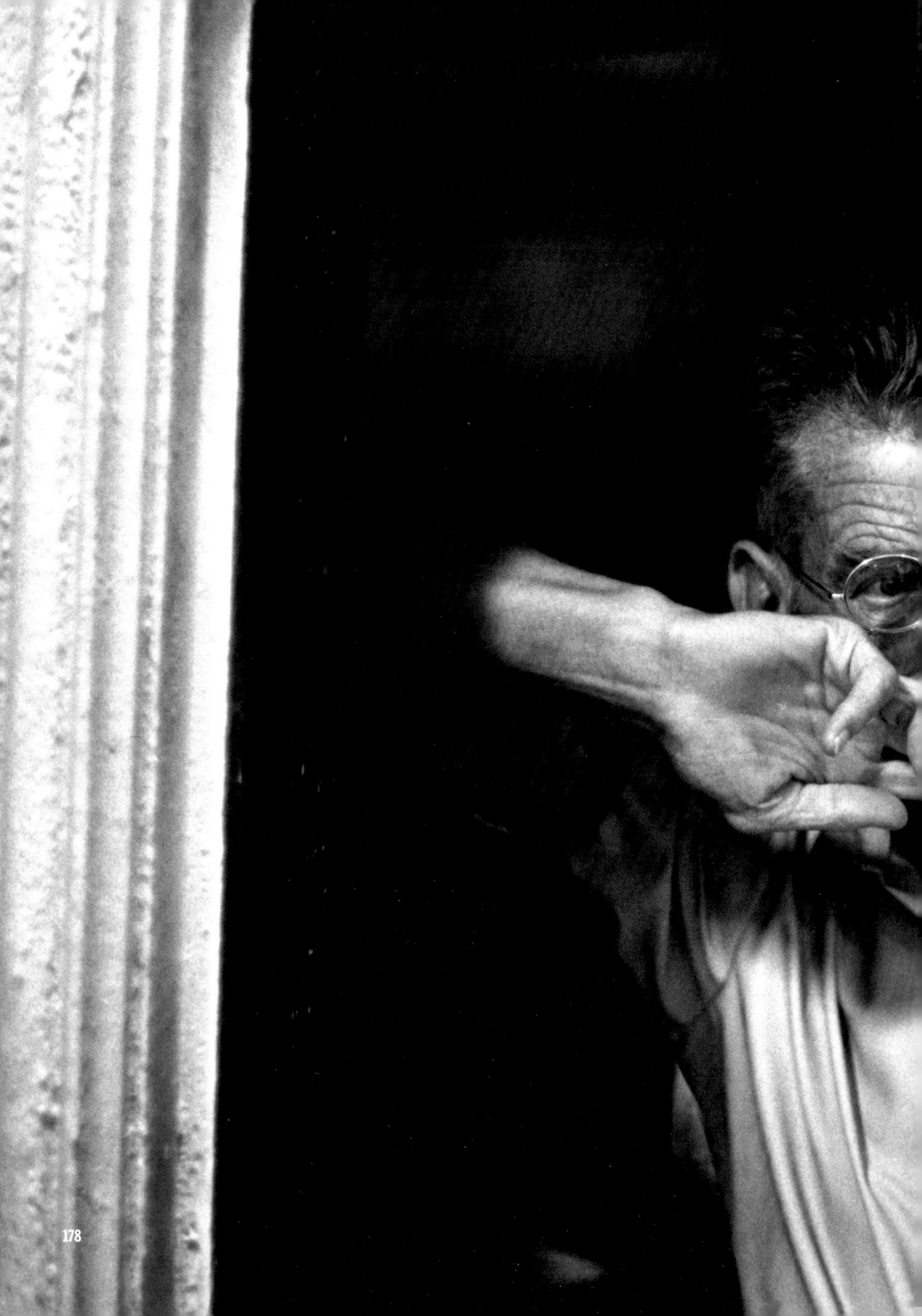

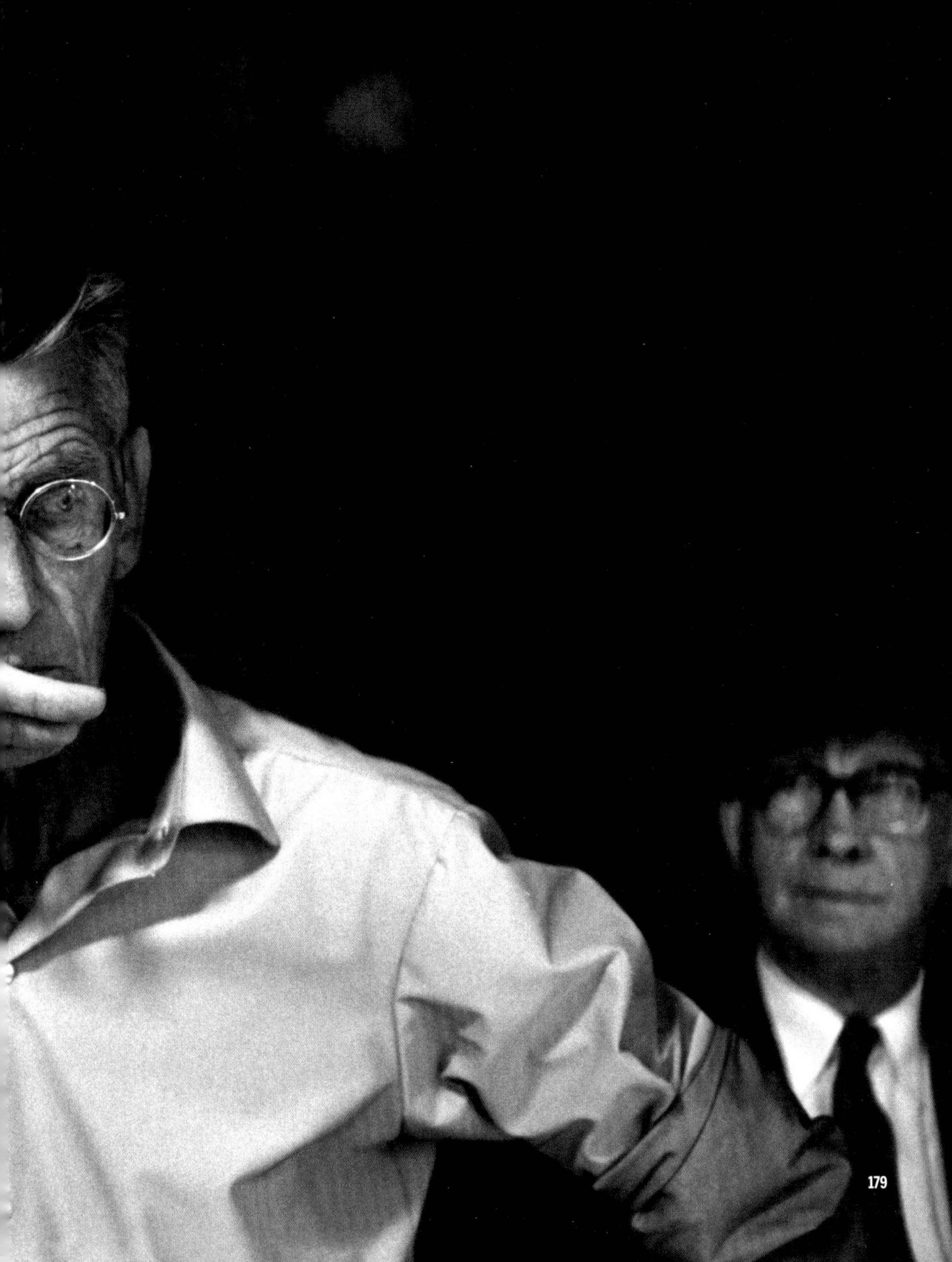

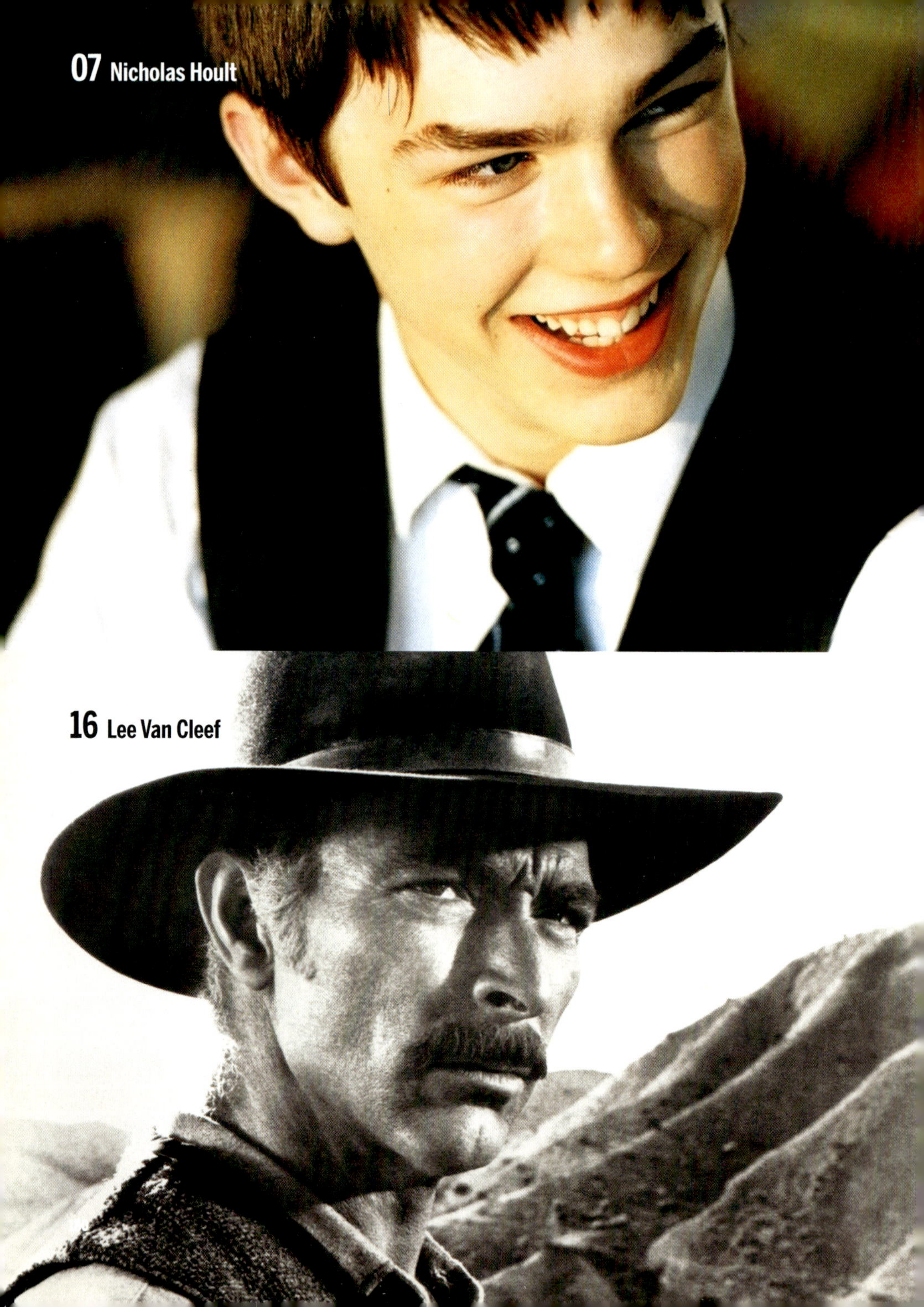
07 Nicholas Hoult
16 Lee Van Cleef

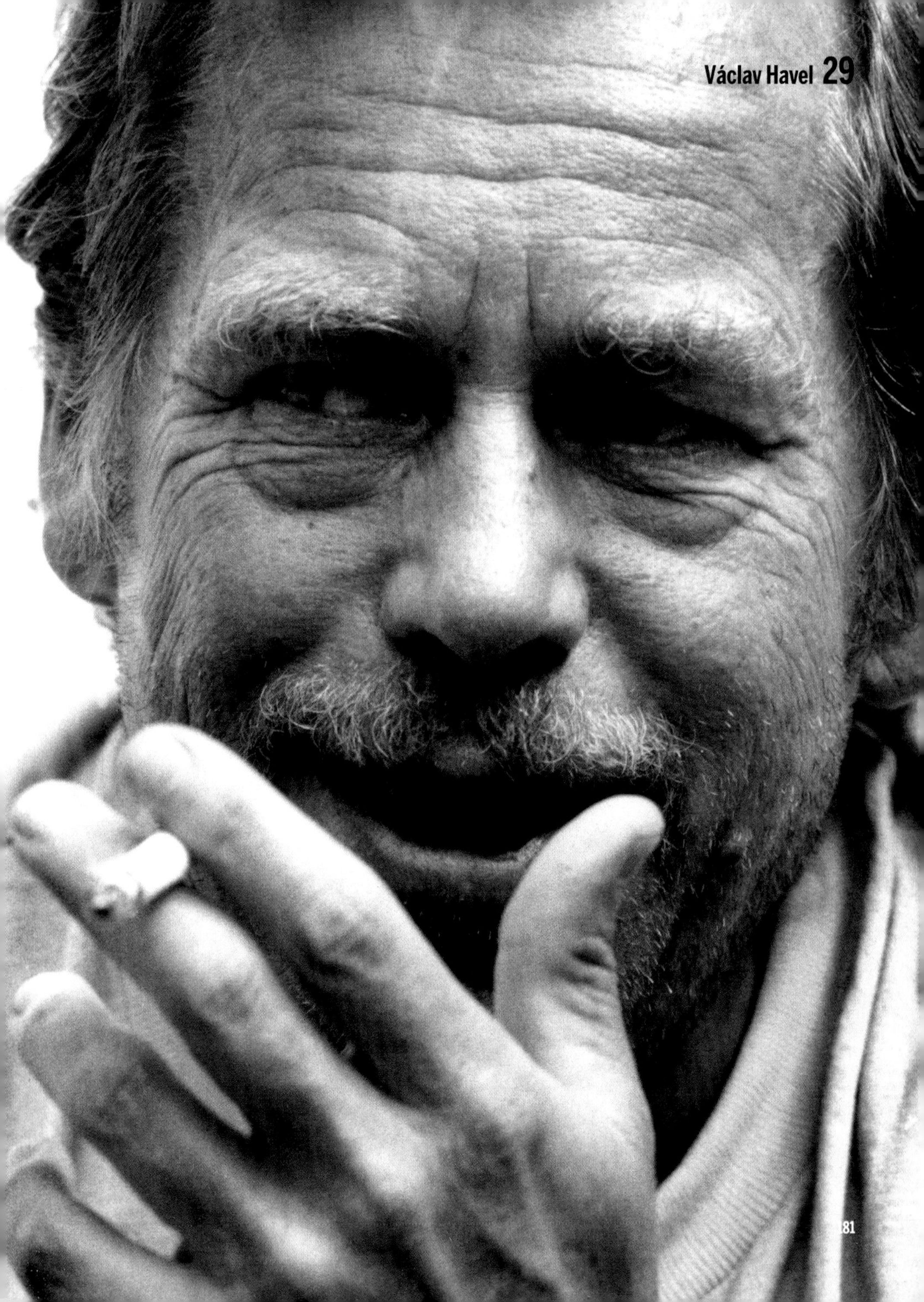

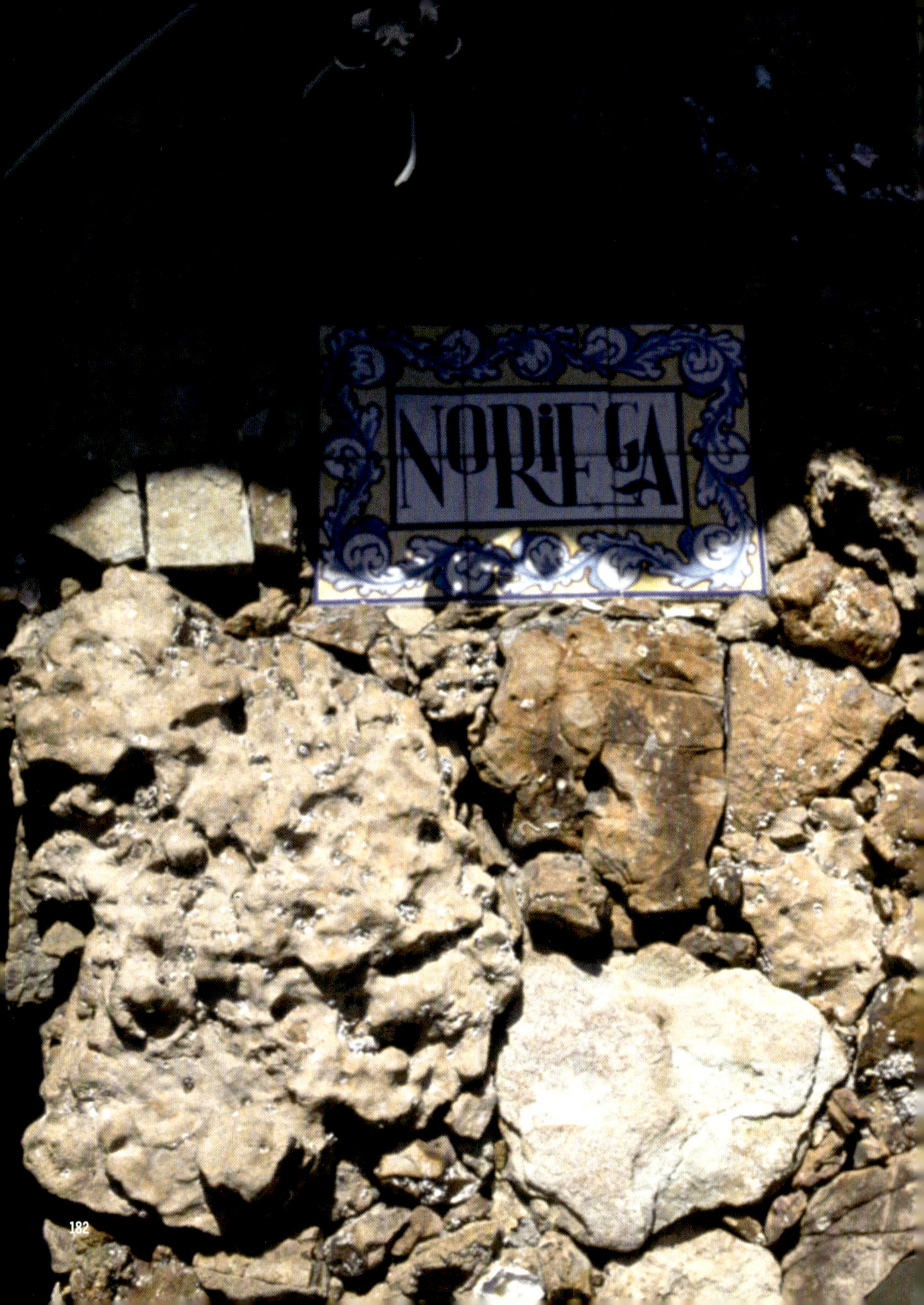
NORiEGA

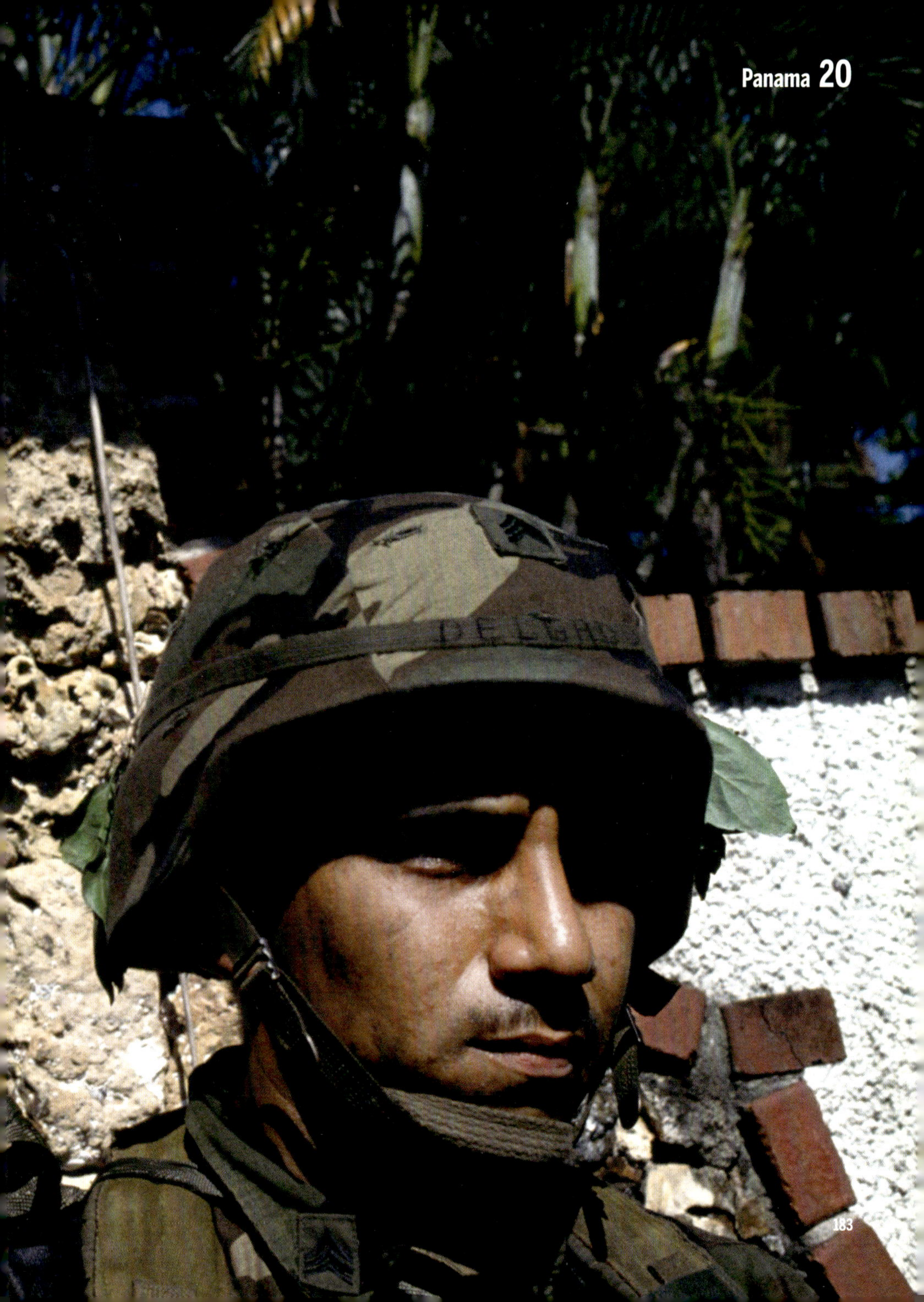

08 "The War of the Roses"

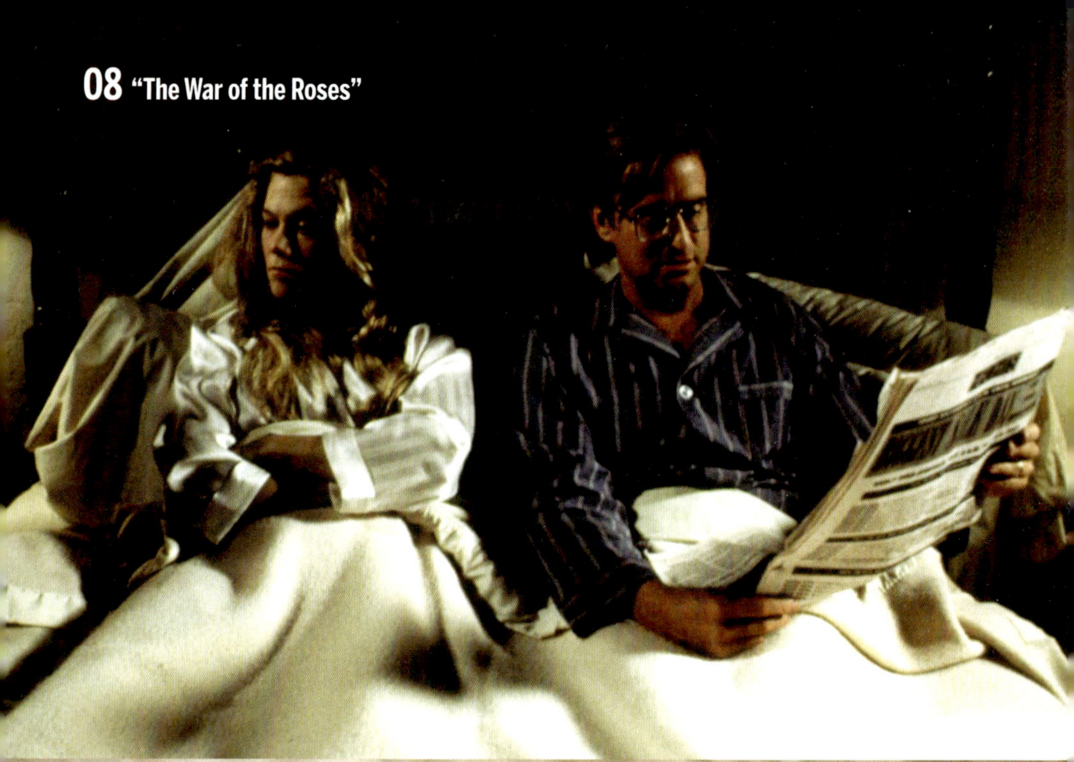

20 "Born on the Fourth of July"

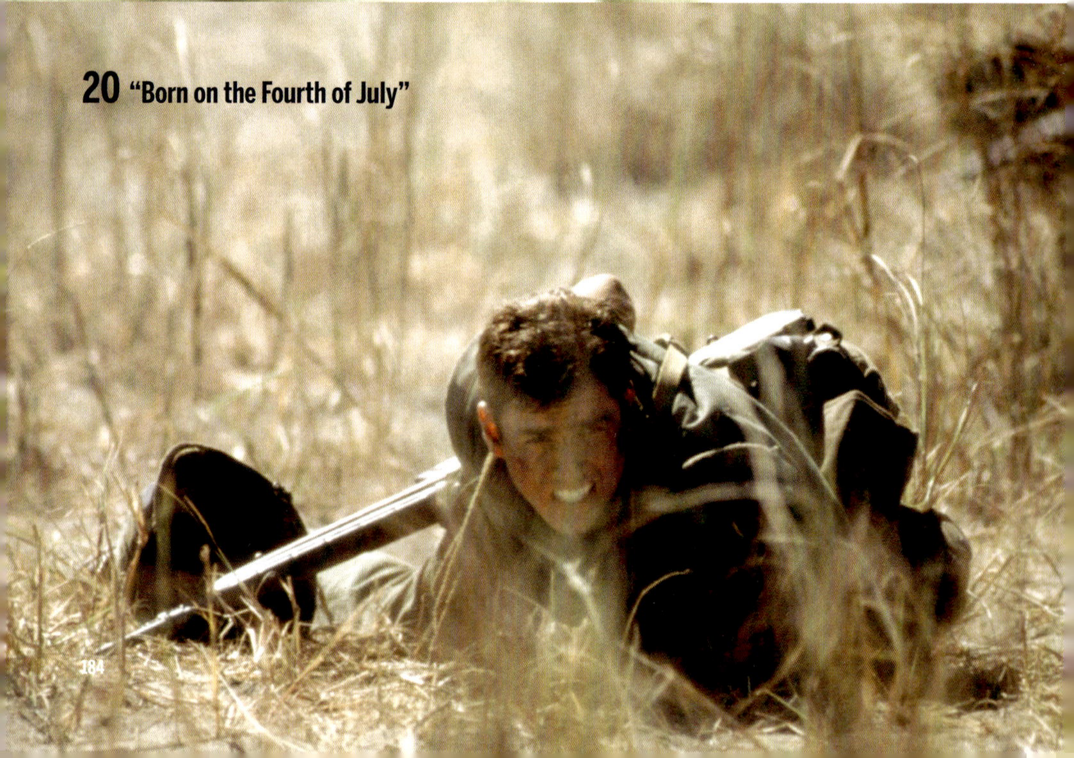

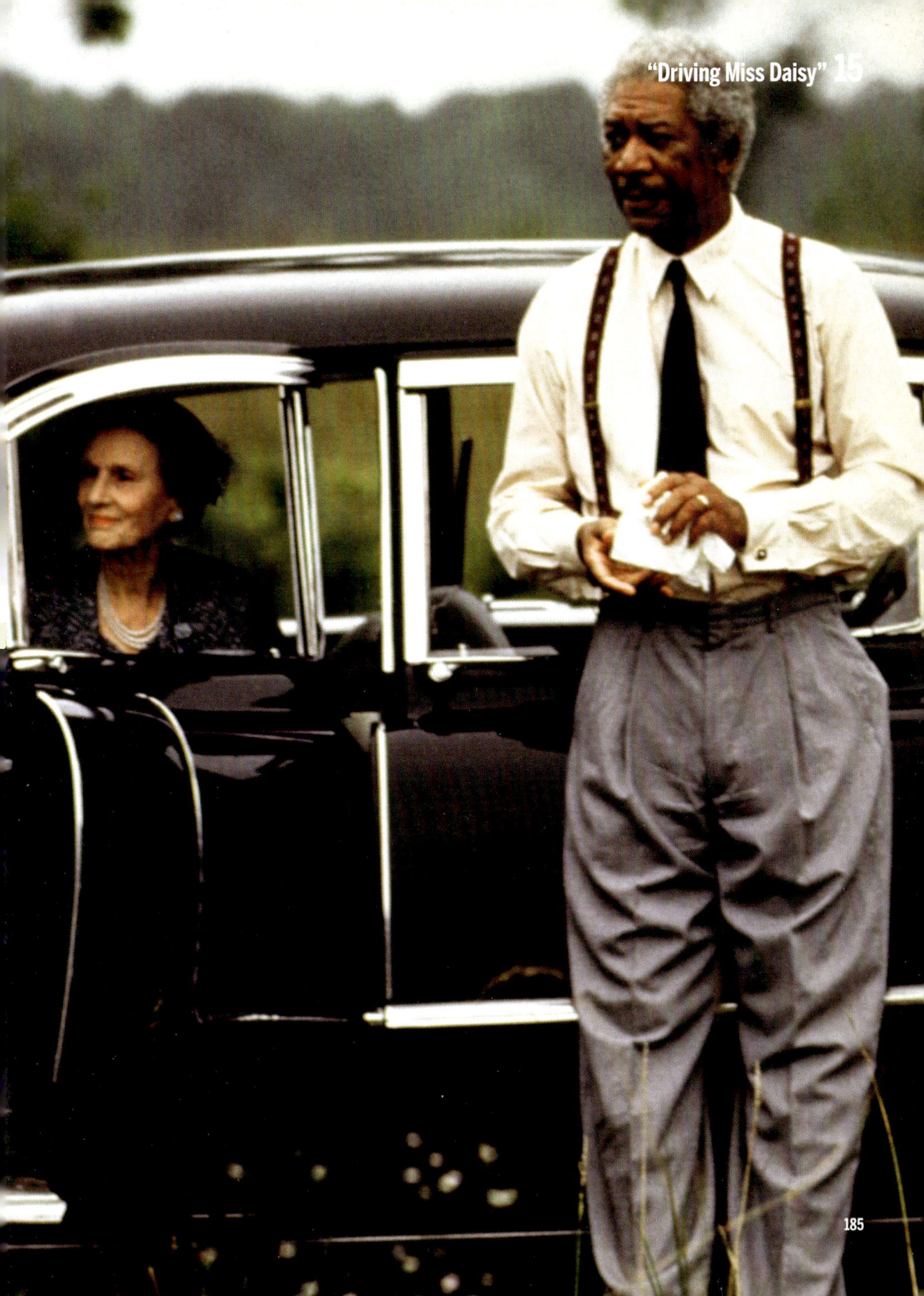

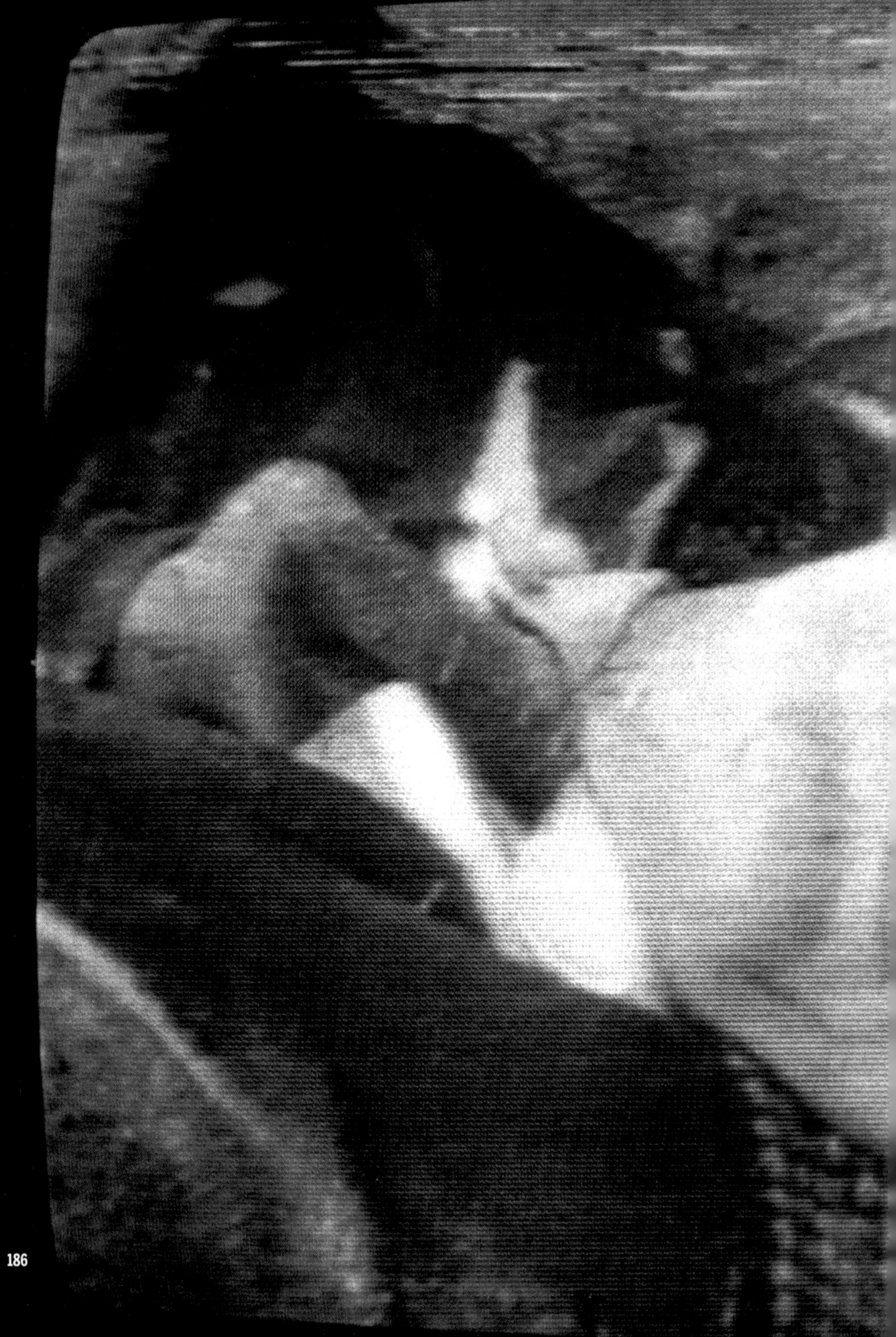

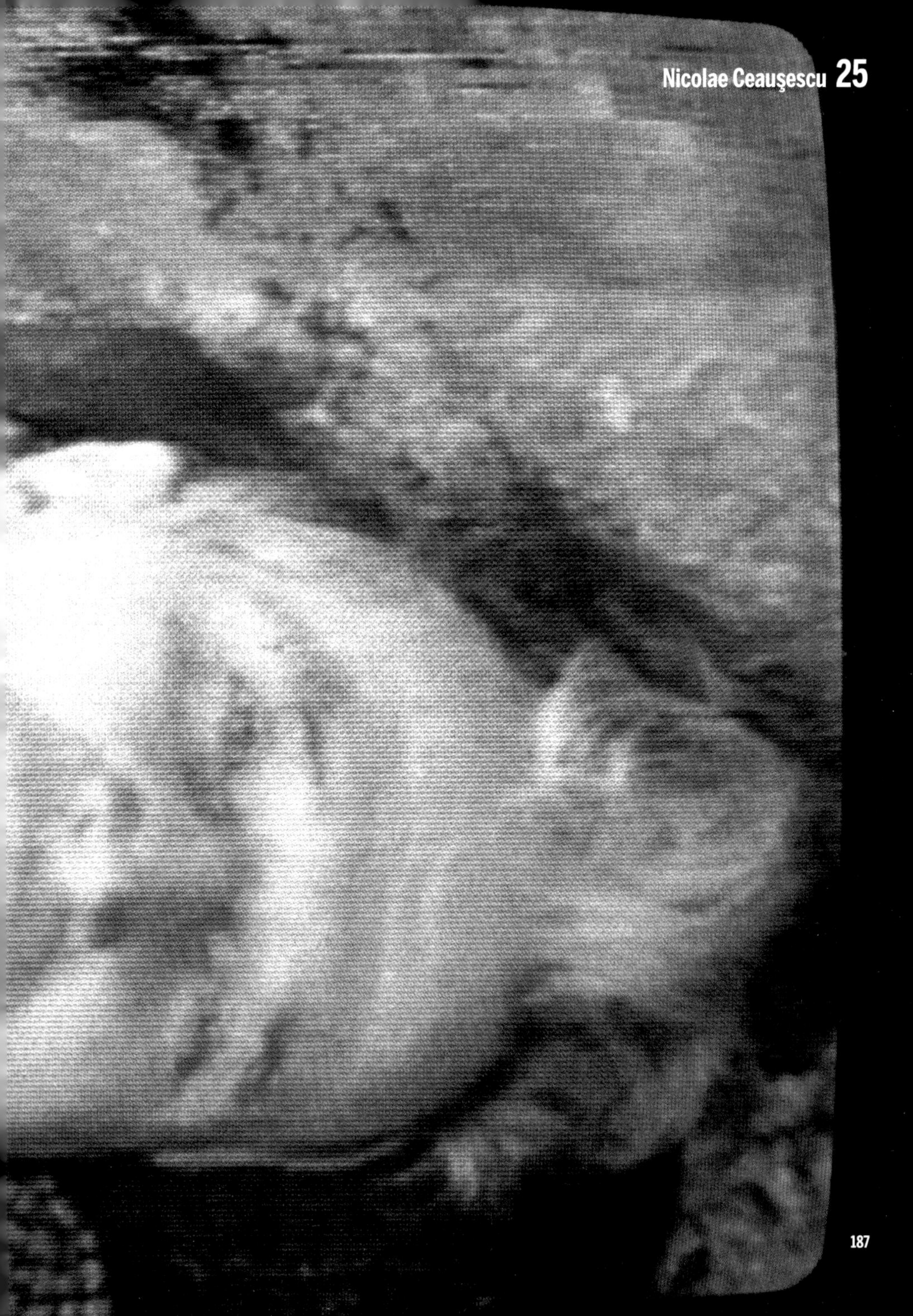

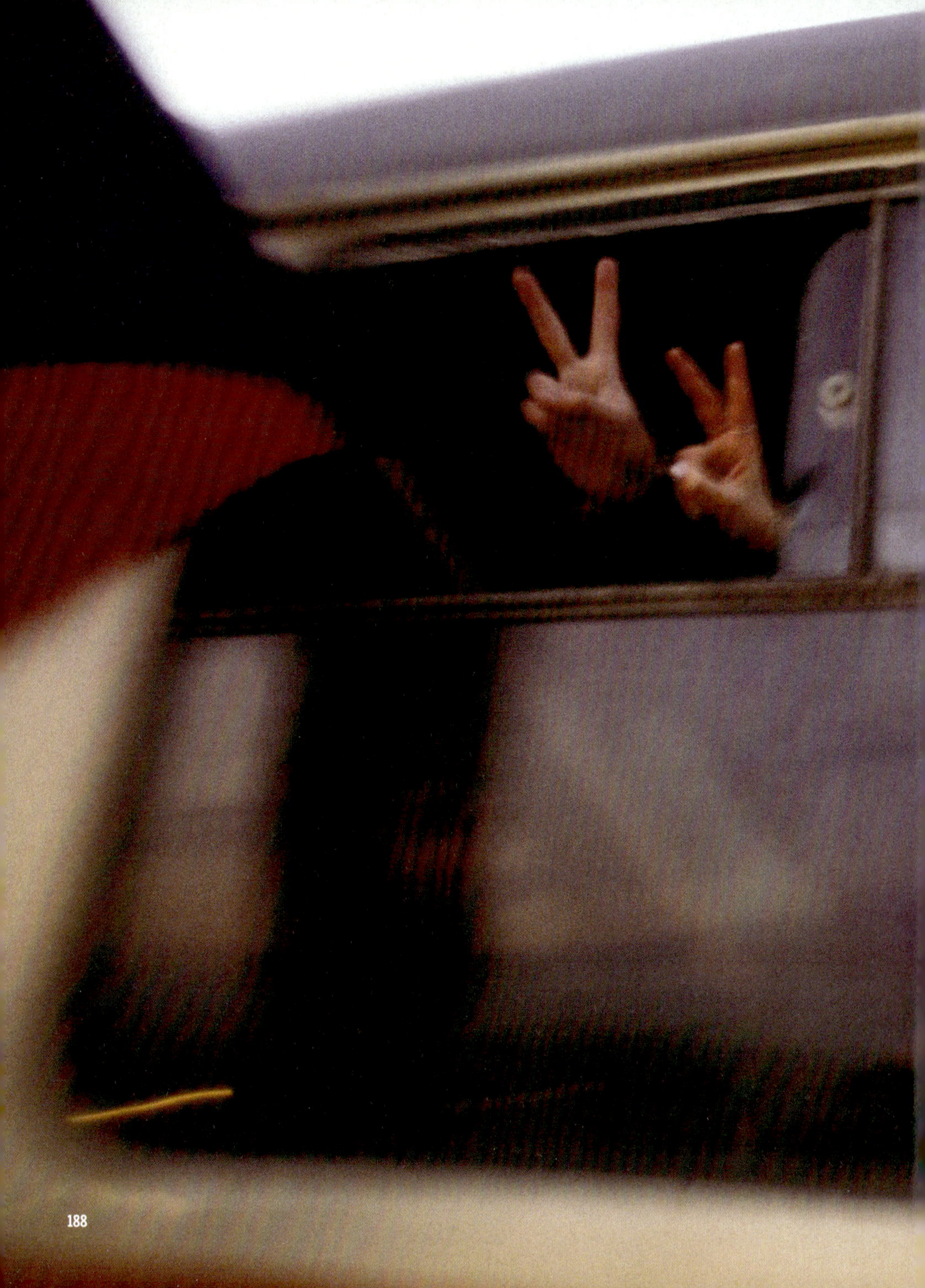

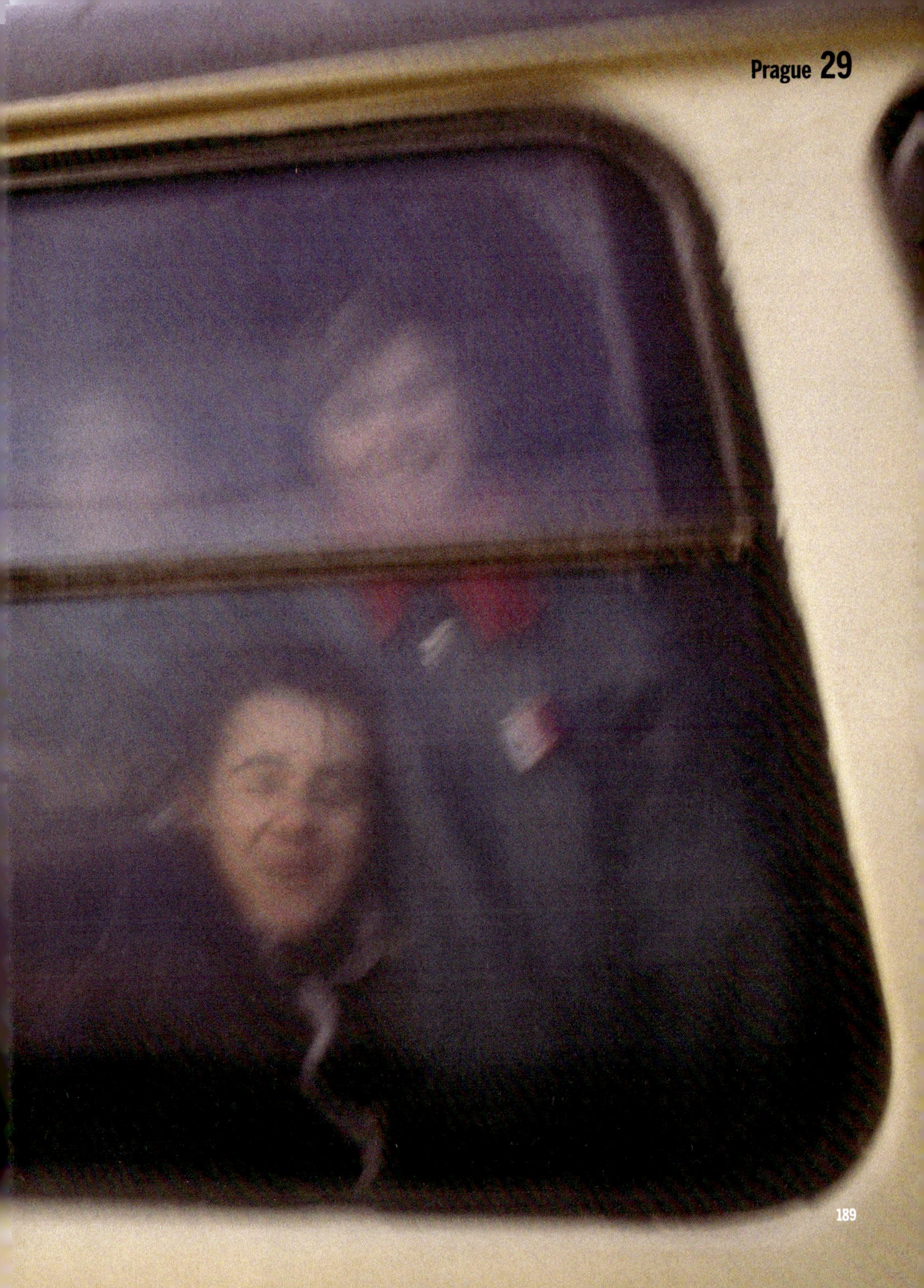

CREDITS

JULY

P108-109: **Gueorgui Pinkhassov** MAGNUM PHOTOS

P110-111: COLUMBIA PICTURES/EVERETT COLLECTION

P112-113: WARNER BROS./EVERETT COLLECTION

P114-115: **Guido Harari** CONTRASTO

P116: **Steve McCurry** MAGNUM PHOTOS

P117: PELE COLLECTION/GAMMA/EYEDEA PRESSE

P118-119: WARNER BROS./EVERETT COLLECTION

P120-121: **Michel Gouverneur** EYEDEA PRESSE

AUGUST

P122-123: **Peter Turnley** CORBIS

P124-125: **Chip Hires** GAMMA/EYEDEA PRESSE

P126-127: **Roger Ressmeyer** CORBIS

P128-129: **Fréderic Meylan** SYGMA/CORBIS

SEPTEMBER

P130-131: **Eisermann** LAIF/CONTRASTO

P132-133: **Ian Berry** MAGNUM PHOTOS

P134-135: DEMANGE/GAMMA/EYEDEA PRESSE

P136: ALBUM

P137: EVERETT COLLECTION

P138: **Erich Hartmann** MAGNUM PHOTOS

P139: **Bruce Gilden** MAGNUM PHOTOS

OCTOBER

P140-141: **Bernard Bisson** SYGMA/CORBIS

P142: EVERETT COLLECTION

P143: **Ferdinando Scianna** MAGNUM PHOTOS

P144-145: **Eli Reed** MAGNUM PHOTOS

P146-147: **Giogowski** LAIF/CONTRASTO

P148: KEYSTONE FRANCE/EYEDEA

P149: EVERETT COLLECTION

NOVEMBER

P150-151: **Raymond Depardon** MAGNUM PHOTOS

P152-153: **Gilles Levent** GAMMA/EYEDEA PRESSE

P154-155: **Steve McCurry** MAGNUM PHOTOS

P156: **Sassaki** GAMMA/EYEDEA PRESSE

P157: **Ari Lago** GAMMA/EYEDEA PRESSE

P158 SOPRA: **Mark Power** MAGNUM PHOTOS

P158 SOTTO: **Guy Le Querrec** MAGNUM PHOTOS

P159 SOPRA: **Mark Power** MAGNUM PHOTOS

P159 SOTTO: **Guy Le Querrec** MAGNUM PHOTOS

P160: UNIVERSAL/EVERETT COLLECTION

P161: **Philippe Halsman** MAGNUM PHOTOS

P162-163: **Fausto Giaccone** ANZENBERGER/CONTRASTO

P164-165: **Maher Attar** SYGMA/CORBIS

DECEMBER

P166-167: **Angelo Turetta** CONTRASTO

P168-169: **Roberto Koch** CONTRASTO

P170-171: **Leonard Freed** MAGNUM PHOTOS

P172: PHOTO NEWS/GAMMA/EYEDEA PRESSE

P173: **Chip Hires** GAMMA/EYEDEA PRESSE

P174-175: **Carlos Carrion** SYGMA/CORBIS

P176: KEYSTONE FRANCE/EYEDEA PRESSE

P177: EVERETT COLLECTION

P178-179: **Bruce Davidson** MAGNUM PHOTOS

P180 SOPRA: SAMUEL GOLDWIN FILMS/EVERETT COLLECTION

P180 SOTTO: EVERETT COLLECTION

P181: **Gueorgui Pinkhassov** MAGNUM PHOTOS

P182-183: **Eli Reed** MAGNUM PHOTOS

P184 SOPRA: 20TH CENTURY FOX FILM CORP./EVERETT COLLECTION

P184 SOTTO: UNIVERSAL/EVERETT COLLECTION

P185: EVERETT COLLECTION

P186-187: **Abbas** MAGNUM PHOTOS

P188-189: BOUVET-HIRES/GAMMA/EYEDEA PRESSE

Printed in Italy

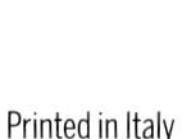

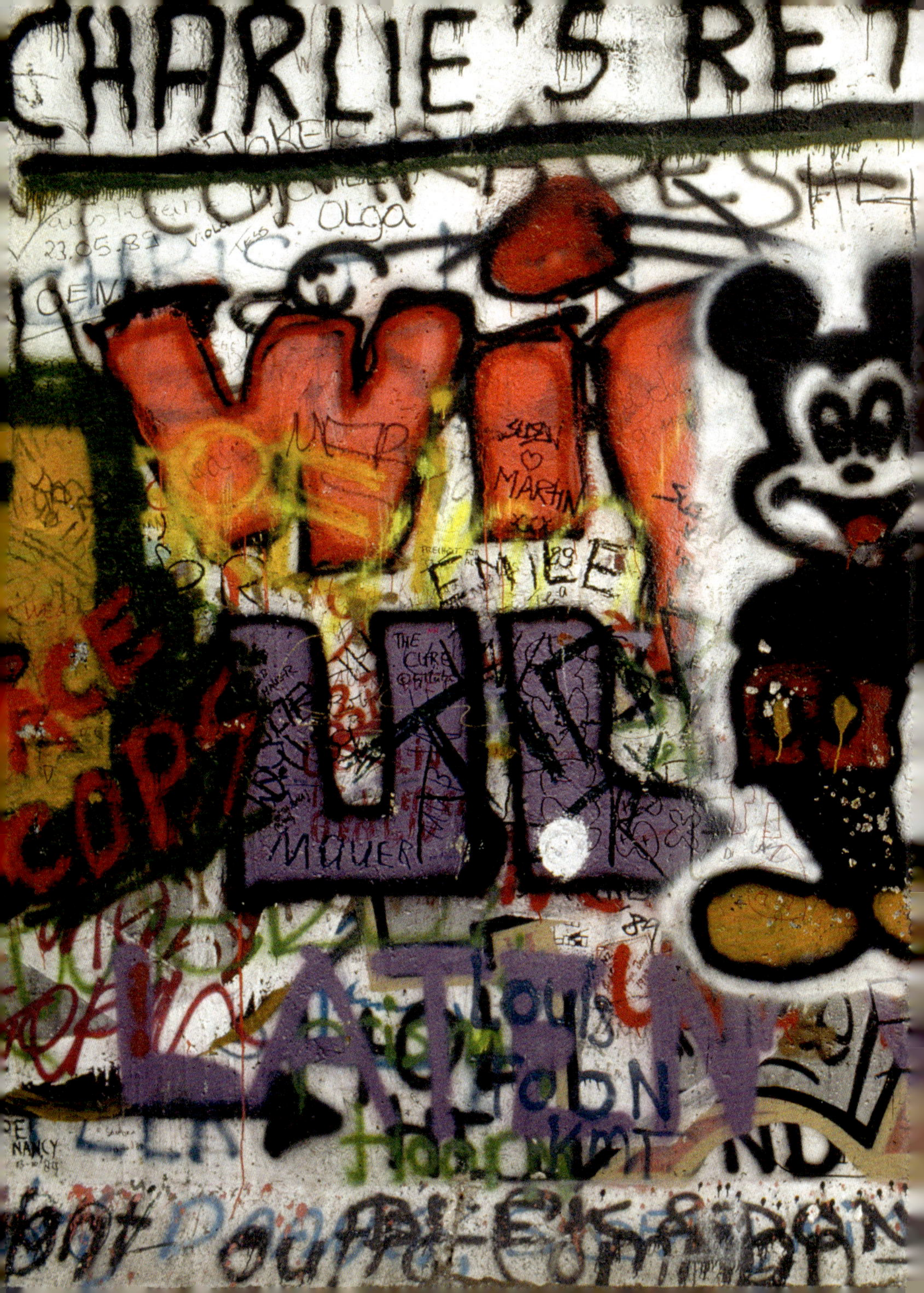
CHARLIE'S RE
Olga
23.05.89
MARTIN
THE CURE
COPS
MAUER
Louis
NANCY